English Translators
and Translations

by

J. M. COHEN

Published for The British Council
and The National Book League
by Longmans, Green & Co.

Two shillings and sixpence

As Mr. Cohen points out in the opening of his survey, the two great periods of excellence in English translation occur at the time of the Renaissance, and again at the present, when "English has become . . . the common cultural language of a vast section of the world".

Helped by a discriminating use of quotation in prose and verse, Mr. Cohen covers the whole story of the English effort to make classics of other languages their own, and he has wise words on the difficulties and achievements of individual translators.

Ezra Pound once said: "English literature lives on translation, it is fed by translation: every new heave is stimulated by translation, every allegedly quiet age is an age of translations." This booklet is a valuable commentary on this judgement by a writer who has himself won distinction as a translator of Cervantes, Montaigne and Rabelais.

Bibliographical Series
of Supplements to 'British Book News'
on Writers and Their Work

GENERAL EDITOR
Bonamy Dobrée

ENGLISH TRANSLATORS AND TRANSLATIONS

by

J. M. Cohen

PUBLISHED FOR
THE BRITISH COUNCIL
and the NATIONAL BOOK LEAGUE
by LONGMANS, GREEN & CO.

LONGMANS, GREEN & CO. LTD.,
48 Grosvenor Street, London, W.1.
Railway Crescent, Croydon, Victoria, Australia
Auckland, Kingston (Jamaica), Lahore, Nairobi
LONGMANS SOUTHERN AFRICA (PTY) LTD.
Thibault House, Thibault Square, Cape Town,
Johannesburg, Salisbury
LONGMANS OF NIGERIA LTD.
W.R. Industrial Estate, Ikeja
LONGMANS OF GHANA LTD.
Industrial Estate, Ring Road South, Accra
LONGMANS GREEN (FAR EAST) LTD.
443 Lockhart Road, Hong Kong
LONGMANS OF MALAYA LTD.
44 Jalan Ampang, Kuala Lumpur
ORIENT LONGMANS LTD.
Calcutta, Bombay, Madras
Delhi, Hyderabad, Dacca
LONGMANS CANADA LTD.
137 Bond Street, Toronto 2

First Published in 1962
© J. M. Cohen 1962

Printed in Great Britain by
F. Mildner & Sons, London, E.C.1

To

E. V. RIEU

In pleasant remembrance of our joint
projects in the last fifteen years

CONTENTS

English Translators and Translations   Page 9

A Reading List   49

ILLUSTRATIONS

I. Dr. E. V. Rieu

II. C. K. Scott Moncrieff (1889–1930)
From a portrait by Mercer in the Scottish National Portrait Gallery, showing the translator in the uniform of the King's Own Scottish Borderers (the Edinburgh Regiment) with which he served with distinction in the field

III. Arthur Waley

IV. Constance Garnett (1862–1946)

. . . between pages 28 *and* 29

ENGLISH TRANSLATORS AND TRANSLATIONS

I

ENGLISH translation has had two great periods of excellence: the first, generally called the Elizabethan though it extends from the reign of Henry VIII until the middle of the 17th century, in which the great works of the Classical past, and some modern books also, were introduced to a country which was from the literary point of view still backward, but whose language was at its freshest and most vigorous; and the second, which began some twenty years ago and still continues, in which English has become and remains the common cultural language of a vast section of the world. Today more copies of the "Odyssey", for example, circulate in English than in any other language, and appearance in an English translation will probably find an author a far wider public than he can hope to reach in his original tongue. Both these great periods of translation coincide with the emergence of a new class of reader in Britain itself. The new rich merchant or landowner of Tudor times, lacking the Latin and French of the medieval noble and cleric, demanded from the new printing-presses the great books of the world in his own tongue; and similarly the new educated classes of our day, whose training has been in the sciences rather than in languages, look to the paper-back industry to give them readable versions of those masterpieces which gather dust on the library shelves until reintroduced in the idiom of their own day.

Every great book demands to be re-translated once in a century, to suit the change in standards and taste of new generations, which will differ radically from those of the past. The Elizabethan translations ignored their author's style and background, intent only on producing a book for their own times; the 18th century made the Classics conform to their own aristocratic standards, ruthlessly pruning away all complexities and digressions that might cause a gentleman's interest to flag; the Victorians conferred on all works alike the brown varnish of antiquarianism; and our own age, in its scientific devotion to simplicity and accuracy, demands plain versions which sacrifice sound to sense, and verbal idiosyncracy to the narrative virtues. It is this preference for plainness that has won our modern translations their wide public in countries where English is only the second language.

II

Up to the 14th Century, the very small body of writers and educated readers in England used Latin and French in preference to the rude tongue of the peasant and citizen. Thomas d'Angleterre, Robert Wace and Marie de France may have written on English soil and certainly treated subjects drawn from English and Welsh history and legend, but which belong to the history of French literature. Geoffrey of Monmouth and John of Salisbury used Latin, and the tradition of Latin writing was very slow to die, since only in the ancient tongue could a writer hope to address a universal audience such as he would today reach with English.

England's first great translator, Geoffrey Chaucer (c.1340–1400), who was also her first great poet, adapted all the leading themes of current Western literature to English uses. Besides acclimatising the ballade, the Boccaccian romance, the *fabliau* or popular story of Flanders, and the animal fable, he translated at least one section—two others are attributed to him—of his century's favourite poem, "The Romaunt of the Rose", and the whole of its favourite work of religious philosophy, Boethius's "De consolatione philosophie", which had been translated into Anglo-Saxon by King Alfred. Chaucer's standard of craftsmanship and accuracy was very high. Indeed a comparison between his description, in the "Romaunt", of the secret garden as the dreamer first saw it (lines 135–146) and a prose rendering by a modern scholar (Brian Woledge: "Penguin Book of French Verse, I", p. 145) provides the reader with one more reason for respecting the father of English poetry. Chaucer used Guillaume de Lorris's original iambic couplet with its four-beat lines, a measure unnatural to modern English which more readily adapts itself to the pentameter:

> And when I had a whyle goon,
> I saugh a GARDIN right anoon,
> Ful long and brood, and everydel
> Enclos it was, and walled wel,
> With hye walles embatailled,
> Portrayed without, and wel entailled
> With many riche portraitures;
> And both images and peyntures
> Gan I biholde bisily.
> And I wol telle you, redily,
> Of thilke images the semblaunce,
> As fer as I have remembraunce.

Chaucer takes the liberty of expanding de Lorris's ten lines to a dozen, and to get the rhyme of his third, fourth and final couplets crudely anglicises the French words in a way that would be forbidden to a modern poet. Yet to a reader with little 13th century French he is almost as good a guide as Professor Woledge, whose version begins:

> When I had gone a little way, I saw an orchard great and wide, all enclosed with a high battlemented wall, painted and carved on its outer side with many richly adorned inscriptions . . .

As translator and adaptor, Chaucer laid the foundations of modern English narrative poetry. But the lyric too received its original impetus from the translation or adaptation of secular French poetry in the Provençal tradition, and of Latin hymns. The very early "Sumer Is Icumen In" was found in a monkish commonplace book which contains no other poem in English, but many in Latin and French. It is itself an exercise in the Provençal manner, a *reverdie* or spring-song, of which examples occur in every literature that was affected by the Troubadours. An equally beautiful though less well-known short lyric of approximately the same date, "When the Turf is the Tower", appears in its manuscript form directly under its Latin original and the handful of poems that survive by Friar William Herebert (?–1330), the first of our lyrical poets to leave us his name, includes translations from the popular Latin hymns, "Vexilla Regis prodeunt", "Hostis Herodis impie", "Veni creator spiritus", and "Ave Maris Stella", which were no doubt improvised for the purpose of preaching in the vernacular, a custom which was responsible also for the Psalter of the more pedestrian Richard Rolle (c.1300–1349), a contemplative more remarkable for his mystical writing than as a poet.

The most important English translation of the 14th century was, however, the Wyclif Bible of 1384, which reveals all the weaknesses of English prose-writing at that date. Whereas the rhythms of verse, both alliterative and rhymed, exploited the character of the language, those of prose lumbered somewhat unhappily in the wake of Latin rhetoric. The passage from St. John's Gospel which tells of the coming of the Baptist is, in Wyclif's phrases, gracelessly repetitious:

> a man was sente fro god: to whom the name was Ioon/ this man cam into witnessynge that he shulde bere witnessynge of the light. that all men should believe by him./ he was not the light: but that he bere witnessynge of the light· it was verrey lighte the which lighteneth eche man comynge into the world.

Tyndale, the next heretical translator, found in his version of 1534 not only the rhythms which would be followed in the Authorized Version, the greatest of all English translations, but words which were taken over almost unaltered by its translating committee. Where Wyclif's phrasing is abrupt, Tyndale's prose flows in a manner that looks forward to that of the Elizabethans. His repetitions display variety of sentence-structure rather than poverty of language.

> There was a man sent from God, whose name was Iohn. The same cam as a witnes to beare witnes of the lyght, that all men through him myght beleve. He was not that lyght: but to beare witnes of the lyght. That was a true lyght, which lyghteth all man that come into the worlde.

Already, towards the end of the 15th century, the first great era of English translation had begun. The invention of printing vastly increased the supply of books, and widened the circle of potential book-buyers. Malory's "Morte D'Arthur", adapted and printed by Caxton in 1485, must count only partly as a translation, since though based on a number of earlier Arthurian romances, it was freely adapted and expanded. There is as much of Malory in the book as of his original sources. Lord Berners' translation of Froissart's Chronicles, on the other hand, though less well-known, hardly falls behind it in the beauty of its prose. John Bouchier, Lord Berners (c.1469–1533) was a soldier, diplomat and writer with a developed taste for that romantic literature which was so popular at the very moment when the invention of gunpowder and printing was reducing the ideas of chivalry to a picturesque absurdity. Berners not only translated Froissart and the romance of 'Huon of Bordeaux', but also that famous Renaissance forgery "The Golden Book of Marcus Aurelius", or "Relox de Principes" of the Spaniard Antonio de Guevara, whose studied anti-theses, internal rhymes and assonances, and repetitions or doublets, provided the germ for the Euphuistic style of the early Elizabethans. Knowing no Spanish, Berners translated the book from a French translation, a precedent followed by many well-known craftsmen even as late as our present century. Berners wrote a fine flowing style which is even and discursive and equally capable of reciting a battle-roll, of describing the loot, intrigue and destruction of a sordid campaign, and of recording a simple moment with overtones of mystery that remind one of Malory. Such a moment is that in which Sir John Froissart rides out on a quite unimportant journey like one of Arthur's knights embarking on a quest:

> The next day we departed and roode to dyner to Mountgarbell, and so to Ercye, and there we dranke, and by sun setting we came to Ortaise. The knight alighted at his owne lodgynge, and I alighted at the Mone, wher dwelte a squier of the erles, Ernalton de Pyne, who well receyved me, bycause I was of Fraunce. Sir Spayne of Leon went to the castell to therle, and found him in his galarye, for he had dyned a lytell before; for the erles usage was alwayes, that it was hyghe noone or he arose out of his bedde, and I supped ever at midnight.

Berners' Froissart was the first of the great English prose translations, commonly called Elizabethan, which were designed for the ever increasing middle-class which had no knowledge of the original tongues, but a great curiosity, nourished by Renaissance scholarship, to make acquaintance with the great writers of the near and distant past. From Berners' Froissart to the unfinished Rabelais of Sir Thomas Urquhart, from 1525 to 1653, the output of distinguished translations was continuous. In general, the style was exuberant and, judged by present day standards, somewhat marred by the tricks of Euphuism, nouns and adjectives generally appearing in pairs, and by a certain syntactical slackness which renders the connexion between one sentence and the next at times imprecise. Exactness of rendering too, yields on most occasions to a certain leisurely readability. The Elizabethans seem to have designed their translations for reading aloud on winter evenings; their habit of repetition, often so foreign to the original, makes for drowsiness, and at the same time guarantees that the listener will not have dropped far behind if for a moment he closes his eyes.

The Plutarch of Sir Thomas North (1523–1601?), most famous because Shakespeare used it as a source-book for his

Roman plays, was translated not from the Greek, but from the French of Jacques Amyot, and because of this double refraction detail is often blurred that was perfectly clear in the original. An anecdote from the early manhood of Alcibiades, for example, becomes almost legendary in its vagueness when handled by North:

> For they saye there was one Diomedes of Athens, a friend of Alcibiades, and no ill man, who desired once in his life to winne a game at the playes Olympicall. This man being enformed that the Argives had a coche excellently furnished, belonging to the common weale, and knowing that Alcibiades could doe very much in the cittie of Argos, bicause he had many friends in the same; he came to intreate Alcibiades to buye his coche for him. Alcibiades thereupon bought it, but kept it to him selfe, not regarding Diomedes request he had made.

Using almost a hundred words, North entirely loses the dramatic quality of the incident, which Ian Scott-Kilvert, a modern translator[1], captures in no more than eighty-five:

> The story is that there was at Athens a certain Diomedes, a respectable man and a friend of Alcibiades, who was keenly ambitious to win a victory at Olympia. He discovered that there was a racing chariot at Argos which was the property of the city and as he knew that Alcibiades had many friends and was extremely influential there, he persuaded him to buy it. Alcibiades made the purchase for his friend, but then entered the chariot for the race as his own.

The Montaigne of John Florio (1533–1625), which is rated even more highly as a masterpiece of Elizabethan translation, also blurs the hard contours of a style which, though intellectually discursive, is far tauter in its reasoning than its Anglo-Italian translator supposed. Florio does not always use more words than his modern successors. He generally fails however to convey the exactness of Montaigne's descriptions, as in this passage from the essay on Cannibals:

[1] Plutarch: *The Rise and Fall of Athens*. Nine Greek Lives (Penguin Books, 1960).

After they have long time used and entreated their prisoners well, and with all commodities they can devise, he that is the Master of them; summoning a great assembly of his acquaintance; tieth a corde to one of the prisoners armes, by the end whereof he holds him fast, with some distance from him, for feare he might offend him, and giveth the other arme, bound in like manner, to the dearest friend he hath, and both in the presence of all the assembly kill him with swords.

The actual meaning is more accurately though perhaps less gracefully conveyed in a modern version[1], which renders the manner of the captive's death in concrete language:

He then ties a rope to one of the prisoner's arms, holding him by the other end, at some yards' distance for fear of being hit; and these two, in front of the whole assembly, despatch him with their swords.

Whereas Plutarch and Montaigne lose their natural outline when clothed in Elizabethan dress, Philemon Holland (1552–1637) seems almost to improve Pliny's "Natural History" by conferring an air of portent and mystery on its farrago of strange information and theory. Despite his Euphuistic doublets, Holland writes a fine, slow-moving prose:

Not in vaine the planet of the moone is supposed to be a Spirit: for this is it which satisfieth the earth to her content: she it is that in her approach and coming toward, filleth bodies full; and in her retire and going away, emptieth them againe. And hereupon it is, that in her growth, all shelle-fish waxe and encrease; and those creatures which have no blood, them most of all do feele her spirit.

H. Rackham's Loeb translation of 1938 renders Pliny's dubious science more accurately, but could never restore the book to the popularity that it enjoyed in Elizabeth's days. He begins the same passage:

[1] Montaigne: Essays, translated by J. M. Cohen (Penguin Books, 1958).

This is the source of the true conjecture that the moon is rightly believed to be the star of the breath, and that it is this star that saturates the earth and fills bodies by its approach and empties them by its departure.

Even in this version the number of words is twice that of the Latin.

A similar exuberance affects the "Don Quixote" of Thomas Shelton, an Irishman, who translated the first part before Cervantes had finished the second. Shelton, whose Spanish was far from perfect, successfully imitates the tone of Cervantes' voice, even though he misses many of his allusions. Written at a time when English was still rich in proverbs, his version conveys the saltiness of Sancho's speech better than any subsequent attempt. Where he fails to understand a phrase, Shelton unashamedly invents a substitute that generally proves to be quite as good. He is at his best at that moment during Sancho's ill-starred governorship of his Isle when he decides to conceal the fact that he cannot write:

"I can set to my name", quoth Sancho, "for when I was constable of our town I learned to make certain letters, such as are set to mark trusses of stuff, which they said spelt my name: besides now, I'll feign that my right hand is maimed, and so another shall firm for me; for there's a remedy for everything but death, and since I bear sway I'll do what I list; for, according to the proverb, (*a troop of absurd speeches still in Sancho's part*) He that hath the judge to his father etc, and I am governor, which is more than judge. Ay, ay, let 'em come and play at bo-peep, let 'em backbite me, let 'em come for wool, and I'll send them back shorn; whom God loves, his house is savoury to him, and everyone bears with the rich man's follies. . . ."

Sancho is never-ending, and Shelton can find an equivalent for every one of his homely phrases. A modern translator may ignore all the rest of his predecessors, but is compelled to steal or adapt something from Shelton.

Masterly though Shelton was, he was eclipsed as an inventor of exuberant language by Sir Thomas Urquhart (1611–c.1660), an eccentric Scottish royalist, who left his Rabelais unfinished to be completed by Peter Motteux (1659–1717), a man of less calibre and the first of the professional translators-for-profit. Urquhart was not only capable of matching and freely expanding the French monk's most complicated passages of associative verbiage. He could also write with an exactness that would have been beyond the powers of the Elizabethan translators. His account of the scholastic argument in dumb-show between Panurge and the Englishman correctly describes even the most complicated gestures of the antagonists.

> Everybody then taking heed, and hearkening with great silence, the Englishman lift up on high into the air his two hands severally, clenching in all the tops of his fingers together, after the manner, which, *a la Chinonnese*, they call the hen's arse, and struck the one hand on the other by the nails four several times. Then he, opening them, struck the one with the flat of the other, till it yielded a clashing noise, and that only once. Again, in joining them as before, he struck twice, and afterwards four times in opening them.

Urquhart's directions are sufficient to enable a reader to imitate each one of Panurge's movements. Unfortunately he had no successors. Motteux's completion was a work-a-day job: nor was his "Don Quixote", though far more popular to this day, the equal of Shelton's. The Restoration and 18th Century translator cut and adapted to the taste of his age. Where Shelton's version is longer than Cervantes', Motteux's and its immediate successor Jarvis's are shorter. Allusions and digressions disappear, as does the conversational tone of the original. Motteux and Sir Roger L'Estrange (1616–1704), whose "Visions", an adaptation of Quevedo's "Sueños" was a very popular work in its day, are typical competent practitioners. Dryden, on the other hand, produced a more faithful Plutarch than North's, and Charles Cotton (1630–1668), who wrote Part two of the

"Compleat Angler", comes nearer to Montaigne than Florio, since he writes a clearer and less congested sentence and is free from Euphuism.

Other competent translations which were widely read throughout the 18th century include L'Estrange's *Seneca* and Jeremy Collier's *Meditations* of Marcus Aurelius, both of which played their part in moulding the Stoical character of the educated man of the day. With these works, which belong to the beginning of the century, the first great period of prose translation ends.

III

The great achievements of the Elizabethan translators were in prose. Though the reputation of Chapman's Homer stands high, the work is readable only in extracts. "Judged as a feat of endurance", writes Doctor Tillyard[1], "Chapman's Homer is indeed a prodigy; judged as a poem, the very things that made it a prodigy destroy its value. Bent beneath his labour, Chapman had no strength left to match poetry with poetry." The judgement is not unfair, and is well borne out by the passage which Doctor Tillyard chooses as his illustration, Priam's speech in the last book of the Iliad, in which he begs Achilles to restore Hector's body:

> See in me, O godlike Thetis' sonne,
> Thy aged father, and perhaps even now being outrunne
> With some of my woes, neighbour foes (thou absent) taking
>> time
> To do him mischiefe, no meane left to terrifie the crime
> Of his oppression; yet he heares thy graces still survive
> And joyes to heare it, hoping still to see thee safe arrive
> From ruin'd Troy. But I (curst man) of all my race shall live
> To see none living. Fiftie sonnes the Deities did give
> My hopes to live in—all alive when neare our trembling shore
> The Greeke ships harbor'd—and one wombe nineteen of these
>> sons bore.

[1] The English Epic and its Background, 1945, p. 359.

Chapman's uses of the rhymed *fourteener* as the equivalent of Homer's hexameter produces, in Matthew Arnold's words, "a jogging rapidity rather than a flowing rapidity".[1] In his "Odyssey", on the other hand, by adopting the rhymed couplet, he exchanged ruggedness for pedestrianism. It was remarkable that an Elizabethan should have the Greek to make this version, but few will greet Chapman's work with the delight of Keats, for each century since Chapman's has produced a better and more Homeric "Iliad" and "Odyssey".

Some other verse translators of the period were faced with less serious problems since the eight-line stanza of their originals was a living measure, which could be written in the tradition of Spenser's nine-line stanza, the measure of "The Faerie Queene". Sir John Harington's version of Ariosto's "Orlando Furioso", Edward Fairfax's of Tasso's "Gerusalemme Liberata", and Sir Richard Fanshawe's of Camoes' "Lusiadas" are all readable substitutes for these three great artificial epics of the Renaissance, and John Sylvester's "Divine Weekes and Works", also, a free translation of du Bartas' "Semaines", which was vastly influential in its day, is in Doctor Tillyard's words "good sound stuff for cut-and-come again reading".[2]

New heights of verse translation were attained by John Dryden (1631–1700) with his version of the "Aeneid", a work attempted by several of his predecessors without conspicuous success. Dryden drew on them all to make Virgil speak, as he says in his "Essay on Translation", "in words such as he would probably have written if he were living and an Englishman". The Restoration poet's easy narrative powers and his mastery of the rhymed iambic couplet gave him advantages that the scrupulous Virgil did not possess. The Roman poet had however a subtlety and richness of meaning which Dryden could not equal with such stock expressions of the day as "his watery way",

[1] On Translating Homer.
[2] Op. cit. p. 353.

"secret springs" and "purple gore". Dryden naturalised
Virgil, however, in a translation that frequently attained
nobility even though it sometimes lapsed into the vulgarity
of what was, compared with the 18th century, an insensitive
age. At his best, in that passage from the second book in
which the dead Hector appears before Aeneas in a dream,
Dryden writes an English epic that is indeed for his age the
equivalent of Virgil's:

> 'Twas in the dead of night, when sleep repairs
> Our bodies, worn with toils, or minds, with cares,
> When Hector's ghost before my sight appears:
> A bloody shroud he seemed, and bathed in tears;
> Such as he was, when, by Pelides slain,
> Thessalian coursers dragged him o'er the plain.
> Swoln were his feet, as when the thongs were thrust
> Through the bored holes: his body black with dust:
> Unlike that Hector who returned from toils
> Of war, triumphant in Aeacian spoils;
> Or him, who made the fainting Greeks retire,
> And launched against their navy Phrygian fire.
> His hair and beard stood stiffened with his gore;
> And all the wounds he for his country bore
> Now streamed afresh, and with new purple ran.

Though Dryden did not always capture with his very
different talents what he himself called the "exactness and
sobriety" of his originals, he went too far when he accused
himself of a failure to do justice to Virgil, and said that he
believed himself better suited to cope with Homer's "fiery
way of writing".[1]

Alexander Pope (1688–1744) certainly failed to catch the
fiery quality in the "Iliad" and "Odyssey", but wrote
magnificent 18th century poetry. Of this failure he was
well aware. While praising Homer as the first of poets in
the opening paragraphs of the introduction to his "Iliad",
he warns his reader that "our author's work is a wild
paradise", which he is setting out to reduce to order. Yet

---

[1] Letter to Charles Montague, quoted by Tillyard, op. cit. p.481.

when he disclaims all intention of "deviating into the modern manners of expression", one cannot suppress a smile. Pope's age was unpropitious to the epic, and more at home in didactic verse, and it is precisely on its didactic and moralizing sides that Pope's translation is farthest from Homer. Very often, indeed, he loses Homer's immediacy, to achieve only a superbly polished reflection. Yet his rendering of the lines already quoted in Chapman's version certainly conveys the majesty of the poem and a depth of simple emotion even though Priam's grief is expressed in highly formalized language:

> Ah think, thou favour'd of the powers divine!
> Think of thy father's age, and pity mine!
> In me that father's reverend image trace,
> Those silver hairs, that venerable face;
> His trembling limbs, his helpless person see!
> In all my equal, but in misery!
> Yet now, perhaps, some turn of human fate
> Expels him helpless from his peaceful state;
> Think, from some powerful foe thou seest him fly,
> And beg protection with a feeble cry.
> Yet still one comfort in his soul may rise;
> He sees his son still lives to glad his eyes,
> And, hearing, still may hope a better day
> May send him thee, to chase that foe away.
> No comforts to my griefs, no hopes remain,
> The best, the bravest, of my sons are slain!
> Yet what a race! ere Greece to Ilion came,
> The pledge of many a loved and loving dame:
> Nineteen one mother bore—Dead, all are dead!

The build-up is slow, and the climax is perhaps disappointing. Yet the speech has a sustained dignity that entirely escaped Chapman, and that no other verse translator of Homer achieved.

The remainder of the 18th century saw much competent prose translation, but little that was remarkable in verse. Early attempts to render poems from Celtic, Norse and

Oriental tongues were marred by an excess of convention-
ality. MacPherson's *Ossian*, though largely a fake, has more
affinities with Gaelic poetry than Gray's attempts at the
Welsh and the Norse, or the Calcutta judge, Sir William
Jones's (1748–1794) more accurate renderings from the
Persian. Not until the blank-verse Dante of H. F. Cary
(1772–1844), Coleridge's scenes from Schiller's "Wallenstein", and Shelley's fragments from Goethe and Calderón
and the Homeric Hymns is a high standard again attained.

Cary's Dante gives a good and even account of the
"Commedia", which retained currency until displaced by
the *terza rima* versions of Laurence Binyon and Dorothy
Sayers, and Coleridge's "Wallenstein" at times improves
on the stock dramatic rhetoric of the original. Shelley,
however, is of another class. He demonstrates the heights
to which translation can rise when a poet of genius chooses
a work to which he feels attuned. In his scenes from "El
mágico prodigioso" he makes no attempt to reproduce
Calderón's antithetical style. Instead he renders its thought
and imagery with a freedom denied to the Spaniard in his
century of ecclesiastical censorship. In the Daemon's speech,
when he appears, as if escaped from the sea, to renew his
temptation of Cyprian, Shelley translated poetry into
poetry, bridging the hundred and fifty years between the
Baroque and the Romantic by a just equivalence of style:

> DAEMON (aside) It was essential to my purpose
> To wake a tumult on the sapphire ocean,
> That in this unknown form I might at length
> Wipe out the blot of the discomfiture
> Sustained upon the mountain, and assail
> With a new war the soul of Cyprian,
> Forging the instruments of his destruction
> Even from his love and from his wisdom. . . .

The scenes do not reveal themselves as a translation, yet
convey, as Fitzgerald's later adaptations from Calderón do
not, the essence of the Spanish poet's intention. Had Shelley

not devoted himself to original poetry, he might well have been the greatest translator of the 19th century.

IV

The theory of Victorian translation appears from our point of view to have been founded on a fundamental error. The aim was to convey the remoteness both in time and place of the original work by the use of a mock-antique language which was called by William Morris "Wardour Street English", after the fake-antique and theatrical costumiers' shops which were to be found there. The theory was set out by J. H. Newman, brother of the Cardinal, who demanded that "the translator should retain every peculiarity of the original, so far as he is able, with the greater care the more foreign it may be". The Elizabethans had viewed Plutarch, Pliny and Homer as moralists, historians, and story-tellers whose climate of thought and world-picture did not greatly differ from their own. Dress them in Elizabethan costume, and like Macbeth, Julius Caesar or Henry V, they were men of the 16th century. Distance of time and place counted for nothing. The Victorians, by contrast, insisted on it as a prime reality of which the reader must be constantly reminded. A leading exponent of this type of translation was Thomas Carlyle (1795–1881), whose versions of German stories outdo their originals in Teutonic ungain-liness of style. But one of the most extreme practitioners was Morris himself, who with his collaborator A. J. Wyatt rendered the Saxon epic "Beowulf" in a language such as English might have been had there been no Norman conquest and no cultural traffic with the Latin world. "Beowulf" certainly presents a special problem. Its language was formal and archaic even at the time when it was first recited. But Morris felt it necessary to stress its antiquity in every line:

> Out then spake Hrothgar; for he to the hall went,
> By the staple a-standing the steep roof he saw
> Shining fair with the gold, and the hand there of Grendel:
> "For this sight that I see to the All-wielder thanks
> Befall now forthwith, for foul evil I bided
> All griefs from this Grendel. . . . "

Even the meaning has become obscure. Much of the antique formality is retained in a twentieth century verse "Beowulf" by C. K. Scott Moncrieff, the translator of Proust. Scott Moncrieff retains the accentual measures and the alliteration, but uses a more modern vocabulary and verse order:

> Hrothgar spake:/ he to the hall going
> Stood on the steps of it,/ saw the steep-pitched roof
> With gold made lovely,/ and Grendel's hand.

The recent prose translation by David Wright[1], on the other hand, goes for the story, remembering that the primitive epic was a tale recited to an audience which could not read, and that, however distant their historical basis, such heroic stories were invariably narrated as if they had happened yesterday. Mr. Wright therefore translated the same passage in this way:

> As he entered the hall Hrothgar paused on the threshold. Seeing the tall golden roof-tree and Grendel's claw, he cried: "For this sight let thanks be at once offered to the Almighty! Much horror and distress I have had to suffer at the hands of Grendel. . . . "

The prose is direct and readable, but retains some hints of the archaism and formality of the work itself. Mr. Wright finds the Scott Moncrieff version "a monument of unreadable ingenuity". His own tells the story, but clearly changes the tone. As he himself says, only Ezra Pound, in his remarkable version of "The Seafarer", actually captures

[1] Penguin Books, 1959.

the real "feel" of old English poetry:

> Days little durable,
> And all arrogance of earthen riches,
> There come now no kings nor Caesars
> Nor gold-giving lords like those gone. . . .

Here the tone is preserved by a free use of the original measure, which is preferable both to the crabbed imitation of the earlier versions and to the plain narrative of David Wright. But Pound's "Seafarer" is an exceptional work, even for him. Most of his other translations, from the Italian and Provençal, are laced with Wardour Street pseudo-antiquities.

The Victorian translator was hampered by his preconceptions. William Morris associated the fire which both Dryden and Pope demanded from any translation of the Classical epics with antiquity of diction and the ring of the narrator's voice. In his version the "Aeneid", a poem designed for a highly cultivated audience and for the most formal recitation, becomes a tale of action such as might have been related around the fire in the depths of an Icelandic winter; and the Italian translations of D. G. Rossetti are similarly partial, since they select those features of the centuries before Raphael that agree best with the vague and languid pessimism of the pre-Raphaelite movement:

> Lo! I am she who makes the wheel to turn;
> Lo! I am she who gives and takes away;
> Blamed idly, day by day,
> In all my acts by you, ye humankind.

These lines, though allegedly based on a Canzone by Dante, in no way differ from the original poetry of Rossetti and his circle.

Robert Browning, on the other hand, in the foreword to his translation of the "Agamemnon" of Aeschylus, states that it is the translator's duty "to be literal at every cost save that of absolute violence to our language": a healthy prescription which he nullifies by granting himself in his next sentence "the use of certain allowable constructions which, happening to be out of daily favour, are all the more appropriate to archaic workmanship". Yet the rough-hewn English which he uses conforms to no language that ever has been in favour; it is a mock-Greek variant of Browning's own style which often, in its pursuit of literalness, does un-pardonable violence to the English language, "Klutaim-nestra's" speech to the "Choros", protesting against her exile, provides an example of this:

> Now, indeed, thou adjudgest exile to me,
> And citizen's hate, and to have popular curses:
> Nothing of this against the man here bringing,
> Who, no more awe-checked than as 'twere a beasts' fate,—
> With sheep abundant in the well-fleeced graze-flocks,—
> Sacrificed *his* child

Here the pedantic use of *popular* for *of the people*, and the curiously Germanic compound nouns and adjectives are more odd than archaic. Browning has invented his own Greek world and placed Aeschylus in it. Similarly, Gilbert Murray (1866–1959) a far more experienced scholar, in the early years of this century, found an equivalent for the Greek verse dialogue and chorus in the measures of Swin-burne, and translated the same lines of Clytemnestra's speech into a clearer but none the less Victorian idiom:

> Aye, now, for me, thou hast thy words of fate;
> Exile from Argos and the people's hate
> For ever! Against him no word was cried,
> When, recking not, as 'twere a beast that died,
> With flocks abounding o'er his wide domain,
> He slew his child . . .

Murray finds it necessary to resort to a stock poetic idiom (*recking not, as 'twere*) in order to give the first of Greek dramatists majesty and temporal distance. A contemporary translator, Louis MacNeice (b.1907), by contrast, still preserves Aeschylus's hieratic dignity when translating the same lines into a timeless though hardly colloquial English:

> Now your verdict—in my case—is exile
> And to have the people's hatred, the public curses,
> Though then in no way you opposed this man
> Who carelessly, as it were a herd of sheep
> Out of the abundance of his fleecy flocks
> Sacrificed his own daughter . . .

MacNeice succeeds by allowing Aeschylus to speak for himself without "deviating into modern manners". A later generation may, however, accuse him of using the language of his own poetry and W. H. Auden's, in much the same way as Murray made use of Swinburne's, which he did to an even greater extent in translating Euripides than when confronted with the greater strictness of the "Agamemnon". The choruses of Murray's "Hippolytus" indeed, are indistinguishable in manner from those of Swinburne's "Atalanta in Calydon":

> There riseth a rock-born river,
> Of Ocean's tribe, men say;
> The crags of it gleam and quiver,
> And pitchers dip in the spray:
> A woman was there with raiment white
> To bathe and spread in the warm sunlight,
> And she told a tale to me there by the river,
> The tale of the Queen and her evil day.

The most famous verse translation of the 19th century, Fitzgerald's "Rubaiyat of Omar Khayyam", has the advantage over these versions from the Greek, in that there was no original to which Fitzgerald (1809–1883) owed a debt of faithfulness. It is merely a Victorian poem in the oriental convention based on some quatrains by the Persian astronomer-poet, which in its use of personification, its

Dr. E. V. Rieu

C. K. Scott-Moncrieff (1889–1930)

From a portrait by Mercer in the Scottish National Portrait Gallery.

Arthur Waley

Constance Garnett (1862–1946)

over-capitalization, apostrophe and stock poeticism recalls all the worst features of minor Victorian poetry. Fitzgerald's Persia, despite his knowledge of the language, most forcibly recalls the divan-room in a 19th century furniture exhibition.

Morris, Rossetti, Browning, Murray and Fitzgerald adapted their authors' styles to their more or less erroneous pictures of the age in which these authors lived and worked. But a more general form of Victorian distortion was practised by lesser men, who were often good scholars, simply in order to underline the greatness of the work they were presenting. The more important the book in the cultural history of mankind, the more self-important the language in which it must be translated. Even "Don Quixote", which continually mocks at pomposities of verbiage and imagination, was subjected by its Victorian translators to a fatal process of verbal inflation. H. E. Watts, in his translation of 1888, shows himself a master of Cervantes' Spanish infinitely superior to Shelton and Motteux and their successor Smollett, who translated from the French. Yet in his awe before this mighty classic, he resorts to tortuous old-world language which turns Sancho from an earthy peasant into a pretentious clown. The squire is speaking the English of no known century when he protests to his master in these words against his rebuke for using too many proverbs:

> 'Fore God, Sir master of ours . . . but your worship makes complaint of a mighty little thing. Why the devil should you fret yourself because I make use of my estate who have none other nor other stock in trade but proverbs, and more proverbs, and just now I have four that offer which come fit like pears in a pottle; but I will not say them for good silence is called Sancho.

Cervantes' colloquial tone has vanished, and Sancho's proverbs have become deliberately quaint. The Spanish is accurately followed, yet if the tale were told by a reincarnate author to a contemporary audience, the introductory apostrophe would certainly be shorter, and the number of dependent clauses fewer. My own solution in the Penguin "Don Quixote" is:

> "Goodness me, my dear master . . . you complain about very small matters. Why the devil do you fret yourself because I make use of my wealth? For I have no other. My only fortune is proverbs and still more proverbs. Why four of them occur to me now that come slick to the point, or like pears in a basket. But I won't say them for Sage Silence is Sancho's name." (II, 43)

Even this retains a slightly archaic tone, and the third and fourth sentences might read still more colloquially; "I've got nothing else. Proverbs and proverbs, that's my whole stock-in-trade."

This Victorian version of "Don Quixote" is on the whole less fusty than the equally scholarly "Arabian Nights" of Sir Richard Burton (1821–1890), which contains such pseudo-Arabic convolutions as the opening of the Second Kalendar's tale:

> Know, O my lady, that I was not born one-eyed and mine is a strange story; an it were graven with needle-graver on the eye-corners, it were a warner to whoso would be warned.

While at other moments the narrator observes with a pomposity equal to that of Watts' Sancho: "Then she stripped off her outer gear and Badr-al-Din arose and doffed his clothes."

The recent translations of a few of these tales by N. J. Dawood preserve the oriental flavour while avoiding the grotesque literalness of Burton. In the same way the excessive archaisms of the Victorian translators of Icelandic sagas, Sir George Dasent, William Morris and others, have been avoided in one or two recent renderings, such as Magnus Magnusson and Hermann Patsson's "Njal's Saga".[1]

---

[1] Penguin Books, 1960.

V

Victorian standards began to mend about the year 1871, which saw the publication of Benjamin Jowett's Plato. Though feeling compelled to convey the importance and the temporal distance of the philosopher by a somewhat ponderous vocabulary and sentence structure, Jowett (1817–1898) saw no need to archaize. Describing the captives in the cave at the opening of the myth in "The Republic", he wrote decently in the language of his century:

> And now, I said, let me shew in a figure how far our nature is enlightened or unenlightened:—Behold! human beings living in an underground den, which had a mouth open towards the light and reaching all along the den; here they have been from their childhood, and have their legs and necks chained so that they cannot move, and can only see before them, being prevented by their chains from turning round their heads. Above and behind them a fire is blazing at a distance, and between the fire and the prisoners there is a raised way; and you will see, if you look, a low wall built along the way, like the screen that marionette players have in front of them, over which they show their puppets.

Jowett renders the Greek accurately and with due Victorian dignity, yet fails to interpret for his reader those sentences which should reveal the exact topography of the cave. How, one asks, can a mouth "reach all along the den"? Is the wall, which is behind the prisoners, above or below the raised way? Such questions of interpretation no doubt seemed to Jowett to be beside the point. His duty as translator was to put the Greek into English, not to make good his author's oversights or explain his meaning to readers who could not grasp it, in whatever language they found him, as readily as those of his own day. To add this duty to that of plain translation has become the task of the 20th century craftsman. In rendering the same passage seventy years later (1941), F. M. Cornford not only put

Plato's Greek into more current English, but conveyed by his more exact choice of words, and with the aid of a couple of footnotes, the precise relation to one another of the fire, the captives, the wall and the raised way:

> Next, said I, here is a parable to illustrate the degrees in which our nature may be enlightened or unenlightened. Imagine the condition of men living in a sort of cavernous chamber underground, with an entrance open to the light and a long passage all down the cave.[1] Here they have been from childhood, chained by the leg, and also by the neck, so that they cannot move and can see only what is in front of them. At some distance higher up is the light of a fire burning behind them, and between the prisoners and the fire is a track[2] with a parapet built along it, like the screen at a puppet show, which hides the performers while they show their puppets over the top.

> [1] The length of the "way in" (eisodos) to the chamber where the prisoners sit is an essential feature, explaining why no daylight reaches them.
> [2] The track crosses the passage into the cave at right angles, and is *above* the parapet built along it.

Cornford has realised the scene and recreated it for his reader, who might not have known from the Jowett version that the captives faced the light, though at such a distance from it that none of it reached them, and that in front of them was a wall of the cave, for the track was a winding one.

Cornford's "Republic" is a typical of the work of our century, which did not seriously begin until after the first World War. The Edwardian era suffered from a Victorian hang-over. Even such accomplished work as Constance Garnett's in the field of Russian and William Archer's in his complete Ibsen (completed 1912) constantly reminds the reader or listener that the characters were speaking Russian or Norwegian, and that only thanks to the translator do we know what they said. Their coy pet names, absurd endearments and stiff sentiments underline their essential foreignness, which is rendered almost unnoticeable in more recent translations of the same novels and plays.

In contrast to the Victorians and Edwardians, whose antiquarian productions are, by a complete reversal of taste, now declared unreadable, craftsmen in the last twenty years have aimed principally at interpretation in current language, even at the risk of reducing individual authors' styles and national tricks of speech to a plain prose uniformity, a danger which they have just succeeded in avoiding in the best of their work. They have also, in common with most writers of their time, modelled their prose closely on common speech rhythms. Where Jowett wrote a convoluted style, rich in semi-colons and unrelated clauses but deficient in full-stops, Cornford reduced his sentences to a 20th century length, even at the cost of sometimes leaving the reader to decide, in default of a guiding conjunction, exactly what relation one sentence bears to another.

As scholarly as the Victorians, the moderns strive to satisfy the vastly increased public which has remained at school till the age of 18, or has taken university courses in non-linguistic subjects and cannot consequently be expected to be primarily concerned with literature. The new translator, therefore, aims to make everything plain, though without the use of footnotes since conditions of reading have radically changed and the young person of today is generally reading in far less comfortable surroundings than his father or grandfather. He has therefore to carry forward on an irresistible stream of narrative. Little can be demanded of him except his attention. Knowledge, standards of comparison, Classical background: all must be supplied by the translator in his choice of words or in the briefest of introductions.

The plain prose narrative has already been discussed in the case of "Beowulf". The first and pioneer exercise in this manner, however, was E. V. Rieu's "Odyssey" of 1946. True, the prose "Odyssey" of S. H. Butcher and Andrew Lang (1879) was among the most successful of Victorian translations. Their language however was ornate, literary, and sometimes as obscure as Browning's through clinging too closely to the phraseology and word-order of the Greek. W. H. Rouse's version is plainer, but lacks distinction and settled purpose. As a successful headmaster, Rouse appears to have addressed himself, perhaps involuntarily, to the young. Rieu, on the other hand, began with the intention of obeying what he himself calls "the principle of equivalent effect", that is to say to create in an adult audience the same impression as was made by the original on its contemporaries. For this reason, since tales today are no longer told in verse, he decided to translate Homer's narrative into contemporary prose. In fact his cadences, if not his choice of vocabulary, are poetic, and his rendering of the Homeric epithet, a stumbling-block to most translators, skilful and various. In his "Iliad", which followed his "Odyssey" four years later, he gave both pathos and eloquence to Priam's plea to Achilles, already quoted in Chapman's and Pope's versions:

> "Most worshipful Achilles", he said, "think of your own father, who is the same age as I, and so has nothing but miserable old age ahead of him. No doubt his neighbours are oppressing him and there is nobody to save him from their depredations. Yet he at least has one consolation. While he knows that you are still alive, he can look forward day by day to seeing his beloved son come back from Troy; whereas my fortunes are completely broken. I had the best sons in the whole of this broad realm, and now not one, not one, I say, is left. There were fifty when the Achaean expedition came. Nineteen of them were born of one mother . . ."

"The frame of mind in which we approach an author", wrote Matthew Arnold in his essay "On Translating Homer", "influences our correctness of appreciation of him; and Homer should be approached by a translator in the simplest frame of mind possible." Arnold further advises any would-be translator of Homer "not to trouble himself with constructing a special vocabulary . . . in obedience to any theory about the peculiar qualities of Homer's style".

Dismissing Chapman for his Elizabethan complexity and the "high intellectualisation" of Pope's version, also he leaves the field open for a future translator who "will have an eye for the real matter". Though Arnold postulated the English hexameter as the best medium and was unduly anxious that this ideal version should satisfy the scholars rather than the Greekless public, the "eye for the real matter" in preference to the manner was first shown by Rieu, who insisted that the "Odyssey", with its well-knit plot, its psychological interest, and its interplay of character, is the true ancestor of the long line of novels that have followed it.[1]

VI

Twentieth century translators, influenced by the spread of science-teaching and the growing importance attached to accuracy even to the exclusion of spirit have, I repeat, generally concentrated on prose-meaning and interpretation, and neglected the imitation of form and manner.

There is, however, a field in which the reverse is true. The translation of lyrical poetry, always the most exacting undertaking, has engaged a number of fine poets who have in the last years added considerable tracts to the territory familiar to the reader of English. Outstanding as pioneer is Arthur Waley (b.1889), whose *Chinese Poems* now represent for our time the poetry of a whole civilization which was scarcely known before, since the few conventionally translated lyrics that had appeared created very little impression. Faced with the alternative of imitating form or content, Waley unhesitatingly chose the latter. His English measure, a variety of stressed verse which owes something to the example of Gerard Manley Hopkins, was adopted as an equivalent and not as an approximate copy. "Each character in the Chinese", wrote Waley in a note to his *170 Chinese*

[1] Introduction to the "Odyssey", p. 10.

Poems of 1918, "is represented by a stress in the English; but between the stresses unstressed syllables are of course interposed." The translation is vouched for as literal, and where padding might have been necessary to fill out a line, Waley has preferred to vary his metre in order to avoid it. He omits rhyme, since it is impossible to produce the same rhyming effects as the Chinese. The prescription, as set out in this note on method, might seem unpromisingly dry. But, as Waley notes, "about two lines out of three have a very definite swing similar to that of the Chinese lines". The translator, in fact, being himself poet as well as scholar, has written poems which stand as such in their own right. The grandeur of language and the subtle changes in pace of 'The Bones of Chuang Tzu' by Chang Heng (A.D. 78–139) represents Waley at his highest level:

> I, Chang P'ing-Tzu, had traversed the Nine Wilds and seen
> their wonders,
> In the eight continents beheld the ways of Man,
> The Sun's procession, the orbit of the Stars,
> The surging of the dragon, the soaring of the phoenix in his
> flight.
>
> In the red desert to the south I sweltered,
> And northward waded through the wintry burghs of Yu.
> Through the Valley of Darkness to the west I wandered,
> And eastward travelled to the Sun's extreme abode
> The stooping Mulberry Tree.
>
> So the seasons sped; weak autumn languished,
> A small wind woke the cold.
>
> And now with rearing of rein-horse,
> Plunging of the tracer, round I fetched
> My high-roofed chariot to westward.
> Along the dykes we loitered, past many meadows,
> And far away among the dunes and hills.
> Suddenly I looked and by the roadside
> I saw a man's bones lying in the squelchy earth,
> Black rime-frost over him . . .

The whole poem is sustained on this level. Vast cosmo-logical prospects are narrowed to a single conversation with the dead man on the value of a recall to life, which he rejects. Many of the poems which Waley has chosen are shorter and more personal. Poets hitherto unknown in English, such as Po Chü-i and Li Po, are called back from their distant centuries to take modern form and yet preserve the individuality of their own lives and age.

Occasional successes in the same manner have been scored by Ezra Pound, in "The Seafarer" already mentioned, and by Robert Graves (b.1895) in his "Instructions to the Orphic Adept"—almost completely adapted from the Greek—and his versions of the Mexican poet, Juana de la Cruz. John Masefield, J. E. Flecker and Stephen Spender, among our poets in their own right, have produced a few translations of authentic merit. However, since Waley set the example, much more systematic work has been done by devoted verse-translators with a view to introducing known and unknown poets from abroad, if not in their entirety, at least in adequate selections. Here the late Norman Cameron's Villon, and J. B. Leishman's renderings of Rilke are out-standing. In undertaking to present a very large proportion of the Austrian poet's output, Leishman set himself a task in which he has perhaps achieved only an uneven success. Unlike Waley, he has not striven merely for an equivalent form. He has aimed at a complete imitation and, faced with Rilke's close-packed reasoning, has sometimes produced poems that fail to sing. Nevertheless, he has made it possible for a large public with no first-hand knowledge to catch something of Rilke's individuality. Certainly Rilke's con-siderable influence on English poetry of the last thirty years has largely been conveyed by way of the Leishman versions. Similarly, Hölderlin, a poet who presents almost equal problems of interpretation though rhythmically easier to transmute, has taken satisfactory English form in the versions of Michael Hamburger.

One poet who devoted much of his energy to translation

was Roy Campbell (1901–1957). Beginning with Baudelaire, who has so far defeated every Englishman who has attempted him, Campbell went on to produce some uneven and rather too colourful Lorca and a complete version of the poems of St. John of the Cross, which cannot be bettered. Campbell possessed a great lyrical strength and boldness, and an almost Victorian power of writing not in single lines but stanza by stanza. His opening of St. John's most famous "En una noche oscura" has a remarkable authenticity, yet carries over almost the full rhyme-scheme of the original:

> Upon a gloomy night,
> With all my cares to loving ardours flushed,
> (O venture of delight!)
> With nobody in sight
> I went abroad when all my house was hushed.
> In safety, in disguise,
> In darkness up the secret stair I crept,
> (O happy enterprise!)
> Concealed from other eyes
> When all my house at length in silence slept.

Campbell's mastery is complete both here and in many single poems which he translated in the later years of his life from the Spanish and the Portuguese. Campbell's taste was individual; he enjoyed a rip-roaring poem even on a spiritual theme, and avoided the subtleties of half thought and shadowy emotion. Baudelaire's, in fact, was too subtle and divided a mind for him, and Lorca's a little too sensitive. So far English versions of Lorca have not been successful. This was however true of St. John up to the moment when Roy Campbell attempted him. The miracle of lyrical translation takes place only when poet and translator are almost evenly matched.

For this reason verse translations of Goethe, and particularly of his *Faust*, have been until recently unsatisfactory. However, in the last few years both Louis MacNeice and Philip Wayne have produced readable and characteristically

racy versions of Goethe's poem. The defects of most
Victorian translators of the play were that they endeavoured
to bring over into English a high seriousness which was not
present in the original. The best of them, such as that by the
American Bayard Taylor, fail for that reason, and because
of a quite un-Goethean obviousness in their rhymes.
Mephistopheles, "prying around" in the Classical Walpur-
gis-night of Part II, reflects somewhat heavy-footedly in
Taylor's version:

> And as among these fires I wander, aimless,
> I find myself so strange, so disconcerted:
> Quite naked most, a few are only shirted;
> The Griffins insolent, the Sphinxes shameless,
> And what not all, with pinions and with tresses,
> Before, behind, upon one's eyesight presses!—
> Indecency, 'tis true, is our ideal,
> But the Antique is too alive and real . . .

Compared with this version, Wayne's leaps briskly into life,
with no *poetic* verbiage or syntactical awkwardness:

> Now, as I wandered through the fields of flame,
> I'd much to vex me, much to disconcert:
> Naked the lot, just here and there a shirt,
> The sphinxes brazen, griffins without shame;
> The crowd of creatures, winged and tressed, displays
> No end of back and front views to the gaze . . .
> We, lewd at heart, can relish the salacious,
> But this antique's too lifelike and vivacious.

Wayne on the whole keeps it up, as indeed does MacNeice
also, from whom it would be easy to quote equal felicities.

Of similar accomplishment to Wayne's Goethe is a work
not strictly in the field of translation, the modernised
Canterbury Tales of Nevill Coghill, which have restored the
speed and immediacy of the original, now lost owing to the
ordinary reader's need to look up or remember the meaning
for Chaucer's time of phrases that have either lapsed from

the language or acquired different significance. Less well-known than Coghill's Chaucer is a similar and somewhat earlier modernization of Langland's *Vision of Piers Plowman* by Henry W. Wells (1938). Wells, a skilful modernizer, does not strain away the flavour of the ancient language though he effectively removes the linguistic difficulty of reading 14th century dialect. Another alliterative poem of the same epoch which presents difficulties to the modern reader, *Sir Gawain and the Green Knight*, has also been rendered into more contemporary English by Brian Stone. It is indeed now possible to read most of the masterpieces of the 14th century without undue puzzlement as to meanings.

Other attempts to naturalize into English tracts of poetry hitherto unknown to those without linguistic accomplishment, include collections of Russian poems made by Professor Maurice Bowra, who has himself contributed a number of splendid translations in full rhyme and exact metre of poems by writers of the revolutionary epoch, in particular of "The Twelve" by Alexander Blok, and of "I believe sang the guns and the squares" of Viktor Khlebnikov. Among the most interesting adaptations from the Russian, however, have been versions of the 19th century poet Fyodor Tyutchev, made by one of our most accomplished younger poets, Charles Tomlinson in collaboration with the Russian and English scholar Henry Gifford. The method of this small collection intrinsically differs from those of previous lyrical translators. The intention is to re-write the essentials of the poem in English, transferring it from its own century into our own, and choosing metres and rhyme-schemes suitable to the new poem but in no way matching the old. The endeavour would seem over-bold. Yet on comparing Tomlinson's versions with the Russian one discovers that new poems have been created and nothing of the originals has been sacrificed except so much as would have made them seem trite derivatives from the German romantics if brought across in the conventional way.

> I knew her erst in days afar
> That full of fairy fancies are . . .

are the opening lines of a Tyutchev lyric rendered by Sir
Cecil Kisch. This translation catches all the qualities in the
Russian poet which bind him to his century. Tomlinson,
on the other hand, lifts him into ours:

> Neither thought not threat
> But a limp and sullen sleep
> This night-sky gloom
> Clouded from every quarter.
> Only the intermittent flare as
> Lightnings, deaf-mute demons
> Converse with one another.

This opening of a short lyric conveys the essence of
Tyutchev, the sense of living nature and its menaced beauty
that gave him so strong an influence over Boris Pasternak.
Several attempts have been made to present selections from
this great poet of modern times, but so far without outstanding success. Herbert Marshall's versions of his contemporary, Vladimir Mayakovsky, on the other hand, catch
the pulsing speed and vigour of a man whose personal
violence made him for a short time the laureate of the
Revolution. Marshall's version of his poem on the suicide
of Yessenin has all the colloquial ease of Philip Wayne's
Goethe in a higher concentration:

> You have passed,
>   as they say,
>   into worlds elsewhere.
> Emptiness . . .
>   Fly
>   cutting your way into starry
>   dubiety,
> No advances,
>   no pubs for you there.
> Sobriety.

No, Yessenin,
                    this
                        is not deridingly,—
    in my throat
                not laughter
                            but sorrow racks
    I see—
            your cut-open hand
                            lingeringly
        swings
                your very own bones
                            like a sack.

Marshall catches to perfection the mixture of curtness, defiance, poeticism and mock-poeticism that went to the making of this remarkable poet.

A final mention must be made of the American poet W. S. Merwin, a recent resident in this country, whose versions of a selection of the traditional Spanish *romances* has for the first time conveyed their individual quality into English. Previous translators since the 18th century had rendered them in English ballad metres, with plangent rhymes to correspond with the alliterative half-rhymes of the Spanish. Merwin, on the other hand, catches the colloquial convention and the unobvious singing quality of the *romance*, as in that most beautiful fragment, "The Prisoner":

It was May, the month of May,
When warm days are with us,
When the grain gets its growth
And the fields are in flower,
When the skylark sings
And the nightingale gives answer,
When those who are in love
Go in love's service,
Except for me, wretch living
In sorrow in this prison,
Not knowing when it is day

Nor when night has come
Except for a little bird
Which sang to me at dawn;
A man killed it with a crossbow,
God give him an ill reward!

It was almost certainly the example of Arthur Waley that prompted this group of poets to make more or less free versions of foreign writers to whom they felt specially attuned. In this way we have acquired a number of extensions to our own rich store of poetry, which have in varying degrees impressed and influenced the poets who are writing today.

VII

It was Rieu's example, however, and not Waley's that set a number of distinguished writers, of talents equal to those of the Elizabethan translators, to the work of retranslating the great works of the past for a 20th century audience. Robert Graves, Rex Warner, Philip Vellacott, Michael Grant, Aubrey de Sélincourt and W. F. Jackson Knight are among the outstanding practitioners of the new "plain prose" method which, upon examination, however, proves to be not a single method, like that of the Elizabethans, but to vary from the direct telling of a somewhat mannered story in Graves's version of Apuleius's "Golden Ass" to a radical expansion which brings out all the telescoped meanings and sub-meanings of the Latin in the case of Jackson Knight's "Aeneid". Verse is rendered in free verse forms by Vellacott and in prose by Jackson Knight. A strict following of Rieu's example is attempted by none.

The contrast between the Elizabethan and the 20th century method is most marked in the case of "The Golden Ass". William Adlington in his translation of 1566, intro-

duced the witch Meroë, the cause of all the hero's misfortunes, with a conversational and slightly Euphuistic
prolixity suitable for leisurely reading aloud:

> And so I fortuned to come to the house of an old woman that sold
> wine, called Meroë, who had her tongue sufficiently instructed to
> flattery: unto whom I opened the causes of my long peregrination
> and carefull travell, and of myne unlucky adventure; and after I
> had declared unto her such things as then presently came to my
> remembrance, shee gently entertained mee and made mee good
> cheere; and by and by beeing pricked by carnall desire, she brought
> mee to her own bed chamber.

Robert Graves writes for a reader in the train or on a
holiday beach. Reducing the whole matter to its bare
narrative bones, he says rather more—he is using a different
text—in a quarter less words:

> I went to an inn run by a woman named Meroë. She was no longer
> young but extraordinarily attractive, and when I told her my sad
> story and explained how anxious I was to return home after my
> long absence, she pretended to be deeply sympathetic, cooked me
> a grand supper for which she charged me nothing, and afterwards
> pressed me to sleep with her.

Graves claims the licence to "alter the order not only of
phrases but of sentences, where English prose logic differs
from Latin",[1] and to avoid the use of footnotes brings their
substance into the story itself whenever it reads obscurely.
He remains true, however, to the tone if not to the complex
language of his original, as he does also in his version of
Suetonius's "Twelve Caesars". When he grows impatient
with his author, on the other hand, he sharply alters the tone
and drops into irony at his expense. When Graves comes to
Lucan's evocation of the witch Erichto in the sixth book of
the "Pharsalia", he parodies rather than elucidates Lucan's
baroque talent:

[1] *The Golden Ass*, Introduction, p. 11.

Witches have introduced the art of dragging the stars from the sky; and know how to turn the moon dim and muddy-coloured, as though she were being eclipsed by the Earth's shadow—after which they pull her close to them and torture her until she secretes poisonous foam on the plants growing underneath.

This reads like a translation of one of the odder anecdotes from Pliny. It not only reduces exalted poetry to humble prose, but obliterates all the poetic content of the original. "Secretes" not only fails to correspond to the Latin, but suggests a modern scientific primer, while "to catch and bottle whatever lightning happened to fall", a few lines further on, makes the whole idea of witchcraft, in which Lucan believed, appear ridiculous.

At the opposite end of the scale Jackson Knight gives a more formal and detailed account of Aeneas's vision of the dead Hector than Dryden's version already quoted:

It was the hour when divinely-given rest first comes to poor human creatures, and creeps over them deliciously. In my sleep I dreamed that Hector stood there before my eyes. He looked most sorrowful, and was weeping plenteous tears. He was filthy with dust and blood, as he had been that day when he was dragged behind the chariot, and his feet were swollen where they had been pierced by the thongs. And, oh, how harrowing was the sight of him; how changed he was from the old Hector, back from battle wearing the spoils of Achilles, or that time when he had just flung Trojan firebrands onto the Greek ships! Now his beard was ragged and his hair clotted with blood, and all those wounds which he had sustained fighting to defend the walls of his homeland could still be seen.

Using more words even than Dryden—and twice as many as Virgil—Jackson Knight gives an exact rendering of his original, in plain and pleasing prose though with considerably less grace than Rieu in his Homer, or Graves in "The Golden Ass".

More strictly comparable to Dryden's is the verse "Aeneid" of C. Day Lewis (b.1904) which although as uneven in its language as Graves's Lucan conveys some of the sweep though not all the majesty of Virgil's poem. But Day Lewis is happier in his version of the "Georgics", which are more capable of translation in the homespun style of the contemporary poet who no longer aims at the epic grandeur postulated by Arnold.

Two recent verse translations of Dante's "Commedia", one by Laurence Binyon (1869–1942) and the other by Dorothy Sayers—the latter left incomplete at her death— fail for another reason to be completely satisfactory. The effort to sustain Dante's *terza rima* is in both cases heroic. Binyon, allowing himself more metrical freedom, comes closer to poetry, and at times writes fine passages. But the slightly pre-Raphaelite prose version of Thomas Okey better represents the essential simplicity of Dante's style and the complexity of his thought.

Standards of modern translation are extremely high, and the competence with which plays and novels with extremely up-to-date dialogue are rendered in unaffected English is quite remarkable. "Translaterese", the legacy of the Victorian amateur, has almost entirely disappeared. Here Scott Moncrieff's Proust set the example, which has been followed by Gerard Hopkins in his versions of Mauriac and other French novelists, by Edwin and Willa Muir in their magnificent versions of Kafka, by Eithne Wilkins and Ernst Kaiser in Robert Musil's novels, by Henry Reed and Archibald Colquhoun in various plays and novels from the Italian, and by David Magarshack and Rosemary Edmonds in their retranslations of familiar novels from the Russian.

In addition, much has been done in the last twenty years in the field of more specialized translations, such as those of the complete works of Freud and Jung, to provide what must be, in effect, official versions which will represent these most important thinkers in the wide regions where English is read in preference to German has necessitated the recruiting of translators not only skilled in their craft but well acquainted with the subject-matter of their originals. Theology too has attracted translators with more than literary talents capable of rendering the abstruse thought of such men as Kierkegaard, Heidegger and Karl Barth. The English translator has, in fact, in these fields the double responsibility of writing well and of representing his author's meaning so accurately that there shall be no appreciable difference between the English and the original. In this most exacting task a very high level of success has been achieved.

Much work of the past also has been presented afresh to the English-reading public in a form suitable to the straightforward requirements of this century. The next may, as E. V. Rieu expects, demand that the whole task be done over again to meet its different conventions. For the life of a translation rarely exceeds a hundred years, and those few which achieve greater longevity owe the continued favour of their readers to their intrinsic merits rather than to their faithfulness. We do not now turn to Dryden's "Aeneid" or Pope's "Iliad" in order to make acquaintance with Virgil and Homer, but value them as the greatest long poems of their own age. Future generations may read Rieu's "Odyssey" and Graves's "Golden Ass" as examples of first-rate 20th century writing, even when fashions of translation have radically altered once more. The translators of this mid-century may then be generally compared, as they have been in this essay, to the masters of the first Elizabethan age.

ENGLISH TRANSLATORS AND TRANSLATIONS

A READING LIST

I

General Works:

PREFACE TO OVID'S EPISTLES, by John Dryden (1680)
—included, with other material concerning translation, in W. P. Ker's 2 volume edition of Dryden's Essays, Oxford, 1926.

AN ESSAY ON TRANSLATED VERSE, by the Earl of Roscommon (1684; enlarged 1685).

ESSAY ON THE PRINCIPLES OF TRANSLATION, by A. F. Tytler (Lord Woodhouselee) (1791)
—included in Everyman's Library, 1907.

ON TRANSLATING HOMER, by Matthew Arnold (1861).

MODERN TRANSLATION, by E. S. Bates. Oxford (1936).

INTERTRAFFIC: STUDIES IN TRANSLATION, by E. S. Bates (1943).

ASPECTS OF TRANSLATION (1958)
—No. 2 in 'Studies in Communication' published by the Communication Research Centre, University College, London.

THE READER'S GUIDE, edited by W. Emrys Williams (1960)
—includes 'Classics in Translation' by E. V. Rieu, with special references to Penguin translations.

BOOKMAN'S MANUAL: A GUIDE TO LITERATURE, by B. Graham (9th ed. revised by H. Hoffman, New York, 1960)
—a standard handbook which includes numbers of translations by British and American translators.

THE ENGLISH BIBLE, A HISTORY OF TRANSLATIONS, by F. S. Bruce (1961)

II

¶ *A select alphabetical list of authors and translations, including the principal versions referred to in the text of the essay:*

AESCHYLUS
Works   Translated by L. Campbell, 1890
             „   Gilbert Murray, 1920-39
             „   Philip Vellacott, 1956 and 1961

Agamemnon	,,	Robert Browning, 1877
		(Included in John Murray editions of Poetical Works, 1896 and 1919)
	,,	Louis MacNeice, 1936
Prometheus Bound	,,	Rex Warner, 1947

APULEIUS

Metamorphoses Translated as "The Golden Asse" by William Adlington, 1566

Reprinted, revised by S. Gaselee, 1915

Translated as "The Golden Ass" by Robert Graves, 1950

THE ARABIAN NIGHTS Translated by John Payne, 1882-89
,, Richard Burton, 1885-6
,, N. J. Dawood, 1954 and 1957 (a small selection in two volumes, entitled "The Thousand and One Nights" and "Aladdin").

ARIOSTO

Orlando Furioso Translated by Sir John Harington, 1591

BALZAC

Cousin Bette Translated by Kathleen Raine, 1948
Cousin Pons ,, ,, Norman Cameron, 1950
Domestic Peace and Translated by M. A. Crawford, 1958
Other Stories
Lost Illusions ,, ,, Kathleen Raine, 1951
Old Goriot ,, ,, M. A. Crawford, 1951

BEOWULF Translated by William Morris and A. J. Wyatt, 1895
,, C. K. Scott Moncrieff, 1921
,, G. D. Bone, 1946
(Prose versions) J. R. Clark Hall, Revised C. L. Wrenn, 1950
David Wright, 1957

THE BIBLE

The Wyclifite Bible Translated by John Wyclif and his followers from the Latin Vulgate, 1384, and improved and revised, 1396.

The New Testament	Reprinted, 1848, by Charles Whittingham from the 14th century translation manuscript.

From the original texts:

The New Testament (1525) revised (1534) and *The Pentateuch* (1530)	Translated by William Tyndale. The Pentateuch and the New, Testament reprinted from the edition of 1534, in the 'Matthew Bible', 1537 and the 'Great Bible', 1539.

Miles Coverdale's translation of the whole Bible, 1535

The Authorized Version, which was the work of 47 Scholars, 1611

The Revised Version (New Testament, 1881 and Old Testament, 1885)

The New Testament	Translated into modern English by James Moffat, 1913
The Old Testament	Translated into modern English by James Moffat, 1924
The Gospels	Translated by E. V. Rieu, 1952
Acts of the Apostles	Translated by C. H. Rieu, 1957
	„ „ J. B. Phillips, 1955 as 'The Young Church in Action'

The New English Bible, the New Testament only in modern English, Oxford and Cambridge, 1961

BOETHIUS

De Consolatione Philosophiae	Translated by Geoffrey Chaucer, and included in standard editions of his Works.
	Translated by 'I.T.', revised by H. F. Stewart, Loeb Library, 1918.

LUIS DE CAMOES

The Lusiads	Translated by R. Fanshawe, 1655
	„ „ Leonard Bacon, New York, 1950
	„ „ W. C. Atkinson (prose version) 1952

CERVANTES

Don Quixote	Translated by T. Shelton, 1612-20. Reprint edited by J. Fitzmaurice Kelly, 1896
	Translated by Peter Motteux, 1700-12. Reprinted in Everyman's Library, 1933
	Translated by C. Jarvis, 1742, and frequently reprinted
	„ „ T. Smollett, 1755
	„ „ J. Ormsby, 1885

Translated by H. E. Watts, 1888 and 1895
  ,, ,, J. M. Cohen, 1950

CHEHOV
 Works   Translated by Constance Garnett, 1916-1922
 The Cherry Orchard, ,, ,, Elisaveta Fen, 1951, 1954
 Three Sisters, Ivanov,   reprinted in one volume 1959
 The Seagull, Uncle
 Vania, The Bear, The
 Proposal, A Jubilee

CHINESE POETRY
 Chinese Poems   Translated by Arthur Waley, 1946. The col-
          lection includes the greater part of "*170
          Chinese Poems*", 1918, "*More Translations
          from the Chinese*", 1919, and "*The Temple*",
          1923. Paper-back edition 1961.

DANTE
 The Divine Comedy Translated by H. F. Cary, 1805-1814. Reprinted
          in Everyman's Library, 1955
          Prose Translation facing original:
          Inferno by J. A. Carlyle, 1900
          Purgatorio by Thomas Okey, 1900
          Paradiso by P. H. Wicksteed, 1899
          Translated by Laurence Binyon, 1933-43
       ,, ,, Dorothy Sayers, *Hell*, 1949
       ,, ,, Dorothy Sayers, *Purgatory*, 1955
       ,, ,, Dorothy Sayers and Barbara
            Reynolds, *Paradise*, 1962

DOSTOYEVSKY
 Crime and Punishment, Translated by David Magarshack, 1952-58
 The Devils, The Idiot,
 The Brothers Karamazov

EURIPIDES
 Works   Translated by A. S. Way, Loeb Library, 1912,
          translation facing text
 Alcestis, Bacchae, Translated by Gilbert Murray, 1902-15
 Electra, Hippolytus,
 Iphigenia in Tauris,
 Medea, Trojan Women
 and Rhesus

Alcestis, Iphigenia in   Translated by Philip Vellacott, 1953
Tauris and Hippolytus
Ion, Women of Troy,   Translated by Philip Vellacott, 1954
Helen, The Bacchae

FROISSART
Chronicles   Translated by Lord Berners, 1901–3. (Edited
                 W. P. Ker, The Tudor Translations)

GOETHE
Faust: Parts I and II   Translated by Sir Theodore Martin, 1865-87.
                 Reprinted in Everyman's Library, 1954
                 Translated by Philip Wayne, 1949-59
                 Abridged and translated by Louis MacNeice,
                 1951
Scenes from the Faust   Translated by P. B. Shelley, included in
  of Goethe   Poetical Works, 1905

GOGOL
Dead Souls   Translated by George Reavey, 1949
                 ,,   ,,   David Magarshack, 1961

HOMER
The Works   Translated by George Chapman, 1611-16,
                 edited Allardyce Nicol, 1957
The Iliad and   Translated by Alexander Pope, 1715-25, (*The
  The Odyssey   Iliad,* reprinted in World's Classics, 1902-3
                 and frequently reprinted)
                 Translated by William Cowper, 1791
                 Prose translation by W. H. Rouse, 1937-8 (as
                 'The Story of Achilles' and 'The Story of
                 Odysseus')
                 Prose translation by E. V. Rieu, 1945 and 1950
The Iliad   Prose translations by A. Lang, W. Leaf and
                 E. Myers, 1883; by Samuel Butler, 1898
The Odyssey   Prose translations by S. H. Butcher and A.
                 Lang, 1879; by Samuel Butler, 1900; by
                 T. E. Shaw (T. E. Lawrence), 1935

IBSEN
The Pillars of the   Translated by Una Ellis-Fermor, 1950
Community, The Wild
Duck, Hedda Gabler

Rosmersholm, The Master Builder, John Gabriel Borkman	Translated by Una Ellis-Fermor, 1958
Enemy of the People *The Wild Duck* *Rosmersholm*	Translated by I. W. MacFarlane, 1960

KAFKA

The Castle	Translated by Willa and Edwin Muir, 1930
The Great Wall of China	,, ,, ,, ,, ,, ,, 1933
The Trial	,, ,, ,, ,, ,, ,, 1937
In the Penal Settlement	,, ,, ,, ,, ,, ,, 1949

LUCAN

Pharsalia	Translated by Nicholas Rowe, 1718
	Prose translation by Robert Graves, 1956

MOLIÈRE

The Misanthrope, The Sicilian, Tartuffe, A Doctor in Spite of Himself, The Imaginary Invalid	Translated by John Wood, 1959

MONTAIGNE

The Essays	Translated by John Florio, 1603
	Reprinted in Everyman's Library, 1910
	Translated by Charles Cotton, 1685
	,, ,, E. J. Trechmann, 1927
A Selection	Translated by J. M. Cohen, 1958

OMAR KHAYYAM

The Rubaiyat	Translated by Edward Fitzgerald, 1859 4th edition, revised, 1879

PLATO

The Works	Translated by Benjamin Jowett, 1871
The Republic	Translated by F. M. Cornford, 1941
The Republic	Translated by H. D. P. Lee, 1955
Gorgias	Translated by W. Hamilton, 1960
The Last Days of Socrates	Translated by Hugh Tredennick, 1954
The Symposium	Translated by W. Hamilton, 1951

PLINY THE ELDER
The Natural History   Translated by Philemon Holland, 1601 as "The Historie of the World"
A Selection   Edited by Paul Turner, 1962

PLUTARCH
Lives   Translated by Sir Thomas North, 1579, from the French of Jacques Amyot

Collective translation edited by ʃ ohn Dryden, 1683-6

Edition revised by A. H. Clough, 1864

Reprinted in Everyman's Library, 1910
Six Roman Lives   Translated as "Fall of the Roman Republic" by Rex Warner, 1958
Nine Greek Lives   Translated as "The Rise and Fall of Athens" by Ian Scott-Kilvert, 1960

PROUST
Remembrance of   Translated by C. K. Scott Moncrieff, 1922-30
Things Past   Completed by Stephen Hudson, 1931

QUEVEDO
The Visions   Translated by Sir Roger L'Estrange, 1667

RABELAIS
Gargantua and   Translated by Sir T. Urquhart (Bks. 1-3) and
Pantagruel   Peter Motteux (Bks. 3-5), 1653-94

Reprinted in Everyman's Library, 1929

Translated by J. M. Cohen, 1955

SCHILLER
Wallenstein   Translated by S. T. Coleridge, 1800

Included in the Poetical Works, 1828 and later editions.

SOPHOCLES
Works   Translated by L. Campbell, 1883
Oedipus King of   Translated by Gilbert Murray, 1911-48
Thebes, Antigone,
Wife of Heracles,
Oedipus at Colonus
Theban Plays   Translated by E. F. Watling, 1947
Electra, The Women   Translated by E. F. Watling, 1953
of Trachis, Philoctetes,
Ajax

STENDHAL

The Charterhouse of Parma	Translated by C. K. Scott Moncrieff, 1926
	,, ,, M. R. B. Shaw, 1958
Scarlet and Black	Translated by C. K. Scott Moncrieff, 1927
	,, ,, M. R. B. Shaw, 1953

TASSO

Gerusalemme Liberata	Translated as "Godfrey of Bulloigne or The Recovery of Jerusalem" by Edward Fairfax, 1600
	Reprinted H. Morley, 1890

TOLSTOY

Works	Translated by Louise and Aylmer Maude in World's Classics, 1906-47
Anna Karenin	Translated by Constance Garnett, 1901
	,, ,, Rosemary Edmonds, 1954
The Death of Ivan Ilyich	Translated by Constance Garnett, 1902
	Translated by Rosemary Edmonds, 1960
War and Peace	Translated by Constance Garnett, 1904
	,, ,, Rosemary Edmonds, 1957
The Cossacks, Happy Ever After	Translated by Rosemary Edmonds, 1960

TURGENEV

Works	Translated by Constance Garnett, 1894-99
First Love	Translated by Isaiah Berlin, 1950

VIRGIL

Works	Translated by John Dryden, 1697
The Aeneid	Translated by William Morris, 1875
	Translated by C. Day Lewis, 1952
	Prose translation by W. F. Jackson-Knight, 1956
The Georgics	Translated by C. Day Lewis, 1940
The Pastoral Poems	Translated by E. V. Rieu, 1949

Shakespeare:
The Late Comedies

by G. K. HUNTER

Published for The British Council
and The National Book League
by Longmans, Green & Co.

Two shillings and sixpence

In this essay Mr. Hunter seeks to define "the particular kind of excellence . . . in *Much Ado*, *As You Like It*, and *Twelfth Night*". He finds that the "common element in the different achievements is the power to realise love as a force making for proper happiness and reconciliation over a wide area of human experience, and as a spectrum which shows sanity and eccentricity in their social setting". *A Midsummer-Night's Dream* is grouped with them as a play about love, though it "is constructed by contrast rather than interaction".

All the essays are illustrated, and the bibliographies follow a uniform plan. They assume that Mr. J. R. Brown's bibliography in *Writers and Their Work* No. 58 is available to the reader, and in the main they confine themselves to the plays under immediate consideration. Essays and papers are not ordinarily included in the bibliographies of the Series but, as it is not possible to keep up with Shakespeare studies unless they are added, they duly appear.

Forthcoming:

ROMAN PLAYS: T. J. B. Spencer   HISTORIES: L. C. Knights
CHRONICLES: Clifford Leech   FINAL PLAYS: Frank Kermode
THE POEMS: J. W. Lever

Already Published:

SHAKESPEARE by C. J. Sisson: bibliography by J. R. Brown: a Student's Guide to the texts and the literature.
THE EARLY COMEDIES by Derek Traversi.
THE GREAT TRAGEDIES by Kenneth Muir.
THE PROBLEM PLAYS by Peter Ure.

Bibliographical Series
of Supplements to 'British Book News'
on Writers and Their Work

GENERAL EDITOR
Bonamy Dobrée

WILLIAM SHAKESPEARE

The
LATE COMEDIES

A Midsummer-Night's Dream · Much Ado About Nothing
As You Like It · Twelfth Night

by

G. K. HUNTER

Published for the British Council and
The National Book league by
LONGMANS GREEN & CO.

LONGMANS, GREEN & CO. LTD.,
48 Grosvenor Street, London, W.1.
Railway Crescent, Croydon, Victoria, Australia
Auckland, Kingston (Jamaica), Lahore, Nairobi

LONGMANS SOUTHERN AFRICA (PTY) LTD.
Thibault House, Thibault Square, Cape Town,
Johannesburg, Salisbury

LONGMANS OF NIGERIA LTD.
W.R. Industrial Estate, Ikeja

LONGMANS OF GHANA LTD.
Industrial Estate, Ring Road, South Accra

LONGMANS GREEN (FAR EAST) LTD.
443 Lockhart Road, Hong Kong

LONGMANS OF MALAYA LTD.
44 Jalan Ampang, Kuala Lumpur

ORIENT LONGMANS LTD.
Calcutta, Bombay, Madras
Delhi, Hyderabad, Dacca

LONGMANS CANADA LTD.
137 Bond Street, Toronto 2

First Published in 1962
© G. K. Hunter 1962

Printed in Great Britain by
F. Mildner & Sons, London, E.C.1

CONTENTS

I A MIDSUMMER-NIGHT'S DREAM   *page* 7

II MUCH ADO ABOUT NOTHING   20

III AS YOU LIKE IT   32

IV TWELFTH NIGHT   43

A Select Bibliography   57

NOTE: Shakespeare is quoted here in the text of the *Complete Works*, edited by Peter Alexander (1951), and it is to this edition that the lineation refers.

ILLUSTRATIONS

(Between pages 32 and 33)

I Two images of the 'Melancholy lover' (a) from the title-page of Burton's *Anatomy of Melancholy* [note the hat pulled down, the crossed arms and the cross-garters] (b) from Inigo Jones's design of 'a melancholic, despairing lover' for Ben Jonson's masque "Love's triumph through Callipolis" (by kind permission of the Duke of Devonshire).

II Will Sommers (Summers) King Henry VIII's jester: from a print by Francis Delaram (by courtesy of the British Museum).

III The figure of Hymen from Catari's *Le Imagini . . . de i Dei* (Venice, 1580 edition).

IV *Much Ado* Act IV Sc. II. From the First Folio, 1623, K.4 (by courtesy of the British Museum). Note the substitution of the names of the actors, Cowley and Kemp [misprinted as 'Keeper'] for the parts they played—*Verges and Dogberry*.

¶WILLIAM SHAKESPEARE was born at Stratford-on-Avon and was christened in the Parish Church on 26 April 1564. There, too, he died, on 23 April 1616, and was buried in the chancel, where a monument was erected before 1623.

SHAKESPEARE

I

A MIDSUMMER-NIGHT'S DREAM

Each of Shakespeare's plays is a unique organism, as unique as an individual human being; but a number of them share common elements, and it is a convenience of exposition to dispose of the common elements before discussing the individual variations. This is an especial convenience in works as short as the present; but with the four plays before us it involves certain disadvantages, and I should mention these. The plays in the present pamphlet do not hang together as inseparables: three of them—*Much Ado About Nothing*, *As You Like It*, and *Twelfth Night*—are normally placed in contiguous years of composition (1598-1600), and are often taken together by criticism to represent the peak of Shakespeare's achievement as a comic dramatist; but the perspective drawn by this very tenable view of these plays is unfair to the fourth play on our list—*A Midsummer-Night's Dream*, which is also a great comic drama, but of a very different kind, and of a distinct date (1594/5).

If we wish to define the particular kind of excellence that reaches definitive form in *Much Ado*, *As You Like It*, and *Twelfth Night*, and then passes away, then we have to speak of these plays as comedies of love. The common element in the different achievements is the power to realise love as a force making for proper happiness and reconciliation over a wide area of human experience, and as a spectrum which shows sanity and eccentricity in their social setting. In these comedies, to an extent beyond that of any other comic tradition in Europe (Aristophanes, Plautus, Ben Jonson, Molière, Wilde, Shaw) we *share* a sense of the absurdity of love with characters who know their own absurdity, and whose success we desire. The ideal of social balance and reconciliation (which all comedies show) is realized here in the power to live with one's own absurdity, with ease and with confidence.

Shakespeare's concern for this mode of comic vision could be shown by a detailed comparison of his plays and their source material, but there is not space for this. One must state, however, that the 'comedy of love' as manifested in these three plays is an individual creation; even in Shakespeare's own earlier comedies, love is only one of several modes of reconciling the major characters. In *The Comedy of Errors* the relationship of the individual to the family group is far more important than sexual love. In *The Taming of the Shrew*, wifely obedience (not quite the same thing as love) provides the focus; even in *Two Gentlemen of Verona* the reconciliation of friends is at least as important as the fulfilment of love in marriage. *A Midsummer-Night's Dream* is probably best grouped with these plays, and with *Love's Labour's Lost;* it holds together with unique delicacy of balance the variety of experience which they contain— love, clownishness, obedience to husband or to parent, friendship, woodland romance, sophistication in the court, and royalty of nature—and it is like them (and unlike the later comedies) in seeking to reconcile, without judging, the comparative merits of the different worlds that are shown. *A Midsummer-Night's Dream* is best seen, in fact, as a lyric divertissement, or a suite of dances—gay, sober, stately, absurd. Shakespeare has lavished his art on the separate excellencies of the different parts, but has not sought to show them growing out of one another in a process analogous to that of symphonic 'development'. The play is centred on Love, but it moves by exposing the varieties of love, rather than by working them against one another in a process of argument. This is probably another way of saying that the play contains no personalities, no figures like Beatrice, Rosalind or Olivia, who, being self-aware, are also self-correcting; on the whole, the characters remain fixed in their attitudes; those who change, like Demetrius, Lysander and Titania, are lifted bodily, without conflict of characters, and without volition, from one attitude to another. In the case of Titania, the induced passion for Bottom imprisons her but does not infringe her dignity; she can change back without loss of face; in the case of the lovers, the change must be preserved, to complete the pattern, and is accepted in those terms; it is this pattern and the individuals who compose it that is the play's concern:

> When they next wake, all this derision
> Shall seem a dream and fruitless vision;
> And back to Athens shall the lovers wend,
> With league whose date till death shall never end.
>
> (III. ii. 370–73)

Shakespeare has, of course, made some rudimentary distinctions between the lovers, and these are sometimes seized upon as important clues to his conception of their 'characters': Helena is taller and Hermia more shrewish; but these are, in fact, only 'odorous' comparisons to be thrown around in argument, not important traits, with consequences in action. Puck is told, 'Thou shalt know the man By the Athenian garments he hath on' (II. i. 263 f.); this is a fair enough description of either lover; we should beware of adding to it. As far as the play is concerned, the lovers are like dancers who change partners in the middle of a figure; the point at which partners are exchanged is determined by the dance, the pattern, and not by the psychological state of the dancers:

> But, my good lord, I wot not by what power—
> But by some power it is—my love to Hermia,
> Melted as the snow, seems to me now
> As the remembrance of an idle gaud
> Which in my childhood I did dote upon;
> And all the faith, the virtue of my heart,
> The object and the pleasure of mine eye,
> Is only Helena. (IV. i. 161–68)

The pattern of the dance is what matters, and the pattern is one which works through an alternation of errors, trying out all possible combinations of persons: Helena in love with Demetrius, Demetrius in love with Hermia, Hermia in love with Lysander, and then (change partners) Hermia in love with Lysander, Lysander in love with Helena, Helena in love with Demetrius, Demetrius in love with Hermia—but this is worse, so change again: Hermia in love with Lysander, Lysander in love with Helena, Helena in love with Demetrius, but completely at a loss when Demetrius seems to be pretending to return her love; finally we settle on the only stable arrangement, in which no-one is left out:

> That every man should take his own,
> In your waking shall be shown:
> > Jack shall have Jill;
> > Nought shall go ill;
> The man shall have his mare again, and all shall be well.
>
> (III. ii. 459-63)

The naivety of these 'country proverb' lines sums up the kind of world which Shakespeare has tried to create for his Athenian lovers: a world in which the country superstitions of May Day or Midsummer Eve (when maidens are supposed to dream of the man they will marry), together with the traditional figure of Robin Goodfellow, the Puck, are used to give body and background to the adolescent and unserious (but socially accepted and necessary) process of 'pairing off'.

The dance is a dance of emotions, but the emotions are not subjected to anything like a psychological analysis; Shakespeare limits our response by showing us the lovers as the mere puppets of the fairies. They act on their emotions, but what is action to them is only 'an act' to those who (invisible themselves) watch, manipulate and comment:

> Shall we their fond pageant see?
> Lord, what fools these mortals be!   (III. ii. 114 f.)

The verse itself helps to 'distance' the scenes of the lovers'
cross-purposes.   Many critics have objected to verse like
the following:

> *Helena.* . . . But who is here? Lysander! on the ground!
> Dead? or asleep? I see no blood, no wound.
> Lysander, if you live, good sir, awake.
>   *Lys.* And run through fire I will for thy sweet sake.
> Transparent Helena! Nature shows art,
> That through thy bosom makes me see thy heart.
> Where is Demetrius? O, how fit a word
> Is that vile name to perish on my sword!
>   *Hel.* Do not say so, Lysander; say not so.
> What though he love your Hermia? Lord, what though?
> Yet Hermia still loves you: then be content.
>   *Lys.* Content with Hermia! No; I do repent
> The tedious minutes I with her have spent.
> Not Hermia but Helena I love:
> Who will not change a raven for a dove?
>
>   (II. ii. 100-114)

This is certainly not an exchange one would wish to an-
thologize in 'Great Moments with the Bard', but it does
perfectly what the play requires it to do.   It reduces the
passions to a comic level where we do not feel called upon
to share them; but it remains poetic and charming, and
there is no difficulty in distinguishing the comedy of this
scene from the farce of the Pyramus and Thisbe play.

Seen against the fairies, the lovers are absurd; set against
the rational love of Theseus and Hippolyta, the mature and
royal lovers who frame and explain the occasion of the play,
it is the irrationality of their emotion which is emphasized.
This receives its magisterial definition in Theseus' famous
speech about 'The lunatic, the lover and the poet'.   But
even if Theseus had not spoken, or even if we were disposed
not to allow the objectivity of what he says, there is plenty

of evidence from the lovers' own lips to convict their love
of irrationality:

> Things base and vile, holding no quantity,
> Love can transpose to form and dignity.
> Love looks not with the eyes, but with the mind;
> And therefore is wing'd Cupid painted blind:
> Nor hath Love's mind of any judgement taste;
> Wings, and no eyes, figure unheedy haste:
> And therefore is Love said to be a child,
> Because in choice he is so oft beguil'd.
> As waggish boys in game themselves forswear,
> So the boy Love is perjur'd everywhere.   (I. i. 232-41)

This description of love, which Helena puts forward to
justify her betrayal of friendship and abandonment of reason,
is picked up in the next act in a more obviously fallacious
form.   In Act II, scene ii, when Lysander awakes to find
himself in love with Helena (I have quoted the passage above)
he justifies his change of heart in the following terms:

> The will of man is by his reason sway'd,
> And reason says you are the worthier maid.
> Things growing are not ripe until their season:
> So I, being young, till now ripe not to reason;
> And touching now the point of human skill,
> Reason becomes the marshal to my will,
> And leads me to your eyes; where I o'erlook
> Love's stories, written in love's richest book.
> (II. ii. 115-22)

Helena remarks on the capacity of love to work without
knowing the evidence of the senses (the eyes); in Lysander's
case *reason* is only a means of returning to the *eyes* of his
mistress, and reading irrational love stories.   But the clearest
comment on this infatuation comes not in the adventures
of the lovers at all, but in the parallel situation of Titania
and Bottom.   Titania awakes and finds herself in love with

Bottom, ass's head and all. Like the other lovers, her first care is to justify the *wisdom* of her choice:

> *Titania.* . . . So is mine eye enthralled to thy shape;
> And thy fair virtue's force perforce doth move me
> On the first view to say, to swear, I love thee.
> *Bottom.* Methinks, mistress, you should have little reason for that: and yet, to say the truth, reason and love keep little company together now-a-days; the more the pity that some honest neighbours will not make them friends. (III. i. 127-33)

Just as Bottom is the only mortal to see the fairies, so here he is the only one in the moonlit wood to see the daylight truth about love. But in both cases the knowledge is useless to him, since he supposes that 'man is but an ass, if he go about to expound this'. The advantage he has over the lovers is illusory, for he cannot make use of it.

Seen against the fairies or the royal pair, the lovers—who cannot fight back against either of these—cut rather poor figures. But the play does not leave them in this posture; there is a fourth term which helps to restore their dignity. The play of Pyramus and Thisbe, rehearsed by the mechanicals or handicraftsmen of Athens, shows a similar situation to that of Hermia and Lysander: lovers obstructed by parental opposition agree to run away from home and meet unobserved, at night. But the mechanicals' monumental unawareness of what is happening in their scene of 'very tragical mirth' makes the Athenian lovers seem, by contrast, to be in control of their destinies. The innocence of the lovers reduces them in a comparison with the mature gravity of Theseus or with the omniscience of Oberon, but innocence is a virtue still, and an effective one when set against the *ignorance* of the mechanicals. Indeed there is one moment in the play where the innocence of the lovers is celebrated on its own account; it is, significantly enough, the moment at which the moonlight world of their illusions is passing into the daylight world of their responsibilities:

Demetrius. These things seem small and undistinguishable
Like far-off mountains turned into clouds.
　　Hermia. Methinks I see these things with parted eye,
When every thing seems double.
　　Helena. 　　　　　　　　　So methinks:
And I have found Demetrius like a jewel,
Mine own and not mine own.
　　Demetrius. 　　　　　　　Are you sure
That we are awake? It seems to me
That yet we sleep, we dream. Do not you think
The Duke was here, and bid us follow him?

　　　　　　　　　　　　　　　　(IV. i. 184-192)

The humility, the sense of wonder, the hushed note of gratitude here are not available to anyone else in the play.

The contrast between the lovers and the mechanicals is not one which works exclusively by compensating the former at the expense of the latter. In the final scene the lovers make great fun of the ineptitudes in the play being performed; I think we are intended to see the irony of this. Those who were the unwitting performers in a love-play stage-managed and witnessed by the fairies are now, very self-consciously, the superior spectators of another play. We can laugh with them at the mechanicals, but we also laugh at them. Similarly, the aplomb with which Bottom accepts the advances of the fairy queen contrasts in a double-edged way with the frenetic activity of the lovers; immovable ignorance is set against the levity which reacts to every puff of wind, in a fashion which does not redound to the credit of either.

The play is thus a pattern of attitudes, none of which is central and all of which cast light on the others. Shakespeare has obviously laboured (and not in vain) to create complementary visions, and has sought to make each a complete world in itself. In some cases this latter need not have been difficult: the lovers and the mechanicals live inside fairly standard comic conventions. But in the case of the fairies

Shakespeare is to be credited with the creation, single-handed, of an entirely new world. What the play required was a world which was both benevolent and mysterious, romantically beautiful enough to suggest a life not inferior to that of royalty, and one whose blessing on the royal bed would be appropriate; but at the same time it had to be an inhuman world, which would not compete with the dignity of Theseus. One can see that this problem would be especially pressing for Shakespeare if, as most critics suppose, the play was written to celebrate the wedding of a noble patron, whose greatness Theseus in some way mirrored. At any rate, some felt inappropriateness in the rustic spirits of fertility prompted Shakespeare to invent a new world of miniscule fairy spirits which has become so standard in English literary mythology that we tend to forget the originality that is involved. The power to create and sustain this world is largely a poetic power; the natural beauties of the moonlit wood are sumptuously described in order to evoke the spirits who dwell among them:

> I know a bank where the wild thyme blows,
> Where oxlips and the nodding violet grows,
> Quite over-canopied with luscious woodbine,
> With sweet musk-roses and with eglantine:
> There sleeps Titania sometime of the night,
> Lull'd in these flowers with dances and delight;
> And there the snake throws her enamell'd skin,
> Weed wide enough to wrap a fairy in.   (II. i. 249-56)

Shakespeare's fairies are not only different in size from those who were part of folk-lore; their rulers are concerned not with mischief, as traditionally, but with *order* in a quasi-human fashion, and this of course makes it easier to fit their action into that of the play. The quarrel of Oberon and Titania has caused natural havoc, which may serve throughout the play as an image of discord in matrimony, and therefore as a warning to all the intending couples:

The seasons alter: hoary-headed frosts
Fall in the fresh lap of the crimson rose;
And on old Hiems' thin and icy crown
An odorous chaplet of sweet summer buds
Is, as in mockery, set . . .
And this same progeny of evils comes
From our debate, from our dissension.   (II. i. 107-116)

Shakespeare has indicated the difference between his fairies and the traditional spirits by having one of the latter as a member of his fairy court—I mean Puck or Robin Good-fellow, whose traditional role is described in a full-scale exposition:

Fairy. Either I mistake your shape and making quite,
Or else you are that shrewd and knavish sprite
Call'd Robin Goodfellow. Are not you he
That frights the maidens of the villagery,
Skim milk, and sometimes labour in the quern,
And bootless make the breathless housewife churn,
And sometime make the drink to bear no barm,
Mislead night-wanderers, laughing at their harm?
Those that Hobgoblin call you, and sweet Puck,
You do their work, and they shall have good luck.
Are you not he?
    Puck.   Thou speakest aright:
I am that merry wanderer of the night.
I jest to Oberon and make him smile
When I a fat and bean-fed horse beguile
Neighing in likeness of a filly foal.   (II. i. 32-46)

Puck supplies the element of mischief and even malice which is lacking in Shakespeare's other fairies, As jester to Oberon, he shares some features with Shakespeare's later jesters, Touchstone and Feste—detachment from the problems of those around him and attachment to his own off-beat conception of wit:

Then will two at once woo one.
That must needs be sport alone;
And those things do best please me
That befall prepost'rously.   (III. ii. 118-121)

As Oberon's agent in the affair of the lovers he also serves
to keep the lovers apart from the fairy world proper, so
that neither the benevolence of Oberon nor the slow
development of the plot is infringed.

Another world of the play which Shakespeare has been
at some pains to define effectively is the antique heroic
world of Theseus and Hippolyta. It is obviously in an
effort to create an image of antique chivalry that he gives
them their resonant hunting speeches in Act IV:

> *Hippolyta.* I was with Hercules and Cadmus once
> When in a wood of Crete they bay'd the bear
> With hounds of Sparta; never did I hear
> Such gallant chiding; for, besides the groves,
> The skies, the fountains, every region near,
> Seem'd all one mutual cry: I never heard
> So musical a discord, such sweet thunder.
> *Theseus.* My hounds are bred out of the Spartan kind . . .
> Slow in pursuit, but match'd in mouth like bells,
> Each under each. A cry more tuneable
> Was never holla'd to, nor cheer'd with horn
> In Crete, in Sparta, nor in Thessaly.   (IV. i. 109-23)

Shakespeare is obviously concerned to fix this image of har-
monious control over brute impulse, for this idea of
achieved self-possesion which Theseus, I take it, represents,
cannot be projected through external action, and the
psychological dimension of inner debate is not one that this
play employs. All Shakespeare can do is to show Theseus
and Hippolyta, set in graceful posture of power at rest,
like antique statuary, larger than life size. Larger than any
other characters, they foreknow the nature of the play
between the opening speech and their marriage—the focal
point towards which all the action of the play tends:

> *Hippolyta.* Four days will quickly steep themselves in night;
> Four nights will quickly dream away the time;
> And then the moon, like to a silver bow
> New-bent in heaven, shall behold the night
> Of our solemnities.
>   *Theseus.*   Go, Philostrate,
> Stir up the Athenian youth to merriments;
> Awake the pert and nimble spirit of mirth;
> Turn melancholy forth to funerals;
> The pale companion is not for our pomp.
> Hippolyta, I woo'd thee with my sword,
> And won thy love doing thee injuries;
> But I will wed thee in another key,
> With pomp, with triumph and with revelling.   (I. i. 7-19)

The combination of romance and merriment here nicely catches the prevailing tone of the play, and suggests a settled and rational state of loving that has lived through the violent half-knowledge of passion; the concluding lines with their image of violence transposed into revelry (a Feast of the Lapithae in reverse) suggests a Theseus who has also lived in the moonlit wood, and who, led by Titania

> through the glimmering night
> From Perigouna, whom he ravished
> [Did] with fair Ægles break his faith,
> With Ariadne and Antiopa;   (II. i. 77-80)

but who has learned (as Titania does) to

> Think no more of this night's accidents
> But as the fierce vexation of a dream.   (IV. i. 65 f.)

The image of Theseus and Hippolyta is a magnetic one, built up with a marvellous economy of means. But it seems a mistake to see the whole play from their point of view. Theseus is no Rosalind: he does not control what happens in the wood—that is Oberon's province; and he does not have to deal with the assaults and temptations of other kinds of love—no-one in the play is involved in that kind of interaction. The play is constructed by contrast rather than interaction, and the difference between it and later comedies may be expressed as the difference between a two-dimensional art (like that of Matisse) which sets clear colours against one another, and an art (like that of Rembrandt) which asks us to peer into the luminous depths where colour lies behind colour. The relationship between Rosalind's love and Touchstone's is one which helps to define Rosalind's own nature, for she has to absorb Touchstone's parody (of Orlando's poems, for example) before she can declare her own position. The relationship between Theseus and Bottom is, formally, of a similar kind: the poise and self-confidence of one, in the courtly world of Athens, is met by an equal poise, among

Hard-handed men that work in Athens here.

Self-knowledge and self-ignorance face one another across the play; but they do not interact; neither learns from the other. The meanings that each establishes only meet in the total meaningful pattern of the play.

The problem posed between moonlight or dream, on the one hand, and daylight or 'reality' on the other, is one that the play does not solve but rather *uses;* and it is one whose usefulness is disrupted by too rigorous an attempt to *judge* the different levels. Was the adventure of the lovers true or false, real or imaginary? The play would seem to answer, 'both true and false'. For Theseus it is false, for Theseus lives in a rational daylight world where, as for any good ruler, things have to be defined before they can be accepted. But the lovers can live in the result of their 'dream' without worrying about the status of its truth. For them, as for most men, unconscious adjustments are acceptable if they work, and are not made more effective by being understood. It is often asked if the lovers develop in the course of the play, and the assumption that their love is immature while Theseus' is mature, may suggest that they grow to be more like him. But this is an unwarranted assumption; there is nothing in the play to support it. The virtues of a ruler are not required of the lovers, and there is no ground for judging them sub-standard, though they never possess these heroic virtues, nor even seek to acquire them.

Something of the same kind can be said of the mechanicals in this play, and it may be useful to make a general point here about Shakespeare's clowns, citizens and rustics. They are unfit for the court and make fools of themselves when they try to appear there, but our laughter is not entirely scornful. There is an absurd truth in Bottom's dignity, as in Dogberry's, which touches an awareness of the genuine limitations on *anyone's* understanding, and catches our involvement even if it does not control our sympathy. Here among the muddled roots of humanity it is dangerous to laugh too loud, for Shakespeare makes it clear that it is *ourselves* we are laughing at.

II

MUCH ADO ABOUT NOTHING

Much Ado About Nothing is a play which is commonly remembered as a comedy of wit, focussed on Beatrice and Benedick. It is rather remarkable that this should be so, for these persons are not essential to the plot, and seem originally to have been designed as foils to the inherited characters of Hero and Claudio. But we do not need to read very far in the play to understand why memory rests on this aspect. From the very beginning, the poetic tone of the play is balanced between courtly 'compliment'— graceful social manners and their verbal equivalents—and the war-in-words which expresses basic, and more or less rugged, individualism; each shows up the other, but it is the latter that makes the more immediate appeal, and that we choose today to call 'realism'. We *do* respond to the evocation of high-strained chivalry as we find it in the opening lines:

> *Leonato*. . . . . I find here that Don Pedro hath bestowed much honour on a young Florentine called Claudio.
>
> *Messenger*. Much deserv'd on his part, and equally rememb'red by Don Pedro. He hath borne himself beyond the promise of his age, doing, in the figure of a lamb, the feats of a lion; he hath, indeed, bett'red expectation than you must expect of me to tell you how.
>
> *Leon*. He hath an uncle here in Messina will be very much glad of it.
>
> *Mess*. I have already delivered him letters, and there appears much joy in him; even so much that joy could not show itself modest enough without a badge of bitterness.
>
> *Leon*. Did he break out into tears?
>
> *Mess*. In great measure.
>
> *Leon*. A kind overflow of kindness. There are no faces truer than those that are so wash'd. How much better is it to weep at joy than to joy at weeping!　　　　　(I. i. 8-25)

But these noble and generous sentiments about loving, gifted and valiant people could easily cloy, were it not for a dash of bitterness in the line following, which whets our appetite:

> *Beatrice*. I pray you, is Signior Mountanto return'd from the wars or no?

and from this point we are carried forward naturally on a counter-current of scorn and scoffing:

> *Mess*. He hath done good service, lady, in these wars.
>
> *Beat*. You had musty victual, and he hath holp to eat it; he is a very valiant trencherman; he hath an excellent stomach.
>
> *Mess*. And a good soldier too, lady.
>
> *Beat*. And a good soldier to a lady; but what is he to a lord?
>
> *Mess*. A lord to a lord, a man to a man; stuff'd with all honourable virtues.
>
> *Beat*. It is so, indeed; he is no less than a stuff'd man; but for the stuffing—well, we are all mortal.　　　　(I. i. 40-50)

The scoffing of Beatrice could, of course, easily become
tedious, no less than the honeyed compliment of her uncle
Leonato; a play which so nicely balances the sweetness of
romance against the bitterness of wit, makes it difficult for
critics to avoid taking sides and judging one group by the
standards of the other; and the assertiveness of Beatrice's wit
is most often played down in the interest of a romantic vein
of love which Claudio and Hero are thought unfit to present.
But the nearness of Beatrice to a shrew must be faced and
admitted if we are to preserve the balance of the play.
Admitting the quality of aggression in her nature is not
quite the same thing as condemning her; and a comparison
with *The Taming of the Shrew* will show how thoroughly
Shakespeare has, on this occasion, integrated the effective
violence of mind into a coherent vision of the good life,
without weakening its force.

Katherine the Shrew belongs to the same family as the
'gentle' Bianca, but there is little common ground between
the romantic sister of Comedy and the shrewish sister,
whose natural milieu is Farce. In *Much Ado*, on the other
hand, there is no difficulty about fitting Beatrice into the
'gentle' household of Leonato. She is a lady; she does not
indulge in fisticuffs; and her aggressiveness of temperament
can be allowed, accepted and admired as 'high spirits', as a
self-sufficient gaiety:

> she is never sad but when she sleeps; and not ever sad then; for . . .
> she hath often dream'd of unhappiness, and wak'd herself with
> laughing.   (II. i. 310-13)

Beatrice is admirable, moreover, as an independent
person, whose high spirits express an individual control
over her own happiness. It is not for her, in following the
downward path described by Congreve's Millamant as 'by
degrees dwindl[ing] into a wife', to have the independence
knocked out of her by masculine violence, however jovial.
Katherine is starved into submission by the routine of a
hawk-trainer:

My falcon now is sharp and passing empty;
And, till she stoop, she must not be full-gorged,
For then she never looks upon her lure . . .
She eat no meat today, nor none shall eat;
Last night she slept not, nor to-night she shall not.

                                   (*Shrew*, IV. i. 174-82)

Beatrice does not need a hawk-tamer husband; she can act
as her own trainer:

And Benedick, love on; I will requite thee,
Taming my wild heart to thy loving hand;
If thou dost love, my kindness shall incite thee
To bind our loves up in a holy band.   (III. i. 111-14)

Her admirable independence of mind requires that she be
able to correct herself, free of any pressure but that of her
own understanding.

   The balance that Beatrice brings to the somewhat over-
honeyed world of Messina's maidens and old men—the
world with which the play begins—is soon reinforced by
the major action, the entry of the warrior-noblemen, Don
Pedro, Don John, Benedick and Claudio.   For their arrival,
like that of a rout of maskers, submerges the certainties of
Messina in a flood of deceptions (as most obviously in the
masked ball of II. i.), of actions protected by wit or by
disguise, and balanced between good and evil ends. The two
princes, Don Pedro and Don John, between them control
a world in which wit and evil walk hand in hand, and in
which love may be protected or may be destroyed according
to the hairs-breadth difference between the two kinds of
deception; one in which self-sufficiency is necessary for
survival.   Don Pedro is an unamiable figure to most modern tastes: he is unpleasingly self-satisfied with a power to
deceive and manipulate which is chiefly notable as providing the breeding-ground for his brother's evil.   In fact,
each of his deceptions-for-good is reversed by Don John,
the final fulfilment of the good intention is not due to him

but to the Friar and Leonato in one case—they provide the
second Hero to make good the loss of the first—and to
Beatrice and Benedick in the other case—they accept the
trick as a trick and then turn it into a reality:

> *Benedick.* A miracle! here's our own hands against our hearts.
> Come, I will have thee; but, by this light, I take thee for pity.
> *Beatrice.* I would not deny you; but, by this good day, I yield
> upon great persuasion; and partly to save your life, for I was told
> you were in a consumption.
> *Bene.* Peace; I will stop your mouth. [*Kissing her.*]
> *D. Pedro.* How dost thou, Benedick the married man?
> *Bene.* I'll tell thee what, Prince: a college of wit-crackers cannot
> flout me out of my humour . . .   (V. iv. 91-100)

But for all this Shakespeare clearly means Don Pedro to be
viewed with some deference, as providing an image of
power at play, well-disposed to lesser creatures and unselfish in his outlook.

Don John, on the other hand, is seen as incapable of play:
his melancholy vision of human nature is totally un-
protected by irony:

> I cannot hide what I am; I must be sad when I have cause, and
> smile at no man's jests; eat when I have stomach, and wait for no
> man's leisure . . . though I cannot be said to be a flattering honest
> man, it must not be denied but I am a plain-dealing villain.
>   (I. iii. 11-27)

In terms of psychology this makes little sense, but seen in
relation to his half-brother Don John fits into the vision of
the play, as evil itself makes sense as a 'rogue' variant of wit,
where self-defensiveness has become self-infatuation, and
where a proper suspicion of others had turned into a con-
suming hatred for them. In the spectrum of wit that the
visitors bring to Messina, Don John has his own clear place
at the bottom of the scale.

In the world of deception that the gallants bring with

them, there is much ado about noting [or overhearing] as well as much ado about nothing [or self-deception]—*noting* and *nothing* were homonyms at that time—and wit is the essential means of keeping a balance between the two kinds of deception:

> What a pretty thing man is when he goes in his doublet and hose and leaves off his wit!
>
> (V. i. 191-93)

For all the elegance of Messina, no one (except a Dogberry) can be confident about the identity of anyone else, where all is a prey to supposition and 'seeming'. In this context the wariness and defensive banter of Beatrice and Benedick, their unwillingness to abandon self-sufficiency or commit themselves too far—as we may suppose Claudio does, with his 'I give myself away for you, and dote upon the exchange'—can be seen as a proper poise. It has been argued that Shakespeare has simply imposed marriage on Beatrice and Benedick here, substituting for the physical pressure of *The Taming of the Shrew* a social pressure which is not much less external. But the play hardly allows us to treat the social pressure involved in rumour, gossip, and overhearing in this way, or to suppose that a discovery of other people's opinions, however contrived, is a serious infringement of liberty. The romantic love of Claudio and Hero, for all its battery of 'words, vows, gifts, tears' collapses at the breath of scandal; the play provides no obviously superior alternative to the wary, begrudged and finally betrayed emotions of Beatrice and Benedick; for marriage is a social act and requires a fitness to the society to which the lovers belong. Moreover their emotions are responsibly accepted and self-supported to this extent, that they know the limitations on all relationships of their world —'for man is a giddy thing, and this is my conclusion'— and they are too well integrated into society to dream of escaping into a merely private relationship.

The self-sufficiency and responsibility of these two lovers

in their choice of one another is further emphasized by
making their relationship, in hate or in love, seem not only
equal but also inevitable. Social pressure does not create
the relationship; it only alters its mode of expression. From
Leonato's point of view, it is true:

> By my troth, niece, thou wilt never get thee a husband if thou be
> so shrewd of thy tongue.

But love need not be restricted to the modes understood by
Leonato, and the violent repudiation of one another that
Beatrice and Benedick indulge in clearly involves an attraction, even an inverted kind of courtship 'which hurts and
is desired'. Each of them self-consciously sets up as a wit,
and therefore is bound to seek out the other as the rival
claimant; each seeks opportunities to display the rapid
manoeuvre, 'the privy nip', 'the fleering frump' and other
figures that Puttenham lists, and treats the other as the obvious testing ground. The fascination of rivalry draws
Beatrice and Benedick together even when their ostensible
purpose is to hurt one another; and we in the audience
share their enjoyment, fear and thrill in the game, taking
their sharp words as weapons of display rather than of
self-expression. Shakespeare uses the detachment of the
person speaking from the thing spoken, which is an essential
feature of *wit*, to limit our sense of these characters' ir-
revocable psychological involvement in the attitudes they
deploy. Comic exaggeration of one's own standpoint is
one obvious way of doing this. This is how Beatrice sets
up the image of herself as anti-man:

> Lord! I could not endure a husband with a beard on his face; I had
> rather lie in the woollen . . . What should I do with him? Dress
> him in my apparel, and make him my waiting gentlewoman? He
> that hath a beard is more than a youth, and he that hath no beard is
> less than a man; and he that is more than a youth is not for me, and
> he that is less than a man I am not for him . . . Would it not grieve

a woman to be over-master'd with a piece of valiant dust? to make an account of her life to a clod of wayward marl? No, uncle, I'll none: Adam's sons are my brethren; and, truly, I hold it a sin to match in my kindred.

(II. i. 25-55)

What we respond to here is the gaiety of the manner, rather than the truth of the matter. Remembering her own avowal: 'I was born to speak all mirth and no matter', we are not likely to be shocked by a reversal of the attitude when a change seems appropriate. As Benedick remarks: 'When I said I would die a bachelor, I did not think I should live till I were married.'

This comic exaggeration works effectively in soliloquy as in dialogue, for the delights of self-dramatization do not require an immediate audience to make them plausible:

May I be so converted, and see with these eyes? I cannot tell; I think not. I will not be sworn but love may transform me to an oyster; but I'll take my oath on it, till he have made an oyster of me he shall never make me such a fool. One woman is fair, yet I am well; another is wise, yet I am well; another virtuous, yet I am well; but till all graces be in one woman, one woman shall not come in my grace. Rich she shall be, that's certain; wise, or I'll none; virtuous, or I'll never cheapen her; fair, or I'll never look on her; mild, or come not near me; noble, or not I for an angel; of good discourse, an excellent musician, and her hair shall be of what colour it please God.

(II. iii. 19-32)

Benedick's comic *hubris* here marks him out as a victim; the comic exaggeration of his independent stance prepares us for the need to change it; and we wait with excitement the new paroxysms of wit that will be required to extract him from shame.

On both sides, the problem of change for Beatrice and Benedick is seen in terms of wit rather than emotion: both have so long sharpened their tongues on the weaknesses of others, that there can be no expectation of mercy for them. But, so they believe, social pressure is equally strong against their scorn of one another. This may seem, in a totally romantic period, to be a bad reason for marriage; but the play supposes that the attraction between the two (already established), and the fair-mindedness and genuine humility, which each shows separately, are in combination enough to complete an image of content. There may indeed be a further suggestion that a relationship which, like that of Hero and Claudio, omits to notice the self-will, suspiciousness and acerbity of the individual is incomplete and riding for a fall.

The tension between self-will and social responsiveness which the witty poise of Beatrice and Benedick keeps in a measure of control shows itself, in the main plot of Claudio and Hero, running out of control. The bitterness that Beatrice's wit, by expressing, is able to temper, is no sooner dissolved in her self-awareness than evil appears elsewhere, betraying others who cannot so temper the deception. The scenes in which Beatrice and Benedick 'learn' of one another's love, come between the planning of Don John's revenge against Claudio and its consummation in the church scene (IV. i.). The counterpoint between the match-makers and the match-marrers (between the end of II. i and the beginning of II. ii) is effective drama, but even more effective is the new source of bitterness arising from Claudio's repudiation of Hero. At this point the pairs of lovers may be said to change places, the 'sweet' lovers, Hero and Claudio, having become bitter, while the 'bitter' lovers, Beatrice and Benedick, seek to become sweet (more or less). It might be argued, of course, that the exchange is not at all between like things, the near-tragic happenings of IV.i. being of a different order of magnitude from the astringent wit of Beatrice, and that (in consequence) the romantic world of loving emotions is not so much balanced in Act IV as overwhelmed. *Much Ado* is sometimes called a tragi-comedy, and there is much in IV. i. (especially when taken in isolation) that would seem to justify this. At the beginning of the scene we have a sense of the exhaustion of all the fragile good-will that has been painstakingly built up throughout the play. The geniality of Leonato, the merry banter of Benedick, the loving trust of Hero are all brought forward, and one by one they wilt in the glare of Claudio's new-found rhetoric:

> Out on thee! Seeming! I will write against it:
> You seem to me as Dian in her orb,
> As chaste as is the bud ere it be blown;
> But you are more intemperate in your blood
> Than Venus or those pamp'red animals
> That rage in savage sensuality.   (IV. i. 55-60)

The perception here of the unbearable gap between appearance and reality is of the essence of Shakespeare's tragic vision. But Shakespeare is able to use the tragic gestures here without requiring the full tragic response. We feel the effect on Hero, Claudio and on Leonato; but we see these characters isolated in their agony from a context which is still comic. The tragic, Troilus-like self-torment of Claudio, 'This is and is not' [Hero] and the blank horror of Hero herself can be felt as their individual purgatories, without implying any claim to interpret the whole of experience. It is true that Beatrice and Benedick are at a disadvantage in this scene. But a number of factors outside the scene itself help to redress the balance. We know from the preceding action (III.v.) that the plot against Hero has already been uncovered and that only Dogberry's incompetence has allowed the denunciation to take place at all. Moreover we have already seen, in the masked ball (II.i), that Don John has a triumphant power to deceive and disillusion Claudio, but that the triumph is liable to be reversed when other people hear of it. For these reasons we may regard, with some sympathy, Benedick's view that his own life is not seriously changed by what has happened to Hero. But the love-conversation he attempts to have with Beatrice on those terms turns out

to be no less vexed than their earlier interviews. It is no
longer from the shafts of wit that 'four of his five wits went
halting off'; but the threat of violence now lies in the whole
tenor of the dialogue:

> *Beat.* You have stayed me in a happy hour; I was about to
> protest I loved you.
>
> *Bene.* And do it with all thy heart?
>
> *Beat.* I love you with so much of my heart that none is left to
> protest.
>
> *Bene.* Come, bid me do anything for thee.
>
> *Beat.* Kill Claudio.
>
> *Bene.* Ha! not for the wide world.
>
> *Beat.* You kill me to deny it. Farewell.
>
> *Bene.* Tarry, sweet Beatrice.
>
> *Beat.* I am gone though I am here; there is no love in you; nay,
> I pray you, let me go.
>
> *Bene.* Beatrice—
>
> *Beat.* In faith, I will go.
>
> *Bene.* We'll be friends first.
>
> *Beat.* You dare easier be friends with me than fight with mine
> enemy.
>
> *Bene.* Is Claudio thine enemy?
>
> *Beat.* Is 'a not approved in the height a villain that hath slandered,
> scorned, dishonoured, my kinswoman? O that I were a man!
> What! bear her in hand until they come to take hands, and then
> with public accusation, uncover'd slander, unmitigated rancour—
> O God, that I were a man! I would eat his heart in the market-
> place.
>
> *Bene.* Hear me, Beatrice.
>
> *Beat.* Talk with a man out at a window! A proper saying!
>
> *Bene.* Nay, but Beatrice—
>
> *Beat.* Sweet Hero! She is wrong'd, she is sland'red, she is undone.
>
> *Bene.* Beat—
>
> *Beat.* Princes and Counties! Surely, a princely testimony, a
> goodly count, Count Comfect; a sweet gallant, surely! O that I
> were a man for his sake! or that I had any friend would be a man
> for my sake! But manhood is melted into curtsies, valour into
> compliment, and men are only turn'd into tongue, and trim
> ones too.   (IV. i. 281-316)

There is much that is comic here, in the would-be love dialogue that runs into the quicksands of hate, and in Benedick's fumbling and incoherent attempts to find his feet again, and regain control of what he has started. But the sinister and deadly seriousness of Beatrice's 'Kill Claudio' should not escape us either. The violence of Beatrice's nature, the contempt for mere sweetness or for 'compliment' is still a factor that Benedick and the play have to cope with, though in a different key. The remaining wit-dialogues between Benedick and Claudio are often disliked for this very combination of the sinister and the flippant, but they catch very fairly an essential interest of the play in the limits of wit, in the mutual antagonism of social poise and individual passion. We dislike the episodes because the contrast makes both men seem so unattractive; Benedick is absurd, shackled, as it were, to the interests of Beatrice; and Claudio is repellent for his very lack of involvement. But the scenes are not, for this reason, ineffective in the total economy of the play. The whole work is more bitter than is usually allowed; the world of Messina buys its elegance dearly; it is a world where wit is a weapon for the strong, where the comic vision of happiness is available only to those with enough poise to remain balanced and adaptive throughout conflict and deception.

The blind self-interest of Don John and the social expertise of Don Pedro frame between them an action in which these qualities are perpetually at odds. In this society only a Dogberry could suppose that 'Self-love and Social be the same', expect it to be of general concern whether or not he was 'writ down an ass', or indeed be assured that the English language means to others what in his own 'nice derangement' it plainly means to himself. It is this sublime but also pathetic self-confidence, no less than their function in the intrigue, that fits the comic watchmen into the structure of the play. They remind us that beneath the brittle wit of the courtlings, forever turning expectation inside out 'like a cheveril glove', there is a world of untroubled (though unsupported) certitudes about justice, communication and dignity, which is no less true for being richly comic. The play shows us the growth of individual self-awareness out of these comic pieties as indeed depending on the witty knowledge that we are all, somewhere, 'writ down an ass'.

III

AS YOU LIKE IT

Of all Shakespeare's comedies, *As You Like It* is the most completely centred on the vision of the happiness that is available in this world through personally satisfying, humanely poised and socially accepted love. This does not mean that the play contains no evil or foolish characters: Frederick, the usurping duke who displaces and exiles his elder brother, and Oliver, who seeks to kill and forces into exile *his* brother, are violent and destructive in their attitudes. Even in the Forest of Arden, which provides a space temporarily free from the operations of vice, and so available for the comic and romantic manipulations of Rosalind—even here Jaques the forest moralist and retired libertine, and Phebe the shepherdess-cocotte are unbalanced enough in their attitudes to make the equation of Arden with Eden an absurd over-simplification. The point is not that folly and vice do not exist in this comic world, but that the central figures, Rosalind, Celia and Orlando can face the reality of vice and yet escape contamination, can face the deviations of folly and yet, through self-knowledge and self-discipline, dismiss them with an effortless superiority.

In its most generalised form this capacity for love, seen to be connected with both self-knowledge and the willing acceptance of hardship, is exemplified by the court of the Duke in exile: the Duke tells us that when the winter's wind

(a)

I. Two images of the 'Melancholy lover' (a) from the title-page of Burton's *Anatomy of Melancholy* [note the hat pulled down, the crossed arms and the cross-garters] (b) from Inigo Jones's design of 'a melancholic, despairing lover' for Ben Jonson's masque "Love's triumph through Callipolis"

(b)

Will Sommers — Ringe Henceyes Jester

Are the [...] by [...] as [...] what bears in Cornewall Franc Delaram
Went kings ta: kinges mee clad in strange attire: | This Horne I haue, betokens Sommers gone
Knowes I am suted to my owne desire: | Which sportiue tyme will bid thee make
And yet the Characters describ'd vpon mee | All with my Nature well agreeing too
Say shewe thee, that a King bestowd them in | As both the Name, and Tyme, and He

II. Will Sommers, Henry VIII's fool, wearing a 'motley'
petticoat, after a print by Francis Delaram (*British Museum*).

II. The figure of *Hymen*, from Cartari's 'Le Imagini de i'Dei'
Venice, edition of 1580).

is dead, and so farewell.

Enter the Constables, Borachio, and the Towne Clerke
in gownes.

Keeper. Is our whole dissembly appeard?
Cowley. O a stoole and a cushion for the Sexton.
Sexton. Which be the malefactors?
Andrew. Marry that am I, and my partner.
Cowley. Nay that's certaine, wee haue the exhibition
to examine.
Sexton. But which are the offenders that are to be ex-
amined, let them come before master Constable.
Kemp. Yea marry, let them come before mee, what is
your name, friend?
Bor. Borachio.
Kem. Pray write downe *Borachio.* Yours sirra.
Con. I am a Gentleman sir, and my name is *Conrade.*
Kee. Write downe Master gentleman *Conrade:* mai-
sters, doe you serue God : maisters, it is proued alreadie
that you are little better than false knaues, and it will goe
neere to be thought so shortly, how answer you for your
selues?
Con. Marry sir, we say we are none.
Kemp. A maruellous witty fellow I assure you, but I
will goe about with him : come you hither sirra, a word
in your eare sir, I say to you, it is thought you are false
knaues.
Bor. Sir, I say to you, we are none.
Kemp. Well, stand aside, 'fore God they are both in
a tale : haue you writ downe that they are none?
Sext. Master Constable, you goe not the way to examine, you must call forth the watch that are their ac-
cusers.
Kemp. Yea marry, that's the eftest way, let the watch
come forth : masters, I charge you in the Princes name,
accuse these men.

IV. First Folio (1623) p.116 (Sig.K4ᵛ)—actual size—from the
text of *Much Ado*; note the substitution of the names of the
actors, Cowley and Kemp [misprinted as 'Keeper'] for the parts
they played—Verges and Dogberry (*British Museum*).

. . . bites and blows upon my body
Even till I shrink with cold, I smile and say,
'This is no flattery; these are counsellors
That feelingly persuade me what I am'.
Sweet are the uses of adversity;
Which, like the toad, ugly and venomous,
Wears yet a precious jewel in his head;
And this our life, exempt from public haunt,
Finds tongues in trees, books in the running brooks,
Sermons in stones and good in everything.
I would not change it.
 Amiens.   Happy is your Grace
That can translate the stubbornness of fortune
Into so quiet and so sweet a style
 Duke. Come, shall we go and kill us venison?
And yet it irks me the poor dappled fools,
Being native burghers of this desert city,
Should, in their own confines, with forked heads
Have their round haunches gor'd.   (II. i. 8–25)

This generalised benevolence could easily become sentimental; Shakespeare guards against the possibility by immediately parodying it. Straight on top of the Duke's
speech comes Jaques' self-indulgent 'moralizing' of the
same situation:

First, for his weeping into the needless stream;
'Poor deer', quoth he, 'thou mak'st a testament
As worldlings do, giving thy sum of more
To that which had too much': then being there alone
Left and abandoned of his velvet friends;
'Tis right', quoth he; 'thus misery doth part
The flux of company': anon a careless herd
Full of the pasture, jumps along by him
And never stays to greet him; 'Ay', quoth Jaques,
'Sweep on, you fat and greasy citizens,' etc. (46–55)

This 'placing' of an attitude by relating it to a deviation of
the same response is typical of the play.

But in presenting the sanity and self-awareness of noble love, the Duke and his court form only a background. The central image of the love which can effortlessly see through and put aside folly, and yet retain its own exuberant vision of happiness, is found in Rosalind, and around her. The more than cousinly love of Rosalind and Celia easily defeats the less than brotherly relationship between their respective fathers (the two Dukes):

> *Celia.* O my poor Rosalind, whither wilt thou go?
> Wilt thou change fathers? I will give thee mine.
> I charge thee, be not thou more griev'd than I am.
>   *Rosalind.* I have more cause.
>   *Celia.*   Thou hast not, cousin;
> Prithee, be cheerful: know'st thou not the Duke
> Hath banish'd me, his daughter?
>   *Rosalind.*   That he hath not.
>   *Celia.* No, hath not? Rosalind lacks then the love
> Which teacheth thee that thou and I am one:
> Shall we be sund'red? shall we part, sweet girl?
> No: let my father seek another heir.   (I. iii. 86–95)

Even the flight from the court is presented as if it was of choice and not of necessity, as if the two loving cousins were in command of the situation:

> Now go we in content
> To liberty and not to banishment.   (I. iii. 133 f.)

The dangers of the venture are evoked:

> Alas, what danger will it be to us,
> Maids as we are, to travel forth so far!   (I. iii. 104 f.)

But they are evoked only to be dismissed by common sense and a knowledge of the world:

> We'll have a swashing and a martial outside,
> As many other mannish cowards have
> That do outface it with their semblances.   (I. iii. 116–18)

The disguise of the heroine as a boy could lead to all kinds of amusing and embarrassing situations, but Rosalind is never cornered in her disguise—these straits are reserved for Viola in *Twelfth Night*.

The easy assurance of love and the bubbling vision of happiness that it offers are seen as the basis of Rosalind's unassertive but terrifyingly accurate perception of shams and follies. As we have suggested, The Forest of Arden is no mere haunt of sentimental self-indulgence, where self-control is unnecessary. The ease with which Rosalind detects the follies of Phebe and Jaques is directly connected with her self-awareness and capacity for self-mockery. Her disguise as Ganymede gives Shakespeare a unique opportunity to make this point. In stressing the force and independence of Beatrice's mind Shakespeare made her into something dangerously close to a shrew; but Rosalind, in order to sustain her role as a quasi-man, *must* play a swaggering part of this kind, and there is no danger that we will take her play-role as an infringement of her true personality, or have difficulty in separating out the mocking part from the loving part. Indeed, the golden assurance of the conquering good in love that this play presents is necessarily connected with the assumption that lovers are absurd; to know one's own absurdity, yet not to be oppressed by it, indeed to enjoy it, is the basis of romantic heroism as the play shows it.

The scene in which we can most clearly see Shakespeare balancing the wonder against the absurdity of love is Act III, scene ii, and a look at the details of this scene may indicate the methods by which the effect is built up. Here Shakespeare puts the poet, the lover and the madman together (once again), but here, if not in *A Midsummer-Night's Dream*, it is clear what he means by the conjunction. The scene opens with Orlando as pastoral poet-lover hanging his verses on a tree. There is much that is inherently absurd here: the very action of tying love-verses on trees takes us far away from practical behaviour; then there are

the verses themselves, which reflect the attempt to be
poetical rather than the success; the central image of Orlando
'abusing young plants with carving Rosalind on their barks'
(III.ii. 334 f.) leads forward to the climactically absurd lines:

> Run, run, Orlando; carve on every tree
> The fair, the chaste and unexpressive she,   (III. ii. 9 f.)

where the idea of the fervent lover sprinting from tree to
tree, with his jacknife at the ready, seeking to express what
he knows already is inexpressible ('unexpressive'), cannot
possibly be taken seriously. But though the poet-lover is
shown as absurd here, he is not really satirized; he is lovably
absurd; we sympathise with the noble and poetical madness,
whose victim he is, and whose name he bears.

Orlando's poeticizing makes the prologue to the scene,
and the verses remain dangling from the stage tree to remind
the audience what has passed. For what follows has no
obvious continuity with what we have seen: Corin and
Touchstone enter and debate the traditional topic of court
versus country. Shakespeare, as is usual in his handling of
debates, does not prefer one side to another; he is content
to establish the social and psychological backgrounds which
give coherence to the separate views. Most important for
the development and balance of the scene is the view of
Touchstone that emerges: against Corin, his slick wit and
uncommitted cleverness is clear enough, but it is also clear
that his lack of commitment to any way of life makes him
incomplete as a man:

> *Corin.* Sir, I am a true labourer: I earn that I eat, get that I wear,
> owe no man hate, envy no man's happiness, glad of other men's
> good, content with my harm, and the greatest of my pride is to
> see my ewes graze and my lambs suck.
> *Touchstone.* That is another simple sin in you, to bring the ewes
> and the rams together and to offer to get your living by the
> copulation of cattle; to be a bawd to a bell-weather, and to betray

a she-lamb of a twelve-month to a crooked-pated, old, cuckoldly ram, out of all reasonable match. If thou beest not damn'd for this, the devil himself will have no shepherds; I cannot see else how thou shouldst 'scape.

(III. ii. 65-75)

This 'placing' of Touchstone is important to the economy of the scene, for it is Touchstone who appears in the next episode as the chief critic of Orlando's verses. We have already seen that these are delightfully absurd. Now we hear Touchstone scoffing at them while Rosalind demurs; but having observed already that Touchstone is more clever than understanding we are in a position to enjoy Touchstone's parodies:

> If a hart do lack a hind
> Let him seek out Rosalind, etc.

knowing that they reflect on the parodist at least as much as on the poet. Likewise we can enjoy Rosalind's embarrassment when still more poems appear, and at the same time share her delight in being praised. Rosalind (in so far as she is a lover) is also absurd, and the dialogue which follows, between Rosalind and Celia, makes this point abundantly clear:

> *Ros.* Alas the day! what shall I do with my doublet and hose? What did he when thou saw'st him? What said he? How look'd he? Wherein went he? What makes he here? Did he ask for me? Where remains he? How parted he with thee? and when shalt thou see him again? Answer me in one word. (III. ii. 204-09)

In such a situation we laugh *at* her, but we laugh with her as well, for she takes us on to her side by laughing at herself.

The climax of this scene is the confrontation of the self-aware but passionate Rosalind and the noble but absurd Orlando; but before Shakespeare moves on to this he interposes another of those interlude-like dialogues (we have already seen one involving Corin and Touchstone) which prolong the pleasure of anticipated resolutions, and at the same time prepare us for, give depth to, the characteristics about to be displayed. This time we meet Orlando, not as a pastoral poet-lover, but, in contrast to Jaques, as a well-balanced *Man*, contemptuous of affectation. Jaques' ridicule of Orlando, like Touchstone's earlier ridicule of the verses, reflects back on himself: love may be absurd, but compared to melancholy it is not at all disabling.

Now comes the climax which all that has gone before has prepared for; Jaques having slunk away, Rosalind takes up the challenge and issues forth herself:

> Ros. [*Aside to Celia*] I will speak to him like a saucy lackey, and under that habit play the knave with him.   (III. ii. 278-80)

Her wit succeeds where Jaques' had failed; it is quicker than Orlando's on the turn, and more acute in its social reference. Without ever reversing our impression that she is deeply in love she is able to keep Orlando at wit's distance, to play the opposing role of 'A very beadle to a humorous sigh' and remain in control of the situation while revealing (to us) how far she is emotionally involved in it. The scene ends with the preparations for further interviews in which the lover will give his mistress (and us) the pleasures of romantic wooing, without ever knowing how far his play of love with 'Ganymede' is the reality of love with Rosalind.

This scene we have been looking at is not only beautifully balanced in itself, but reflects the central achievement of the play—the achievement of a point of view in which love is known for its absurdity, and yet retained with laughing certainty at the centre of human experience, able to put aside the self-indulgent anti-love jaundice of Jaques, and the self-regarding and prettified love of Phebe. It is sometimes supposed that Touchstone's name indicates that *he* is the central and normative figure in the play, but this would seem to be a confusion of his role with that of Feste in

Twelfth Night. Touchstone is, of course, though a jester, no fool; he is faithful to the ladies and he sees through Jaques. But his deliberate downgrading of his desires to what he can get cheaply, his sophisticated version of earthiness, is seen by the play as only a very restricted kind of virtue; the dialogue with Corin reveals his shallowness, and even the clodhopping William shows him up. Set beside Rosalind, Touchstone is no touchstone at all.

The first part of the play is concerned with the escape from evil; the central episodes (of which I hope the scene I have chosen—III. ii—is sufficiently representative) show a series of contrasting attitudes to love and to the country; these are developed through the meaningful *play* of Rosalind (pretending to be 'Ganymede' pretending to be Rosalind) and Orlando. This *play* is a uniquely powerful way of presenting the richness and complexity of a relationship; but it requires a suspension of place, time and intrigue, and this becalming of the play makes it difficult to steer it to a satisfactory conclusion. Shakespeare has to rescue his characters from their 'dream' or 'holiday' at the end of the play, and to tie up the various strands of interest and intention, and do so in such a way that we can believe that the knots will last.

He solves the problem in an unexpected way. He achieves the fulfilment of a character as real as Rosalind by keeping his *play* motif open, and deliberately exploiting its theatrical naivety. The couples are paired off with comic efficiency:

> *Jaques.* There is, sure, another flood toward, and these couples are coming to the ark.   (V. iv. 35 f.)

Rosalind acts as impresario, not only for their wedding but also for her own, seeing as well as enjoying the naivety that underlies the proper ceremonial of a great social occasion:

> *Rosalind.* Pray you, no more of this; 'tis like the howling of
> Irish wolves against the moon. [*To Silvius*] I will help you if I can.
> [*To Phebe*] I would love you if I could. —Tomorrow meet me all
> together. [*To Phebe*] I will marry you if ever I marry woman, and
> I'll be married tomorrow. [*To Orlando*] I will satisfy you if ever I
> satisfied man, and you shall be married tomorrow. [*To Silvius*]
> I will content you if what pleases you contents you, and you shall
> be married tomorrow. [*To Orlando*] As you love Rosalind, meet.
> [*To Silvius*] As you love Phebe, meet; —and as I love no woman,
> I'll meet. (V. ii. 102–111)

Shakespeare wishes to emphazise his heroine's control over
the environment, and she hangs on to her role as impresario
for as long as possible; but even she has to step down
eventually and join the Dance of Life:

> commanded
> By such poor passion as the maid that milks
> And does the meanest chares.

Many critics have objected to the recession of character
involved in this substitution of pattern for individual
response. An extremely acute recent appraisal of
'Shakespeare's Rituals' has stated that 'what might have
been an emotion becomes in effect a conundrum'. Given
the structure of the play as I have sketched it, this does not
seem to be a necessary judgement. There is, of course, a
'critical war' being fought in this century between those
who stress the symbolism and ritual of Shakespeare's plays
and those who stress the naturalistic elements; and any
statement on the subject should be seen against this polemical
background. Granting this, however, one must still point
out that Shakespeare is easy to defend in the denouement of
As You Like It. The formal arrangement of the lovers and
the final appearance of Hymen, to bless and organize, only
reflects the formality which life, no less than art, thinks
appropriate to the presentation of marriage. Hymen admits
that these are 'strange events' and instructs the bystanders
(including the theatre audience):

Whiles a wedlock-hymn we sing,
Feed yourselves with questioning;
That reason wonder may diminish,
How thus we met, and these things finish.   (V. iv. 131-34)

But this *wonder* is not a new or unprepared element in the play; it has sustained Rosalind throughout the action, not only in the sense that the world shows itself extraordinarily amenable to her control and full of most convenient coincidences:

O wonderful, wonderful, and most wonderful wonderful! and yet again wonderful, and after that, out of all whooping!
(III. ii. 178-80)

but also in the sense that her control seems to be supported by a force outside herself or a tendency in the world—call it the Life-force if you will; Hymen is as good a name as any, and Shakespeare does not seem too anxious to make definitions—which can emerge and take charge on its own account, when this is required. We may see the formality of Hymen as only the emergence of a subdued current which has run through the play.

What is more, the Masque of Hymen serves to bring to the surface an idea which has had recurrent emphasis throughout the play, the idea of life itself as a 'play', which only the most poised can master, and in which the others are tied to stage-struck or incoherent roles. It is no accident that the most famous and perhaps even the 'keynote' speech of the play is Jaques' 'All the world's a stage' which is so well-known that we have ceased to ask what it means in the play. It may be worth while to remember, therefore, the context in which the speech appears. The Duke, hearing Orlando's tale of the 'good old man', Adam, sends Orlando to succour him, and then turns to the rest of the company:

Thou seest we are not all alone unhappy;
This wide and universal theatre
Presents more woeful pageants than the scene
Wherein we play in.
 Jaques.   All the world's a stage, etc.
                                   (II. vii. 136-39)

A tradition of reciters and of 'speeches from Shakespeare'
has taught us to accent this, 'All the *world's* a stage', but in
the context it must be, '*All* the world's a stage'; that is, 'not
only are we not alone in presenting a 'woeful pageant', but
we are in fact only doing what *everyone* must do—playing a
part'. The words are given to Jaques, and the instances are
presented with his characteristic bile, but the idea is appropriate to the play as a whole; it is Rosalind, not Jaques,
who exemplifies in the dramatic action the knowledge that
play is itself a mode (and often the most accessible mode)
of reality.

Jaques himself is in some ways a frustrated impresario:
he has no sooner ended his seven-ages speech on the 'tragedy
of life' with:

Last scene of all,
That ends this strange eventful history,
Is second childishness, and mere oblivion,
Sans teeth, sans eyes, sans taste, sans everything
                                   (II. vii. 163-66)

than we are given physical demonstration of a different
view of age. Orlando enters carrying old Adam, whose
age has earned him reverence and respect:

O good old man, how well in thee appears
The constant service of the antique world.   (II. iii. 56 f.)

It is Jaques' constant effort to find or invent or organize
occasions which he can moralize into food for melancholy,
but he fails to convince others, for he has his eye fixed
constantly on his own obsessions. Touchstone, on the
other hand, is disabled by precisely the opposite defect:

his life is organized too obviously with an eye fixed on an audience that can be amused by wit. His wooing of Audrey is conducted in the same spirit as his memory of Jane Smile:

> I remember when I was in love I broke my sword upon a stone and bid him take that for coming a-night to Jane Smile: and I remember the kissing of her batler and the cow's dugs that her pretty chopt hands had milk'd. (II. iv. 43-47)

In the final scene Jaques tries to *present* Touchstone as an example of the melancholy observation that fools are wiser than wise men:

> Is not this a rare fellow, my lord? he's as good at anything, and yet a fool. (V. iv. 98 f.)

The Duke sees well enough that Touchstone's *folly*, his personality as he shows it, is not a real thing:

> He uses his folly like a stalking-horse and under the presentation of that he shoots his wit. (V. iv. 100 f.)

Touchstone is imprisoned in his detachment as surely as Jaques is imprisoned in his obsession. It is the same final scene that shows us the superiority of Rosalind in these terms by making her step down from her role as presenter and stand in line with the other country copulatives. She has as much wit as Touchstone and as much morality as Jaques, but her wit is a function of her feeling heart, and her morality springs from the experience or expectation of being one in the final dance of comedy.

IV

TWELFTH NIGHT

A reading of *As You Like It* together with *Twelfth Night* will soon reveal that the two plays are by the same hand. Both centre on the vision of happiness through love as it is

seen by a highly-born heroine who is condemned to serve
her love in a strange country, disguised as a boy. Both
plays set the loving self-awareness of this heroine against a
gallery of poseurs, lamed by self-love (and the consequent
lack of self-awareness) and show her depth of sanity in her
capacity to play the strange role that the harsh world sets
her, with efficiency but without losing faith in the true
identity to which fate and her own efforts will eventually
return her. Both plays contain important 'wise-fool' roles,
in which the fool (Touchstone or Feste) is largely detached
from the loving and self-loving world, knowing better than
most the inevitability of self-deception, but less than at
least one (the heroine) the value of implication in the Human
Dilemma.

The likeness of the two plays is considerable, but it
appears in the mechanics rather than the effects. The two
professional fools may indeed serve to focus the differences
as well as the similarities. A. C. Bradley remarked of Feste
that 'he would never have dreamed of marrying Audrey'.
Critics today are properly chary about the kind of criticism
which tries to fit characters out of one play into another
('we can imagine the difference at Elsinore if only Hamlet
could have been married to Lady Macbeth') but in this case
the remark seems to compress conveniently an important
difference between the two plays. Feste (unlike Touchstone)
has no history, and this affects his function in the play. I
have already quoted Touchstone's use of his own experience,
past and present, of Jane Smile in the past and Audrey in the
present to make points about love and pastoralism. Feste
has no personal life to use as a 'stalking horse'; there is no
self-parody in his statements; his gaze is fixed relentlessly
on the temperaments and actions of others, with a clear eye
for their foibles and weaknesses, for the self-indulgent
melancholia of Orsino:

> the tailor make thy doublet of changeable taffeta, for thy mind is
> a very opal.   (II. iv. 72 f.)

For the wilful grieving of Olivia:

> the more fool [you] Madonna, to mourn for your brother's soul,
> being in heaven.   (I. v. 65 f.)

For the self-love (and so self-ignorance) of Malvolio:

> I say there is no darkness but ignorance, in which thou art more
> puzzled than the Egyptians in their fog.   (IV. ii. 41-3)

It is typical of Feste's role as the detached onlooker that we
are uncertain if he was ever fully involved in the plot against
Malvolio. Certainly he was willing to appear as the 'wise'
Sir Topas ministering to the 'fool' Malvolio, for that
demonstrates neatly how 'the whirligig of time brings in
his revenges', but the involvement seems limited to this
intellectual kind of pleasure in consequences. Feste is not to
be circumscribed by the subplot grouping of Sir Toby,
Maria, Sir Andrew, nor can he be supposed to share their
'eat, drink and be merry' philosophy, except as it suits his
purpose. He is the onlooker who judges but is never judged;
in this way he is bound to be much nearer to the centre of
the play than is Touchstone.

The changed and more central role of the fool in this
play is symptomatic of a change of focus in the whole
design. No longer is affectation or self-indulgence a
weakness which can be put aside blandly, as it is by Rosalind.
In *As You Like It* Phebe and Jaques can be put in their
places, in a dance of living and loving, by self-control and
self-awareness, but without self-sacrifice. In *Twelfth Night*,
affectation is everywhere—among the heroic as among the
foolish, among the central characters as among the marginal
—and self-sacrifice is necessarily involved if it is to be defeated.
Rosalind is able to use her disguise as a genuine and joyous
extension of her personality; Viola suffers constriction and
discomfiture in *her* role. It is properly representative that
the most famous speeches by the disguised Rosalind are her
teasing comments on Orlando, such as that at IV.i. 83 ff.:

The poor world is almost six thousand years old, and in all this time there was not any man died in his own person, videlicet, in a love-cause . . . men have died from time to time, and worms have eaten them, but not for love.

While the most famous speech of the disguised Viola is the melancholy description of her own imagined fate:

> She never told her love,
> But let concealment, like a worm i' th' bud,
> Feed on her damask cheek. She pin'd in thought;
> And with a green and yellow melancholy
> She sat like Patience on a monument
> Smiling at grief. Was not this love indeed?   (II. iv. 109-14)

—further constricted, as the speech is, in the context of Orsino's assumption that women cannot love.

The vision of happiness is thus for Viola a smiling through tears, a vision all the more poignant for its unlikeliness to be fulfilled. To say this is to make Viola sound like the archetype for much modern 'brave little woman' sentimentality. And she is not: the play is too busy to let her seem so. The sentiment is placed in a current of cross-intrigues which keeps it from the stagnation of sentimentality. Happiness is a perpetual possibility which has to be shelved away as soon as it is exposed (for matters, not hostile, but more immediately pressing, always intervene); it is a single thread in a broadloom that is largely made up of threats and deceptions. It is one of the functions of the large-scale and fully developed subplot of this play to complicate each of the visits that Viola makes to the house of Olivia, and to cross-hatch the final comedy of errors between Sebastian and Viola.

But the complications introduced by the sub-plot are not to be limited to the intrigues it contains; what we have here is not a simple world of below-stairs bumbling and aping (as in *Much Ado*) but a real, even if easily deflected, threat to the security of princely natures and developed sensibilities. On the self-indulgence of Olivia and Orsino must be laid at least some of the blame for the presumptuousness of Malvolio and the idle mischief of Sir Toby. Malvolio's aspiration to join the aristocracy is not absurd; his disguise in smiles and yellow stockings can be seen as a nastier variant of the 'mental disguise' of Orsino and Olivia—their willingness to act on temporary obsessions, and to forget the continuity of their lives. All are presented as victims of a need to hide from the isolated truth (and here Viola, though her disguise is forced on her and not chosen, must be joined with the others): Olivia cannot bear to be known for what she is—a healthy and nubile woman; Viola cannot permit herself to be known for what she is—a girl; Orsino cannot bear to be known for what he is—a lover in love with the idea of love; Sir Toby cannot bear to be known for a parasite, Sir Andrew for a fool, Malvolio for a steward. The process of the play is one which allows these truths to be bearable (or socially organized) at the end of the action, not by developing characters to a greater understanding, but simply by moving the plot around till the major characters each find themselves opposite a desirable partner and an escape hatch from absurdity. The new pattern at the end is seen not only as personally satisfying, but also as socially desirable, certain pretenders to civility (notably Malvolio and Sir Andrew) being rejected from the pattern (as in Restoration Comedy), in which the others express their own superior natures. It is true that there is a degree of 'Jonsonian' social realism in the play's image of an effete aristocracy threatened by a determined upstart; the economic basis of the relationship between Sir Toby and Sir Andrew is clearly stated (II.iv. 170 ff.), and the marriage of Sir Toby and Maria is more a piece of social justice than a contribution to any final dance of reconciliation. But this dance itself is not to be explained in social terms; the principal emotion involved in the denouement is the sense of release from the complexity and isolation of outer disguise or inner obsession; and this is a personal and individual matter, to which society is merely accessary:

> When . . . golden time convents,
> A solemn combination shall be made
> Of our dear souls. Meantime, sweet sister,
> We will not part from hence. Cesario, come;
> For so you shall be, while you are a man;
> But when in other habits you are seen,
> Orsino's mistress, and his fancy's queen.   (V. i. 368-74)

But we may well feel that the play has related the dream world of 'golden time' too securely to the class struggle around it to allow this to be more than a partial reconciliation. The amount of space that the denouement gives to Malvolio (about one hundred lines out of a total of one hundred and seventy-five) may seem to be indicative of Shakespeare's waning interest in these glamorous aristocrats. In *As You Like It* the dance of lovers was broken by the solitary Jaques but was not marred by him, for he too had found a milieu in which he could be himself:

> [*to Duke*] You to your former honour I bequeath;
> Your patience and your virtue well deserves it.
> [*to Orlando*] You to a love that your true faith doth merit;
> . . .   So, to your pleasures:
> I am for other than for dancing measures.   (V. iv. 180-87)

But the exit of Malvolio:

> I'll be reveng'd on the whole pack of you.   (V. i. 364)

is more difficult to fit in. The Duke instructs servants to

> Pursue him, and entreat him to a peace,

but we are hardly convinced that this will be effective. The happiness of the lovers would seem to have been bought at a price which excludes Malvolio, and we may feel that this circumscribes and diminishes the final effect of their happiness.

It is another function of the subplot in *Twelfth Night* to complement the lyric world of the high-born characters with a robust and self-sufficient grossness so that a more complete image of society emerges. I have already suggested that the combination of wit and sentiment serves, in both *Much Ado* and *As You Like It*, to keep the comedy from extremes of either harshness or pulpiness. *Twelfth Night* is not, however, a comedy of wit. It is, on the other hand, the most poetical (and musical) of the comedies; this is not to say that a higher proportion of the lines are poetry, but that it is more shot through and through by the lyric abandon of poetic utterance:

> *Viola.* If I did love you in my master's flame,
> With such a suff'ring, such a deadly life,
> In your denial I would find no sense;
> I would not understand it.
> > *Olivia.*   Why, what would you?
> *Viola.* Make me a willow cabin at your gate,
> And call upon my soul within the house;
> Write loyal cantons of contemned love
> And sing them loud even in the dead of night;
> Halloo your name to the reverberate hills,
> And make the babbling gossip of the air
> Cry out 'Olivia!' O, you should not rest
> Between the elements of air and earth
> But you should pity me.   (I. v. 248-60)

Poetic abandon of this kind is required in *Twelfth Night*, because there is so little that the characters, disguised, obsessed and frustrated as they are, can *do;* they are obliged to live out their potentialities rather than their deeds—potentialities (here as in the 'she never told her love' speech) dramatically enlarged in the mirror of a nostalgia for the impossible. This powerfully affects the image of the lover that the play gives us. In *As You Like It* we met the absurdity of the lover in Orlando's verses; but the verse is only a by-product of the loving personality. In Orsino, on the other hand, as in Olivia, the poetic abandon of love is given its bent and allowed a full range of languorous evocation:

> If music be the food of love, play on,
> Give me excess of it, that, surfeiting,
> The appetite may sicken and so die.
> That strain again! It had a dying fall;
> O, it came o'er my ear like the sweet sound
> That breathes upon a bank of violets,
> Stealing and giving odour! Enough, no more;
> 'Tis not so sweet now as it was before.   (I. i. 1-8)

The situation is somewhat similar to that of Silvius and Phoebe in *As You Like It*, high poetical but illusory; this time, however, because it stands at the centre of the play, it cannot be shot down by wit; Orsino and Olivia are too powerful to be scored against and pushed aside.   Both indeed are, as has been remarked, 'unlikely candidates for affectation'; Orsino is categorically stated, in the exposition, to be

> A noble duke, in nature as in name.   (I. ii. 25)

And Olivia, in her rule of her household and her distinction between Feste and Malvolio, shows a rare poise, even in the midst of her excess:

> O, you are sick of self-love, Malvolio, and taste with a distemper'd
> appetite. To be generous, guiltless, and of free disposition, is to
> take those things for bird-bolts that you deem cannon bullets.
> There is no slander in an allow'd fool, though he do nothing but
> rail; nor no railing in a known discreet man, though he do nothing
> but reprove.   (I. v. 85-90)

If such people are deluded, then their poetical delusions must be *self*-cured; it is for this reason, I suppose, that the play offers, beside *their* worlds, other worlds of experience which they can react to and discover, and discovering, evaluate properly (because of their fundamental nobility); with this evidence we judge them on their potential insight, seen against the others' incurable blindness. That love is both absurd and ennobling is a point that all these comedies have made; here in a world where all are disguised or deluded we need the grosser loves (and delusions) of Andrew, Toby and Malvolio, whose sensuality is an important element in his character, to give a scale to the high poetical delusions of Orsino and Olivia. A glance at a long and complex scene, like Act III, scene iv, may indicate how this is achieved. The scene opens with the comic incoherence of an Olivia plagued by love—very similar to the comedy of Rosalind already quoted (from III.ii. 204-09), but moves immediately to the related love-madness of Malvolio, the relevance of this being stated categorically:

> *Olivia.* Go call him hither. I am mad as he ,
> If sad and merry madness equal be.   (III. iv. 14 f.)

Malvolio's lunatic power to find encouragement in insults reflects directly on Olivia's refusal to accept Viola's words, but it also highlights the self-knowledge she knows in the face of her own madness; for he flies straight into a state where he is the very puppet of his own obsession, incapable of human conversation:

> *Malvolio.* Go, hang yourselves all! you are idle shallow things: I am not of your element: you shall know more hereafter. [*Exit.*
> *Sir Toby.* Is't possible?
> *Fab.* If this were play'd upon a stage now, I could condemn it as an improbable fiction.
> *Sir Toby.* His very genius hath taken the infection of the device, man.   (III. iv. 117-24)

The next episode contrasts the cowardice of Viola with that of Sir Andrew, and again the contrast is handled as one between laughing at the person and laughing at the situation. Andrew is sublimely ignorant of the difference between noble and ignoble behaviour:

> Plague on't; an I thought he had been valiant, and so cunning in fence, I'd have seen him damn'd ere I'd have challeng'd him. Let him let the matter slip, and I'll give him my horse, grey Capilet.
> (III. iv. 270-73)

To Fabian and Sir Toby the comedy of the cowardly Cesario is no different from that of the cowardly Sir Andrew:

> *Sir Toby.* I have his horse to take up the quarrel: I have persuaded him the youth's a devil.
> *Fabian.* He is as horribly conceited of him; and pants and looks pale, as if a bear were at his heels.
> (III. iv. 277-80)

but we react differently. Viola directs our attention to her inner dilemma:

> Pray God defend me! A little thing would make me tell them how much I lack of a man.
> (III. iv. 286 f.)

and so (while we laugh) we share her view of the situation; the gross level of the practical joke that Fabian and Sir Toby are conducting is being judged by Viola's reaction to it no less than she is being judged by their contrived situation.

In among these pranks Shakespeare places two passages of high-bred sensibility. Olivia and Viola meet briefly (for seventeen lines) and reveal their natures:

> *Olivia.* I have said too much unto a heart of stone,
> And laid mine honour too unchary out:
> There's something in me that reproves my fault;
> But such a headstrong potent fault it is,
> That it but mocks reproof.
> *Viola.* With the same 'haviour that your passion bears
> Goes on my master's griefs.
> (III. iv. 191-97)

In the context of the fake conflict of Sir Andrew's challenge, this real conflict of sensibilities and self-awarenesses make an immediate effect of noble honesty; it is not the self-indulgence that we note so much as the effort to deal with emotion. A second and more extended expression of the emotional world of noble persons comes at the end of the scene. Sir Toby's plan to trap Viola in her cowardice is turned back on his own head (quite literally) by the intervention of Antonio; but the farce turns towards tragedy in the arrest and apparent betrayal of Antonio.

Shakespeare's handling of this is extremely complex: the natural release by a just revenge on the bullies is suspended; they are left plotting new torments for Viola, while Antonio is haled away to prison; but the centre of the episode is in none of these, but in the sudden and rapturous vision that the refined sensibility will not always have to endure the context of disguise and discomfiture:

> *Viola.* He nam'd Sebastian: I my brother know
> Yet living in my glass; even such and so
> In favour was my brother; and he went
> Still in this fashion, colour, ornament,
> For him I imitate: O, if it prove,
> Tempests are kind, and salt waves fresh in love!
>
> (III. iv. 363-68)

Beside this vision of escape and reconciliation, the difficulties of denouement fall away, and the threat from the bullies, still crouching in the corner, suddenly seems absurd and unimportant; for the constructive powers of noble minds are not within their scope, and this has been given witness to, once again, even in the face of Antonio's betrayal:

> I hate ingratitude more in a man
> Than lying, vainness, babbling drunkenness,
> Or any taint of vice whose strong corruption
> Inhabits our frail blood.
>
> (III. iv. 338-41)

But the reconciliation is an *escape* here, not a conquest, as in *As You Like It*. The final dance of reconciliation is bound to seem circumscribed, for the role of Chance (which brings Sebastian to Illyria) is (unlike that of Hymen) that of the master and not the servant of the heroine:

> What will become of this? As I am man,
> My state is desperate for my master's love;
> As I am woman—now alas the day!—
> What thriftless sighs shall poor Olivia breathe!
> O time! thou must untangle this, not I;
> It is too hard a knot for me t' untie.   (II. ii. 34-39)

The play ends with a nonsense-song which earlier critics thought was plain nonsense and therefore spurious, but which modern critics usually see as an extended comment on the central ideas of the play:

> When that I was and a little tiny boy,
>   With hey, ho, the wind and the rain,
> A foolish thing was but a toy,
>   For the rain it raineth every day.
>
> But when I came to man's estate, etc.
> 'Gainst knaves and thieves men shut their gate, etc.
>
> But when I came, alas! to wive, etc.
> By swaggering could I never thrive, etc.
>
> But when I came unto my beds, etc.
> With toss-pots still had drunken heads, etc.
>
> A great while ago the world begun, etc.
> But that's all one, our play is done,
>   And we'll strive to please you every day.

Very little is clear in this; maturing seems to be looked at as a process in which folly loses its status, though most things stay the same ('the rain it raineth every day'), and have stayed the same since the world began. The song ends with a deliberate refusal to philosophize even this far, however: 'don't look for causal connections; a play is a play and not a treatise.' In its illogicality and its bitter-sweet sense of the need to submit to illogicality, the song is a fitting conclusion to a play in which happiness itself is seen as illogical and chancy. The very name of the play should suggest the same mood to us. 'Twelfth night' is often taken as meaning simply 'revelry', but though it is still in the season of Misrule, twelfth night is at the very limit of the season:

> Hedge crickets sing; and now with treble soft
> The red-breast whistles from a garden-croft;
> And gathering swallows twitter in the skies.

Seen in the context of Shakespeare's *oeuvre*, this melancholy mood of comedy in *Twelfth Night* cannot well be kept apart from the tragic vision of the plays like *Troilus and Cressida* and *Hamlet* which are its contemporaries. The comedy ends with happiness for some, but the happiness has no inevitability, and the final song sounds perilously like a tune whistled through the surrounding darkness. The fate of Malvolio is proper enough in the context of revelry, but the context is hardly strong enough to drown completely the overtones of *Hamlet*; the malcontented outsider is not *always* despicable. In *Twelfth Night* the impetus towards reconciliation is sufficiently tentative to allow such thoughts, and in such thoughts lies the death of Comedy.

WILLIAM SHAKESPEARE

THE LATE COMEDIES

A Midsummer-Night's Dream · Much Ado about Nothing
As You Like It · Twelfth Night

A SELECT BIBLIOGRAPHY

(Books published in London, unless stated otherwise)

Full bibliographical descriptions of the separate quarto editions and of the first collected edition of *Mr. William Shakespeare's Comedies, Histories, & Tragedies*, 1623 (the FIRST FOLIO) are given in W. W. Greg, *A Bibliography of the English Printed Drama to the Restoration*, 4 vols. 1940-59.

ABBREVIATIONS

ESEA:	*Essays and Studies by members of the English Association*
JEGP:	*Journal of English and German Philology*
MLN:	*Modern Language Notes*
MP:	*Modern Philology*
PMLA:	*Publications of the Modern Language Association*
PQ:	*Philological Quarterly*
ShJ:	*Jahrbuch der Deutsche Shakespeare Gesellschaft*
ShQ:	*Shakespeare Quarterly*
ShS:	*Shakespeare Survey*
UTQ:	*University of Toronto Quarterly*

TEXTUAL

E. K. Chambers, *William Shakespeare: a study of facts and problems.* Oxford, 1930, 2 vols. I., pp. 356-63, 384-88, 401-04, 404-07.

W. W. Greg, *The Shakespeare First Folio.* Oxford, 1955, pp. 240-47, 277-81, 293-95, 296-98.

GENERAL CRITICISM

RICHMOND NOBLE, *Shakespeare's use of song.* Oxford, 1923.

G. WILSON KNIGHT, *The Shakespearian Tempest.* 1932
—Chapter III, 'The romantic comedies'.

WELSFORD, E. *The fool: his social and literary history.* 1935.

STOLL, E. E. *Shakespeare's young lovers.* 1937.

CHARLTON, H. B. *Shakespearian Comedy.* 1938
—a comprehensive treatment, marred by sentimentalism and eccentric chronology.

HUIZINGER, J. *Homo Ludens.* Amsterdam, 1939. English translation, 1949
—a serious view of 'play'.

GORDON, G. *Shakespearean Comedy, and other essays.* 1944
—genial belles lettres.

PALMER, J. *Comic Characters of Shakespeare.* 1946.

STEVENSON, D. L. *The love game comedy.* New York, 1946.

PARROTT, T. M. *Shakespearean comedy.* New York, 1949.

PETTET, E. C. *Shakespeare and the romance tradition.* 1949.

COGHILL, N. H. K. A. 'The basis of Shakespearian comedy: a study in medieval affinities', *ESEA*, n.s. III, 1950, 1-28.

BABB, L. *The Elizabethan malady: a study of melancholia in English literature from 1580 to 1642.* East Lancing, 1951
—especially chapters VI and VII on love-melancholy.

BRADBROOK, M. C. *Shakespeare and Elizabethan poetry.* 1951.

SEN GUPTA, S. C. *Shakespearian comedy.* Calcutta, 1951.

HOTSON, L. *Shakespeare's Motley.* 1952
—the dress and the role of the clown.

THOMPSON, K. F. 'Shakespeare's romantic comedies', *PMLA*, LXVII, 1952, 1079-93.

FRYE, N. 'Characterization in Shakespearian comedy', *ShQ*, IV, 1953, 271-77.

MEADER, W. G. *Courtship in Shakespeare: its relation to the tradition of courtly love.* New York, 1954.

BROWN, J. R. 'The interpretation of Shakespeare's comedies', *ShS*, VIII, 1955, 1-13.

GOLDSMITH, R. H. *Wise fools in Shakespeare.* East Lancing, 1955.

MAXWELL, J. C. 'The middle plays'. *The Age of Shakespeare.* 1955 (Pelican Guide to English Literature, ed. Boris Ford). pp. 201-27.

BROWN, J. R. *Shakespeare and his comedies.* 1957.

MUIR, K. *Shakespeare's Sources.* Vol. I, 1957.

BULLOUGH, G. *Narrative and dramatic sources of Shakespeare*, vol. I (includes *A Midsummer-Night's Dream*), 1957; vol. II (includes *Much Ado, As You Like It* and *Twelfth Night*), 1958.

TILLYARD, E. M. W. *The nature of comedy and Shakespeare.* English Association, 1958.

BARBER, CESAR L. *Shakespeare's festive comedy*. Princeton, 1959.
SEHRT, E. T. 'Wandlungen der Shakespeareschen komödie'. *ShJ*,
XCV, 1959, 10-41
—uncomic elements in the comedies.
EVANS, B. *Shakespeare's comedies*. Oxford, 1960.
MINCOFF, M. 'Shakespeare and Lyly.' *ShS*, XIV, 1961, pp. 15-24.
F. KERMODE, 'The Mature Comedies' in *Early Shakespeare* (Stratford-
upon-Avon Studies 3) 1961. pp. 211-27.

A MIDSUMMER-NIGHT'S DREAM

First edition: A Midsommer nights dreame. As it hath beene sundry
times publickely acted, by the Right honourable, the Lord Chamber-
laine his servants. Written by William Shakespeare . . . 1600. Quarto.
[Facsimile, ed. Ebsworth (1880)]
Reprinted in the First Folio.
Modern editions: New Variorum, ed. Furness. Philadelphia, 1895;
Arden, ed. Cunningham, 1905; Yale, ed. Durham, New Haven, 1918;
New Cambridge, ed. Quiller-Couch and Wilson, Cambridge, 1924;
New Temple, ed. Ridley, 1934; ed. Kittredge, Boston, 1939. Penguin,
ed. Harrison, 1953.

TEXTUAL

GREG, W. W. 'On certain false dates in Shakespearian quartos.' *The
Library*, IX, 1908, 113-31, 381-409
—the 1600 Roberts quarto of the play was printed in 1619.

CRITICAL STUDIES

CHAMBERS, E. K. 'On the occasion of *A Midsummer-Night's Dream* '
A Book of Homage to Shakespeare, 1916, 154-60, [reprinted in
Shakespearian Gleanings, 1946].
LAWRENCE, W. J. 'A plummet for Bottom's dream', *Fortnightly Review*
CXVII, 1922, 833-44 [reprinted in *Shakespeare's Workshop*, Oxford,
1928].
LATHAM, M. W. *The Elizabethan Fairies*, New York, 1930.
LAW, R. A. 'The "preconceived pattern" of *A Midsummer-Night's
Dream*.' *Texas Studies in English*, XXIII, 1934, 5-14.

BETHURUM, D. 'Shakespeare's comment on medieval romance i A Midsummer-Night's Dream.' MLN LX, 1945, 85-94.

WATKINS, R. Moonlight at the Globe: an essay in Shakespeare productic based on performance of A Midsummer-Night's Dream at Harro school. 1946.

SCHANZER, E. 'The central theme of A Midsummer-Night's Dream UTQ, XX, 1951, 233-38

—'The moon and the fairies in A Midsummer-Night's Dream', UTG XXIV, 1955, 234-46

—Preface to Le songe d'une nuit d'été [Oeuvres complètes de Shakespear Paris (Formes et Reflets), 1956, III. 1-17].

SIEGEL, P. N. 'A Midsummer-Night's Dream and the wedding guest ShQ, IV, 1953, 139-44.

BONNARD, G. 'Shakespeare's purpose in Midsummer-Night's Dream ShJ, XCII, 1956, 268-79.

BRADDY, H. 'Shakespeare's Puck and Froissart's Orthon.' ShQ, VI 1956, 276-80.

NEMEROV, H. 'The marriage of Theseus and Hippolyta.' Kenyon Revie XVIII, 1956, 633-41.

OLSEN, P. A. 'A Midsummer-Night's Dream and the meaning of cou marriage.' ELH, XXIV, 1957, 95-119.

BRIGGS, K.M. The English Fairies, 1957.

„   „   The Anatomy of Puck. 1959.

W. M. MERCHANT, 'A Midsummer-Night's Dream: a visual re-creatior in Early Shakespeare (Stratford-upon Avon Studies 3) 1961. pp. 165-8

MUCH ADO ABOUT NOTHING

First edition: Much adoe about Nothing. As it hath been sundrie tim publikely acted by the right honourable, the Lord Chamberlair his servants. Written by William Shakespeare . . . 1600. [Facsimil ed. Daniel, 1886]. Reprinted in the First Folio.

Modern editions: New Variorum, ed. Furness, Philadelphia, 189 Yale, ed. Brooke, New Haven, 1917; New Cambridge, ed. Quille Couch and Wilson, Cambridge, 1923; Arden, ed. Trenery, 192 New Temple, ed. Ridley, 1935; ed. Kittredge, Boston, 1941; e Prouty, New York, 1948; Penguin, ed. Harrison, 1954; Pelican, e Bennett, Baltimore, 1958.

CRITICAL STUDIES

COLLIER, J. P. 'Dogberry and his associates', *Shakespeare Society Papers* I, 1844, 1-4.

SCOTT, M. A. 'The Book of the Courtier; a possible source of Benedick and Beatrice.' *PMLA*, XVI, 1901, 475-502.

SMITH, J. 'Much Ado About Nothing', *Scrutiny*, XIII, 1946, 242-57.

PROUTY, C. T. *The sources of* Much Ado About Nothing. New Haven, 1950.

NEILL, K. 'More ado about Claudio.' *ShQ*, III, 1952, 91-107
—mainly a reply to Prouty.

CRAIK, T. W. 'Much Ado About Nothing.' *Scrutiny*, XIX, 1953, 297-316

JORGENSEN, P. A. 'Much ado about *Nothing.*'*ShQ*, V, 1954, 287-95
—the tradition of discourses on *nothing*.

FERGUSSON, F. 'The Comedy of Errors and Much Ado About Nothing.' *Sewanee Review*, LXIX, 1954, 24-37. [reprinted in *The Human Image in Dramatic Literature*. New York, 1957].

HOCKEY, D. C. 'Notes, notes, forsooth.' *ShQ*, VIII, 1957, 353-58
—on *nothing* and *noting*.

OSBORN, J. M. 'Benedick's song in *Much Ado*', *The Times*, November 17, 1958 (p. 11)
—the full version of the song 'the god of love' (V. ii. 23 ff.).

POTTS, A. F. *Shakespeare and* The Faerie Queene. Ithaca, 1958
—chapter III attempts to trace connections with *Much Ado*.

STOREY, G. 'The success of *Much Ado About Nothing.*' *More Talking of Shakespeare*, ed. Garrett, 1959, 128-43.

ROSSITER, A. P. *Angel with horns.* 1961
—pp. 65-81 contain an essay on *Much Ado*.

AS YOU LIKE IT

First edition: First printed in the First Folio, 1623 [Facsimile, ed., J. D. Wilson, 1929].

Modern editions: New Variorum, ed. Furness. Philadelphia, 1890; Arden, ed. Holme. 1914; New Cambridge, ed. Quiller-Couch and Wilson. Cambridge, 1926; New Temple, ed. Ridley. 1934; ed. Kittredge. Boston, 1939; Yale, ed. Burchell. New Haven, 1954; Penguin, ed. Harrison, 1955; Pelican, ed. Sargent, Baltimore, 1959.

CRITICAL STUDIES

[WHITER, W.] *A specimen of a commentary on Shakespeare, containing I. Notes on* As You Like It, *II. an attempt to explain and illustrate various passages on a new principle of criticism derived from Mr. Locke's doctrine of the association of ideas.* 1794
—pioneer work on imagery.

BOSWELL-STONE, W. G. 'Shakespeare's *As You Like It* and Lodge's *Rosalynde* compared', *Transactions of the New Shakespeare Society*, 1882, 277–93.

THORNDIKE, A. H. 'The relation of *As You Like It* to Robin Hood plays.' *JEGP*, IV, 1901, 59–69.

STOLL, E. E. 'Shakspere, Marston and the Malcontent type', *MP*, III, 1905–6, 281–303
—Jaques derived from Marston's Malevole.

TOLMAN, A. H. 'Shakespeare's manipulation of his sources in *As You Like It*.' *MLN*, XXXVII, 1922, 65–76.

CAMPBELL, O. J. 'Jaques.' *Huntington Library Bulletin*, VIII, 1935, 71–102. Reprinted in *Shakespeare's Satire*, 1943.

FINK, Z. S. 'Jaques and the malcontented traveller.' *PQ*, XIV, 1935, 237–52.

SMITH, J. 'As You Like It.' *Scrutiny*, IX, 1940, 9–32.

CHEW, S. C. 'This strange eventful history.' *J. Q. Adams Memorial Studies*, Washington, 1948, 157–82
—the 'seven ages' speech.

JENKINS, H. 'As You Like It.' *ShS*, VIII 1955, 40–51.

GARDNER, H. L. 'As You Like It.' in *More Talking of Shakespeare*, ed. Garrett, 1959, 17–32.

LASCELLES, M. 'Shakespeare's pastoral comedy,' in *More Talking of Shakespeare*, ed. Garrett, 1959, 70–86.

MINCOFF, M. 'What Shakespeare did to Rosalynde.' *ShJ*, XCVI, 1960, 78–89.

TWELFTH NIGHT

First edition: First printed in the First Folio, 1623 [Facsimile, ed. J. D. Wilson, 1928].

Modern editions: New Variorum, ed. Furness, Philadelphia, 1901; Arden, ed. Luce, 1906; New Cambridge, ed. Quiller-Couch and Wilson. Cambridge, 1903; New Temple, ed. Ridley. 1935; Penguin, ed. Harrison, 1937. ed. Eccles. New York, 1948; Yale, ed. Holden. New Haven, 1954; Pelican, ed. Harbage. Baltimore, 1958.

TEXTUAL

SCHROEDER, J. W. *The Great Folio of 1623.* New Haven, 1956
—delays in the printing of the Folio.

CRITICAL STUDIES

TILLEY, M. P. 'The organic unity of Twelfth Night.' *PMLA*, XXIX,
1914, 550–66.

BRADLEY, A. C. 'Feste the jester.' *A Book of Homage to Shakespeare*,
1916, 164–69 [reprinted in *A Miscellany.* 1929].

GOLLANCZ, I. 'Bits of Timber', *A Book of Homage to Shakespeare.* 1916,
170–78
—Malvolio and contemporary scandal.

SYMONS, A. 'Twelfth Night.' *Studies in the Elizabethan Drama*, 1920.

MUESCHKE, P. and FLEISHER J. 'Jonsonian elements in the comic
underplot of *Twelfth Night.*' *PMLA*, XLVIII, 1933, 722–40.

GORDON, D. J. '*Twelfth Night* and *Gli Ingannati.*' *Bollettino degli studi
inglesi*, VII, 1939.

WEST, E. J. 'Bradleian Reprise', *Shakespeare Assoc. Bulletin*, XXIV,
1949
—a reply to Bradley's article on Feste, cited above.

HOTSON, L. *The first night of* Twelfth Night. 1954
—attempts to reconsruct the occasion of the play.

SUMMERS, J. 'The Masks of *Twelfth Night.*' *University of Kansas City
Review*, XXII, 1955, 25–32 [reprinted in Dean, *Shakespeare: Modern
Essays in Criticism.* New York, 1961].

SALINGER, L. G. 'The design of *Twelfth Night.*' *ShQ*, 1958, 117–39.

JENKINS, H. 'Shakespeare's Twelfth Night.' *Rice Institute Pamphlet*,
XLV, 1959, 19–42.

HOLLANDER, J. '*Twelfth Night* and the morality of indulgence.' *Sewanee
Review*, LXVII, 1959, 220–38.

L. P. Hartley
by PAUL BLOOMFIELD

and

Anthony Powell
by BERNARD BERGONZI

Published for The British Council
and The National Book League
by Longmans, Green & Co.

Two shillings and sixpence net

This is the first issue in the *Writers and Their Work* series to include not one author or a group of authors but two contemporaries. It will be followed shortly by others.

Mr. L. P. Hartley, born in 1895, and Mr. Anthony Powell, born in 1905, are among the most distinguished living novelists in Britain. Mr. Hartley has had the distinction of seeing an entire number of *Adam*, the international review, given to his work, and Mr. Powell's 'Music of Time' series has been the subject of critical papers of the highest standing.

Mr. Bloomfield, who writes about Mr. L. P. Hartley, wrote the booklet on *Disraeli* which appeared as No. 138 in the present series, and his last book, a life of the Colonial reformer, E. G. Wakefield, was published last year. Mr. Bergonzi, the author of the essay on Mr. Anthony Powell, has recently published *The Early H. G. Wells*.

Bibliographical Series
of Supplements to 'British Book News'

★

GENERAL EDITOR
Bonamy Dobrée

L. P. HARTLEY
from a photograph by Mark G

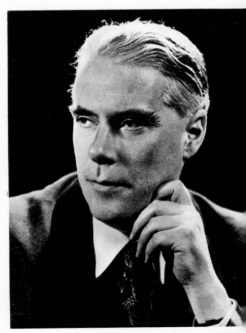

ANTHONY POWELL
Photograph by Camera Press

L. P. HARTLEY

by Paul Bloomfield

★

ANTHONY POWELL

by Bernard Bergonzi

Published for the British Council and
The National Book League by
LONGMANS GREEN & CO.

LONGMANS, GREEN & CO. LTD.,
48 Grosvenor Street, London, W.1.
Railway Crescent, Croydon, Victoria, Australia
Auckland, Kingston (Jamaica), Lahore, Nairobi

LONGMANS SOUTHERN AFRICA (PTY) LTD.
Thibault House, Thibault Square, Cape Town,
Johannesburg, Salisbury

LONGMANS OF NIGERIA LTD.
W.R. Industrial Estate, Ikeja

LONGMANS OF GHANA LTD.
Industrial Estate, Ring Road South, Accra

LONGMANS GREEN (FAR EAST) LTD.
443 Lockhart Road, Hong Kong

LONGMANS OF MALAYA LTD.
44 Jalan Ampang, Kuala Lumpur

ORIENT LONGMANS LTD.
Calcutta, Bombay, Madras
Delhi, Hyderabad, Dacca

LONGMANS CANADA LTD.
137 Bond Street, Toronto 2

Printed in Great Britain by
F. Mildner & Sons, London, E.C.1

L. P. Hartley

I

'I<small>T</small> must happen', said Hazlitt, 'that, in the course of time . . . some people will have struck out finer observations, reflections and sentiments than others. These they have committed to books . . . as a lasting legacy to posterity; and such persons have become standard authors.' Such a person is L. P. Hartley, who is read and will go on being read for the reason Hazlitt gives. Another and equally good reason is that he is a novelist who tells a first-rate tale. So far he has published ten novels and five books of short stories. The strange thing is that nearly twenty years should have elapsed between the appearance of this prolific writer's first novel, *Simonetta Perkins*, and of his second. It was a mature man who wrote *The Shrimp and the Anemone*—yet there seems nothing immature about *Simonetta*, so artfully are virtues made of its limitations.

All the same it is a young man's book, a gay book. It reads delightfully. Only if we consider it together with what has followed do we find significance in the pseudo-Simonetta's frustration. Her real name was Lavinia Johnstone. On a visit with her mother to Venice, this well-brought-up girl from Boston, U.S.A., had to be frustrated—her infatuation for the handsome gondolier Emilio had to come to nothing or Hartley would have been obliged to start again and write a quite different kind of book. Indeed, her non-frustration would almost certainly have meant tragedy. We had better note that a tragedy may or may not be a tragedy of frustration and that frustration may or may not be tragic. In *Simonetta* it is not, in Hartley's Eustace and Hilda's trilogy it is.[1] Still, there is significance in Simonetta's frustration because it foreshadows her creator's interest in certain kinds of temperament. In a word, he feels for those

[1] *The Shrimp and the Anemone; The Sixth Heaven; Eustace and Hilda.*

people who, because of their sensibility, are their own worst enemies—at any rate where adjusting themselves to life is concerned.

We shall find that Hartley has drawn his subjects from the past, from contemporary life, and in one instance, *Facial Justice*, from the future. But of course his true subject is human nature, so for 'subjects' as used above it would be better to say 'situations'. His plots are sometimes more sometimes less complex, and now and again, in some of the short stories particularly, they trail away, as life itself is apt to do, into indeterminacy—*exeunt in mysterium*.

But now back to *Simonetta Perkins*. No 'light' book was ever more acceptable intellectually or freer from clichés. Though most of the persons in it are caricatures they are absolutely not *gross* caricatures. They are all sophisticated, including in his way the gondolier Emilio, and Stephen too —Stephen, the unromantic young American whom Lavinia's bustling and hypochondriac mother wants her to marry. Now Lavinia, till Emilio begins to attract her, is no friend to love and very self-sufficient:

> "Should I call myself an egoist?" Miss Johnstone mused. "Others have called me so. They merely meant I did not care for them.'

A shrewd remark. Then, when Stephen first sets eyes on Emilio we get this little dialogue:

> "There's a good-looking man if you like", Lavinia's companion remarked.
> "Yes, he's considered good-looking", Lavinia concurred.
> "I call him very good-looking", Stephen repeated, as though there were nothing beautiful or ugly but his thinking made it so.

Is this not a prig in a nutshell?

There are several ways in which a novelist can describe his characters. He can describe them himself, or let them speak for themselves, or let the other characters allude to them; or of course he can do two or all three of these things. We have just seen with what neatness Stephen's self-exposure is confirmed by the author's aside. If a character has to be allowed to develop, such finality has its dangers, and if they are to be warded off, the writer has to have (what Hartley has) an unusual talent for catching idioms and idiosyncrasies, inflexions, tones of voice, the breath of life. Even more dangerous in a book is letting the evocation of someone's personality depend too much on what other people say about him. The reason is that allusions *are* so evocative, and raise expectations which it is then very hard for the person concerned, when he appears, to live up to. *In The Waves* Virginia Woolf got out of the difficulty by not letting Perceval, whom there is so much talk about, appear at all. In the last book of his Eustace and Hilda trilogy, Hartley, as we shall see, takes the risk of keeping the all-important Hilda off the stage till towards the end.

Among the people in *Simonetta* who establish their identities in a moment is Lord Henry de Winton. He is the first of the English aristocrats whom Hartley does so well, forerunner of the amusing Lord Morecambe in *Eustace and Hilda* and the more grave Lord Trimingham in *The Go-Between*. Lord Henry and his wife, seeing Lavinia shy and sad (sad because of her repressed passion for Emilio), make a most civilised effort to flatter her into a better humour. They even invent kind things alleged to have been said about her by a mutual friend, Caroline:

"Thank you", Lavinia said, ". . . but before I go will you tell me what vices Caroline said I had? I know her", she went on, looking down at them without a smile. "She must have mentioned some." They looked at each other in dismay.

"Be fair", Lavinia said, turning away. "Think of the burden I carry, with all those recommendations round my neck."

"We didn't mean to give you a character", Lord Henry said, distressed.

"Couldn't you", said Lavinia, turning to them again, "take just a little of it away?"

They do so for unawares, later, when she overhears them discussing her—not maliciously, but candidly; it is this which begins to give her the impulse to risk losing her 'character' altogether.

Hartley's aristocrats—the men—are on the whole *gentlemen*, with the self-confidence they actually so often have, and with a turn of wit as richly comic and irreverent after its fashion as that of any brick-layer or meat-porter. Like Lord Henry they have a regard for other people's feelings at any rate if those people are on their own social level, and know how to show it undemonstratively. In *Simonetta*, too, we get a first taste of the introspective monologue in which so many of the characters in the later books freely indulge. Our suspicions that Lavinia is preparing to rebel against the strictness of her upbringing are roused when we find her talking to herself as follows:

> To do wrong against one's will, as I did last night, how disagreeable! But with the full approval of conscience . . . how intoxicating. Before, when I felt I must only be good, my choice was confined, in fact I had no choice. Now, at last, I see the meaning of free will, which no one can see who has not wilfully done wrong. Even the people who say they always act for the best, and do so much harm, never get an inkling (it is their punishment) of the pleasure they would have if they knew, as others do, that they are really acting for the worst.

So much for *Simonetta Perkins*, one of the best constructed, ripe, entertaining and characteristic of first novels; and then after all those years comes *The Shrimp and the Anemone*. This, with *The Sixth Heaven* and *Eustace and Hilda*, makes a great English social comedy of the period between the world wars—but intending readers must not be led to suppose there is a happy outcome for the brother and sister whose close but tortured relationship is the thread on which the episodes are strung.

II

The Shrimp rates as a classic among studies of childhood, even if the boy child, the shrimp, the nervous, ingrown Eustace, is in some respects such an un-classic, unusual little creature. The story of the dominating elder sister (there is a charming 'ordinary' sister as well) and her adoring brother takes us from a sea-coast village in East Anglia, through school, Oxford and Venice back to where it started. This is not a working-class saga. The orders of society involved are the middle, upper middle and highest. Minney, the old nurse in the Cherrington home, is a feudal type, and her values are therefore bourgeois *in excelsis* (as indeed working-class ideals are everywhere, including Russia: petty bourgeois for a start). Minney's sights are however raised higher than that, for the children she is looking after rather than for herself.

It will not be giving too much away to mention that the first volume of the trilogy turns on Eustace in his gentle way dancing attendance—Hilda drives him to it—on an old lady, Miss Fothergill, who dies and leaves him quite a large fortune. This he insists on sharing with Hilda. The children's father being a widower, a professional man, not very well off, a strict but kindly aunt (their late mother's sister) acts as his housekeeper and their foster-mother. Perhaps their mother herself had a vein of strictness, a streak of puritanism. For something of the sort is ingrained in Hilda—she has a confidence in her own rectitude which at once mesmerises and desolates her young brother. And now Miss Fothergill's money is not only going to allow Eustace to have the best English public-school and University education, but also further Hilda's plans for devoting herself to social welfare.

On the first page of *The Shrimp* Hartley performs a feat the impressiveness of which is at once, though not at once fully, apparent. Hilda's personality leaps out of the very first line, Eustace's is established in the rest of the paragraph.

Eustace paddling by a pool on the sea shore has noticed a shrimp being eaten by an anemone:

> A tumult arose in Eustace's breast. His heart bled for the shrimp but on the other hand how could he bear to rob the anemone of its dinner? The anemone was more beautiful than the shrimp more interesting and much rarer . . . If he took the shrimp away, the anemone might never catch another, and die of hunger. But while he debated the unswallowed part of the shrimp grew perceptibly smaller.

There we have it—the predicament of a humane man with so often no choice except between courses repugnant to him. The incident which begins like this also symbolises the peculiar relationship of Eustace and Hilda, born to kill each other (figuratively) by kindness.

Another memorable episode in the book is the dialogue between Eustace and Minney while she is giving him a bath on her return from old Miss Fothergill's funeral. Eustace, being such a delicate child, has not been allowed to go.

> "Now, where are you the dirtiest? Shall I do your face first and get it over?"
> Taking the flannel she leaned forward and screwing her face bent on Eustace a look of ferocious scrutiny. He saw that his eyes were red.
> "Why, you've been crying", he said.
> "Well, can't I cry sometimes?" Minney brushed away a tear she spoke. "You often do."

One would like to quote the whole of it; many more tears have been started by the little boy's questions than those which Minney brushed away.

A peculiar little boy, but still a little boy trailing 'clouds of glory', thinking thoughts which remind us of the puzzling contradiction between natural selection and the Platonic intimations many of us have of the non-Darwinian ancestry of our human kind . . . And again there is the unforgettable scene, once more on the beach, when Eustace is persuading his sister to let him divide his legacy with her so that she should not have to be a governess:

> "And you could go to school too, if you liked!" Eustace saw that he had scored a hit. Hilda's head sank backwards, and her long eyelids drooped over her eyes.
> Speaking in her deepest voice, she said, "What's the good of talking about it? Miss Fothergill didn't leave the money to me."
> "No", said Eustace, "but", he added triumphantly, "I can share it with you if you'll let me."
> "I won't."
> "You will."
> "I won't."
> "You will".
> "All right", said Hilda. "Anything to keep you quiet."

There is no real inconsistency in the circumstance that Eustace, for all those clouds of glory, is afflicted with a sense of life being tainted, and suffers morbid apprehensions. And his love for Hilda, after all how ambivalent it is! As he grows up his whole ambition seems to be for her. Though he is clever, does well at school and wins a scholarship to Oxford, it is with Hilda's work at a home for crippled children he is most concerned, work she could not have been doing unless she had accepted half his legacy . . . and he wants her to make a splendid marriage. To rid himself of her on such terms would be agreeable even to *his* tender conscience.

The Sixth Heaven, then, turns on Eustace in his mild but obstinate way planning to throw Hilda into the arms of the virile and impetuous Dick, heir of Sir John Staveley of Anchorstone Hall. This in spite of the fact that his sympathetic Oxford friend Stephen shows sign of falling in love with her. Stephen is a brilliantly conceived character, the élite of a generation in epitome. They were the young ex-officers of the first world war, with more or less success trying to recapture their lost youth by Oxford's life-giving

springs. Stephen's affectations are disarming; we are perfectly
aware of the serious person he really is. We shall not be
surprised to find him developing, in the course of this book
and its sequel, into a pillar of his substantial family firm of
lawyers.

One of Hartley's regular expedients for letting his
characters reveal themselves is to make them write each
other long letters, and Stephen's letters are first rate; but
they do not deflect Eustace from his purpose. Perhaps it is
too much to say that *all* his ambition is for Hilda. He
early shows a decided inclination to enter the *Grand Monde*
of English 'Society'—charmed circle by no means so shrunken
even today, after another quarter-century of social revolution. Eustace is drawn to these people, who had, and have,
style, and the money to keep up that style, people whose
discipline, humour and willingness to raise families are
characteristics of a breed with great survival value. English
social life has the subtleties and variety of English poetry,
aesthetic traits which appeal to Hartley much as they did
to Henry James. His soft spot for ease and elegance combined
with the authority of tradition, as they sometimes are in the
'well-born soul' (if one may borrow a telling French idiom)
has by no means blurred his vision, though curiously enough
he overlooks, at any rate in his books, and as James did, the
effectiveness and viability mentioned above. *The Sixth
Heaven* is only a qualified testimonial to the Landed Gentry
here represented by the Staveley family into whose bosom
Eustace is so anxious to precipitate Hilda.

Sir John is having it broken to him by his wife that the
brother and sister are coming for the week-end. He asks

"Who on earth are they?"
"Miss Hilda Cherrington", said Lady Staveley, speaking slowly
and patiently and rather loudly as if she were addressing a foreigner
or a refractory child—a bluff that on such occasions she sometimes
tried—"is the Secretary of the Clinic for Crippled Children at
Highcross Hill . . ."
"Never heard of her", said Sir John.

"Perhaps not, because you don't move in high medical circles.
She's doing an extremely fine work there."
"But what's she doing here?" asked Sir John.

Not exactly a snob, he is more conservative than the
really grand member of the family, Lady Nelly. This delightful character is one of Hartley's triumphs, nor is it a flaw
in the third book of the trilogy that he should have almost
allowed her to steal the thunder. Lady Nelly is too much a
real aristocrat to be a snob. Such women, rare birds at any
time, can usually choose their company, and when they
cannot, can choose their moral plumage from a trousseau
no item of which is unbecoming. Their technique for
adjusting themselves socially is not a bit less wonderful
than putting rockets into orbit, and one would think more
relevant to the problems of our human condition.

We are never told how old Lady Nelly is supposed to
be. Evidently a woman 'of a certain age', she has something
of Cleopatra's immunity to the ravages of time:

> Her features might have been called blunt, for all their finish; to
> Eustace they never seemed quite visible, some effluence of her
> personality lay over them like a ground mist, and sometimes
> her spirit seemed to retreat, leaving her face untenanted save by
> its beauty.

The Sixth Heaven ends on a note of mystery. We are
made to share Eustace's anxiety about the progress of Hilda's
relations with Dick. Eustace has a dream—a dream while
asleep in bed (he often day-dreams)—and what he dreams
and our unsatisfied curiosity about what happened when
Dick took Hilda up in his aeroplane leaves us in suspense;
the answers are to come in *Eustace and Hilda*. Strictly, then,
the middle book of the trilogy is less complete in itself
than the other two, but since Hartley seldom writes a
page without enchanting us by his powers of observation,
this matters much less than it would otherwise. Hartley's
style is in general that of the best intelligent talk fortified

by the usages of prose diction—of the prose diction meant to be understood. He is not an 'experimental' novelist; with few exceptions who is, who has anything to say? The day-dreaming we get from Eustace and others is unforced—nothing to suggest theories about the 'stream-of-consciousness'.

We pick up *Eustace and Hilda* impatient to find out what is going to happen. But at once we come under a number of spells. The spell of Lady Nelly; the spell of Venice, where Eustace is Lady Nelly's guest; the spell of Hartley, at the top of his form in the first two-thirds of the book, which is divided into two parts of unequal length, Venice and home again. Eustace at Lady Nelly's is kept informed of developments in England—that is to say of the course of Hilda's relations with Dick—by letters from his family and from friends, and by a newspaper paragraph to which Lady Nelly draws his attention. Meanwhile Eustace's experience of life is being enlarged (and how brilliantly this is done!), for round Lady Nelly revolve social notabilities of many nations, on the whole not stupid people but most of them gilded and idle. These chapters are really a study of decadence. Indeed one asks oneself whether Hartley has not here proved himself a Balaam in reverse—whether he did not set out to bless but stayed to denounce. . . .

Lady Nelly, always considerate, wants Eustace to be prepared for a disappointment over Hilda and Dick. Dick, she warns him, 'hasn't much to give a woman'.

> "What kind of things hasn't he?"
> "The kind of things women value—gentleness, affection, small attentions, fussing about after them, you know. We like to be always in someone's thoughts."

In her tactfulness she passes over the question: What kind of things has *Hilda* to give a *man*? We readers, however, had already begun asking ourselves just this, and may feel by now we have the material for framing an answer. There

are times, after all, when a woman's duty, not to mention
her interest, is to be Woman, and this, we have noticed, is
beyond the beautiful Hilda's power except when she is in
a condition bordering on hysteria. And perhaps by letting
himself be so dominated by her the mild Eustace was
helping to spoil her for Dick—and to some extent for us.
A criticism to which this third book of the trilogy is open
is that Hilda is made to suffer from the many allusions to
her beauty and personality. She is less convincing as the
complete image than she was at her chrysalis stage, when
we saw more of her for ourselves.

Before Eustace leaves Venice he sees a ghost. Hartley
often introduces the uncanny into his work, especially
into the short stories, sometimes just to make our flesh creep,
sometimes, as here, in accordance both with the intimations of Hoffmann and Poe and the findings of modern
psychical research, that there are times when our psyche
projects itself outwards in mysterious ways. Eustace's
ghost-woman clearly bodes no good. But we had our
warning on the page facing the beginning of the whole
story—the quotation from Emily Brontë:

> I've known a hundred kinds of love,
> *All* made the loved one rue.

To judge love by most of its effects', said La Rochefoucauld,
it bears a closer resemblance to hate than to friendship.'
Whatever Hartley 'means' by his memorable story of
Eustace and Hilda, his outlook is no more pessimistic than
that of Heracleitus with his 'Character is Fate'. And after
all the whole of the life of any of us is greater than the sum
of our disappointments. Most of Hartley's books are about
the trials of the sensitive or the thin-skinned in a world
where good seems less fairly matched against evil than in
the Zoroastrian philosophy. But we put down the last book
of the trilogy, probably with a tear in our eye, knowing
which side we are on.

Though *The Boat* and *My Fellow Devils* were Hartley's next books, the one after—the famous *Go-Between*—seems to belong to the same group as the trilogy, being about a little boy of twelve, Leo, a kind of Eustace. The scene is set as far back as the year 1900. A very large public has comfortably stomached this retreat to a social ambiance in a way more strange than earlier 'period' worlds which seem more familiar for having been more written up. The narrative is straight enough, built up of a thousand perceptive touches. It is told in the first person by Leo, who has been persuaded to carry letters secretly between Marian, a young woman of good family, and her lover Ted, a farmer 'below' her in social status. The trouble is that Leo does not know the 'facts of life'. In the following extract from one of his dialogues with Ted he is using the now obsolete verb 'to spoon' for our 'to flirt'.

> "Could you be in love with someone without spooning with them?" I asked.
> He shook his head.
> "It wouldn't be natural."
> For him the word "natural" seemed to be conclusive. I had never thought of it as justifying anything. Natural! So spooning was natural! I had never thought of that. I had thought of it as a kind of game that grown-ups played.
> "Then if you spoon with someone, does it mean they will have a baby?"

When Leo's eyes are at last opened—and it is under circumstances of great emotional tension—the sociologist in us is grateful for the disappearance of the prudery which, not so very long ago, could expose a child of Leo's delicate constitution to such a shock. And there is something else to be said about that particular climax. One might hold it against an author lacking Hartley's finesse that he should work us, as well as Leo, into such a fever over the act which is simply, in the words of the poet Donne, 'the right true end of love', and especially where a pair of true lovers is concerned. But at any rate Leo is Leo, he does not stand for childhood in general, and it is for him we feel—it may be in spite of ourselves. Older and tougher persons, who *know* the facts of life, do not always reconcile themselves easily to the nature which is our mother or feel altogether at home in this world.

III

The sense of not quite *belonging* is the most conspicuous feature of the leading character's make-up in *The Boat:* one would not care to call him the 'hero', but neither would 'anti-hero' describe Timothy Casson. Would it be fair to say he is Eustace—grown up, still frustrated but no longer enjoying frustration, ready at last to enjoy being alive? The moment is hardly propitious, for Hitler's war is raging, and in the secluded village where Timothy, a middle-aged writer, has taken a house, the tenour of daily life has lost its humdrum ordinariness. But although Hartley, in this rich book, ruthlessly stigmatizes both the more sinister and the merely niggling aspects of civilian existence during the war years, his subject is not war at second hand. It is those traits of human nature which make it so difficult for men and women to live in harmony with each other even in the comparative peace and quiet of an Upton-on-Swirrel.

Now though Timothy may be Eustace grown-up he is no longer the innocent victim of other people's egoisms, he has his own quirks, and he does not always behave very well himself. Thus he allows his modest hope to sail his boat on the river, against the wishes of the local fishermen, to harden into an *idée fixe*, with far-reaching and tragic consequences . . . This is the longest and psychologically the most complex of Hartley's books, and from internal evidence one would guess that, in spite of the usual suavity of the narrative, the author's spirit was perhaps never more tormented than while he was at work on it. On feels that he, as well as Timothy, was struggling to allocate responsibility for what goes wrong between people when there seems no sufficient reason for it, and to trace good as far as he can to its hidden springs. The most virtuous character in *The Boat*, Mrs. Purbright the parson's wife, reminds us of somebody. Why of course!—she could be own cousin to Lady Nelly. In her less grand social context she shows the same concern for others as Lady Nelly, the same tact, and having more occupation seems to have done her no harm. It is among middle-aged *women* of a certain kind, then, that Hartley finds his Bodhisattvas, come down again from Nirvana to save or at least to encourage us. What are they like when they are young? Hartley never tells us.

Mrs. Purbright analyses a part of Timothy's trouble. She says:

> "Do you know, I sometimes think you bring out the worst in people."
> "Do I?" exclaimed Timothy.
> "Yes, somehow with you it is difficult not to give way to one's besetting sins. I believe you expect it of us."
> "I'm quite sure I don't", said Timothy, bewildered by this novel view of his requirements.
> "Where would you be", said Mrs. Purbright suddenly, "how would you feel about yourself, if nearly everyone in Upton hadn't done something to hurt and mortify you?"
> "I must have notice of that question", Timothy said.

The beam in his own eye! . . . The critique this deep, sometimes baffling book deserves would take up many pages The numerous characters include a large selection from the 'working class', a dog as true to life as any of the human beings, and a young woman, Vera, who had not waited for Timothy to bring out the worst in her (he certainly brings out no good in her): she is one of the most callous reprobates in modern fiction.

Then in *My Fellow Devils* Hartley leaves the Eustace-Timothy motif; it and *A Perfect Woman* and *The Hireling* are written with a new detachment. Hartley is for the time being above the battle. In *My Fellow Devils* he sets in opposition the infinite variety of delinquency and the absolute of Roman Catholicism: it is a coalition of obtuse-angles versus the right-angle. Colum MacInnes, the dishonest film star, represents that grimace which Hartley sees on the face of unregenerate humanity, while his unhappy wife Margaret, by nature a woman of integrity, vacillates between conscience and her love for her husband. The book is a kind of exploration; Hartley has not become a Roman Catholic. Roman Catholics might be surprised, for what a persuasive character (in both senses) is Father McBane! Speaking to Margaret of Colum on the screen he asks:

> "If the audience could bare their breasts when he is playing to them, what kind of shape would you expect to see?"
> Margaret was startled by the intensity of his voice. "I don't know", she said.
> "Nor do I", said the priest, "but I can guess. What is the name of his new film to be?" he asked inconsequently.
> "Oh", said Margaret, "such a silly name. I hardly like to tell you. It's called *The Devil is so Distinguished*."
> "Ah", said the priest, "he must have a talent for the role."
> "Do you know", said Margaret, "he hasn't. He's been worried all along because he doesn't do it well. He blamed me—he said I'd taken the devil out of him."

Just so; hence the acuteness of her conflict. We are so often in league with those who are most fatal to our peace or happiness (as we are to theirs) to prevent them from relaxing their hold on us.

The note Hartley strikes in *A Perfect Woman* is different again, the social setting is for once petty bourgeois, and the mixture of mischief, humour, shoddiness and decency has an almost photographic likeness to the world about us. There is tragedy, though love does not make *all* the loving and loved ones rue. It may be that the author's heart was less in this than in any of his other novels, for more readily than the tangled skein of the plot one is apt to remember admirable details, like the children comically asking awkward questions and the Welsh Inland Revenue man who, out of his Celtic sympathy for 'bards', allows the third-rate novelist Alec Goodrich to class his garden as a *market* garden and so pay less tax.

But *The Hireling* is felt; it is a strong book, working up from a situation that grips at once to the catharsis of its issue. Leadbitter, an ex-soldier, drives a car for hire. He often takes the attractive and talkative Lady Franklin, a young widow, and falls in love with her. Another of his clients is Hugh, whom she is preparing to marry and who, Leadbitter cannot help overhearing, means to go on with his liaison with his present mistress. Here we obviously have combustible materials. The significance of what happens? It is not a question that needs be pressed. Hartley does not suggest that because Lady Franklin feels Leadbitter's advances are incongruous, granted their different positions in society, 'class' should be abolished; on the other hand he does suggest that Hugh's social advantages are no excuse for his rudeness to the chauffeur. If Hugh had been less arrogant—here too many ifs could rear their heads; a writer is entitled to premise what he thinks fit about his characters. By altering the balance of temperaments another writer—or indeed this one —could have given the story a different end. I believe the end Hartley chooses is less a moralizing one than an illustration of the old Latin sentiment 'sunt lachrymae rerum et mentem mortalia tangunt'—roughly 'there are tears in the affairs of life and human suffering touches the heart'.

As to the question of 'class' and its abolition, Hartley has thought about it—which of us has not?—and his last novel up to date, *Facial Justice*, which is set in the future, is about just this. Well, it is about the *motive* which he believes inspires many people who wish to abolish class, and this motive, according to him, is envy. Hazlitt, with a quotation from whom I began this essay, was much more radical than Hartley, but he would have agreed with this diagnosis.

Then suppose social justice has been achieved, and that everybody is as well off as everybody else, will envy have been rooted up at last? No, for some girls will still most unjustly be born with prettier faces than others. In the egalitarian Utopia of Hartley's England—what is left of it after the Atomic War—society has no hesitation over setting *that* to rights. The usual thing is for alpha girls to ask to be 'beta-fied' (among us it pays plastic surgeons better to alphafy betas).

Jael, our heroine, has voluntarily *kept* her nice looks, and when she decides to visit the tower of Ely Cathedral, an indulgence looked upon as evidence of deviationist tendencies, her brother utters a warning:

> "The Voluntary Principle, as the Dictator has said, is like the appendix in the human body—it is of no use, but unless it gives serious trouble it had better be retained. If it gives serious trouble—"
> "Yes?" said Jael.
> "Well, there might be an order for the V.P. to be removed. By clinging to your face—"
> "I don't exactly cling to it", objected Jael.
> "Well, by refusing to be betafied, you have shown that your Voluntary Principle is unhealthy, and if you now go on this expedition you will prove it is inflamed. Besides—"
> "Besides what?" Jael asked.
> "Besides, there is the danger of an accident."

Yes, accidents can be arranged by a benevolent dictator. When Jael goes to Ely there is an accident . . .

This is a remarkable book, an achievement comparable with Huxley's *Brave New World* and Orwell's *1984*, its predecessors in this *genre*. If the more civilised part of the human race were to find itself in the clutches of a scientific dictator, cunning enough to wear a velvet glove over his iron fist, from what inward impulses might a renaissance of freedom still be hoped? Readers of *Facial Justice* should try to detect Hartley's opinions on this head—absorbed though they will find themselves by Jael's adventures, which are told with a wealth of circumstantial and indeed horrific detail. It is a question worth a good deal of thought; let us therefore consider what this very thoughtful writer has to say about it.

Hartley's short stories are made of the same paste as his novels, and though a surprising number of them are macabre many are in the straight mandarin vein; there is Venice to be revisited, there is a little supplement to the history of Eustace and Hilda, one way and another there is a good deal of self-revelation, and there is much pleasure to be got from the commentary, the dialogues, the touches bringing out the imponderabilia of temperament, the nuances of social intercourse.

Among our contemporary novelists Hartley is the master of sensibility. Of the sensibility, or susceptibility to impressions, of a man in whom the finer manifestation of civilised life meet with immediate response—in whom, indeed, they are to an unusual degree realised. Hartley was born more adult than most people; this, even if it seems a paradox, is why he has written so understandingly about children. But he has written with no less insight about grown-ups, and very sophisticated ones at that. His function as a writer, then, is not so much to be a moralist, and not at all to be a rebel. He is the transmitter of a civilised ethos. If we want a more civilised world we had better know all we can about what it is like to be civilised. And this is yet another reason why Hartley's novels and tales are so well worth reading.

L. P. HARTLEY

Bibliography:

'Adam International Review', Nos. 294, 295, 296 (1961) includes a bibliography of books, stories, etc. by L. P. Hartley

Separate Works:

NIGHT FEARS (1924) *Short Stories*
SIMONETTA PERKINS (1925) *Novel*
THE KILLING BOTTLE (1932) *Short Stories*
THE SHRIMP AND THE ANEMONE (1944) *Novel*
THE SIXTH HEAVEN (1946) *Novel*
EUSTACE AND HILDA (1947) *Novel*
THE TRAVELLING GRAVE. Wisconsin (1948) *Short Stories*
—published in London 1951.
THE BOAT (1949) *Novel*
MY FELLOW DEVILS (1951) *Novel*
THE GO-BETWEEN (1953) *Novel*
THE WHITE WAND (1954) *Short Stories*
A PERFECT WOMAN (1955) *Novel*
THE HIRELING (1957) *Novel*
FACIAL JUSTICE (1960) *Novel*
TWO FOR THE RIVER (1961) *Short Stories*

Critical Study:

THE NOVEL TODAY, by W. Allen (1955)
—includes a consideration of Hartley's work. Mr. Allen re-wrote his survey in 1960, bringing it up to date.

¶ L. P. Hartley's contributions to collections &c. are listed in *Adam*, Nos. 294, 295, 296 which also contains a symposium of critical articles in French and English, edited by Miron Grindea.

Anthony Powell

I

ANTHONY Powell has been writing novels for over thirty years, but it is only comparatively recently that he has been recognised as a major living novelist. His first book, *Afternoon Men*, came out in 1931, when he was twenty-five, and was followed, during the next few years, by four more novels. The war interrupted Mr. Powell's literary career, but whilst in the army he was able to do a certain amount of work on a project he had begun in the late thirties: a life of the seventeenth-century antiquarian, John Aubrey, in whom he had been interested for some years. This book was completed after the war, and was published in 1948 under the title of *John Aubrey and His Friends*; Mr. Powell also edited a selection from Aubrey's *Brief Lives*. About this time he resumed the writing of fiction. In a recent interview he remarked:

> After the war when I came out of the army and returned to the writing of novels, I decided that the thing to do was to produce a really large work about all the things I was interested in—the whole of one's life, in fact—for I have no talent for inventing plots of a dramatic kind in a comparatively small space—80,000 words.

This 'really large work' was to be *The Music of Time*, a work which Mr. Powell regards as one long novel, even though it appears, for convenience, in separate volumes. So far the following sections have appeared: *A Question of Upbringing* (1951), *A Buyer's Market* (1952), *The Acceptance World* (1955), *At Lady Molly's* (1957), and *Casanova's Chinese Restaurant* (1960). It is expected that the whole work will be complete in twelve volumes.

Although Mr. Powell's reputation rests largely on *The Music of Time*, some critics dislike its subtle elaboration of manner and prefer the crisper, more immediate effect of the pre-war comedies. I sympathise with this view; though *The Music of Time* is the major achievement, *Afternoon Men* is, I think, Mr. Powell's most sustainedly brilliant book. It can be classed with Evelyn Waugh's *Decline and Fall* as one of the few outstanding first novels published in England between the wars. The novel describes a society already made familiar by such books as Aldous Huxley's *Antic Hay* and Evelyn Waugh's *Decline and Fall* and *Vile Bodies*, the world of more-or-less fashionable London in the twenties, when the traditional social and moral patterns of English life had been badly shaken by the First World War, and outrageous behaviour was cultivated for its own sake. In this society, the circles of the minor aristocracy, certain of the professions, and literary and artistic Bohemia, though preserving their separate identities, overlapped and mingled. It is these circles that provide the setting and characters of *Afternoon Men*. In this novel, it must be admitted, the glamour of the 'bright young things' is somewhat tarnished, for though it describes a world which had come into existence in the twenties, the book was published in 1931, when Britain was in the grip of an economic depression and life had become distinctly grimmer. *Afternoon Men* is a magnificently comic novel, but the dominant note is drily sardonic rather than gay.

On the first page we encounter Atwater, the central figure—in no sense could he be called a 'hero'—in a seedy but smart drinking club, talking to a painter called Pringle:

> Atwater did not answer. He read a newspaper that someone had left on the table. He read the comic strip and later the column headed "Titled Woman in Motor Tragedy". He was a weedy-looking young man with straw-coloured hair and rather long legs, who had failed twice for the Foreign Office. He sometimes wore tortoiseshell-rimmed spectacles to correct a slight squint, and through influence had recently got a job in a museum. His father was a retired civil servant who lived in Essex, where he and his wife kept a chicken farm.
>
> 'How long has this place been open?' said Pringle.

'Not long. Everybody comes here.'

'Do they?'

'Mostly.'

This passage with its detached, laconic understatement, and short, simple sentences giving an air of calculated bathos, is characteristic of the whole work. Atwater, the dim, ineffectual young man with an upper-middle-class background, incapable of getting a job without 'influence', is neatly drawn. When he picks up a newspaper he inevitably turns from to the trivial to the sensational. The brief snatch of futile dialogue is, again, typical (technically, it owes an obvious debt to the early work of Hemingway); though inarticulate, it is highly expressive, and throughout the novel Mr. Powell uses these fragmentary exchanges to develop the story and sustain an atmosphere. Yet though *Afternoon Men* brilliantly anatomizes a world of futility and boredom, it is not an indictment; Mr. Powell is content to bring out the absurdity of his characters' lives, and to leave the moral indignation to others. This acute awareness of the absurd leads to comic scenes which are, I think, hardly surpassed by anything in English. As, for instance, when Pringle, who has been entertaining a party of friends at his cottage by the sea, disappears one day and leaves behind a suicide note, announcing his intention of not returning from bathing. A few hours later he is discovered in a fisherman's clothes, looking round the dining-room for the note; he announces that he changed his mind, and was picked up by some fishermen. A little later, when one of the fishermen returns to claim his clothes, a complex discussion arises between Pringle and his friends about how much he should give the man for saving him; ten shillings seems too little, and a pound too much, so he compromises by giving fifteen shillings. The man simply says 'Tar' when handed the money, and Pringle remarks, 'That was obviously the right sum'.

Afternoon Men, with its laconic wit, and stylized manner disguised as artlessness, is a small masterpiece, and certainly the best of Mr. Powell's pre-war novels. Its immediate successor, *Venusberg*, (1932), which describes the adventures of another ineffectual young man in a Baltic capital, contains some fine exotic characters and a number of entertaining interludes, but is a rather slight and static work. *From a View to a Death* (1933)—the title is a term used in fox hunting—is a good deal more interesting. Here Mr. Powell turns his attention to a world of declining county families, disturbed by the impact of a vulgar, social-climbing young artist, Zouch. The prose is less economical and more explicit than in *Afternoon Men*; the novel has greater solidity if less sharpness. It portrays a segment of society in greater depth than the first two novels, and to this extent looks forward to *The Music of Time*. Mr. Powell also indulges an interest in the grotesque, even the macabre, in his portrayal of the transvestite Major Fosdick, and the three organ-grinding dwarfs. Of all Mr. Powell's novels, *From a View to a Death* is the least unambiguously comic, even though much of it is extremely funny, for it ends with the death of Zouch, and the work is permeated by an atmosphere of lassitude and frustration. *Agents and Patients* (1936) seems to me the slightest of Mr. Powell's books. It is a farce rather than a comedy, which moves across Europe with somewhat breathless rapidity, and deals with the efforts of two genial adventurers to extract money from a young man who, at the start of the novel, has rather more money than sense. The last of the pre-war novels, *What's Become of Waring* (1939), which takes its title from a poem by Browning, embodies a good idea—the attempt to discover an author called T. T. Waring, whom no-one has ever seen—but is rather lacking in inventiveness. However, in its use, for the first time in Mr. Powell's fiction, of a first-person narrator (a somewhat shadowy figure, whose name we are never told), it anticipates the later novels. Mr. Powell's books of the thirties contain evidence of a lively talent—and *Afternoon Men* has something more—but one which tends to lack staying power; there is not a great deal in them to suggest his subsequent achievement.

Mr. Powell's work on John Aubrey, though in a sense marginal to his career as a novelist, is by no means irrelevant to it. Aubrey, the antiquarian, was a man in love with the past; but in his *Brief Lives*, his most celebrated work, he is revealed as equally fascinated by the oddities of human behaviour; as a great collector of gossip and a retailer of anecdotes, no matter how improbable or scurrilous, about the men of his age. It is this aspect of Aubrey, one imagines, that aroused Mr. Powell's sympathetic interest; throughout his novels, snatches of gossip or hints of anecdotes about figures off stage (who may never appear) frequently tantalise the reader. The following casual exchange from *Afternoon Men* is highly characteristic:

> 'William has had a letter from Undershaft. He's in New York, living with an Annamite and playing the piano.'
> 'Is he making any money?'
> 'Doing very well, he says.'

This anecdotal technique is used in a far more complex form in *The Music of Time*, which is, in essentials, a vast collection of anecdotes about a large, amorphous group of acquaintances in fashionable London between the wars. In fact, Professor Arthur Mizener, in a brilliant essay on the sequence, has remarked, 'the heart of Powell's work is his "Brief Lives"'

II

The Music of Time describes a similar world to that portrayed in *Afternoon Men*, though perhaps centred more closely on aristocratic circles. But the modes of description are strikingly different; Mr. Alan Brownjohn has remarked that 'the later sequence seems to fill in the social detail sketched lightly and to probe the emotions treated flippantly. Solid flesh is added to the grotesque bones.' Hence, the careful elaboration of the prose and the leisurely, analytical passages that we find particularly in the first two or three volumes, and which seem to disconcert readers who prefer the sharper outlines of Mr. Powell's early comedy. Yet the rewards for persevering with the admittedly more difficult prose of *The Music of Time* are very great; though less than half the work has so far appeared, one can already say that it is a major achievement in the kind of English social comedy exemplified above all in the work of Jane Austen. English society, with its complex and seemingly arbitrary class divisions and snobberies, and the collisions that arise from them, has always offered rich material to the novelist with an eye for the comic. Mr. Powell himself has observed, 'very few people can believe the routine of their lives when it is shown to them'. There is a further element, however, in *The Music of Time* which gives the comedy a unique flavour, and this springs from Mr. Powell's ability to create extravagant but convincing characters. Here he has affinities with Dickens.

Whereas *Afternoon Men* had opened abruptly with the terse sentence, " 'When do you take it?' said Atwater," *A Question of Upbringing*—the first of *The Music of Time* series—begins with a long, detailed, very careful description of a group of workmen warming themselves round a coke brazier, with snow falling on them. This image releases in the narrator's mind a number of potent suggestions; he thinks of the classical world, and then, by association, of a painting by Poussin:

in which the Seasons, hand in hand and facing outward, tread in rhythm to the notes of the lyre that the winged and naked greybeard plays. The image of Time brought thoughts of mortality: of human beings, facing outward like the Seasons, moving hand in hand in intricate measure: stepping slowly, methodically, sometimes a trifle awkwardly, in evolutions that take recognisable shape: or breaking into seemingly meaningless gyrations, while partners disappear only to reappear again, once more giving pattern to the spectacle: unable to control the melody, unable, perhaps, to control the steps of the dance. Classical associations made me think, too, of days at school, where so many forces, hitherto unfamiliar, had become in due course uncompromisingly clear.

The image of the dance sets the tone for the whole work and dominates everything which is to follow. The innumerable characters do indeed 'dance to the music of time', moving in and out of each others' lives, sometimes for long periods, but rarely disappearing completely. The dance gives a pattern to the memories of Nicholas Jenkins, an upper-middle-class young Englishman, whom we encounter first at his public school in 1921, and whose progress we follow to university and then into London society, and the worlds of publishing and the films. He has love affairs, marries, and forms a large and growing circle of acquaintances. The novels so far published cover a period of sixteen years; *Casanova's Chinese Restaurant* takes us up to 1937, and Mr. Powell's next novel will carry the story on to the outbreak of war in 1939. The novels do not cover Jenkins' life in a continuous fashion; they concentrate on key periods in it— or, very often, in the lives of his friends—and it is not altogether easy to plot the time sequence in detail (Professor Mizener gives an outline chronology, but this is not completely accurate; for instance, certain references to international politics make it clear that *At Lady Molly's* is set in 1934, and not 1935, as he suggests). Although Jenkins is the central figure, it is not true to describe *The Music of Time* as Jenkins' life story. The emphasis is always on the people he moves among, the other partners in the dance; some critics, in fact, have described him as a 'recessive narrator', who never really emerges as a personality. Mr. Powell has expressed surprise at this view. It is true that Jenkins is usually more explicit about the lives of his friends than about his own; he tells us practically nothing about his engagement and marriage to Isobel Tolland, for instance. Nevertheless, on subsequent readings of the sequence it becomes clear that Jenkins does have a genuine personality, of an elusive kind; he is more than the simple 'camera-eye' that we find in the early novels of Christopher Isherwood, for example. But he is, at all times, more concerned with the dance as a whole than with his particular part in it. The narrator's relative lack of preoccupation with himself is one of the things which distinguishes *The Music of Time* from Proust's *A la Recherche du Temps Perdu*, a work with which it has evident affinities.

In the five volumes that have so far appeared, nearly two hundred characters, major and minor, have been introduced. Even if they are given only a sentence or two, one can never be quite certain that they will not reappear at a later point in the sequence, perhaps to play a larger part in Jenkins' life. This reflects, not only the intricacy of Mr. Powell's fictional dance, but also the extreme cohesiveness of English upper-class or upper-middle-class society, where contact between a great many people in different circles is preserved by a large network of friends, or friends of friends, and few people are lost sight of altogether. At intervals throughout the sequence we will be reminded of the existence of absent figures by the kind of casual anecdotal reference to which I have referred. Some of the characters, admittedly, disappear for very long periods, such as Sunny Farebrother, who appears in *A Question of Upbringing* and then, says Jenkins, 'passed out of my life for some twenty years'. In time Jenkins realises that not only do persons reappear and converge at key points in the story, but that this converging movement is true also of the social worlds they occupy, of ways of life, and even of moral qualities. The underlying pattern of *The Music of Time* is constantly revealing unexpected correspondences and affinities. Jenkins expresses his feeling of this in the complex reflection that opens Chapter 3 of *A Buyer's Market*:

> I used to imagine life divided into separate compartments, consisting, for example, of such dual abstractions as pleasure and pain, love and hate, friendship and enmity; and more material classifications like work and play: a profession or calling being, according to that concept—one that seemed, at least on the surface, unequivocally assumed by persons so dissimilar from one another as Widmerpool and Archie Gilbert, something entirely different from 'spare time'. That illusion, as such a point of view was, in due course, to appear —was closely related to another belief: that existence fans out

indefinitely into new areas of experience, and that almost every additional acquaintance offers some supplementary world with its own hazards and enchantments. As time goes on, of course, these supposedly different worlds draw closer, if not to each other, then to some pattern common to all; so that, at last, diversity between them, if in truth existent, seems to be almost imperceptible except in a few crude and exterior ways: unthinkable, as formerly appeared, any single consummation of cause and effect. In other words, nearly all the inhabitants of these outwardly disconnected empires turn out at last to be tenaciously inter-related; love and hate, friendship and enmity, too, becoming themselves much less clearly defined, more often than not showing signs of possessing characteristics that could claim, to say the least, not a little in common; while work and play merge indistinguishably into a complex tissue of pleasure and tedium.

Professor Mizener has described *The Music of Time* as the product of 'an enormously intelligent but completely un-theoretical mind': a passage such as this is the closest one gets to a general statement of the vision of life that dominates the work.

III

Discussing the problems involved in handling such a vast collection of characters, Mr. Powell has remarked that 'inevitably certain groups of characters and their friends and relations get, as it were, preferential treatment'. Prominent among the figures who play a central part in the dance are two friends of Jenkins, sharply opposed types, whom we first encounter at school with him in the opening chapter of *A Question of Upbringing*. Jenkins is returning from a walk towards dusk on a winter afternoon when a boy called Kenneth Widmerpool hobbles past in sweater and running shoes, returning from a solitary run. Widmerpool was already notorious in the school as an oddity, and an unusual overcoat he had once owned had become a legend; but, says Jenkins, it was at that point that 'Widmerpool, fairly heavily built, thick lips and metal-rimmed spectacles giving his face as usual an aggrieved expression, first took coherent form in my mind'. Widmerpool, an unattractive but powerful personality, is to recur at many points in Jenkins' life subsequently. A little later Jenkins joins his friend Charles Stringham for tea; at all points Stringham offers a contrast to the earnest, ungainly Widmerpool:

> He was tall and dark, and looked like one of those stiff, sad young men in ruffs, whose long legs take up so much room in sixteenth-century portraits: or perhaps a younger—and far slighter —version of Veronese's Alexander receiving the children of Darius after the Battle of Issus: with the same high forehead and suggestion of hair thinning a bit at the temples. His features certainly seemed to belong to that epoch of painting: the faces in Elizabethan miniatures, lively, obstinate, generous, not very happy, and quite relentless. He was an excellent mimic, and, although he suffered from prolonged fits of melancholy, he talked a lot when one of these splenetic fits was not upon him: and ragged with extraordinary violence when excited.

At this early point in the story, Stringham—elegant, witty, self-assured—seems an immeasurably superior person to Widmerpool. But in time Stringham is defeated by his own inherent weakness, and Widmerpool becomes the dominating figure. The difference between them can perhaps be described as the difference between personality and character; Professor Mizener has said that Widmerpool and Stringham embody 'a major contrast of twentieth century natures'.

In Mr. Powell's description of Stringham we have a good example of his use of images taken from painting and the other visual arts to establish a character or capture an atmosphere. This is already apparent in the use of the Poussin image in the passage which opens the novel; the device will be familiar to readers of Proust. It is perhaps significant that when Jenkins calls on Widmerpool and his mother at their London flat, in *A Buyer's Market*, almost the first thing he sees is a vaguely symbolic painting called 'The Omnipresent'.

A picture called 'Boyhood of Cyrus' by Edgar Deacon, an elderly painter who had been a friend of Jenkins' parents, assumed a great significance for him, not because of its artistic merits, but because it hangs in the house of Sir Gavin and Lady Walpole-Wilson, with whose niece, Barbara Goring, Jenkins is for a time in love. Again in the same book, at lunch at a country house, Jenkins finds himself contemplating a large tapestry, one of a set illustrating the Seven Deadly Sins, which depicts 'Luxuria' with a wealth of appropriate detail. He then discovers that the girl sitting next to him, Jean Duport, is the sister of a school-friend of his. Some time afterwards they have a love affair.

All these events occur in *A Buyer's Market*, which shows us Jenkins moving into London fashionable and artistic society in the late twenties. The greater part of the novel is taken up with the happenings of a single evening and night: Jenkins and Widmerpool meet, to their mutual surprise, at dinner at the Walpole-Wilsons', and then go on to Lady Huntercombe's dance. Later they run into Edgar Deacon and a young girl called Gipsy Jones in the street; they all go on to a coffee-stall, where they have a chance encounter with Stringham, who invites them to a large party given by Mrs. Milly Andriadis, a society hostess of some notoriety. Returning to his flat in the early morning Jenkins encounters his elusive and rather disreputable Uncle Giles, who mysteriously describes himself as 'just up from the country'.

It is at the Huntercombes' dance that Widmerpool undergoes a spectacular humiliation at the hands of Barbara Goring, a pretty but irresponsible girl with whom both he and Jenkins are, at the time, in love. Remarking 'Why are you so sour tonight? You need some sweetening', she picks up a heavy sugar castor, meaning to sprinkle a few grains over Widmerpool. But the top falls off, and Widmerpool is covered in a cascade of sugar. It is one of the few overtly farcical incidents in *The Music of Time*, but the effect is considerably heightened by the exaggeratedly elaborate way in which the event is described:

Widmerpool's rather sparse hair had been liberally greased with a dressing—the sweetish smell of which I remembered as somewhat disagreeable when applied in France—this lubricant retaining the grains of sugar, which, as they adhered thickly to his skull, gave him the appearance of having turned white at a single stroke; which, judging by what could be seen of his expression, he might very well in reality have done underneath the glittering incrustations that enveloped his head and shoulders.

In *The Acceptance World*, which is set in the early thirties, Jenkins pursues his affair with Jean Duport, and is much involved with St John Clarke, an elderly novelist who, late in life, starts dabbling in Marxist politics. J. G. Quiggin, an able literary critic of strongly left-wing views, whom Jenkins had known at Oxford, is another central figure; he proudly asserts his humble origins, and adopts a resolutely proletarian mode of dress and speech: nevertheless, he illustrates the remarkable capacity of the English Establishment for absorbing those who are apparently its most radical critics. Quiggin, like Widmerpool, is a figure embodying the force of the will. Widmerpool appears later in the novel at one of the annual Old Boys' dinners attended by various members of Jenkins' school. It is at this dinner that Widmerpool is revealed at his most shockingly ludicrous: he is rising in the business world, and insists on delivering a lengthy speech, full of incomprehensible jargon, about the economic state of the country. It is interrupted when the elderly master, Mr. Le Bas, for whom the dinner is being given, collapses with a stroke. Jenkins imagines that Le Bas had been 'bitterly regretting that he was no longer in a position to order Widmerpool to sit down at once'.

Jenkins also meets Stringham at the dinner, obviously the worse for drink, and when they have left an incident occurs which graphically illustrates the change in the relative positions of Widmerpool and Stringham. Stringham collapses in Piccadilly, helplessly drunk; Jenkins is trying, rather ineffectually, to assist him when Widmerpool appears and briskly takes charge of the situation: 'A cab seemed to rise out of the earth at that moment. Perhaps all action, even summoning a taxi when none is there, is basically a matter of the will.' Jenkins and Widmerpool take Stringham home, and there Widmerpool succeeds in putting the reluctant Stringham to bed by sheer physical force:

> The scene was so grotesque that I began to laugh; not altogether happily, it was true, but at least as some form of nervous relief. The two of them wrestling together were pouring with sweat, especially Widmerpool, who was the stronger. He must have been quite powerful, for Stringham was fighting like a maniac. The bed creaked and rocked as if it would break beneath them. And then, quite suddenly, Stringham began laughing too. He laughed and laughed, until he could struggle no more. The combat ceased. Widmerpool stepped back. Stringham lay gasping on the pillows.

Here we see Widmerpool, who is crude, insensitive, but utterly determined, and who always emerges successfully from the humiliations he undergoes, standing triumphant, while Stringham, the man of wit and charm and sensibility, lies prone and defeated. Professor Mizener has suggested that Mr. Powell sees the twentieth century as 'a world nearly transformed by Widmerpools though still haunted by Stringhams'.

IV

The Acceptance World closes the first phase of the sequence, the period of Jenkins' youth and early manhood, when he was still growing up and receiving impressions of the world. In the later volumes we see him increasingly involved with the responsibilities of life. Critics have remarked that as the sequence develops, the passages of leisurely Proustian reflection that marked the early books become fewer in number, and the narrative style rather more clear-cut; this is true, I think, and may be due to a number of causes. It may be that Mr. Powell's approach to his material changed whilst he was writing, or that now Jenkins and his world have become firmly established in the reader's mind, the author can afford to be more direct and less tentative and exploratory. Or it may be that as the narrative draws closer to the point of time from which Jenkins tells the story, he has less need deliberately to evoke his memories of the remoter past.

The fourth volume, *At Lady Molly's*, is a rich, packed book, which introduces a wealth of new characters. Most prominent, perhaps is Lord Warminster, usually known by his second title of Erridge (and, to his intimates, as 'Alf'). Erridge has strong left-wing leanings, like many public figures in the thirties, and adopts a completely *déclassé* mode of life; indeed, he is thought by his family to have become a tramp at one time, and he certainly presents the unkempt appearance of one. Nevertheless, he preserves unexpected traces of his aristocratic origin, and is notoriously mean. He is one of the great characters of *The Music of Time*, in the true line of genuine English eccentrics. Jenkins falls in love with and marries Erridge's sister, Isobel Tolland, though we are told little about her. *At Lady Molly's* shows us Widmerpool, who is continuing to rise in the world, also contemplating marriage; he has become unexpectedly engaged to a Mrs. Haycock, a highly sophisticated widow several years older than himself, who already has two children. There is a delightful sequence in which Widmerpool circumspectly asks Jenkins whether his fiancée might not expect him to sleep with her before they are married:

> 'In fact my fiancée—Mildred, that is—might even expect such a suggestion?'
> 'Well, yes, from what you say.'
> 'Might even regard it as *usage du monde*?'
> 'Quite possible.'
> Then Widmerpool sniggered. For some reason I was conscious of embarrassment, even of annoyance. The problem could be treated, as it were, clinically, or humorously; a combination of the two approaches was distasteful. I had the impression that the question

of how he should behave worried him more on account of the
figure he cut in the eyes of Mrs. Haycock than because his passion
could not be curbed.

Here we see how the laconic dialogue of *Afternoon Men* is
made to carry an immense range of social nuance, while
Jenkins' incisive comment illustrates the clear-eyed awareness of human folly that is at the heart of Mr. Powell's
comedy. It is not surprising to learn, as we do, that
Widmerpool's experiment was unsuccessful, and that the
engagement has been broken off. There is much more in
At Lady Molly's that I would like to refer to; I will merely
single out the splendid figure of General Conyers, who, at
the age of nearly eighty, embarks on the serious study of
psychology, and engages Jenkins in weighty conversation
about Freud and Jung. He is a triumph of characterization.

Casanova's Chinese Restaurant is a rather more sombre
work. It begins in 1936, when Europe is divided by the
Spanish Civil War, and English society is, in addition, badly
shaken by the crisis over the abdication of King Edward VIII.
We are introduced to more new characters, and see rather
less of some of the old ones. Erridge is in Spain, enthusiastically if naively supporting the Republican cause. Stringham
makes a brief pathetic reappearance; he is now a hopeless
alcoholic, and is looked after by a Miss Weedon, formerly
his mother's secretary, from whose benevolent attentions
he makes ineffectual efforts to escape. Widmerpool, on the
other hand, is as pompously ebullient as ever: he remarks
to Jenkins that he has been 'moving in very exalted circles',
though certain of his plans are shattered at the Abdication.

But for the most part Jenkins is involved with a new set
of acquaintances, drawn from the world of music; the
principal ones are the young composer, Moreland, and the
sad, disgruntled music critic, Maclintick and his pathological
virago of a wife, who are both superbly realised. Jenkins'
own marriage means that he is more aware of the marital
problems of others. Moreland's marriage undergoes a crisis

but survives, while the Maclinticks' fantastically unhappy relationship ends in tragedy. The sombre note is emphasised by the entry of death: Jenkins' wife has a miscarriage, the Morelands' baby dies, and Maclintick commits suicide. And since the coming volumes of *The Music of Time* will take the story into the war years, when some of the characters will no doubt disappear, this darker, more serious note is only to be expected. Jenkins himself, though we never know what he looks like, seems to have aged.

At this stage, when so much of the work is still to come, one cannot hope to make a final assessment of *The Music of Time*. But I hope to have given some hint of the quality of this intricate fictional dance. Mr. Powell's central achievement is one which he shares with the great novelists of the past, the invention of a world of rich, complex characters, who, though extravagant and in some ways larger than life, are ultimately credible. Until recently, criticism of the novel tended to dismiss characterization much too lightly, but there are now signs of a change of emphasis; if that comes about, we may expect Mr. Powell's achievement to get even wider recognition. He himself has said of Aubrey's *Brief Lives*, 'there, loosely woven together, is a kind of tapestry of the good and evil; the ingenuity and the folly; the integrity and the hypocrisy; the eccentricity, the melancholy, and the greatness of the English race'. This could serve as an apt summary of *The Music of Time*, though admittedly the greatness is not much in evidence. The work describes what is in many respects a profoundly shabby society, still suffering from the demoralising effects of the First World War, when so many of the best men in England had perished. But if Mr. Powell's characters have little greatness or conspicuous virtue they are still human, and it has always been the achievement of the great comic writers —Chaucer, Shakespeare, Rabelais, Joyce—to make memorable comedy out of radically imperfect human material.

ANTHONY POWELL

Separate Works:

AFTERNOON MEN (1931) *Novel*

VENUSBERG (1932) *Novel*

FROM A VIEW TO A DEATH (1933) *Novel*

AGENTS AND PATIENTS (1936) *Novel*

WHAT'S BECOME OF WARING (1939) *Novel*

JOHN AUBREY AND HIS FRIENDS (1948) *Biography*

BRIEF LIVES AND OTHER SELECTED WRITINGS BY JOHN AUBREY, edited with an introduction by Anthony Powell (1949) *Biography*

A QUESTION OF UPBRINGING (1951) *Novel* ⎫

A BUYER'S MARKET (1952) *Novel* ⎪

THE ACCEPTANCE WORLD (1955) *Novel* ⎬ The 'Music of

AT LADY MOLLY'S (1957) *Novel* ⎪ Time' Series

CASANOVA'S CHINESE RESTAURANT (1960) *Novel* ⎭

Note:

¶ Anthony Powell contributed an essay on Eton, *The Wat'ry Glade* to THE OLD SCHOOL edited by Graham Greene, 1934; an Introduction to NOVELS OF HIGH SOCIETY, three Victorian Novels, 1947, and Preface to THE COMPLETE FIRBANK, 1961.

Some Critical Studies:

'From a Chase to a View', *Times Literary Supplement*, 15 February 1951.

THE NOVEL TODAY, by W. Allen (1955)

—includes a consideration of Anthony Powell's work. Mr. Allen re-wrote his survey in 1960 bringing it up to date.

'The Social Comedy of Anthony Powell', by A. Brownjohn, *Gemini* No. 2, Summer 1957.

'A Who's Who of the Music of Time', *Time and Tide*, 2 and 9 July 1960.

'A Dance to the Music of Time' by Arthur Mizener, *Kenyon Review* Winter, 1960.

'Taken from Life' (an Interview), *Twentieth Century*, July 1961.

¶ Other articles on Anthony Powell's work include one by Adriaan van der Veen, in the *Nieue Rotterdamse Courant*, June 1960; one by Jocelyn Brooke in the *London Magazine*, September 1960, and by Giocomo Antonini in *La Nazione*, Florence, November 1960.

The Detective
Story in Britain

by JULIAN SYMONS

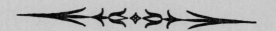

Published for The British Council
and The National Book League
by Longmans, Green & Co.

Two shillings and sixpence net

Mr. Julian Symons, in this concise and beguiling retrospective view of the British detective story, divides his subject into 'The Begetters', 'Sherlock Holmes', 'The Great Detective', 'Fair Play and the Revolt against It', and, towards the end of his survey, he introduces a monitory note under the heading 'The Weakening Form'. Mr. Symons's select bibliography includes most of the greater writers in the *genre*, but he has modestly refrained from emphasising his own works such as *The Colour of Murder* and *The Progress of a Crime*, which received awards as the best crime novels of 1957 and 1960 respectively. Mr. Symons has also written on the General Strike of 1926, on the Thirties and on that astonishing figure Horatio Bottomley.

Bibliographical Series
of Supplements to 'British Book News'
on Writers and Their Work

GENERAL EDITOR
Bonamy Dobrée

THE DETECTIVE
STORY IN BRITAIN

by JULIAN SYMONS

PUBLISHED FOR
THE BRITISH COUNCIL
and the NATIONAL BOOK LEAGUE
by LONGMANS, GREEN & CO.

LONGMANS, GREEN & CO. LTD.
48 Grosvenor Street, London, W.1
Railway Crescent, Croydon, Victoria, Australia
Auckland, Kingston (Jamaica), Lahore, Nairobi

LONGMANS SOUTHERN AFRICA (PTY) LTD.
Thibault House, Thibault Square, Cape Town
Johannesburg, Salisbury

LONGMANS OF NIGERIA LTD.
W. R. Industrial Estate, Ikeja

LONGMANS OF GHANA LTD.
Industrial Estate, Ring Road South, Accra

LONGMANS, GREEN (FAR EAST) LTD.
443 Lockhart Road, Hong Kong

LONGMANS OF MALAYA LTD.
44 Jalan Ampang, Kuala Lumpur

ORIENT LONGMANS LTD.
Calcutta, Bombay, Madras
Delhi, Hyderabad, Dacca

LONGMANS CANADA LTD.
137 Bond Street, Toronto 2

First published in 1962
© Julian Symons 1962

Printed in Great Britain by
F. Mildner & Sons, London, E.C.1

CONTENTS

I.   THE NATURE OF THE FORM   *page* 7

II. THE BEGETTERS   10

III. SHERLOCK HOLMES   13

IV. THE GREAT DETECTIVE   18

V.   FAIR PLAY, AND THE REVOLT AGAINST IT   22

VI. THE WEAKENING FORM   28

VII. TOWARDS THE CRIME NOVEL   32

VIII. CONCLUSION   34

A Select Bibliography   36

ILLUSTRATIONS

I.   Wilkie Collins (1824-1889) after a portrait by J. E. Millais of 1850 in the National Portrait Gallery.

II. Sir Arthur Conan Doyle (1859-1930).

III. Dorothy Sayers (1893-1957).

IV. Agatha Christie.

between pages ** 24 and 25

¶ Reconstruction of the living room at 221b Baker Street. Drawing by Ronald Searle. Reproduced by permission of *Punch*, page 14.

THE DETECTIVE STORY IN BRITAIN

(I) THE NATURE OF THE FORM

AS a literary form, the detective story has a place of importance in twentieth century English literature. It is important, first of all, through sheer weight of volumes. Several hundred detective stories or crime stories have been produced each year for the past forty years, and their total sales in paperback editions probably exceed those of any other sort of literature. It is well known that they are a favoured form of reading among British politicians and clerics who regard them (the compliment is ambiguous) as an agreeable relaxation from the cares of life. A small minority of them have a claim to be considered on level terms with other imaginative literature, but they receive little critical attention, and certainly most of them are not very well written. They are, however, likely to have considerable significance for future sociologists trying to interpret the nature of twentieth century man.

First of all, what is a detective story? What does an intelligent reader look for when he opens a book which is called by that name? He expects to find a situation in which a crime has been committed, and in which there is doubt about the means, the motive and the criminal. The crime may be of any kind, but in nine cases out of ten it is murder. The most important thing about the story will always be the puzzle that is set to the reader. Certain rules govern the formulation of this puzzle, and the revelation of the criminal.

The intelligent reader assumes that the writer will be fair to him. Without formulating the idea very exactly, he expects that a fair trail of clues will be laid, and that the author will not be deliberately misleading or untruthful, although the characters may lie as much as they wish. The reader will be annoyed if unsuspected facts are suddenly revealed at the end of the book. He is likely to say to a friend, if provocation has been carried far enough, that the author has 'cheated'. He may be annoyed, also, if a book which is called a detective story turns out to be a thriller.

A detective story, then, is not a thriller. A detective story asks questions about Who, Why and When; a thriller, dealing also in violent matters, simply tells us How. The lines of demarcation are sometimes vague, but books which can be classed quite positively as thrillers have been omitted from this survey. This is no denigration of John Buchan, Eric Ambler, and many other admirable writers, but simply an acknowledgement of the fact that there is a difference in kind between the two forms.

It becomes apparent to a student, however, that our intelligent reader's view of the detective story is a partial one: that the crime was not always murder, that the detective story was at first generally a short story and only latterly a novel, and that the rules he invokes when he says indignantly that the author has cheated held sway only for a period of some twenty years, between the two World Wars. During this period, which is sometimes called the Golden Age of the detective story, conventions as strict as those of Restoration comedy were established. Those writers invited to become members of the Detection Club had to swear, on their initiation, that they would abjure the use of twin brothers, secret passages and mysterious Chinamen, and exact rules were drawn up by various critics and writers, which we shall consider in detail a little later on. The detective story, as established within these conventions, was an exercise in logic. At a fairly advanced point in it the author should ideally have been able to say to the reader: 'All the clues to the puzzle are in your possession. Interpret them correctly, and they will lead to one inevitable solution.'

The pleasure the intelligent reader gets from reading detective stories is thus partly the fascination of engaging in a battle of wits with the author, something more nearly akin to a game of chess or a crossword puzzle than to the emotional rewards commonly looked for in reading fiction. But that is only the acknowledged part of the pleasure: the rest of it, often unacknowledged, rests in the fact that detective stories are concerned with violent crime. It would be facile to say simply that respectable readers sublimate their own tendencies towards violence by reading about it in detective stories. Nevertheless, the form arose in the latter part of the nineteenth century, its increasing popularity ran parallel to the development of the police force in Britain, and it does seem to be true that a high degree of personal security is necessary to the full enjoyment of the detective story.

In a social sense the detective story expresses in an extreme form the desire of the middle and upper classes in British society for a firm, almost hierarchical, social order, and for an efficient police force. Classical detective stories, with their strict rules, their invariable punishment of subtle and intelligent wrongdoers, and their bloodhound policemen supplemented when necessary by private detectives of almost superhuman intelligence and insight, are the fairy tales of Western industrial civilization. Mr. Nicholas Blake puts it extremely well when he suggests that some anthropologist of the next century may consider the detective story primarily as an outlet for the sense of guilt:

> He will call attention to the pattern of the detective-novel, as highly formalised as that of a religious ritual, with its initial necessary sin (the murder), its victim, its high priest (the criminal) who must in turn be destroyed by a yet higher power (the detective). He will conjecture—and rightly—that the devotee identified himself both with the detective and the murderer, representing the light and the dark sides of his own nature.

Mr. Blake is writing about the detective stories of the Golden Age. But this is the most curious of literary forms. Most of the greatest masters have been ignorant of or

heretical about the rules; and these rules are generally disregarded to-day.

(II) THE BEGETTERS

Some historians of the detective story have found its
origins in Archimedes' discovery of his principle in
hydrostatics, or in the deductions by which Voltaire's Zadig
was able accurately to describe the King's horse and the
Queen's dog by the traces they had left behind them, but
these are mere fragments of deductive reasoning. The tales
of terror that were so popular in England at the end of the
eighteenth century, with their emphasis on supernatural
appearances and on the romantic qualities of ruined castles
and sinister aristocrats, have also only the most tenuous
links with the severe logic of the detective story. The father
of detective fiction, in any serious sense, was undoubtedly
Edgar Allan Poe. It was a freakish chance that made the
generator of this conspicuously British literary form an
American, but Poe was a rarity, a writer of original genius
who was deeply interested in cryptograms and in the
processes of deduction, and who was fascinated also by
violent death. In his *Tales of Mystery and Imagination* may
be found many of the elements that later writers developed.
'The Gold Bug' depends upon the solution of a crypto-
gram; 'Thou Art the Man' offers the most unlikely
person as the criminal; and the three tales involving the
Chevalier C. Auguste Dupin show him as the first 'great
detective' of fiction. Dupin is a nobleman, a man of
culture, and a thinking machine. We are told little of his
appearance, but a great deal about his methods of reasoning.
See how cunningly Poe introduces the solution to a story
right at the beginning of 'The Purloined Letter', when
the prefect of the Paris police comes to see Dupin and tells
him of the problem of a stolen letter, a problem which is,
as he says, simple yet extraordinarily baffling:

'Perhaps it is the very simplicity of the thing which puts you at fault', said my friend.

'What nonsense you *do* talk!' replied the prefect, laughing heartily.

'Perhaps the mystery is a little *too* plain', said Dupin.

'Oh, good heavens! who ever heard of such an idea?'

'A little *too* self-evident.'

'Ha! ha! ha!—ha! ha! ha!—ho! ho! ho!' roared our visitor, profoundly amused; 'oh, Dupin, you will be the death of me yet!'

The police know that the letter is hidden in a certain house. They have probed cushions with fine needles, unscrewed chair legs, opened packages and parcels, measured the thicknesses of book covers, looked beneath carpets and floor boards, examined the joints of pieces of furniture—and have overlooked what is beneath their noses. The letter, torn almost in two, has been placed with apparent carelessness in 'a trumpery filigree card-rack'. Dupin, understanding the daring of the man he is dealing with, discovers it immediately.

Poe died in 1849, and his influence upon English writers was at first indirect. Charles Dickens and Wilkie Collins, the first important writers in this country to use detective themes, owe very little to Poe. Dickens was deeply interested in the work of the recently-established detective police force, and wrote several articles about it for the magazine he edited, *Household Words*. He created the first detective in English fiction, 'Inspector Bucket of the Detective', who plays a minor but important part in *Bleak House*, and is even permitted a chapter in which he recounts the course of his deductions. Dickens, however, never wrote a detective story. His last book, *The Mystery of Edwin Drood*, offers problems which even now are not definitively solved, but it is a mystery only because it remained unfinished.

The honour of writing the first detective novel (for Poe wrote only short stories in the field of detection) belongs to Dickens's close friend and occasional collaborator, Wilkie Collins. The book is *The Moonstone*, and the year of its appearance 1868. Mr. T. S. Eliot has called *The Moonstone* the first and best detective story, and certainly it is an original and fascinating book, notable because of its wonderfully ingenious construction, and also because Collins anticipated the standards of fair play already mentioned, which at the time he wrote were of course unknown. As Dorothy Sayers has pointed out, almost every clue needed for solution of the mystery is set out in the early chapters, and although the solution itself may be disappointing to our sophisticated tastes, it is perfectly fair. Collins's professional detective, Sergeant Cuff, is based upon Sergeant Whicher of the detective department. He is described with loving care by the house-steward, Gabriel Betteredge:

> A fly from the railway drove up as I reached the lodge; and out got a grizzled, elderly man so lean that he looked as if he had not got an ounce of flesh on his bones in any part of him. He was dressed all in decent black, with a white cravat round his neck. His face was as sharp as a hatchet, and the skin of it was as yellow and dry and withered as an autumn leaf. His eyes, of a steely light grey, had a very disconcerting trick, when they encountered your eyes, of looking as if they expected something more from you than you were aware of yourself. His walk was soft; his voice was melancholy; his long lanky fingers were hooked like claws. He might have been a parson, or an undertaker—or anything else you like, except what he really was.

Cuff is the first master of the apparently irrelevant report, the unexpected observation. Faced with a difficult problem and asked what is to be done, he trims his nails with a pen knife and suggests a turn in the garden and a look at the roses; asked who has stolen the missing yellow diamond that gives a title to the book he says blandly that nobody has stolen it. The fascination of such remarks is that their meaning just eludes us. By making the proper deduction we feel that we should be able to grasp it.

Collins, who wrote a number of other novels and short stories with some detective interest, as well as the masterly thriller *The Woman in White*, did not realise that he was working in a new form. He would have been astonished by the distinction made to-day between the 'serious' novel and the detective story which is regarded as being, to quote one of the few historians of the *genre*, Mr. Howard Haycraft, 'a frankly non-serious, entertainment form of literature'. Collins might have been moved to indignation by such a remark, and so might the other masters in this period who dealt with detective themes, Poe, Dickens, the Frenchman Emile Gaboriau (whose detective, Lecoq, is modelled partly on Dupin and partly on Vidocq, the ex-convict who founded the Sûretè), and the under-rated Irish novelist Sheridan Le Fanu, who wrote two remarkable detective stories *Wylder's Hand* and *The House By The Churchyard*. The radical change, through which the detective story was regarded as a 'frankly non-serious' form of literature came with Sherlock Holmes.

(III) SHERLOCK HOLMES

The first Sherlock Holmes story was the novel, *A Study in Scarlet*, written by Dr. Arthur Conan Doyle in 1886 and published in the following year. A second novel, *The Sign of Four*, appeared three years later. The first series of short stories appeared in the *Strand Magazine* in 1891, and they brought instant and immense success to their author. At the end of the second series, Holmes and Moriarty went to their presumed deaths over the Reichenbach Falls, and Doyle wrote thankfully to a friend that he had killed off his hero:

> I have had such an overdose of him that I feel towards him as I do towards *pâté de foie gras*, of which I once ate too much, so that the name of it gives me a sickly feeling to this day.

Frank Wiles June 6.
221 B Baker Street

But the insistence of readers, and Doyle's own need for money, brought Holmes back in three more collections of short stories and two more novels. Doyle wrote several admirable historical novels, and it was by these that he wished and expected to be remembered. The fact that his fame, as the years passed, rested more and more upon the Holmes stories, was something to which he never became reconciled. 'I have never taken them seriously myself', he wrote, and he made a sharp distinction between his serious fiction and what he regarded as the trivia of the Holmes stories. In vain: as a writer Conan Doyle was the victim of the legend he had so casually created.

Within a very short time Sherlock Holmes became a legend so vivid that criminal or emotional problems were addressed to him for solution, and pilgrimages made in search of his consulting rooms at 221b Baker Street. Doyle wrote many of the early short stories quickly, without worrying about consistencies of date in the history of his hero or of his faithful chronicler, Doctor Watson. From these inconsistencies there grew and flourished, after Doyle's death in 1930, a whole literature dealing with such matters as Holmes's interest in music, his relations with women, his early life and career as a student. There is a smaller, but still considerable, literature devoted to Watson. There is even a London public house called the ' Sherlock Holmes ' where the sitting room at Baker Street, complete with its occupant, may be regarded while one dines, and where many mementoes of Holmes's famous cases are preserved on the walls of the saloon bar. With Holmes the Great Detective really came to flower.

The Great Detective has certain strongly marked characteristics, which fascinated Victorian and Edwardian readers because they were so alien to their own deep-seated respectability. He is eccentric and often anti-social; Holmes, when we are first introduced to him takes drugs, and has fits of depression when he lies upon a sofa 'for days on end . . . hardly uttering a word or moving a muscle from morning to night'. He plays the violin extremely well, but when left to himself will merely 'scrape carelessly at the fiddle thrown across his knee'. He is also deeply and narrowly egotistical. When Watson expresses astonishment that Holmes is ignorant of the Copernican theory and of the composition of the Solar System, Holmes says that such information can be of no use to him:

> 'But the Solar System!' I protested.
> 'What the deuce is it to me?' he interrupted impatiently. 'You say that we go round the sun. If we went round the moon it would not make a pennyworth of difference to me or to my work.'

The Great Detective is above, or at any rate outside, human emotions:

> He was, I take it, the most perfect reasoning and observing machine that the world has seen: but as a lover, he would have placed himself in a false position. He never spoke of the softer passions, save with a gibe and a sneer . . . Grit in a sensitive instrument, or a crack in one of his own high-power lenses, would not be more disturbing than a strong emotion in a nature such as his.

In later stories Doyle found it necessary to soften and humanise Holmes's nature, but there can be no doubt that his presentation as an eccentric genius was part of his attraction; and attractive, too, in a highly conventional society, was Holmes's readiness to place himself above the the law. In 'The Abbey Grange' Holmes and Watson jointly decide that they will not reveal to the police the identity of the man who killed Sir Eustace Brackenstall; in 'Charles Augustus Milverton' they actually see a woman shoot the man who is blackmailing her, grind her heel into his upturned face, and do nothing about it; in 'The Blue Carbuncle' Holmes condones a felony with the reflection that it is possible he is saving a soul. In these, and in some other cases, Holmes has decided that the law is not adequate to mete out justice, and that he must do so himself. This dangerous doctrine is endorsed by other Great Detectives, including Chesterton's Father Brown, Dorothy Sayers's Lord Peter Wimsey and the American S. S. van Dine's Philo Vance. The exploits of Sherlock Holmes fulfilled much the same psychological function for their early readers that those of Superman fulfil to-day.

To stress the psychological basis of the Holmes legend is not to deny that these are excellent stories. Something in Doyle's Victorian romanticism responded to the figure he was inventing, and in the creation of Sherlock Holmes he wrought better than he knew. The character based originally on Doyle's old teacher Joseph Bell, the consulting surgeon at Edinburgh's Royal Infirmary, was enlarged far beyond the scope of Bell's character or deductive abilities. Doyle perfected the puzzling but meaningful retort, and used it with a skill that no other writer of detective stories has ever approached.

> 'Is there any other point to which you would wish to draw my attention?'
> 'To the curious incident of the dog in the night-time.'
> 'The dog did nothing in the night-time.'
> 'That was the curious incident', remarked Sherlock Holmes.

The dog did not bark, although somebody had entered the stables where he was on watch, and had taken out a horse. The significance of the incident is that the intruder must have been somebody well known to the dog.

Holmes is also unequalled in the brilliant deductions he is able to make from apparently trifling pieces of evidence. Given a battered old black felt hat, of which Watson can make nothing, he says:

> 'That the man was highly intellectual is of course obvious upon the face of it, and also that he was fairly well-to-do within the last three years, although he has now fallen upon evil days. He had foresight, but has less now than formerly, pointing to a moral retrogression, which, when taken with the decline of his fortunes, seems to indicate some evil influence, probably drink, at work upon him. This may account also for the obvious fact that his wife has ceased to love him.'

It is not surprising that Watson exclaims, 'My dear Holmes!' But Holmes has a reasonable basis for these, and for the six other deductions that he makes from the battered hat. Very often it would be easy to reach different conclusions, but in our dazed pleasant astonishment at Holmes's skill we do not notice that until afterwards.

The formula to which many of Holmes's exploits were written—the introduction of a new client, either by letter or in person, Holmes's startling deductions from very fragmentary evidence, the introduction of the other characters and the setting of the puzzle, Holmes's enigmatic remarks in relation to it, and the final solution—is perfectly suited to the short story form, much less well to the novel. Of the four Holmes novels, only *The Hound of the Baskervilles* is a real success, and this less for the puzzle, which is not difficult to solve, than for the skill with which Doyle makes us feel the terror and loneliness of the Devon moors, implied in the disturbed feelings of the sane and sober doctor who discovered footprints beside the dead body of Sir Charles Baskerville. A man's or a woman's footprints? Holmes asks, and Doctor Mortimer almost whispers his reply:

'Mr. Holmes, they were the footprints of a gigantic hound!'

The romantic excitement we feel in the Holmes stories springs from the strength with which Doyle conceived this vanished world of hansom cabs and gas lamps, of fogs and impenetrable disguises, of an incognito King of Bohemia and of the great coal-black hound whose "muzzle and hackles and dewlap were outlined in flickering flame."

(IV) THE GREAT DETECTIVE

The technique of the detective short story changed rapidly, and among the dozens of writers who tried to emulate the form and manner of the Holmes stories, very few are read to-day. Their stories are out-of-date, yet they lack almost entirely the period feeling that we value in the Holmes stories. Nobody to-day reads the work of Arthur Morrison, whose Martin Hewitt stories were at one time popular; or of McDonnell Bodkin, who created the first lady detective, Dora Myrl, and also the first father and son detective collaboration, in young Beck and his father; nor is it easy to find Baroness Orczy's ingenious tales about *The Old Man in the Corner*, who claims that 'there is no such thing as a mystery in connection with any crime, provided intelligence is brought to bear upon its investigation', and who solves a number of crimes without moving from his place in the corner of an A.B.C. teashop; nor the short stories which recount the exploits of Ernest Bramah's blind detective Max Carrados, who like Holmes is given to amending the law, in one case to the point of ordering a murderer to commit suicide. Few nowadays look at the books of the once-famous R. Austin Freeman, a doctor who created the first truly scientific detective in Doctor Thorndyke. It is a pity that Thorndyke is so nearly lost to us, because Freeman was an innovator of importance who wrote, in *The Singing Bone*, a collection of 'inverted' stories, in which we see a crime committed and then watch Thorndyke reveal the criminal, with the aid of the square green box covered with Willesden canvas, in which he keeps an extraordinary variety of materials for the detection of crime. The truth is, however, that Freeman, like many of his fellows, was an extremely poor writer, and in the end it is the quality of the writing that preserves all forms of art. In G. K. Chesterton's Father Brown stories the plots are often of dazzling ingenuity, but it is above all the zest and sparkle of the writing that makes us return to them again and again with pleasure.

In one of his essays Chesterton says that 'of (the) realisation of a great city itself as something wild and obvious the detective story is certainly the *Iliad*. The lights of the city are the guardians of some secret, however crude, which the writer knows and the reader does not. Every twist of the road is like a finger pointing to it; every fantastic skyline of chimney-pots seems wildly and derisively signalling the meaning of the mystery.'

This is wonderful special pleading for Chesterton's own stories. His dumpy little Catholic priest-detective, who finds difficulty in rolling his umbrella and does not know the right end of his return ticket, is the most preposterous of detectives. He is made acceptable by the genius that places him among scenes which also outrage realism: a secret garden where there are found two severed heads but only one body; a desolate house in the West Country in which the body of a man looking like an enormous bat is found spreadeagled among unspotted snow. In Chesterton's stories we meet stars that fly, feet that bound along a corridor like those of a panther and then change to a slow shuffling tread, an image in a passage which appears differently to each witness. In the field of detection Chesterton wrote only short stories, and the first two of his five collections, *The Innocence of Father Brown* and *The Wisdom of Father Brown* are much the best. Chesterton was a Catholic convert, and it has been said that he carried his faith too much and too obviously into his detective stories, but really the complaint seems a churlish one. If we accept Father Brown as a character—and Chesterton makes us do so—then we must accept also the fact that he is a priest, who may draw from any crime its religious moral. Chesterton is not a model for any other writer to copy, and the later logicians of the detective story, who drew up the 'fair play' rules, complained bitterly that Chesterton outraged them all, that he would not tell you whether all the windows were fastened or whether a shot in the gun-room could be heard in the butler's pantry. But the genius of Chesterton lay in his ability to ignore all that, to leave out everything extraneous to the single theme he wanted to develop, and yet to provide us with a clue that is blindingly obvious once we have accepted the premises of the story.

A dog whines because a stick sinks in the sea, the red light from a closed door looks like 'a splash of blood that grew vivid as it cried for vengeance', the priest of a new religion does not look round when he hears a crash and a scream, and these are clues by which we may solve mysteries if we have wit enough to understand them.

The detective story is particularly rich, if that is the word, in books which are of historical importance, although they are no longer of much interest to modern readers. Pre-eminent among them is *Trent's Last Case*, written by Chesterton's friend E. C. Bentley, and published in 1913. It is difficult nowadays to account for the high regard in which this book was held for many years. The writing seems stiff and characterless, the movement from one surprise to another, and the final shock of revelation, rather artificial. Perhaps it was the fact that Philip Trent, the detective, was such an ordinary human being that gave the book its great popularity. Mr. Howard Haycraft has remarked perceptively that 'its deceptive *un*-remarkableness, in fact, is the chief reason for its uniqueness in an era in which flamboyance and over-writing were the hall-marks of the crime novel'.

To-day A. E. W. Mason's first detective story, *At The Villa Rose*, published three years before Bentley's book, seems much more interesting than *Trent's Last Case*. Mason was an accomplished novelist, who wrote also four books, in which, as he says, he tried to 'combine the crime story which produces a shiver with the detective story which aims at a surprise'. His detective is M. Hanaud of the Sûreté, a stout broad-shouldered bourgeois who looks like a prosperous comedian. His very distinctive Watson is an over-fastidious dilettante and uxorious bachelor named Ricardo, who has made a fortune in Mincing Lane and feels it a point of honour to keep himself thoroughly up to date both in his very sound knowledge of red wine and in the criminal affairs of his friend Hanaud. Of Mason's four crime stories, which were published at wide intervals, *The*

House of the Arrow is perhaps the best, but all stand the most important test applicable to the detective story: they can be read again with pleasure.

(V) FAIR PLAY AND THE REVOLT AGAINST IT

The idea that the detective story is a distinctive literary form for which rules can be laid down was formulated during the nineteen twenties by many writers, perhaps most lucidly by Father (later Monsignor) Ronald Knox. The detective story, he said, was a game between two players, 'the author of the one part and the reader of the other part', and when one talked about rules it was not 'in the sense in which poetry has rules, but . . . in the sense in which cricket has rules—a far more impressive considera-tion to the ordinary Englishman'. He then laid down a 'Detective Decalogue', too long to be printed in full, which is summarised here:

(i)   The criminal must be mentioned early on.
(ii)   Supernatural solutions are ruled out.
(iii)   Only one secret room or passage is allowed.
(iv)   No undiscovered poisons are permitted.
(v)   No Chinamen should appear in the story.
(vi)   The detective must not be helped by lucky accidents, or by intuitions.
(vii)   The detective must not himself commit the crime.
(viii) Nor must he conceal clues from the reader.
(ix)   The thoughts of the 'Watson' must not be concealed.
(x)   There must be special warning of the use of twin brothers, or doubles.

It was easy to show by reference to the rules that the Sherlock Holmes stories erred in many ways, particularly in the matter of concealing clues from the reader. The American S. S. van Dine, the creator of Philo Vance, thought that all characterisation should be excluded from the detective story, and that 'style' had no more business in it than in a crossword puzzle.

It seems strange to-day that such rules can ever have been taken seriously, but during the years between the wars a great many writers worked carefully within them, and produced books which had almost invariably been plotted with a slide rule, but were written without style or savour. Among them were Freeman Wills Crofts, a railway construction engineer who turned to writing detective stories and specialised in apparently unbreakable alibis which were often connected with the intricacies of railway time tables; the Socialist economists G. D. H. and Margaret Cole, who like Crofts employed principally a police detective; E. R. Punshon, J. J. Connington, Ronald Knox himself, and a host of other writers now almost forgotten. To these writers, who were almost all novelists rather than short story writers, a plot constructed in accordance with the rules (and very often accompanied by a plan of the Manor House or of the library) was all; wit, characterisation, and consideration of the psychology of the people involved in the books, nothing.

The most interesting books produced by a firm adherent to the rules are undoubtedly those of John Dickson Carr, who wrote also as Carter Dickson, an American who qualifies for consideration here because his subjects and characters are so often English. Mr. Carr is a disciple of Chesterton, and his detectives, Doctor Fell and H. M., are in manner distinctly Chestertonian. He is a specialist in 'locked room' mysteries, in which an apparently impossible situation is always ingeniously resolved, and he has exceeded even his master in dramatic inventiveness. In recent years his work has shown a falling-off in quality, perhaps because of the human difficulty in ringing the changes so often on a single theme, but *The Hollow Man*, *The Black Spectacles*, and a Carter Dickson book, *The Reader is Warned*, are three books (and a dozen others almost equally as good might be mentioned) which delight us simply by their staggering ingenuity. *The Hollow Man* contains a chapter which is in effect a brilliant essay on the many varieties of locked room mysteries.

Carr is an exception. Upon the whole the flowering of talent that caused the years between the wars to be called the Golden Age came, in Britain, not by adherence to the rules but through a measure of revolt against them. The revolt came principally through three writers: Anthony Berkeley, Agatha Christie and Dorothy Sayers.

Anthony Berkeley began writing straightforward detective stories with an amateur detective named Roger Sheringham playing the central part. He soon, however, demonstrated considerable irreverence in relation to the rules. *The Poisoned Chocolates Case* offers six separate solutions to the stated problem: who sent the box of poisoned chocolates that killed Joan Bendix? In a sense this is an academically perfect puzzle, but it is also something near to a parody of the whole form. The book was published in 1929 and a year later, in the preface to *The Second Shot*, Berkeley wrote:

> I am personally convinced that the days of the old crime-puzzle, pure and simple, relying entirely upon the plot and without any added attractions of character, style, or even humour, are in the hands of the auditor; and that the detective story is in the process of developing into the novel with a detective or crime interest, holding its readers less by mathematical than by psychological ties.

In 1931, under the pseudonym of Francis Iles, he published *Malice Aforethought*, and in the following year an equally brilliant successor to it, *Before the Fact*. What was new about these books may be expressed in the first sentences of *Malice Aforethought*:

> It was not until several weeks after he had decided to murder his wife that Dr. Bickleigh took any active steps in the matter. Murder is a serious business.

I. Wilkie Collins (1824-1889) after a portrait by J. E. Millais of 1850 in the National Portrait Gallery

II. Sir Arthur Conan Doyle (1859–1930)

III. Dorothy Sayers (1893-1957)

Howard Coster

IV. Agatha Christie

We have here not a detective story, but a crime novel. We see Doctor Bickleigh's plans for murdering his wife, the progress of those plans, the police investigation after her death. But the effect created is quite different from that of a Thorndyke 'inverted' story. The fascination of this book, and of its successor, is in the interplay of character, the gaps between plan and execution, and in the dramatic ironies permitted himself by the author. The third Iles book, *As For The Woman*, was interesting, but much inferior to the first two: and unhappily, since then both Francis Iles and Anthony Berkeley have been silent. It was a long time before Iles's approach to the crime story was to bear any considerable fruit.

Berkeley-Iles was a conscious heretic, Agatha Christie perhaps an unconscious one. In *The Murder of Roger Ackroyd*, published in 1926, she replaced her usual extraordinarily stupid Watson, Captain Hastings, with an amiable country doctor named Sheppard. The doctor's first meeting with the little Belgian private detective, Hercule Poirot, comes when a vegetable marrow is thrown over the garden wall:

> I looked up angrily. Over the wall, to my left, there appeared a face. An egg-shaped head, partially covered with suspiciously black hair, two immense moustaches, and a pair of watchful eyes.
> He broke at once into fluent apologies.
> 'I demand of you a thousand pardons, monsieur. I am without defence. For some months now I cultivate the marrows. This morning suddenly I enrage myself with these marrows. I seize the biggest. I hurl him over the wall. Monsieur, I am ashamed. I prostrate myself.'

So the relationship is established. The friendly country doctor, who is telling the story, becomes Poirot's helper. Then in the last chapter, he is revealed as the murderer. The outcry was long and loud. This, it was said, was a deliberate cheat on the reader. And one or two of Mrs. Christie's later books, like *The A.B.C. Murders* and *Ten Little Niggers*, provoked almost as much discussion. Mrs.

Christie was accused of an unscrupulous use of the least-likely-person motive, and of failure to pay attention to the probabilities and to 'the canons of fair play'. Some pundits, including S. S. van Dine, brought in a verdict of guilty, others, like Ronald Knox, were graciously 'inclined to let her off', others still, like Dorothy Sayers, cast votes for acquittal. Undisturbed by this flurry of argument, Mrs. Christie went on to produce during the nineteen thirties a whole series of books which with great ingenuity play variations on the theme of tricking the reader. The first string to her detectival bow has always been Hercule Poirot, who has become less eccentric in speech and appearance with the passing years. The second string is a quiet spinster named Miss Marple.

Mrs. Christie has become more and more tired of Poirot, but has been obliged by public demand to go on writing books about him. Miss Dorothy Sayers, by contrast, could never have enough of Lord Peter Wimsey, and one might change Wilde's epigram a little by saying that to fall in love with one's detective is the beginning of a lifelong romance. We meet Lord Peter in her first novel, *Whose Body?*, published in 1923. He is an elegant aristocrat, and a devoted bibliophile who has such faith in his man Bunter that, when criminal affairs press, he is able to send Bunter off to a sale with the vaguest instructions:

> 'I don't want to miss the Folio Dante nor the De Voragine—here you are—see? *Golden Legend*—Wynkyn de Worde, 1493—got that?—and, I say, make a special effort for the Caxton Folio of the *Four Sons of Aymon*—it's the 1489 folio and unique.'

Lord Peter then changes hurriedly to go to see an architect who has found a dead body in his bath.

> He selected a dark-green tie to match his socks and tied it accurately without hesitation or the slightest compression of his lips; substituted a pair of brown shoes for his black ones, slipped a monocle into a breast pocket, and took up a beautiful Malacca walking-stick with a heavy silver knob.

Lord Peter drops the last letters of a good many words, and uses slang which is at times reminiscent of P. G. Wodehouse's Bertie Wooster ('I'll toddle round to Battersea now an' try to console the poor little beast', he says before going round to see the architect). Miss Sayers eventually equipped him with a 'Who's Who' entry and a lengthy 'biographical note' written by his uncle, Paul Austin Delagardie, which were printed in the new editions of every book about him.

Dorothy Sayers's originality certainly did not rest in the creation of Lord Peter, who is one of the purest fragments of feminine wish-fulfilment in fiction. In her early books, indeed, she was a fairly conscientious adherent to the rules. There was, she thought, great difficulty about letting real human beings into a detective story. 'At some point or other, either their emotions make hay of the detective interest, or the detective interest gets hold of them and makes their emotions look like pasteboard.' She was particularly severe upon 'the heroes who insist on fooling about after young women when they ought to be putting their minds to the job of detection' and concluded that, upon the whole, 'the less love in a detective story, the better'.

It is doubtful if one should give more weight to Dorothy Sayers's wish to provide Lord Peter with a love affair, or to her recognition that the 'rules' were absurdly restrictive: but in her later books she strove to create real human beings, and placed no restriction upon their emotions. In *Strong Poison* Lord Peter clears Harriet Vane of a charge of murder, and falls in love with her in the process; in *Gaudy Night* a puzzle (not a murder) is blended with an account of Lord Peter's love affair, and *Busman's Honeymoon* is frankly subtitled: 'A love story with detective interruptions.' Nor was this the limit of her experimentation. Implicit in the fair play rules was the idea that the setting of a story should not be too obtrusive, since its function was simply to serve as background for the puzzle and not to provide a distracting interest in itself. The lively picture of an advertising agency in *Murder Must Advertise* disregarded this idea, and so did the picture of the Fens and the campanological lore in *The Nine Tailors*.

It cannot be said that Miss Sayers's rebellion against the rules was completely successful. Her formidable intellect and learning were perfectly employed in writing the several essays in the form that appeared as introductions to collections of 'Great Short Stories of Detection, Mystery and Horror', but she never produced the masterpiece which her admirers had expected. The plots of her best books are shaped with wonderful skill, but there seems to be a softness at the centre of them. Her infatuation with Lord Peter, and her attempt to turn the detective story into a 'novel of manners' ended in a weakening of the detective element almost to the point where it ceased to exist. In the end she became dissatisfied with what she contemptuously called "the artificial plot-construction" of her own and other people's books. During the last twenty years of her life she wrote no more detective stories, and often referred slightingly to her own work within the detective form.

(VI) THE WEAKENING FORM

In detective fiction, as in any other *genre* of literature there comes a moment when fresh blood is needed, not only for its novelty but for its tonic effect as a whole. For some time now little has appeared, except from the pens of the old masters, which has been above a mediocre level.

So wrote the *Times Literary Supplement* reviewer in 1936, welcoming Michael Innes's first book, *Death at the President's Lodging*, which he called 'the most important contribution to detective literature that has appeared for some time'. This book and its immediate successors, *Hamlet, Revenge!* and *Stop Press* were certainly something new in detective fiction. These books followed the letter of the fair play rules in presenting a puzzle and the clues by which it might be solved, but flouted the spirit of them outrageously by a frivolity which turned the detective story into a literary conversation piece. There is no greater quotation-spotter or quotation-capper in detective literature than Inspector, later Sir John, Appleby, no conversations so recondite or so witty as those carried on by the guests at Scamnum Court, the seat of the Duke of Horton, where the Lord Chancellor is murdered during an amateur performance of *Hamlet*. Few Innes characters will flinch at playing a parlour game which involves remembering quotations about bells in Shakespeare, and Appleby, when confronted by the 'fourteen bulky volumes of the Argentorati Athenaeus' murmurs:

> 'The *Deipnosophists* . . . Schweighauser's edition . . . takes up a lot of room . . . Dindorf's compacter . . . and there he is.'

Appleby shows off sometimes in these early books, but not as Lord Peter shows off, by appearing a superior being to those surrounding him: it is rather that Appleby has to be a man of letters in order to survive in the highly cultured environment of Mr. Innes's imagination. At the time of writing these books Mr. Innes (the pseudonym of J. I. M. Stewart) was professor of English at Adelaide University. Asked to comment on his work in the field of detection he said that it had a somewhat literary flavour, and that some of his books were on the frontier between the detective story and the fantasy. Mr. Innes is now a don at Christ Church. His later detective stories are always amusing and original, but perhaps his most successful books in recent years have been thrillers, among which *The Journeying Boy* and *The Man From the Sea* should be mentioned as quite exceptionally good. His most recent detective stories lack the literary high spirits of the earlier books, and some-times show a certain carelessness in craftsmanship. The detective story was momentarily freshened, but finally weakened, by this attempt to treat it as an occasion for a display of literary fireworks in the manner of Aldous Huxley.

Nicholas Blake belonged like Innes to the post-Sayers generation. Blake (the pseudonym of the poet Cecil Day Lewis) invented a 'literary' detective, Nigel Strangeways, who solved one mystery by his recognition of a quotation from the Jacobean dramatist, Tourneur. His first book, *A Question of Proof*, was a lively and accomplished mystery set at a boys' prep school, and his fourth, *The Beast Must Die*, which appeared in 1938, was an extraordinarily clever variation of Agatha Christie's trick in *The Murder of Roger Ackroyd*. Like Innes again, Blake at first wrote detective stories in which the most engaging thing was the bubbling high spirits of the author, the obvious pleasure he felt in playing the detective game. With the years the high spirits have faded, and too often Blake's later detective stories bear the mark of being chores rather than pleasures. But there are several of his books to which such a stricture does not apply, among them his wartime *Minute for Murder*, a post-war book set in a publishing firm and called *End of Chapter*, and *A Tangled Web*, a fictional modern reconstruction of an Edwardian murder case, which alone among Blake's books is written with intense personal feeling.

In the thirties Innes and Blake were acclaimed by their admirers as giving a new direction to the detective story, and criticised by some detractors as too highbrow. To-day both praise and detraction seem exaggerated. In their writing there is no real break with the detective story's traditional features. Both employed a detective who appeared in a series of books, and who showed much of the omniscience carried down from the days of Sherlock Holmes. Both regarded the detective story as 'entertainment' literature, in which it was not advisable to dig deeply into character or motive. Both, Innes more than Blake, ignored the events of their day and set their stories in a setting that in a political and social sense was timeless. The innovations that they made were minor, the rejection of the railway time table and eventually of the drawing showing the scene of the crime, and the abandonment of that most limited of all detective story conventions by which the body is found in the library at a house party where every guest has a reason for wishing the victim dead.

Much the same could be said of two other talented writers who came to literary maturity in the years before the war, Margery Allingham and Ngaio Marsh. Both used a detective, in Miss Allingham's case the aristocratic amateur Albert Campion, in Miss Marsh's the gentlemanly, unobtrusive professional Detective-Inspector (later Superintendent) Roderick Alleyn; both wrote with an ease and elegance unknown to the stricter purists of the fair play school; both were prepared to investigate the psychology of their characters, and also to provide a background which was seen with a most agreeably satirical eye. Miss Allingham's progress has been particularly interesting. She began with some light-hearted and rather sentimental books in which Campion seems at times almost a figure of caricature:

> The Inspector had a vision of a lank immaculate form surmounted by a pale face half obliterated by enormous horn-rimmed spectacles. The final note of incongruity was struck by an old-fashioned deerstalker cap set jauntily upon the top of the young man's head.

That is Campion in 1931, in *Police at the Funeral*. Here he is fourteen years later, in *Coroner's Pidgin*, after some arduous war service:

> He had changed a little in the past three years; the sun had bleached his fair hair to whiteness lending him a physical distinction he had never before possessed. There were new lines in his over-thin face and with their appearance some of his old misleading vacancy of expression had vanished. But nothing had altered the upward drift of his thin mouth nor the engaging astonishment which so often and so falsely appeared in his pale eyes.

Campion has not merely aged and matured; he is regarded with deeper seriousness by his creator, and so is the world in which he moves. As the years went by Miss Allingham felt herself less and less confined by the bonds of the fair play detective story, and began to write books which in effect were novels with a detective element in them. Miss Marsh never went so far, but there was noticeable in her books also a greater interest in the settings than in the puzzles to be solved. The first third of *Overture to Death* gives a fascinating picture of the squabbles in a village about what play shall be done to raise money for the Young People's Friendly Circle, how it shall be cast and, most significant of all, who shall perform the overture. The first half of *Opening Night* gives in a rather similar way a picture of the intrigues taking place before the opening of a new play. In both of these books we are fascinated by the relationships between the characters, and want to see them developed fully. The murder, with its following investigation and interrogation of suspects, puts a halt to this process and causes a distinct lowering of our emotional temperature.

The experiments of these four writers, and some others of less importance, had little obvious effect on the apparent supremacy of the detective novel produced according to the fair play rules. It was not until a new generation of crime writers appeared, after the second World War, that the decline of the detective story as a literary form became obvious.

(VII) TOWARDS THE CRIME NOVEL

At the heart of the classical detective story, as Ronald Knox said, was the Great Detective, who appeared in story after story and created a bond of familiarity between writer and reader:

It is personality that counts (Ronald Knox wrote). You are not
bound to make your public *like* the Great Detective; many readers
have found Lord Peter Wimsey too much of a good thing, and I
have even heard of people who were unable to appreciate the
flavours of Poirot. But he must be real; he must have idiosyncrasies,
eccentricities; even if he is a professional policeman, like Hanaud,
he must smoke those appalling cigarettes, and get his English
idioms wrong.

There could be no clearer indication of the move away
from the detective story since the war than the fact that
only one of the crime writers who have come into prominence during the past fifteen years has made any attempt
to create a Great Detective. This is Mr. Edmund Crispin, a
talented writer who would probably acknowledge Michael
Innes as his exemplar. Crispin's highly individual sense of
light comedy and his flair for verbal deception make all of
his books extremely enjoyable. The best of them, *The
Moving Toyshop*, is a most successfully mystifying frolic.
But Crispin and his Professor Fen were swimming against
the stream, and he has been silent now for several years.
Many of the practitioners firmly established before the war
have changed their approach to the detective story. Agatha
Christie has trimmed Poirot's eccentricities and has abandoned altogether his faithful Watson, Captain Hastings,
because she thought that Hastings seemed too ridiculous.
Margery Allingham has retained Albert Campion, but his
activities seem an unnecessary intrusion in *The Tiger in the
Smoke* and *Hide My Eyes*, two of her most recent books.
Nigel Strangeways, Sir John Appleby and Superintendent
Roderick Alleyn are still active, but they are much muted
nowadays, for it is the object of their creators to soften
rather than to emphasise those idiosyncrasies that Ronald
Knox thought so important. And it is not seriously disputed
that the work of these practitioners nowadays is much
below their best writing. Mr. Howard Haycraft, when
asked to name books published within the last ten years
which might come within the canon of the best hundred

detective stories, mentioned only *The Daughter of Time*, a brilliantly freakish performance by Josephine Tey (a pseudonym of the dramatist Gordon Daviot) in which a police inspector 'solves' from his hospital bed the mystery of Richard III and the Princes in the Tower. The Detection Club, once so austerely concerned about candidates' credentials under the fair play rules, now requires from them only a high degree of professional skill.

There were two main reasons for the changed attitude of new crime writers. The first was a general feeling, earlier voiced by Dorothy Sayers, that it had become extremely difficult to devise new methods of murder and new ways of deceiving the reader. The tricks of Sherlock Holmes, protected as they are by the patina of age, still have power to fascinate us: but how ludicrous we should find it if any modern detective adopted the device used by Holmes in his attempt in *A Scandal in Bohemia* to discover Irene Adler's secret, of pretending injury in a street fight so that he may obtain entry into her house, and then having a plumber's smoke rocket thrown into the sitting room, so that she will rush to the safe that holds her secret. Proof that puzzles and deceptions have become harder to devise is not lacking in the work of such exponents of apparent impossibilities as John Dickson Carr, and in the most recent work of Agatha Christie.

(VIII) CONCLUSION

An even more potent cause of change was the fact that the post-war crime writers looked at the world in a different way from their predecessors. Behind the detective stories written before the war there was a belief that human affairs could be ruled by reason and that virtue, generally identified with the established order of society, must prevail in the end. The post war crime writers did not identify themselves with such a point of view. They saw, instead, a world in which German force had been defeated only by the greater force employed by the Allies, and in which concentration camps and the atomic bomb mocked a liberal dream of reason. The new writers had no wish to create locked room puzzles. They have turned instead to stories which, while often retaining a puzzle element, are primarily concerned with crime in relation to character and motive. We have seen what Dorothy Sayers thought about the difficulty of letting 'real human beings' enter a detective story. The compromise she effected was very much on the side of the detective story—that is to say, her human beings were not very real: but recent writers have had no hesitation in admitting 'real human beings' into their books, and working out stories of which the central interest was the investigation of human motives. They have been prepared to discuss sex with reasonable freedom (the writers of the Golden Age showed an astonishing prudishness about this most potent motive for crime), and have even been prepared to question the way in which the police treat those under suspicion. It was a tradition of the British detective story that the police might be stupid, but could never be seriously corrupt or brutal. The abandonment of this shibboleth, in such books as John Bingham's *My Name is Michael Sibley* or in my own *The Progress of a Crime* showed that the defences were really down.

The new crime novel has retained many elements of the detective story, but its interests are much more like those of a novel. It looks back to Francis Iles, much more than to Conan Doyle or Dorothy Sayers. Its practitioners vary in style, feeling and treatment. They include Margot Bennett, who writes at her best with a wit and elegance lacking in a great many 'serious' novelists, Edward Grierson whose best work stems fairly directly from Francis Iles, Shelley Smith, Patrick Hamilton and John Bingham, as well as several Americans among whom the remarkably talented Patricia Highsmith should be particularly mentioned. There has been a loss, certainly, in the collapse of the detective story, and many readers will regret the passing of the Great Detective: but the loss is more than counterbalanced by what has been gained in characterisation, in psychological analysis, and in a more nearly realistic approach to crime and punishment. It may be too soon to announce the death of the detective story: but not, surely, to say *Long live the crime novel*.

THE DETECTIVE STORY IN BRITAIN

A Select Bibliography

(Place of publication London, unless stated otherwise)

NOTE: Many detective story writers have published dozens of books, and a complete list of their works would have occupied a disproportionate amount of space. Consequently, in the case of writers who have published a considerable number of books, or of writers whose work today seems of mainly historical interest, only the most important of their works have been listed, the rest being subsumed under 'And Others'. Otherwise, it is understood that a writer's contributions to detective fiction have been listed in full. One or two items which are not strictly detective stories have been included. The most important of them is Wilkie Collins's *The Woman in White*. This is a thriller; but it would be absurd to exclude what is, by general agreement, one of Collins's most important books.

An asterisk indicates a volume of short stories

Check-List of Authors and Titles:

ALLINGHAM, Margery

The White Cottage Mystery (1928).
The Crime at Black Dudley (1929).
Mystery Mile (1930).
Police at the Funeral (1931).
Look to the Lady (1931).
Sweet Danger (1933).
Death of a Ghost (1934).
Flowers for the Judge (1936).
The Case of the Late Pig (1937).
Dancers in Mourning (1937).
The Fashion in Shrouds (1938).
*Mr. Campion and Others (1939).
Black Plumes (1940).
Traitors' Purse (1941).
Coroner's Pidgin (1945).
More Work for the Undertaker (1948).
The Tiger in the Smoke (1952).
The Beckoning Lady (1955).
Hide my Eyes (1958).

BENNETT, Margot

Time to Change Hats (1945).
Away Went the Little Fish (1946).
The Widow of Bath (1952).
Farewell Crown and Goodbye King (1953).
The Man who Didn't Fly (1955).
Someone from the Past (1958).

BENTLEY, E. C.

Trent's Last Case (1913)
—with H. Warner Allen.
Trent's Own Case (1936).
*Trent Intervenes (1938).

BERKELEY, Anthony (pseudonym of A. B. Cox).

The Layton Court Mystery (1925)
—published anonymously.
Mr. Priestley's Problem (1927)
—as by A. B. Cox, later republished under the name of Anthony Berkeley.
Roger Sheringham and the Vane Mystery (1927).
The Silk Stocking Murders (1928).
The Piccadilly Murder (1929).
The Poisoned Chocolates Case (1929).
The Second Shot (1930).
Top Storey Murder (1931).
Murder in the Basement (1932).
Jumping Jenny (1933).
Panic Party (1934).
Trial and Error (1937).
Not to be Taken (1938).
Death in the House (1939).
                    See also ILES, Francis below.

BINGHAM, John (Lord Clanmorris).

My Name is Michael Sibley (1952).
Five Roundabouts to Heaven (1953).
The Third Skin (1954).
The Paton Street Case (1955).
Marion (1958).
Murder Plan Six (1958).
Night's Black Agent (1961).

BLAKE, Nicholas (pseudonym of C. Day Lewis).

A Question of Proof (1935).
Thou Shell of Death (1936).
There's Trouble Brewing (1937).
The Beast Must Die (1938).
The Smiler with the Knife (1939).
Malice in Wonderland (1940).
The Case of the Abominable Snowman (1941).
Minute for Murder (1947).
Head of a Traveller (1949).
The Dreadful Hollow (1953).
TheWhisper in the Gloom (1954).
A Tangled Web (1956).
End of Chapter (1957).
A Penknife in my Heart (1958).
The Widow's Cruise (1959).

BRAMAH, Ernest

*Max Carrados (1914).
*The Eyes of Max Carrados (1923).
*Max Carrados Mysteries (1927).

CARR, John Dickson

It Walks by Night (1930).
Poison in Jest (1932).
The Hollow Man (1935).
The Arabian Nights Murder (1936).
The Four False Weapons (1937).
The Burning Court (1937).
The Crooked Hinge (1938).
The Black Spectacles (1939).
The Problem of the Wire Cage (1940).
The Emperor's Snuff Box (1943).
He Who Whispers (1946).
*The Exploits of Sherlock Holmes (1954)
—with Adrian Conan Doyle.
And Others

See also DICKSON, Carter below.

CHESTERTON, G. K.

*The Innocence of Father Brown (1911).
*The Wisdom of Father Brown (1914).
*The Man who Knew too Much (1922).
*The Incredulity of Father Brown (1926).
*The Secret of Father Brown (1927).
*The Poet and the Lunatics (1929).
*The Scandal of Father Brown (1935).

A selection of Father Brown stories, with an introduction by
Ronald Knox, is available in the World's Classics series, 1955.

CHRISTIE, Agatha

The Mysterious Affair at Styles (1920).
The Secret Adversary (1922).
The Murder on the Links (1923).
The Man in the Brown Suit (1924).
The Secret of Chimneys (1925).
The Murder of Roger Ackroyd (1926).
Peril at End House (1932).
Lord Edgware Dies (1933).
Why Didn't They Ask Evans (1934).
Murder on the Orient Express (1934).
Three Act Tragedy (1935).
Murder in Mesopotamia (1936).
Cards on the Table (1936).
The A.B.C. Murders (1936).
Appointment with Death (1938).
Ten Little Niggers (1939).
N. or M? (1941).
Five Little Pigs (1942).
The Moving Finger (1943).
Towards Zero (1944).
Death Comes as the End (1945).
Sparkling Cyanide (1945).
They do it with Mirrors (1952).
After the Funeral (1953).
4.50 from Paddington (1957).
And Others

COLLINS, Wilkie

*After Dark (1856).
The Dead Secret (1857).
The Woman in White (1860).
Hide and Seek (1861).
No Name (1863).
Armadale (1866).
The Moonstone (1868).
And Others
The Moonstone is available in the World's Classics series, with an important introduction by T. S. Eliot; and in Everyman's Library, with an introduction by Dorothy Sayers.

CRISPIN, Edmund (pseudonym of Robert Bruce Montgomery)

The Case of the Gilded Fly (1944).
Holy Disorders (1945).
The Moving Toyshop (1946).
Swan Song (1947).
Love Lies Bleeding (1948).
Buried for Pleasure (1948).
Frequent Hearses (1950).
The Long Divorce (1951).
*Beware of the Trains (1953).

CROFTS, Freeman Wills

The Cask (1920).
The Pit-Prop Syndicate (1922).
The Groote Park Murder (1924).
Inspector French's Greatest Case (1925).
The 12.30 from Croydon (1934).
Death of a Train (1946).
And Others

DICKENS, Charles

Bleak House (1853).
The Mystery of Edwin Drood (1870).
An edition of *Edwin Drood*, with an interesting introduction by Michael Innes, was published in 1950.

DICKSON, Carter (pseudonym of John Dickson Carr).

The Bowstring Murders (1934).
The Plague Court Murders (1935).
The Ten Teacups (1937).
The Judas Window (1938).
Death in Five Boxes (1938).
The Reader is Warned (1939).
*The Department of Queer Complaints (1940).
Seeing is Believing (1942).
He Wouldn't Kill Patience (1944).
My Late Wives (1947).
And Others

See also CARR, John Dickson above.

CONAN DOYLE, Arthur

A Study in Scarlet (1888)
—first published in *Beeton's Christmas Annual*, 1887.
The Sign of Four (1890).
*The Adventures of Sherlock Holmes (1894).
The Hound of the Baskervilles (1902).
*The Return of Sherlock Holmes (1905).
The Valley of Fear (1915).
*His Last Bow (1917).
*The Case-Book of Sherlock Holmes (1927).

FREEMAN, R. Austin

*John Thorndyke's Cases (1909).
*The Singing Bone (1912).
*Dr. Thorndyke's Case-Book (1923).
The Mystery of Angelina Frood (1924).
The D'Arblay Mystery (1926).
Mr. Pottermack's Oversight (1930).

GRIERSON, Edward

Reputation for a Song (1952).
The Second Man (1956).

HAMILTON, Patrick

Hangover Square (1941).

ILES, Francis (pseudonym of A. B. Cox).

Malice Aforethought (1931).
Before the Fact (1932).
As for the Woman (1939).

See also BERKELEY, Anthony above.

INNES, Michael (pseudonym of J. I. M. Stewart).

Death at the President's Lodging (1936).
Hamlet, Revenge! (1937).
Lament for a Maker (1938).
Stop Press (1939).
There Came Both Mist and Snow (1940).
Appleby of Ararat (1941).
The Weight of the Evidence (1944).
Appleby's End (1945).
From London Far (1946).
A Private View (1952).
The Long Farewell (1958).
The New Sonia Wayward (1960).
And Others

KNOX, Ronald

The Viaduct Murder (1925).
The Three Taps (1927).
The Footsteps at the Lock (1928).
And Others

LE FANU, J. Sheridan

The House by the Churchyard (1863).
Wylder's Hand (1864).
The Wyvern Mystery (1869).
Checkmate (1871).
*In a Glass Darkly (1872).

MARSH, Ngaio

Death in a White Tie (1938).
Artists in Crime (1938).
Overture to Death (1939).
Death at the Bar (1940).
Death and the Dancing Footman (1942).
Colour Scheme (1943).
Died in the Wool (1945).
Final Curtain (1947).
Opening Night (1951).
Scales of Justice (1955).
Singing in the Shrouds (1959).
And Others

MASON, A. E. W.

At the Villa Rose (1910).
The House of the Arrow (1924).
The Prisoner in the Opal (1928).
They Wouldn't be Chessmen (1935).

MORRISON, Arthur

*Martin Hewitt, Investigator (1894).
*Chronicles of Martin Hewitt (1895).
*Adventures of Martin Hewitt (1896).
*The Red Triangle (1903).

ORCZY, Baroness

*The Old Man in the Corner (1909).
*Lady Molly of Scotland Yard (1910).
*Unravelled Knots (1925).
*Skin o' my Tooth (1928).

POE, Edgar Allan

Tales (1845).
Tales of Mystery, Imagination and Horror (1852).
Tales of Mystery and Imagination is published in Everyman's Library,
with an introduction by Padraic Colum. Several tales are included
also in *The Tell-Tale Heart and Other Stories*, a selection published
in 1948, with an introduction by William Sansom.

SAYERS, Dorothy

Whose Body? (1923).
Clouds of Witness (1926).
Unnatural Death (1927).
Lord Peter Views the Body (1928).
The Unpleasantness at the Bellona Club (1928).
Strong Poison (1930).
The Documents in the Case (1930)
—with Robert Eustace.
The Five Red Herrings (1931).
Have his Carcase (1932).
*Hangman's Holiday (1933).
Murder must Advertise (1933).
The Nine Tailors (1934).
Gaudy Night (1935).
Busman's Honeymoon (1937).
*In the Teeth of the Evidence (1939).

SMITH, Shelley (pseudonym of Nancy Hermione Bodington).

Come and be Killed (1946).
He Died of Murder (1947).
The Woman in the Sea (1948).
Man Alone (1952).
An Afternoon to Kill (1953).
The Lord have Mercy (1956).
And Others

TEY, Josephine (pseudonym of Elizabeth Mackintosh).

The Man in the Queue (1929)
—published under the pseudonym of Gordon Daviot, later re-published under the pseudonym Josephine Tey.
The Franchise Affair (1948).
Brat Farrar (1949).
The Daughter of Time (1951).
The Singing Sands (1952).

Some Critical and Bibliographical Studies:

The following list includes only works bearing upon detective stories in general; it does not cover particular studies (e.g. of Sherlock Holmes and Dr. Watson), or biographics (e.g. of Edgar Allan Poe, Wilkie Collins, Conan Doyle, etc.).

CARTER, John

'Detective Fiction' (1934)
—in *New Paths in Book-Collecting*. Separately issued as *Collecting Detective Fiction*, 1938. This is a short study of primarily bibliographical interest, now inevitably out of date in certain respects, but still of considerable value.

CHESTERTON, G. K.

'A Defence of Detective Stories' (1902)
—in *The Defendant*.
'On Detective Novels' (1928)
—in *Generally Speaking*.
'On Detective Story Writers' (1931)
—in *Come to Think of It*.
These are the best of Chesterton's short essays dealing with detective stories.

GILBERT, Michael (editor)

Crime in Good Company (1959)
—a collection of essays by several members of the Crime Writers' Association.

HAYCRAFT, Howard

Murder for Pleasure (1942)
—with an introduction by Nicholas Blake. This, although it shows perhaps a slight bias towards American writers, is much the best and most comprehensive survey of detective fiction up to the year of its publication.
Notes on Additions to a Cornerstone Library (1951)
—Mr. Haycraft's choice of the best detective stories up to the year 1948. Originally published in *Ellery Queen's Mystery Magazine*, it was later separately issued as *A Decennial Detective Digest*.

KNOX, Ronald

Introduction to *The Best Detective Stories of 1928* (1929)
—contains his 'Detective Decalogue'.

MAUGHAM, W. Somerset

'The Decline and Fall of the Detective Story' (1952)
—in *The Vagrant Mood*.

MORLAND, Nigel

How to write Detective Novels (1936).

MURCH, A. E.

The Development of the Detective Novel (1958)
—very good on developments up to around 1914, sketchy in dealing
with later work.

QUEEN, Ellery

Queen's Quorum (1953)
—a choice of the 101 best books of detective stories, with very interesting notes and commentaries.

SAYERS, Dorothy (editor)

Introductions to *Great Short Stories of Detection, Mystery and Horror*,
First series (1928); Second series (1931); Third series (1934).
Introduction to *Tales of Detection* (1936)
—in Everyman's Library.
Read together, these Introductions form an admirably balanced
short history of the detective story up to the dates they were
written.

SUTHERLAND, Scott

Blood in Their Ink (1953)

SYMONS, Julian (editor)

The 100 Best Crime Stories (1959).
—a survey first published in the *Sunday Times*.

THOMSON, H. Douglas

Masters of Mystery (1931)
—a survey of historical interest, but of very limited value today.

TIMES LITERARY SUPPLEMENT

Important supplements have been published on 'Detective Fiction' (25 February 1955) and 'Crime, Detection and Society' (23 June 1961).

VAN DINE, S. S.

The Philo Vance Omnibus (1936)
—contains his 'Twenty Rules for Writing Detective Stories'.

WRONG, E. M. (editor)

Introduction to *Crime and Detection* (1926)
—in the World's Classics series.

Shakespeare:
The Chronicles

by CLIFFORD LEECH

Published for The British Council
and The National Book League
by Longmans, Green & Co.

Two shillings and sixpence

In this essay Professor Leech, head of the Department of English at Durham University, discusses "Shakespeare's 'open-textured' historical writing, the kind of drama in which there is not a persistent consciousness of an ineluctable march of events". The plays concerned are: Henry VI, Henry IV, Henry VIII and The Merry Wives of Windsor.

As is the case with certain companion essays in the Shakespeare series, the illustrations have been chosen with particular reference to the best recent productions. The bibliographies follow a uniform plan. They assume that Mr. J. R. Brown's bibliography in *Writers and Their Work* No. 58 is available to the reader, and in the main they confine themselves to the plays under immediate consideration. Essays and papers are not ordinarily included in the bibliographies of the Series but, as it is not possible to keep up with Shakespeare studies unless they are added, they here duly appear.

Forthcoming:

ROMAN PLAYS: T. J. B. Spencer   HISTORIES: L. C. Knights
FINAL PLAYS: Frank Kermode   THE POEMS: J. W. Lever

Already Published:

SHAKESPEARE by C. J. Sisson: bibliography by J. R. Brown: a Student's Guide to the texts and the literature.

THE EARLY COMEDIES by Derek Traversi.

THE GREAT TRAGEDIES by Kenneth Muir.

THE PROBLEM PLAYS by Peter Ure.

THE LATE COMEDIES by G. K. Hunter.

Bibliographical Series

of Supplements to 'British Book News'
on Writers and Their Work

GENERAL EDITOR
Bonamy Dobrée

'The England of *HENRY VI*.'

WILLIAM SHAKESPEARE

The Chronicles

Henry VI. Henry IV. The Merry Wives of Windsor.
Henry VIII.

by

CLIFFORD LEECH

Published for the British Council and
The National Book league by
LONGMANS, GREEN & CO.

LONGMANS, GREEN & CO. LTD.
48 Grosvenor Street, London, W.1
Railway Crescent, Croydon, Victoria, Australia
Auckland, Kingston (Jamaica), Lahore, Nairobi

LONGMANS SOUTHERN AFRICA (PTY) LTD.
Thibault House, Thibault Square, Cape Town
Johannesburg, Salisbury

LONGMANS OF NIGERIA LTD.
W.R. Industrial Estate, Ikeja

LONGMANS OF GHANA LTD.
Industrial Estate, Ring Road South, Accra

LONGMANS, GREEN (FAR EAST) LTD.
443 Lockhart Road, Hong Kong

LONGMANS OF MALAYA LTD.
44 Jalan Ampang, Kuala Lumpur

ORIENT LONGMANS LTD.
Calcutta, Bombay, Madras
Delhi, Hyderabad, Dacca

LONGMANS CANADA LTD.
137 Bond Street, Toronto 2

Printed in Great Britain by
F. Mildner & Sons, London, E.C.1

CONTENTS

I. HISTORY FOR THE ELIZABETHANS   *page* 7

II. THE THREE PARTS OF *HENRY VI*   12

II. THE TWO PARTS OF *HENRY IV*   22

V. *THE MERRY WIVES OF WINDSOR*   31

V. *HENRY VIII*   33

    A Select Bibliography   41

ILLUSTRATIONS

The frontispiece map of the England of HENRY VI, is reproduced from the New Arden edition of 2 HENRY VI by kind permission of Messrs. Methuen & Co.

I. The title-page of the Quarto of 2 HENRY IV (1600)
     By courtesy of the British Museum

II. The Old Vic production of 2 HENRY IV, staged 1945-6, showing Ralph Richardson as Falstaff and Laurence Olivier as Shallow. (*Photograph: John Vickers*)

II. The death of Clifford in 3 HENRY VI, as produced by the Birmingham Repertory Theatre, 1952-3. (*Photograph: Lisel Haas*)

V. William Blake: 'Queen Katharine's Dream' from the Fitzwilliam Museum, Cambridge

(between pages 24 and 25)

¶ WILLIAM SHAKESPEARE was born at Stratford-on-Avon and w
christened in the Parish Church on 26 April 1564. There, too,
died, on 23 April 1616, and was buried in the chancel, where
monument was erected before 1623.

SHAKESPEARE'S CHRONICLES

I

HISTORY FOR THE ELIZABETHANS

Most of us to-day know that history does not repeat itself, that few things are more dangerous than responding to present circumstances as if they duplicated those that a previous generation had to cope with. Of course, some of our public men and some of our military strategists do exactly that, but the colder manner of contemplation, difficult to maintain in a position of power, makes us recognise a dynamic principle in men and society. Such a principle is incompatible with the notion of repetition. In the sixteenth century, however, men commonly saw the world as essentially static. Each man's life throughout history showed a conflict between an unchanging good and evil, and the threats to a society's health were similarly unchanging. In *The Thre Bokes of Chronicles* (1550) translated by Walter Lynne from the German of Johann Carion, it is argued that rulers must study history in order to see how disasters of the past may be avoided in the future, and this is buttressed by an assertion of constancy in the world's pattern. From a knowledge of past attacks on government, Lynne's readers are told, rulers:

> maye learne to beware in theyr governaunce, lest any such lyke do befall: For such cases do dayly befall. Yea though the persons do sometyme chaunge in commune welthes, neverthelesse so much as is concernynge the qualytye of mattiers, the worlde is and alwayes abydeth lyke to hym selfe.

This view of the value of history underlies the historiography that Shakespeare knew, and for this reason it is common to find him giving utterance to a generalisation concerning a recurrent political condition. Thus in Part I of

Henry VI on the danger that threatens when the King is a
child and dissensions grow among the nobles:

> 'Tis much when sceptres are in children's hands;
> But more when envy breeds unkind division:
> There comes the ruin, there begins confusion.   (IV.i.192–4)

And his eight histories covering the sequence of events from
the time of Richard II to the accession of Henry VII show
certain events virtually repeated: Bolingbroke and the
Percies rebel against Richard II; the Percies rebel against
Henry IV, formerly Bolingbroke; Northumberland deserts
the rebels in Part I of *Henry IV*, and again in Part II; Edward
of York, on returning from exile in Part III of *Henry VI*
declares that he has returned only for his father's dukedom,
not for the crown, exactly as Bolingbroke did in *Richard II*
and in *Henry VIII* we shall see that the substance of the play
is a series of falls from high estate, with an implication that
such a fall is part of a regular pattern of things. Of course
both Shakespeare's sources and his own observation told
him that there was always an element of variation within
any repetition, but the repetitive character of the action is
emphasised and embodies the political lesson.

So simply didactic is historiography outside the drama in
the sixteenth century, so obviously does Shakespeare depend
on the sixteenth-century chroniclers in his history plays
that the assumption is often made that these plays are merely
a dramatic exposition of the chroniclers' ideas, that, however much the didacticism may be enlivened by the judicious
employment of stirring incident and characterisation and
comic admixture, the writer's dominating purpose is to
urge a political lesson on the dangers of civil dissension and
the glories of national well-being. But such an assumption
is hardly compatible with a recognition of Shakespeare's
status as a poet. Whatever a major poet's intellectual

---

* Quotations from Shakespeare are from *The Tudor Shakespeare*, edited
by Peter Alexander. Line-references are to the Globe edition.

starting-point may be—and, of course, in any age he may as a member of society adhere to a particular religion or political party—he will be characterised ultimately by his power to enter into an experience that he has directly known or deeply imagined, and by his ability to relate that experience to the sum total of the human story. In the *Henry VI* plays one of the characters that does most harm is Queen Margaret, the French princess who married Henry VI and became notorious for the major part she played in the disturbance of England's peace and the savagery with which she treated her adversaries. Yet, though Shakespeare shows all this, what we remember most sharply in his presentation of her is the scene in 3 *Henry VI* when she is finally defeated and her son Prince Edward, a prisoner of war, is stabbed to death by his captors. At this point she becomes a representative of suffering humanity, she is at one with that king-husband of hers whom she had despised for his gentleness and compassion and sense of powerlessness. What, in fact, impresses us most in Shakespeare's history plays, and what makes them much more than merely approximately accurate records of past events, is the presentation within them of struggling and suffering humanity. Of course, they also have an interest as enshrining much of the sixteenth-century attitude to history and its lessons, but that would not in itself give them high status as literature.

But, if Shakespeare's plays transcend, not merely in literary skill but in poetic insight, the chronicles that he used in his quest for material, it is still important to see his work in relation to those sources. Englishmen of the sixteenth century were profoundly interested in the history of their own nation, and this interest was ministered to by a whole series of writings and compilations. The most important of these were Edward Hall's *The Union of the two Noble and Illustre Famelies of Lancastre and Yorke* (1548), which more directly than any other piece of sixteenth-century historiography devoted itself to demonstrating how the establishment of the Tudor monarchy in 1485 had

rescued England from the long period of disturbance ensuing on the deposition of Richard II in 1399, and Raphael
Holinshed's *Chronicles of England, Scotlande and Irelande*
(1577; second edition, used by Shakespeare, 1587), which
was a compilation incorporating much of the earlier history-
writing of the century. Underlying all such historiography
is not only the growing thirst for information of all kinds
that characterised the men of the Renascence but the desire
to understand the present through a knowledge of the past.

History became material for narrative poetry as well. *A
Mirror for Magistrates* (1559; seventh edition, 1587) demonstrated through its title the informing notion that rulers
could learn from the mistakes of their predecessors. William
Warner's *Albion's England* (1586-89), Samuel Daniel's *Civil
Wars* (1595-1609), and Michael Drayton's *The Barons' Wars*
(1603) show how, at the apex of English literary achievement, the poets went to history for their material. It cannot
surprise us that in the last decade of the sixteenth century
many dramatists looked in the same direction. New plays
in quantity were needed for the recently built theatres and
their growing audiences. In English history as presented by
the prose chroniclers and the contributors to *A Mirror for
Magistrates* there was material both immediately available
and sure to command the interest of Elizabethans. In addition to Shakespeare, Marlowe and Peele and Heywood
were among the writers who contributed to the history
plays during the years immediately preceding 1600. After
that date the play on an English historical theme became
much rarer, although Shakespeare contributed *Henry VII.*
in 1613 and Ford's *Perkin Warbeck* came about twenty years
later than that. It appears that the popular concern with the
country's recent past was at its height in the second half of
the sixteenth century, and that the drama (as often, a
consolidating rather than a pioneering force) ministered to
that concern in its final phase.

In the First Folio of 1623, the title-page indicates a three-
fold division of Shakespeare's plays into comedies, historie

and tragedies, and the plays are arranged in these three sections. By 'histories' were meant the plays on English historical themes of comparatively recent date—not plays on Roman history or on stories taken from the chronicles of Britain but set in very early times (e.g. *Macbeth*, *Lear*, *Cymbeline*). The history-section of the Folio therefore comprised ten plays, arranged in chronological order of subject-matter, beginning with *King John* and ending with *Henry VIII*. In the present series of essays on Shakespeare, it has been decided to make a somewhat arbitrary division beween 'chronicles' and 'histories': 'chronicles' is the term used for the plays on the reigns of Henry VI, Henry IV and Henry VIII; 'histories' is used for *King John*, *Richard III*, *Richard II*, *Henry V*. The division is not chronological, either in composition or in subject-matter: *Henry VI* was the earliest of Shakespeare's histories, *Henry VIII* the last; the historical sequence runs from *King John* to *Henry VIII*. Nevertheless, the plays we shall be concerned with in the present essay have certain features in common which distinguish them from those that will be dealt with separately as 'histories'. *Henry VI* is in three Parts, *Henry IV* in two Parts: both of them have therefore an amplitude which makes possible the incorporation of a greater range of incident, and facilitates a longer time-sequence, than we find in the other plays. *Henry VIII* is a single drama, but we shall see that its construction is such as to bring it in some measure closer to *Henry VI* and *Henry IV* than to the other historical plays: it has not the integrated action of *Richard III* or *Richard II*, for example, but surveys in turn the fate of a variety of the King's subjects, approaching the manner of an historical pageant rather than a sequence of events governed by a cause-effect relation.

We can thus say that this essay is concerned with Shakespeare's 'open-textured' historical writing, the kind of drama in which there is not a persistent consciousness of an ineluctable march of events. It is writing which incorporates some incidents almost haphazardly, like the bogus miracle

at St. Alban's in 2 *Henry VI* or the Gadshill robbery in
1 *Henry IV*; in *Henry IV*, moreover, this kind of writing
can make use of fictitious characters along with historical
ones, and these creatures of the imagination can take on a
life of their own, can be felt as having an existence outside
the historical frame. Shakespeare, in response to popular
and perhaps royal desire (for there is a legend that it was
the Queen who suggested the idea to the dramatist), could
even transport his Sir John Falstaff from the reign of Henry
IV to his own times and put him in a play set in Elizabethan
Windsor. The fact that the present essay will include a brief
comment on *The Merry Wives of Windsor* will underline
the 'open-textured' character of the historical writing in
this group of plays.

II

THE THREE PARTS OF *HENRY VI*

It is impossible to discuss the *Henry VI* plays without
referring first to the problems of authorship and chronology.
They were published together in the Folio of 1623, but
although this is the first occasion of the printing of Part I,
the other two Parts had appeared long before in corrupt
versions. In 1594 there was published a quarto volume with
the title *The First part of the Contention betwixt the two famous
Houses of Yorke and Lancaster*, and in 1595 an octavo with
the title *The true Tragedie of Richard Duke of Yorke*. These
two texts were published together as *The Whole Contention
betweene the two Famous Houses, Lancaster and Yorke* in 1619.
There is thus a strong bibliographical link between Parts
II and III. There is a link, too, in subject-matter. These two
Parts present a continuous narrative from the King's mar-
riage with the French princess Margaret to the murder of
Henry VI and the establishment on the throne of the
Yorkist Edward IV. Part I, on the other hand, is principally

concerned with the wars in France at the beginning of Henry VI's reign, although it also includes the beginning of the York-Lancaster opposition, the planning of Henry's marriage to Margaret, and a number of incidents that historically were later than some that occur in Part II.

There is a good case for assuming that Part I was a play acted by Strange's Men, for Henslowe's *Diary* records their performance of '*Harey the vj*' as a new play in March 1592, and in the same year Thomas Nashe in *Pierce Pennilesse* refers to the current acting of a play in which Talbot's military triumphs were displayed: as 1 *Henry VI* has Talbot's campaigns as one of its chief concerns, we can reasonably identify the play in the 1623 Folio with the play referred to by Henslowe and Nashe. Yet Part III must have been written by September 1592, for Robert Greene parodies a line from it in his death-bed tract *Greenes Groats-worth of Witte*. And Part III (doubtless with Part II, for the two can hardly be separated) was, according to the title-page of the 1595 edition, acted by Pembroke's Men.

There has been much discussion of the extent of Shakespeare's contribution to the three Parts. Edmund Malone believed that the publications of 1594 and 1595 were source-plays re-written by Shakespeare as 2 and 3 *Henry VI*, and that this had occasioned the attack on Shakespeare in *Greenes Groats-worth of Witte*, where he is described as 'an vpstart Crow, beautified with our feathers'. Now, however, Professor Alexander has won almost universal support for his view that *The First part of the Contention* and *The true Tragedie* are 'bad quartos', i.e. texts derivative from the plays now known as 2 and 3 *Henry VI* but contaminated through memorial transmission. There is still disagreement concerning the extent to which we can find Shakespeare's hand in the three Parts and concerning the order in which they were written. There will probably always be speculation on these matters, but the present weight of opinion is on the side of recognising a much larger Shakespearian element in the 'trilogy' than was formerly the case. Although no certainty is possible, it seems likely that Shakespeare wrote a two-part play on the Wars of the Roses for Pembroke's Men, and that the play recorded by Henslowe as *Harey the vj* was adapted by him when, in 1594, he joined the newly-formed Lord Chamberlain's Men along with some of the actors who had belonged to Strange's. In this way a trilogy was put together out of an original two-part Shakespearian play and a play (originally non-Shakespearian) that concentrated on the earliest events of Henry VI's reign. It may well be that Part I was written later than Parts II and III, but was made into a forepiece for the other two plays when Shakespeare revised it.

If this line of speculation is followed, we must regard Part I as only partially Shakespeare's and Parts II and III as mainly, if not wholly, his. And that will fit our response to the plays as dramatic achievements. Those who saw the Birmingham Repertory Theatre's performances of the three Parts in 1951-53 are likely to hold a more favourable view of their quality than was formerly common. Nevertheless, there can be no doubt that a higher level is reached in Parts II and III than in Part I.

In view of the theory of composition and authorship here suggested, we need not linger for more than a moment with Part I. It is a fairly shapeless piece of writing, beginning with some pomp and indeed impressiveness with the funeral of Henry V, where the Lancastrian nobles are quickly at odds, but soon falling into an anecdotal kind of drama in which incidents are presented in turn for the sake of immediate dramatic effect rather than for their contribution to a total pattern. An extreme example of this is the introduction of a French Countess who plans to murder Talbot by inviting him to her castle. Talbot shows his shrewdness by accepting the invitation but ensuring that his troops are in reach when the Countess shows her hand. The incident has no effect on later action: it is a mere anecdote of the war. Nevertheless, there is vigorous drama in the opposition between the Lord Protector, Humphrey of Gloucester, and the Bishop of Winchester, in the display of Talbot's prowess and his bravery in death, in the crude but lively portrayal of Joan of Arc, and in the first indications of Richard Plantagenet's rise to a position of importance in the kingdom. Concerning this last strand in the play, there is common consent that Shakespeare wrote the Temple Garden scene, where Plantagenet and the Earl of Somerset, having quarrelled in the Temple hall about a point of law (we are never told what it is), pluck respectively a white and a red rose and invite those who support them to do likewise. This scene, for which the sixteenth-century chronicles provide no source, most dramatically presages the state of open conflict between York and Lancaster.

The French wars of Henry VI's reign were hardly to be seen as a reason for national pride, but the author of 1 *Henry VI* did what he could to make them palatable. He put considerable stress on the achievements of Talbot, he presented Joan as a witch and a wanton, and he ended the play, quite unhistorically, with peace terms that declare the French King to be a viceroy under Henry VI, paying tribute to England: Professor Dover Wilson has pointed out that these terms are derived from those offered to, and rejected by, the French in 1435.

Parts II and III tell a continuous and wide-ranging story. For spectators it cannot be easy to grasp the exact relationships between the main characters and the genealogical details that made it possible for Richard Plantagenet, now Duke of York, to lay claim to the throne. For that reason, in Act II scene ii of Part II, the author inserted a scene in which York, addressing the Earl of Salisbury and his son the Earl of Warwick, gives a full account of the ancestry of both himself and Henry VI. The scene is not great drama, but it was necessary if the audience were to see the grounds for the dynastic quarrel. For modern readers a further aid is desirable, and Professor Dover Wilson has presented a most useful genealogical tree in his New Cambridge edition of 2 *Henry VI*. The action of the two plays is widely spread through England, with a short excursion into France in Part III, and the dramatist has clearly wanted to bring home to his audience the sense of a civil war ranging destructively over the country. For non-English readers, in particular, the many references to place-names may be confusing and will certainly not have the impact that was intended in the writing. Mr. Andrew S. Cairncross, in the New Arden edition of 2 *Henry VI*, has provided a map indicating the places scattered through the country that are prominently mentioned in the text, used as a frontispiece to this essay.

Part II differs from Part III in material and consequently in structure. Open war between York and Lancaster does not begin until Part II is almost over, and the greater part of the play is concerned with the gradual development of York's plans, with his waiting until Humphrey Duke of Gloucester is dead (helping modestly in his downfall), and with the enmities stirred up by Henry's Queen Margaret. Departing from his sources, for in fact Margaret did not come to England until after the Duchess of Gloucester's disgrace, the author has made dramatic capital out of a rivalry between the Queen and the wife of the Lord Protector. In addition, he gives the audience a thrill of horror in showing the Duchess of Gloucester using witchcraft in order to pry into the future, where she sees herself as England's Queen, and another thrill when Cardinal Beaufort dies in terror for his guilt in the killing of Gloucester. We have, too, a host of small incidents which, like the story of the Countess in Part I, can be regarded as dramatic anecdotes. There is the pretence of Simpcox that he has been miraculously cured of blindness—a 'miracle' quickly exposed by Humphrey of Gloucester. There is the grim comedy of Horner, an armourer, and his man Peter. The man accuses his master of speaking in favour of York's title to the crown. The issue is put to trial by combat between these two men who are quite unfitted to the test. Peter is terrified, but the armourer comes drunk to the contest and is killed. There is the execution of the Earl of Suffolk, who is captured by pirates when he has been banished from England: they refuse to accept ransom for him because of his opposition to Gloucester and to York and his consorting with Margaret. Yet, unlike the Countess story in Part I, these incidents all play their parts in the economy of the play. The exposure of the Simpcox 'miracle' exhibits the shrewdness and commonsense of Gloucester, so badly needed in the England of Henry VI. The affair of Horner and Peter displays the common people taking part in the nobles' quarrel about the royal title, as does the killing of Suffolk by men who are pirates but claim to be concerned for England's welfare. Moreover, the formal combat between the armourer and his man is a parody of chivalric encounter: in a way remarkably sophisticated for this early drama, it implies a critical attitude towards the warring nobles whose quarrels are grotesquely mirrored in this fight between two simple men, one terrified, one drunk.

This use of a mirror-image appears more fully in the scenes towards the end of Part II showing Jack Cade's rebellion. In Act III York is made regent of Ireland. This, he tells us in soliloquy, will give him his opportunity, for he will have an army at his disposal in Ireland. He is encouraging the 'headstrong Kentishman' Jack Cade to rebel, under the pretence that he is descended from the Mortimers from whom York himself derives his claim to the throne. From Cade's degree of success York will be able to see how the country is affected to the Yorkist claim. Whatever happens, York can come from Ireland with his army and reap the harvest that Cade's rebellion has prepared for him. The greater part of Act IV is taken up with Cade's rebellion. It is a revolt of common men against nobility, of ignorance against learning, of nonsense against sense: it presents a vision of anarchy in which a man can be put to death for being able to read, in which savagery is unchecked by any accepted code of manners, in which the rebels foolishly dream that by a mere proclamation they can refashion the country according to their hearts' desire. It is not a pleasant picture of a mob at work that Shakespeare gives us here, but we should note that some of Cade's followers can, in their asides, make fun of him, and that York's speech in Act III makes it clear that the Kentishman has been deluded by an ambitious noble. Moreover, the anarchy into which London is plunged when Cade is briefly lord of the city is an anticipation of the state of the whole country when the nobles' quarrel comes fully into the open and a whole series of battles is fought between York and Lancaster. The armourer Horner spoke treason on York's behalf and was killed for it. Cade sets himself up as a Mortimer, and having killed London citizens and a noble or two, is deserted by his followers and is himself killed as a fugitive. He provides the occasion for York to bring his army from Ireland, under the pretence that he has come to put down Cade (now defeated). The small revolt of ignorant men is a prelude and a mirror for the larger and much crueller contest between their superiors in the realm. With this in mind, we shall not see Shakespeare here as primarily concerned with the mob's folly and barbarity: rather, he recognises the nature of an armed mob, but sees in it an image of what civilised men can be when their weapons too are out.

This Second Part gains in strength as it proceeds. When battle has been joined in Act V, the Lancastrian Old Clifford is killed by York and the dead body is found by his son, Young Clifford. The character of this son is to be important in Part III, representing an extreme of Lancastrian ruthlessness. Here he addresses his father in words that usher in the grim slaughter of the Third Part:

> O, let the vile world end
> And the premised flames of the last day
> Knit earth and heaven together!
> Now let the general trumpet blow his blast,
> Particularities and petty sounds
> To cease! Wast thou ordain'd, dear father,

To lose thy youth in peace and to achieve
The silver livery of advised age,
And in thy reverence and thy chair-days thus
To die in ruffian battle? Even at this sight
My heart is turn'd to stone; and while 'tis mine
It shall be stony. York not our old men spares;
No more will I their babes. Tears virginal
Shall be to me even as the dew to fire;
And beauty, that the tyrant oft reclaims,
Shall to my flaming wrath be oil and flax.
Henceforth I will not have to do with pity.   (V.ii.40-56)

The balancing of the grand generalities of the Last Judgement in the first six lines with the intimate picture of Old
Clifford, murdered in 'ruffian battle' at a time poignantly
described as his 'chair-days', and then the severity of the
resolution that follows, reaching its climax in the terrible
bareness of the last line—these things belong to a mature
Shakespeare, and it has been thought that the passage was
inserted some considerable time after the first acting of the
play. That guess may be correct, yet the authority of the
speech is something we shall meet again in Part III.

This last Part has a concentrated power that can make it
highly impressive in the theatre. It is a play of battles, yet
with manifest skill the dramatist avoids a sense of repetition.
The first, at Wakefield, is a Lancastrian victory: first we
see Young Clifford's murder of the boy Rutland, the young
son of York, and then the formal mockery and elaborate
killing of York himself. Queen Margaret and Clifford will
not at once dispatch their great enemy. They make him
stand on a molehill, in mockery of the height he aspired to;
they put a paper crown upon his head; and Margaret
shows him a napkin stained with Rutland's blood. York is
allowed a long speech of reply, in which he rebukes
Margaret for her cruelty and weeps for Rutland. Then
Clifford and Margaret stab him in turn. This is followed by
a Lancastrian defeat at Towton. Here we see the battle
through the King's eyes. First, having been chidden from

the field by the Queen, he takes his stand on a molehill
(as York was forced to do after Wakefield) and shows his
envy of the simple countryman's life, patterned according
to the seasons, yielding peacefully to the years as they go,
solaced with plain comforts beyond a king's reach:

> O God! methinks it were a happy life
> To be no better than a homely swain;
> To sit upon a hill, as I do now,
> To carve out dials quaintly, point by point,
> Thereby to see the minutes how they run—
> How many makes the hour full complete,
> How many hours brings about the day,
> How many days will finish up the year,
> How many years a mortal man may live.
> When this is known, then to divide the times—
> So many hours must I tend my flock;
> So many hours must I take my rest;
> So many hours must I contemplate;
> So many hours must I sport myself;
> So many days my ewes have been with young;
> So many weeks ere the poor fools will ean;
> So many years ere I shall shear the fleece:
> So minutes, hours, days, months, and years,
> Pass'd over to the end they were created,
> Would bring white hairs unto a quiet grave.   (II.v.21-40)

But in a moment there enters a son that has killed his father
because they have been fighting on opposite sides in the
battle, and then a father that has killed his son. The three
characters do not speak to each other: they engage in a
shared ritual utterance which voices lamentation for the
war's destruction. This passage has the formal nature of
drama around 1590—profoundly animated, however, by a
sympathy with human loss. It shows, moreover, that
Henry's envy for the simple countryman has no basis in
fact: the war has brought chaos into every man's family.
Then our attention is turned to the fighting itself, with the

Yorkists triumphant. Clifford is mortally wounded. The three sons of York find him at the point of death: he dies as they begin to mock him, and their frustrated desire for verbal revenge, and for the blow that severs life, stands in antithesis to the achieved mockery and killing of York at Wakefield. And we see the war growing more savage. The sons of York hurling their taunts at a dead body reveal a special barbarity as well as grim comedy.

In the third and fourth acts of the play there is no open battle, but in turn the two sides win tactical advantages through each other's mistakes. The King is captured by the Yorkists; Edward, his father's successor as Duke of York, falls into political error in marrying Lady Grey, an obscure but attractive widow, instead of the French King's sister to whom he had sent the powerful Earl of Warwick as an ambassador of love; Margaret through this wins help from France and from the indignant Warwick; Edward is captured by the Lancastrians, but quickly escapes; he rallies the Yorkist armies, captures Henry again. Then in the last act the formal battles are resumed, and again there is skilful variation in the ways they are presented. At Barnet, Warwick is killed in a Yorkist victory, and his body is quietly borne off by his supporters. At Tewkesbury, Margaret and her son Prince Edward are captured: Edward of York with his brothers Clarence and Gloucester stab the boy to death when he displays courage. The incident, recalling the boy Rutland's death at Wakefield, is no mere repetition of that. Rutland's death was certain as the revengeful Clifford faced him: the boy begged for mercy. Prince Edward's death is unexpected, brutally casual: he has for his killers words of confident rebuke. The play ends with Gloucester's murder of Henry VI in the Tower and then with Edward of York, now Edward IV, rejoicing in his possession of the crown:

> Sound drums and trumpets. Farewell, sour annoy!
> For here, I hope, begins our lasting joy.   (V.vii.45-6)

But the audience knew that the reign of Richard of Gloucester, as Richard III, was not far away; and before long Shakespeare was to use that reign for one of the most assured plays of his earlier career. We have seen that 2 and 3 *Henry VI* are at their most interesting when irony is most evident. Here at the end the irony is prominent, dependent not merely on the audience's knowledge of the ensuing history but on the feebleness of 'I hope' in Edward's proclamation of felicity.

Shakespeare was to penetrate, in his later years, far deeper into human suffering, affection, aspiration, and far deeper also into the mystery of things. But the writer of 2 and 3 *Henry VI* was already a dramatist of major stature in England. Only Christopher Marlowe could compare with him.

III

THE TWO PARTS OF *HENRY IV*

In turning to *Henry IV*, we come near the mid-point of Shakespeare's career. The two Parts can be dated 1597-98. They were written close together, and there has been controversy over whether or not Shakespeare originally planned them to make up a single ten-act play. Dr. Tillyard and Professor Dover Wilson are convinced that he did, but Professor M. A. Shaaber, editor of the New Variorum edition of 2 *Henry IV*, is among those who see Part II as an unpremeditated addition to the original plan. We may remember, on the one hand, that 2 and 3 *Henry VI* were manifestly planned as a unit; on the other, that the Second Part of Marlowe's *Tamburlaine* is described in its Prologue as a play written because Part I had achieved popular favour. The key to the problem may well be Falstaff. Were it not for him, it is difficult to see how Shakespeare could have sustained the interest in his *Henry IV* material through ten acts, and even Shakespeare could not know, until he had written words for the character, the size of the Falstaff achievement. Professor Harold Jenkins has recently revived an old theory that Shakespeare developed the notion of a Second Part while he was writing Part I. That would explain, for example, why Falstaff travels in Part II from London to Yorkshire via Gloucestershire: originally the Gloucestershire scenes were to be incorporated in Part I, appropriately enough on the journey between London and Shrewsbury. This view of the matter has a strong ring of probability. Shakespeare was a dramatist whose work grew under his hand, and we have seen that in the histories here examined he was ready to follow a divergent interest as it arose. He had a sense of the whole, but he would keep that in reserve, would allow it to be modified by the developing structure.

However in detail they came into being, we have a Part I and a Part II which in many ways differ. In the first we have three centres of interest among the historical characters. There is the King, Henry IV, a usurper whose old allies— the Earl of Northumberland, his brother the Earl of Worcester, and his son Harry nicknamed Hotspur—are turning against him and making friends of the Scots, the Welsh, and Edmund Mortimer. Of these Mortimer is particularly dangerous, for in lineal descent he has a better claim to the throne than Henry. There is Hal, Prince of Wales, who spends his time with the drunken and dissolute Sir John Falstaff and lesser companions. And there is Hotspur, eloquent and fiery, avid for honour, at once the most admired young man in the kingdom and one who inspires devotion in wife and friend. Henry IV wishes that Hotspur were his own son: Northumberland could have Prince Hal. When the expected rebellion breaks out, Hotspur and his friends show themselves unfit for rule: they plan to divide England into three small kingdoms, and they plan even this haphazardly, as a matter for mere sociable bargaining. And they are unreliable friends to each other. Northumberland holds his forces back, unwilling to risk open battle with the King. The Welsh leader Glendower announces that he is not yet ready to join his allies. Hotspur, the Scot Douglas, and Worcester have to fight at Shrewsbury against the odds. And, while the rebels are thus critically shown, Prince Hal redeems expectation. He saves his father's life in the battle, and then fights and kills Hotspur. At the end of Part I, he is in his father's favour, the rebellion is more or less crushed, the Lancastrian throne is more firmly held than before.

Yet Part I is no simple story of Prince Hal's triumph. It is complicated partly through comedy, partly through irony. Falstaff is rightly Shakespeare's most famous comic character. As he claims in Part II, he is not only witty in himself but the cause that wit is in other men. When he is present, others have a perpetual challenge before them. Hal himself is ever undertaking to put Falstaff down, but never with complete success. Here in Part I the Prince agrees to assist in a highway robbery. He and Poins leave Falstaff and the others and, when the robbery has taken place, they attack the robbers and easily drive them off. When all the companions meet again in the tavern, Falstaff upbraids Hal and Poins for their desertion and recounts how he and the rest were set on by numerous assailants who robbed them. As his story proceeds, the number of the assailants increases fantastically, for Falstaff is not to be discouraged as the passion for fiction grows on him. When the Prince reveals that only he and Poins were responsible for the attack, Falstaff recovers at once, declaring that he knew the King's son by instinct and was therefore powerless to oppose him. This incident is recalled in Part II, when Hal and Poins, disguised as drawers in the inn, overhear Falstaff abusing the Prince. Hal assumes that Falstaff will again assert that he knew the Prince was present. But Falstaff does not repeat himself. He was, he says, doing the Prince a service, by speaking ill of him to the wicked so that the wicked should not fall in love with him. Falstaff is a rogue: Shakespeare makes no doubt of that. He will take a purse on the highway;

THE
Second part of Henrie
the fourth, continuing to his death,
and coronation of Henrie
the fift.

With the humours of fir Iohn Fal-
ftaffe, *and fwaggering*
Piftoll.

As it hath been fundrie times publikely
acted by the right honourable, the Lord
Chamberlaine his feruants.

Written by William Shakefpeare.

LONDON
Printed by V.S. for Andrew Wife, and
William Afpley.
1600.

I. The title-page of the Quarto of 2 HENRY IV (1600)
By courtesy of the British Museum

II. The Old Vic production of 2 HENRY IV, staged 1945-6, showing Ralph Richardson as Falstaff and Laurence Olivier as Shallow

III. The death of Clifford in 3 HENRY VI, as produced
by the Birmingham Repertory Theatre, 1952-3

IV. William Blake: 'Queen Katharine's Dream'
from the Fitzwilliam Museum, Cambridge

he will defraud those who lend him money; he will abuse his position as a recruiting-officer, taking bribes to release all those who can afford to pay; as a captain on the field of battle, he has no concern for his men's fortunes. When Hal comments on the poor state of Falstaff's troop, his reply is shocking as well as comic:

> *Prince.* I did never see such pitiful rascals.
> *Fal.* Tut, tut; good enough to toss; food for powder, food for powder; they'll fill a pit as well as better: tush, man, mortal men, mortal men.
> (IV.ii.70-3)

Along with the roguery and the callousness there is not only wit but an inexhaustible and many-sided vitality. Dr. Tillyard has directed attention to the different ways in which Falstaff makes an appeal to feelings deep within us: he is the eternal child, the adult refusing to grow up, having in this way an odd relationship with Mr. Pickwick's innocence and Samuel Johnson's readiness to 'have a frisk' during the night; he is like the traditional figure of the Fool, an inevitable victim (at Gadshill, at Shrewsbury) but with remarkable powers of quick recovery; he is the adventurer, ever embarking on dangerous undertakings for the thrill of it (replying to Hal's enquiry 'Where shall we take a purse to-morrow, Jack?' with an immediate 'Zounds, where thou wilt, lad'), even though he has no fondness for an exchange of blows; he is the personification of the threat of disorder, both in the state and in the individual, appealing in both instances to an impulse in ourselves that we commonly keep under control. All these aspects of the character put us, more or less unawares, on his side. The sympathy they excite—with the feeling that, though this man can be rejected, the thing he stands for cannot be annihilated—inclines us to see as petty and mechanical the intriguing for power among the historical figures of the play. Of all the other characters in Part I of *Henry IV*, only Hotspur has a comparable fund of natural strength.

Falstaff and Hotspur are in a sense polar opposites. It is Hotspur who thirsts after honour:

> By heaven methinks it were an easy leap
> To pluck bright honour from the pale-fac'd moon;
> Or dive into the bottom of the deep,
> Where fathom-line could never touch the ground,
> And pluck up drowned honour by the locks;
> So he that doth redeem her thence might wear
> Without corrival all her dignities. (I.iii.201-7)

It is Falstaff who, before the battle of Shrewsbury, finds honour a mere word:

> *Prince.* Why, thou owest God a death. [*Exit.*
> *Fal.* 'Tis not due yet; I would be loath to pay him before his day. What need I be so forward with him that calls not on me? Well, 'tis no matter; honour pricks me on. Yea, but how if honour prick me off when I come on? How then? Can honour set to a leg? No. Or an arm? No. Or take away the grief of a wound? No. Honour hath no skill in surgery, then? No. What is honour? A word. What is in that word? Honour. What is that honour? Air. A trim reckoning! Who hath it? He that died o' Wednesday. Doth he feel it? No. Doth he hear it? No. 'Tis insensible, then? Yea, to the dead. But will it not live with the living? No. Why? Detraction will not suffer it. Therefore I'll none of it. Honour is a mere scutcheon. And so ends my catechism. (V.i.127-44)

Hotspur will do anything for glory, Falstaff anything for comfort and survival. Yet they are alike in one thing, in standing away from the cold calculations of the other major figures in the play. At the beginning Henry IV is talking of leading his subjects on a crusade, yet he knows that there is no immediate prospect of that: he has too many problems at home. Hal in a soliloquy in the first act declares that he is deliberately cultivating low company and a soiled reputation in order that he may astonish his subjects the more when he comes to the throne. Northumberland and Glendower and Worcester are cold contrivers of rebellion, the first two withdrawing from danger at a critical moment, the third deceiving Hotspur by withholding from him the King's promise of reconciliation. In the battle Henry IV preserves his life by having many of his followers dressed like himself. Falstaff can play at deceit too, pretending to be dead when Douglas attacks him, pretending that he killed Hotspur when the victorious Prince has left the dead body on the field. But Falstaff's deceits on the battlefield are like his deceits in the tavern: he does not deceive himself concerning motive; he burlesques himself in the very moment of deceit. This First Part shows us the future victor of Agincourt winning his first triumph, schooling himself for the larger task. There is no doubt of his capacity, no doubt that England will not fall apart when he is in control. But there is a power in human nature which he can indeed appreciate—he has words of admiration for Hotspur, of friendship for Falstaff—but which is foreign to him.

In 2 *Henry VI* an irony was established by showing a reflection of the nobles' quarrels in the mortal combat between Horner and his man and in the anarchy that Jack Cade brought to London. Now Shakespeare's handling of human affairs goes deeper. It is not simply that Falstaff's deceits provide a comic parallel to the contrivances of the great. In his precarious existence he is far more alive than they are: he represents the full scope of human nature that they fail to recognise. Hotspur makes the rest of the rebels and all of the King's followers seem shallow men of craft. Falstaff alone of the characters in the play sees the futility of emulation. Nevertheless, the King's government must be carried on; the affairs of the realm must be in capable hands; Falstaff is, even so, an outsider whose 'No' to society needs to be remembered by those who govern. Hal has a glimpse of what it means, and he is the more capable for its recognition.

Although there is a critical strain in this First Part, it is not over-obtrusive. There is plenty of sheer fun in the comedy and plenty of adventure in the story of the rebellion.

The audience's sympathies are stirred by Hotspur's fate, but he does not come close enough for his destruction to be deeply moving. In considerable measure, too, Prince Hal's triumph is to be shared in, and he comports himself with dignity and good feeling in the moment of success. 1 *Henry IV* is one of Shakespeare's most popular plays, and audiences do not go from it with the sense that their minds have been troubled. Only on close consideration does its picture of great affairs appear questioning.

The play in two Parts is a fairly frequent phenomenon in the late sixteenth and seventeenth centuries. Sometimes, as we have seen, a Second Part was added because the First was popular, sometimes the two Parts were planned together. But in either case it often happens that the dramatist, resuming his task with the same characters, taking their story further along the time-dimension, is impelled to look more detachedly at his subject than before. So in 2 *Henry IV* the critical element that is latent in the First Part becomes much more prominent. In Part I we hear of Falstaff abusing his position as a recruiting-officer: in Part II we see him engaged in the task and receiving his bribes. In Part I the King offers terms of reconciliation to the rebels: in Part II Prince John of Lancaster, in his father's name, makes a similar offer and, when it is accepted, orders the rebels to immediate execution. In Part I Falstaff dreams idly of the golden world he will have when Hal comes to the throne: in Part II he hears of Henry IV's death and sets out in haste from Gloucestershire to London, to be on hand for the reign of anarchy:

> Let us take any man's horses: the laws of England are at my com-
> mandment. Blessed are they that have been my friends; and woe
> to my Lord Chief Justice!   (V.iii.141-4)

Part I was predominantly a play of action and of prepara-
tion for action. It had its climax in the battle of Shrewsbury.
Part II is a play where action is threatened but avoided.
There is here not even a Gadshill robbery. The rebels muster

again, but Northumberland flees to Scotland, and the rest are tricked into submission. The only warlike action we see is Falstaff's comic capture of a fleeing rebel. It is a play, too, where old age and sickness are recurrent themes. The King is sick, and death approaches him when he hears of the rebels' final overthrow. Northumberland is old and feeble, readily finding an excuse for abandoning the rebels' cause again. Falstaff's age is emphasised much more than in Part I. There it was merely comic when he cried 'they hate us youth' as he laboriously engaged in robbing peaceful citizens. Here he uses more words in making the absurd claim, and is roundly rebuked by the Lord Chief Justice:

> *Fal.* . . .You that are old consider not the capacities of us that are young; you do measure the heat of our livers with the bitterness of your galls; and we that are in the vaward of our youth, I must confess, are wags too.
>
> *Ch. Just.* Do you set down your name in the scroll of youth, that are written down old with all the characters of age? Have you not a moist eye, a dry hand, a yellow cheek, a white beard, a decreasing leg, an increasing belly? Is not your voice broken, your wind short, your chin double, your wit single, and every part about you blasted with antiquity? And will you yet call yourself young? Fie, fie, fie, Sir John!   (I.ii.196-209)

And his diseases are the subject of close attention when in Act I scene ii his Page gives him his physician's report. The frailty of his body and the proximity of death run through the scene of his merry-making and love-making in the tavern and through the scenes in Gloucestershire where Justice Shallow, also old and infirm, calls back memories of their early days together in London. In Part I we had the opposition of the two young men, Hotspur and Hal, and Falstaff had a carefree spirit that made him at home in the same play. Now the focus of the drama is much more on the aged—the King, Northumberland, Shallow—and Falstaff's claims to youth constitute a joke that has been worn deliberately thin. There is still much occasion for laughter, but there has come to be an element of defiance in it. The prime enemy in this play is not rebellion, or anarchy, but time.

The total effect is indeed not simple. Shakespeare does not depart, in the handling of events, from the didactic notion of history that regularly informed dramatic writing based on the chronicles. The rebels are shown as uncertain of themselves, and the government of the country is obviously more safely entrusted to the Lancastrians. Moreover, the new King at the end of the play, Henry V, indicates that he will rule by law, that he will dissociate himself from his former companions, that he will follow his dying father's shrewd advice by occupying his nobles' minds with a foreign campaign. We have already noted Falstaff's anarchic response to the news of his Hal's accession. To underline the disastrous condition that would have supervened if the new King had not rejected Falstaff, we are shown the trepidation of his brothers and of the Lord Chief Justice before they realise that Hal will henceforth model himself on his father. And we are shown, too, just before the coronation, the arrest of Doll Tearsheet and Mistress Quickly on suspicion of being concerned in a man's death: the arrest indicates the rapid implementation of Henry V's rigorous policy, and at the same time it brings sharply to our notice the less attractive side of the associates he was abandoning. In the last scene of all there is the famous rejection of Falstaff. There is a show of magnanimity about it: Falstaff and his companions will have a pension given them ('That lack of means enforce you not to evils'), but they must not come within ten miles of the King's person: suiting the action to the word, the King sends the Lord Chief Justice to carry them to the Fleet prison. The political need for all this is manifest; the rejection might have been more graciously performed (though that might have lessened the effect for the public that Henry intended to impress); and at the same time we are left with the feeling that Henry is, in the way of governors, necessarily attempting the impossible. To send Falstaff to the Fleet is to put human nature in chains that must be broken. Falstaff the individual can be disposed of, can have his heart pierced (as we learn in *Henry V*), but what he represents is what perpetually challenges the governor's power of control and the very process of government. There is something absurd in the spectacle of the newly crowned King so arrogantly disposing of the anarchic principle in the human mind.

So the play has a double lesson to offer. On the level of immediate apprehension, we are shown the danger of rebellion, the need for discipline, the general good of the King's submission to law. Below that, and standing quite apart from any didacticism that belonged to Tudor historiography, is the hint that a governor must always, in his very moment of triumph, cut an absurd figure.

Some Shakespearian critics have seen 2 *Henry IV* as a mere attempt to exploit an already worked vein. It has even been called a 'pot-boiler'. But such a judgement seems ill-considered. Both Parts of *Henry IV* take high rank in the work of Shakespeare's middle years. The First Part is his most successful blend of chronicle and comedy, and at the same time is rich in its suggestion of complexity in human relationships, both the relationship of man to man and the relationship of ruler to subject. Part II has some of the characteristics of the later 'dark comedies', notably *Troilus and Cressida*. Though less directly satirical than that play, its questionings are more prominent and more searching than the corresponding elements in Part I. And, like so much of the major writing of the Elizabethans, it is pre-occupied with Mutability, with the ruins of time.

IV

THE MERRY WIVES OF WINDSOR

Despite a half-promise in the Epilogue to 2 *Henry IV*, Falstaff was kept out of the immediate sequel, *Henry V*.

But the character was popular and invited resurrection. So, very probably after the writing of *Henry V* (where Falstaff might well have disturbed the King's triumph), the knight was brought back in a play that kept him remote from royal company. Although Fenton, the lover of Anne Page, is described as having consorted with Prince Hal and his rascally companions, the atmosphere of *The Merry Wives* is thoroughly that of an Elizabethan Windsor: topical references, indeed, are to be found. It is a very small play, showing Falstaff's attempt to win, for profit's sake, the loves of Mistress Page and Mistress Ford, the tricks they play on him, and the jealousy of Mistress Ford's husband. Mistress Quickly, no longer the hostess of a tavern, is the housekeeper of a French doctor. Justice Shallow is brought to Windsor from Gloucestershire. Bardolph, Pistol, Nym, and Falstaff's Page are still in their master's company. The farce is eked out with simple merriment concerning the English pronunciation of the French doctor and the Welsh parson, which is reminiscent of the equally tedious juxtaposing of the Irish Macmorris, the Scottish Jamy and the Welsh Fluellen in *Henry V*.

The Merry Wives has often been a success on the stage, and has fittingly lent itself to operatic treatment. It is not an important enough play to spoil, and is principally interesting for its evidence that Falstaff and, by reflection, some of his companions had fixed themselves so firmly in the Elizabethans' minds that they were unwilling to have done with them. But the special power that these characters had in the earlier plays was in considerable measure due to their existence in a highly complicated scheme. It was the magnitude of the impertinence with which they encountered the great that gave their comedy something of grim splendour. Now they have only the burgesses of Windsor in the same world as themselves, and they become simple contrivers simply outwitted.

An audience to-day can bring to *The Merry Wives* a memory of Falstaff elsewhere, and the memory is strong enough to provide an impetus to enjoyment. But in itself the play is citizen-comedy of no high rank. *Eastward Ho!* (1605), a minor work written in collaboration by George Chapman and Ben Jonson and John Marston, is much more lively in device and more adult in its merriment.

V

HENRY VIII

The Folio play called *Henry VIII* is almost certainly the new play on Henry VIII's reign whose performance on 29 June 1613 caused the destruction of Shakespeare's Globe Theatre. Cannon being shot off during the masque-scene at Wolsey's house, the thatch of the roof caught fire. The whole theatre was consumed in less than an hour. The play takes us to the end of Shakespeare's career, and its performance brought to a conclusion a remarkable chapter of theatre-history. The building of the Globe in 1599 marked the full ascendancy of Shakespeare's company—the Lord Chamberlain's Men, renamed the King's Men in 1603— and it was for the Globe that his major dramatic achievements were written. The theatre was rebuilt, but the period of highest eminence in English dramatic writing was over.

There is not common agreement that *Henry VIII* is wholly Shakespeare's. It was published as his in the Folio and no hint of collaboration is to be found in contemporary references. In 1850, however, James Spedding put forward the view that Shakespeare here worked in close association with John Fletcher, and this view is strongly held by many scholars to-day. The opposite view, that the play is wholly Shakespeare's, has at least as strong support. No resolution of the conflict is likely to come in a foreseeable future. On the one hand there is the powerful argument of seventeenth-century silence, when Fletcher's name was a major one. On the other we have the strong resemblance of much of the versification to Fletcher's and the strong probability that the two dramatists worked together on two other plays very close in date to *Henry VIII*—*The Two Noble Kinsmen*, published as their joint work in 1634, and *Cardenio*, now lost but probably surviving in part in Lewis Theobald's adaptation called *Double Falsehood*, published in 1728. Moreover, there is a structural feature of *Henry VIII* that reminds us of Fletcher. Here we do not have the sense that as the play proceeds we are approaching an increasingly complex view of the characters and the situation, penetrating successively to more remote levels of significance: rather, we seem to be given a series of alternations between different views of the characters and situation. It is, for example, hardly possible to reconcile the notion of the King himself as a benevolent monarch unhappily under Wolsey's direction and ultimately, and more happily, freeing himself, with the notion that he is a somewhat shifty person in his public relations and that he masks his sensual attraction to Anne Bullen with a hypocritical display of a troubled conscience. The two images exist side-by-side. That does not mean that Shakespeare is responsible for the one and Fletcher for the other: the verse-tests would not bear that out. Rather, we have here a common phenomenon of Fletcher's writing—an adroit changing of viewpoint, with a consequent disharmony between the several responses set up by a single play. This in Fletcher was not due to incompetence, but to a special kind of approach to the human situation, an approach that depended on a profound, if lightly-worn, scepticism. In reading his plays one learns to reserve judgement on anything that is said.

This is no place to suggest an assured answer to the problem of *Henry VIII*'s authorship. But Fletcher's influence at least seems present, and the feature just mentioned will serve to introduce a sketch of the play's effect in reading and performance to-day.

The Prologue gives an almost full account of what the play will be. Its concern, we are told, is with serious matters and persons of state, whose sad change of fortune will invite pity; it will, moreover, be a true historical record; and it will be pageant-like, offering abundant spectacle. There will not, however, be foolery or bawdry. It is a full programme, and is well lived up to in what follows. But it disregards not only the shifting of attitude already mentioned but the element of satiric comedy that frequently enters when the attitude is shifted.

The play's dominant concern is the operation of Mutability in high places. In Act I the Duke of Buckingham is condemned to death; in Act II Queen Katharine is brought before the court which is trying the matter of her divorce, the verdict being fully anticipated by the King; in Act III Wolsey, considered luke-warm in his furthering of the divorce-action, and with the extent of his wealth unluckily made known to the King, falls from the royal favour; in Act IV Anne is crowned and Katharine dies; in Act V Cranmer is saved from falling by the personal intervention of the King, and the infant Elizabeth, daughter of Henry and Anne, is baptised, Cranmer prophesying England's greatness in her reign and in her successor James's. It will be observed how the fourth act breaks the simple sequence of falls, and how the reversal in Act V provides another variation. But, in counterpoint to the generally repeated pattern of falling, there is another thought-current in the play, an idea that the course of history is deviously working its way to a point of high achievement outside the play, in the dramatist's own life-time. Buckingham and Katharine were good people destroyed. Wolsey had his better side, but at the end of his life he had to experience the bitterness of disgrace. And others, who do not fall within the play itself, will fall in the interim between Elizabeth's baptism and her accession. Anne will be beheaded, as an alleged adulteress; Cromwell, fully in the King's favour as we see him here, will go to the block; Sir Thomas More, not a character in the play but mentioned as rising when Wolsey fell, will come to Cromwell's end; Cranmer will be burned.

If we could take the play at its face-value, and rejoice simply when it bids us rejoice, we should look without serious question on the historical spectacle, counting lost heads as a necessary price for the bright glories of to-day and yesterday.

But the play gives too sharp a picture of human conduct for us to yield unconditionally to the notion of splendour. The coronation-procession of Anne is grandly presented, but as we watch it we hear the shrill and absurd comments of two nameless Gentlemen. It is immediately followed by Katharine's death-scene, and the vision of heavenly spirits that comes into her mind as she sleeps is a companion-picture, and a devastating one, to the glittering pageant in the London streets. Moreover, the plain dignity of Katharine's household suggests that privacy has much to commend it. And the intrigues of man against man that we see throughout the action, though never displayed with strong satire, have a good deal of shabbiness in them. Wolsey wants Buckingham out of the way: the King accepts the evidence of a single witness against the Duke, and assumes the truth of the charge of treason without hearing any defence from Buckingham. This man, on his way to death, speaks at length of his innocence, of his continuing loyalty to the King, of the lesson that his fall may offer to those who now see and hear him:

> I had my trial,
> And must needs say a noble one; which makes me
> A little happier than my wretched father;
> Yet thus far we are one in fortunes: both
> Fell by our servants, by those men we lov'd most—
> A most unnatural and faithless service.
> Heaven has an end in all. Yet, you that hear me,
> This from a dying man receive as certain:
> Where you are liberal of your loves and counsels,
> Be sure you be not loose; for those you make friends
> And give your heart to, when they once perceive
> The least rub in your fortunes, fall away

Like water from ye, never found again
But where they mean to sink ye. All good people,
Pray for me! I must now forsake ye; the last hour
Of my long weary life is come upon me.
Farewell;
And when you would say something that is sad,
Speak how I fell. I have done; and God forgive me!

(II.i.118-36)

The magnanimity and eloquence almost dampen our ability
to consider the nature of the society in which the speaker
was condemned; but later we may remember Buckingham's
fall as due to something other than cosmic necessity. And
Henry, as we have noticed, is eloquent on the subject of
his conscience. With characteristic quietness the play lets
the mere juxtaposition of scenes provide its own comment.
Act II scene ii ends with Henry proclaiming his anguish at
having to abandon Katharine:

O, my lord,
Would it not grieve an able man to leave
So sweet a bedfellow? But, conscience, conscience!
O, 'tis a tender place! and I must leave her.   (II.ii.141-4)

Act II scene iii begins with Anne and an Old Lady discus-
sign the possibility of great place won by marriage:

Anne.   By my troth and maidenhead,
I would not be a queen.
   Old L.   Beshrew me, I would,
And venture maidenhead for't; and so would you,
For all this spice of your hypocrisy.
You that have so fair parts of woman on you
Have too a woman's heart, which ever yet
Affected eminence, wealth, sovereignty;
Which, to say sooth, are blessings; and which gifts,
Saving your mincing, the capacity
Of your soft cheveril conscience would receive
If you might please to stretch it.

> *Anne.*   Nay, good troth.
> *Old L.* Yes, troth and troth. You would not be a queen!
> *Anne.* No, not for all the riches under heaven.
> *Old L.* 'Tis strange: a threepence bow'd would hire me,
> Old as I am, to queen it.   (II.iii.23-37)

There is a notable difference in tone (with continuity of subject-matter) between this and Henry's last words in the previous scene. The juxtaposition would be immediate on the seventeenth-century stage, with no change of setting. In the last act we see the enmity among the lords of the Council, and their crestfallen condition when Henry intervenes on Cranmer's side. And at the ceremony of baptism we are told of the throngs of ordinary people who lose their heads and their hearts in pressing to the show: it is a comic but repellent picture of the monarch's subjects that is left with us, and it brings the ceremony into some question. In the play as a whole we see too intimate a picture of human littleness, self-deception, spite, to be able to respond excitedly to Cranmer's prophecy about the coming glories— glories, moreover, which the first spectators had themselves lived through and whose imperfections were not to be wholly banished from their minds.

Indeed only the most naïve of readers can, on consideration, take Cranmer's words at their face-value. Here he is speaking first of Elizabeth and then of James:

> In her days every man shall eat in safety
> Under his own vine what he plants, and sing
> The merry songs of peace to all his neighbours.
> God shall be truly known; and those about her
> From her shall read the perfect ways of honour,
> And by those claim their greatness, not by blood.
> Nor shall this peace sleep with her; but as when
> The bird of wonder dies, the maiden phoenix,
> Her ashes new create another heir
> As great in admiration as herself,
> So shall she leave her blessedness to one—

When heaven shall call her from this cloud of darkness—
Who from the sacred ashes of her honour
Shall star-like rise, as great in fame as she was,
And so stand fix'd. Peace, plenty, love, truth, terror,
That were the servants to this chosen infant,
Shall then be his, and like a vine grow to him;
Wherever the bright sun of heaven shall shine,
His honour and the greatness of his name
Shall be, and make new nations; he shall flourish,
And like a mountain cedar reach his branches
To all the plains about him; our children's children
Shall see this and bless heaven.   (V.v.34-56)

The writer and the spectators were living in James's time, and a moment's look about them would have suggested other aspects than those here mentioned. We need not assume that the speech is mere tongue-in-cheek writing. It gives, after all, part of the truth, for the last years of the sixteenth century and the first of the seventeenth were years of achievement and some splendour. The writer makes us for a moment entertain the fancy that the time was curiously free from tarnish. But then we remember what the play has shown us, and the seventeenth-century spectators could look about them at their own world: Cranmer becomes only a man with a dream.

Henry VIII was written well after the period when the history play flourished, and it differs remarkably from Shakespeare's previous contributions to this dramatic kind. It has no political lesson to offer. Good subjects and bad come equally to grief; there is no real threat to the strong Tudor rule. It may appear to exhort us to take a good deal of rough for the sake of an imperfectly realised smooth, but we have seen that the effect is more complicated than that. The writer or writers look dispassionately at the flux of time; they see goodness and shabbiness and self-deceit; they offer us a sense of a recurring pattern which is comic, reveals an occasional touch of human dignity and sorrow, and finds its arbitrary termination in a dream.

THE CHRONICLES

Henry VI · Henry IV · The Merry Wives of Windsor
Henry VIII

A SELECT BIBLIOGRAPHY

(Books published in London, unless stated otherwise)

Full bibliographical descriptions of the separate quarto editions and of the first collected edition of *Mr. William Shakespeare's Comedies, Histories, & Tragedies*, 1623 (the FIRST FOLIO) are given in W. W. Greg, *A Bibliography of the English Printed Drama to the Restoration*, 4 vols. 1940-59.

ABBREVIATIONS

MLQ:	*Modern Language Quarterly*
MP:	*Modern Philology*
PMLA:	*Publications of the Modern Languages Association*
RES:	*Review of English Studies*
SB:	*Studies in Bibliography*
ShJ:	*Shakespeare-Jahrbuch*
ShQ:	*Shakespeare Quarterly*
ShS:	*Shakespeare Survey*
SP:	*Studies in Philology*
TLS:	*Times Literary Supplement*

GENERAL: SOURCES AND TEXTUAL STUDIES

BOSWELL-STONE, W. G. *Shakespeare's Holinshed.* 1896. [Reprinted in *The Shakespeare Classics*, ed. I. Gollancz, 1907.]

NICOLL, A. and J. (ed.) *Holinshed's Chronicles as used in Shakespeare's Plays.* 1927.

CHAMBERS, E. K. *William Shakespeare: A Study of Facts and Problems*, Vol. I. Oxford, 1930.

HART, A. *Shakespeare and the Homilies, and other Pieces of Research into the Elizabethan Drama.* Melbourne, 1934.

GREG, W. W. *The Shakespeare First Folio.* Oxford, 1955.

GENERAL: CRITICAL STUDIES

PATER, W. *Appreciations*. 1889. [Essay on 'Shakespeare's English Kings'.]

SCHELLING, F. E. *The English Chronicle Play*. 1902.

TILLYARD, E. M. W. *Shakespeare's History Plays*. 1944.

ELLIS-FERMOR, U. *The Frontiers of Drama*. 1945. [Chapter on 'Shakespeare's Political Plays'.]

ROSSITER, A. P. (ed.) *Woodstock: A Moral History*. 1946. ['Preface' dealing with the history play.]

CAMPBELL, L. B. *Shakespeare's 'Histories': Mirrors of Elizabethan Policy*. San Marino, 1947.

CRAIG, H. 'Shakespeare and the History Play' (in *Joseph Quincy Adams Memorial Studies*, Washington, 1948).

CHAPMAN, R. 'The Wheel of Fortune in Shakespeare's Historical Plays.' *RES*, n.s. I, 1950, 1-7.

BETHELL, S. L. 'The Comic Element in Shakespeare's Histories.' *Anglia*, LXXI, 1952, 82-101.

JENKINS, H. 'Shakespeare's History Plays: 1900-1951.' *ShS*, VI, 1953, 1-15.

LAW, R. A. 'Links between Shakespeare's History Plays.' *SP*, L, 1953, 168-87.

TILLYARD, E. M. W. 'Shakespeare's Historical Cycle: Organism or Compilation.' *SP*, LI, 1954, 34-9. [Rejoinder by R. A. Law, *ibid.*, 40-41.]

RIBNER, I. *The English History Play in the Age of Shakespeare*. Princeton, 1957.

REESE, M. M. *The Cease of Majesty: A Study of Shakespeare's History Plays*. 1961.

HENRY VI

Part I

First edition: in the First Folio (1623).

Part II

First editions: (i) The First part of the Contention betwixt the two famous Houses of Yorke and Lancaster (1594) [the 'bad quarto': Facsimile, ed. F. J. Furnivall (1889)]; (ii) in the First Folio (1623).

Part III

First editions: (i) The true of Tragedie Richard Duke of Yorke (1595) [the 'bad quarto': Facsimile, ed. T. Tyler (1891)]; (ii) in the First Folio (1623).

Modern editions (of the three Parts except where otherwise stated):
 Bankside, ed. C. W. Thomas (1892) [Part II with *Contention*], and ed.
 A. Morgan (1892) [Part III with *True Tragedie*]; Arden, ed. H. C.
 Hart (1909-10); Yale, ed. C. F. T. Brooke (1918-23); New Temple,
 ed. M. R. Ridley (1936); New Cambridge, ed. J. D. Wilson (1952);
 New Arden, ed. A. S. Cairncross (1957) [Part II]; Penguin, ed. G. B.
 Harrison (1959).

SOURCES AND TEXTUAL STUDIES

MALONE, E. *A Dissertation on the Three Parts of King Henry VI, tending
 to show that these Plays were not originally written by Shakespeare.* 1787,
 1792 (expanded). [Reprinted in the Boswell-Malone edition of
 Shakespeare, Vol. XVIII, 1821.]

COURTHOPE, W. J. *A History of English Poetry,* Vol. IV. 1903. [Appendix
 entitled 'On the Authenticity of Some of the Early Plays Assigned to
 Shakespeare'.]

GAW, A. *The Origin and Development of* 1 *Henry VI.* Los Angeles, 1926.

DORAN, M. *Henry VI, Parts II and III, their Relation to the Contention
 and the True Tragedy.* Iowa City, 1928.

ALEXANDER, P. *Shakespeare's Henry VI and Richard III.* Cambridge, 1929.

WILSON, J. D. 'Malone and the Upstart Crow.' *ShS,* IV, 1951, 56-68.

BULLOUGH, G. (ed.) *Narrative and Dramatic Sources of Shakespeare,* Vol.
 III. 1960.

CRITICAL STUDIES

STIRLING, B. *The Populace in Shakespeare.* New York, 1949.

BRADBROOK, M. C. *Shakespeare and Elizabethan Poetry.* 1951. [Chapter
 on 'Tragical-Historical'.]

BOAS, F. S. 'Joan of Arc in Shakespeare, Schiller, and Shaw.' *ShQ,* II,
 1951, 35-45.

KIRSCHBAUM, L. 'The Authorship of 1 *Henry VI.*' *PMLA,* LXVII,
 1952, 809-22.

CLEMEN, W. H. 'Anticipation and Foreboding in Shakespeare's Early
 Histories.' *ShS,* VI, 1953, 25-35.

JACKSON, B. 'On Producing Henry VI.' *ShS,* VI, 1953, 49-52.

WILSON, F. P. *Marlowe and the Early Shakespeare.* Oxford, 1953.

LEECH, C. 'The Two-Part Play: Marlowe and the Early Shakespeare.'
 ShJ, XCIV, 1958, 90-106.

BROCKBANK, J. P. 'The Frame of Disorder: *Henry VI*' (in *Early Shake-speare*, Stratford-upon-Avon Studies III, 1961).

HENRY IV

Part I

First editions: (i) The History of Henrie the fourth (1598) [Facsimile, ed. H. A. Evans (1881)]; (ii) in the First Folio (1623).

Part II

First editions: (i) The Second part of Henrie the fourth (1600) [Facsimile, ed. H. A. Evans (1882)]; (ii) in the First Folio (1623).

Modern editions (of both Parts except where otherwise stated):
Bankside, ed. W. H. Fleming (1890) [parallel texts of quarto and folio versions]; Arden, ed. R. P. Cowl and A. E. Morgan (1914 and 1923); Yale, ed. S. B. Hemingway (1917-21); New Temple, ed. M. R. Ridley (1934); New Variorum, ed. S. B. Hemingway (1936) [Part I] and M. A. Shaaber (1940) [Part II]; Penguin, ed. G. B. Harrison (1938); ed. G. L. Kittredge (1940) [Part I]; New Cambridge, ed. J. D. Wilson (1946); New Clarendon, ed. W. R. Rutland (1946) [Part II]; Crofts, ed. R. C. Bald (1946) [Part I]; Pelican, ed. M. A. Shaaber (1957) [Part I] and A. Chester (1957) [Part II]; Yale, ed. C. F. T. Brooke and S. B. Hemingway (1961).

SOURCES AND TEXTUAL STUDIES

HART, A. *Shakespeare and the Homilies.* Melbourne, 1934. [Chapter on 'Was the Second Part of *King Henry the Fourth* censored?']

WALKER, A. *Textual Problems of the First Folio.* Cambridge, 1953. [Chapter on 2 *Henry IV.*]

——'The Folio Text of 1 *Henry IV.*' *SB*, VI, 1954, 45-50.

FIEHLER, R. 'How Oldcastle Became Falstaff.' *MLQ*, XVI, 1955, 16-28.

SHAABER, M. A. 'The Folio Text of 2 *Henry IV.*' *ShQ*, VI, 1955, 135-44.

CRITICAL STUDIES

MORGANN, M. *An Essay on the Dramatic Character of Sir John Falstaff.* 1777.

HALLIWELL[-PHILLIPPS], J. O. *On the Character of Sir John Falstaff, as originally exhibited by Shakespeare in the Two Parts of King Henry IV.* 1841.

BRADLEY, A. C. *Oxford Lectures on Poetry.* 1909. [Lecture on 'The Rejection of Falstaff'.]

LAW, R. A. 'Structural Unity in the Two Parts of *Henry IV*.' *SP*, XXIV, 1927, 223-42.

WILSON, J. D. *The Fortunes of Falstaff*. Cambridge, 1943.

PALMER, J. *Political Characters of Shakespeare*. 1945. [Chapter on 'Henry of Monmouth'.]

WALDOCK, A. J. A. 'The Men in Buckram.' *RES*, XXIII, 1947, 16-23.

SHAABER, M. A. 'The Unity of *Henry IV*' (in *Joseph Quincy Adams Memorial Studies*, Washington, 1948).

RIBNER, I. 'Bolingbroke, A True Machiavellian.' *MLQ*, IX, 1948, 177-84.

TRAVERSI, D. A. '*Henry IV*—Part I.' *Scrutiny*, XV, 1948, 24-35.

———'*Henry IV*—Part II.' *Scrutiny*, XV, 1948, 117-27.

RIBNER, I. 'The Political Problem in Shakespeare's Lancastrian Tetralogy.' *SP*, XLIX, 1952, 171-84.

CAIN, H. E. 'Further Light on the Relations of 1 and 2 *Henry IV*.' *ShQ*, III, 1952, 21-38.

WILSON, J. D., and WORSLEY, T. C. '*Shakespeare's Histories at Stratford*, *1951*.' 1952.

LEECH, C. 'The Unity of 2 *Henry IV*.' *ShS*, VI, 1953, 16-24.

DAVID, R. 'Shakespeare's History Plays: Epic or Drama?' *ShS*, VI, 1953, 129-39.

SPRAGUE, A. C. 'Gadshill Revisited.' *ShQ*, IV, 1953, 125-37.

HUNTER, G. K. '*Henry IV* and the Elizabethan Two-Part Play.' *RES*, n.s. V, 1954, 236-48.

STOLL, E. E. 'A Falstaff for the "Bright".' *MP*, LI, 1954, 145-59.

JENKINS, H. *The Structural Problem in Shakespeare's Henry the Fourth*. 1956.

TRAVERSI, D. *Shakespeare from Richard II to Henry V*. 1957.

WILLIAMS, P. 'The Birth and Death of Falstaff Reconsidered.' *ShQ*, VIII, 1957, 359-65.

SPIVACK, B. 'Falstaff and the Psychomachia.' *ShQ*, VIII, 1957, 449-59.

HUNTER, G. K. 'Shakespeare's Politics and the Rejection of Falstaff.' *Critical Quarterly*, I, 1959, 229-36.

THE MERRY WIVES OF WINDSOR

First editions: (i) A Most pleasaunt and excellent conceited Comedie, of Syr John Falstaffe, and the merrie Wives of Windsor (1602) [the 'bad quarto': Facsimile, ed. P. A. Daniel (1881), ed. W. W. Greg (1939); type-facsimile, ed. W. W. Greg (1910)]; (ii) in the First Folio (1623).

Modern editions: Bankside, ed. A. Morgan (1888) [parallel texts of quarto and folio versions]; Arden, ed. H. C. Hart (1904); New Cambridge, ed. A. T. Quiller-Couch and J. D. Wilson (1921); Yale, ed. G. van Santvoord (1922); New Temple, ed. M. R. Ridley (1935); Penguin, ed. G. B. Harrison (1957).

SOURCES AND TEXTUAL STUDIES

GREG, W. W. Introduction to his type-facsimile edition of the quarto. 1910.

POLLARD, A. W., and WILSON, J. D. 'The "Stolne and Surreptitious" Shakespearian Texts: *The Merry Wives of Windsor* (1602).' *TLS*, 7 August 1919.

CRITICAL STUDY

HAZLITT, W. *Characters of Shakespeare's Plays.* 1817. [Section on *The Merry Wives.*]

HENRY VIII

First edition: in the First Folio (1623).

Modern editions: Warwick, ed. D. Nichol Smith (1899); Arden, ed. C. K. Pooler (1915); Yale, ed. J. M. Berdan and C. F. T. Brooke (1925); New Temple, ed. M. R. Ridley (1935); New Arden, ed. R. A. Foakes (1957); Penguin, ed. G. B. Harrison (1958).

SOURCES AND TEXTUAL STUDIES

SPEDDING, J. 'On the Several Shares of Shakspere and Fletcher in the Play of *Henry VIII.*' *Gentleman's Magazine*, n.s. XXXIV, 1850, 115-23, 381-2.

MAXWELL, B. 'Fletcher and *Henry VIII*' (in *Manly Anniversary Studies*, Chicago, 1923).

LAWRENCE, W. J. 'The Stage Directions in *King Henry VIII.*' *TLS*, 18 December 1930.

ALEXANDER, P. 'Conjectural History, or Shakespeare's *Henry VIII.*' *Essays and Studies*, XVI, 1931, 85-120.

PARTRIDGE, A. C. *The Problem of Henry VIII Reopened.* Cambridge, 1949.

LAW, R. A. 'Holinshed and *Henry the Eighth.*' *Studies in English* (Texas), XXXVI, 1957, 3-11.

CRITICAL STUDIES

KNIGHT, G. W. *The Crown of Life*. 1947.

KERMODE, F. 'What is Shakespeare's *Henry VIII* About?' *Durham University Journal*, n.s. IX, 1948, 48–55.

BYRNE, M. St. C. 'A Stratford Production: *Henry VIII*.' *ShS*, III, 1950, 120–29.

LEECH, C. *The John Fletcher Plays*. 1962. [Chapter on 'Fletcher and Shakespeare'.]

ROBERT BRIDGES

by John Sparrow

Published for The British Council
and The National Book League
by Longmans, Green & Co.

Two shillings and sixpence

Mr. John Sparrow, in his appreciation of Robert Bridges (1844-1930), remarks that "he is surely the author of the largest body of entirely beautiful poetry in the language". Bridges's longest and most thoughtful poem, *The Testament of Beauty*, expounds the poet's doctrine that "the Artist, and the Poet as such, is the man who is possessed by the idea of Beauty", and the many quotations that adorn this essay illustrate how he himself fulfilled his conception of the poet's rôle. The study will be valued by those who know Bridges's work and will introduce him to many who do not.

¶ Thanks are due to the Clarendon Press for their kindness in allowing quotations from Robert Bridges's works. In the text, SP stands for 'Shorter Poems', NP for 'New Poems', LP for 'Later Poems' and NV for 'New Verse'. The references are to, and the texts taken from, the Oxford Standard Authors edition.

Bibliographical Series
of Supplements to 'British Book News'
on Writers and their Work

★

GENERAL EDITOR
Bonamy Dobrée

Robert Seymour Bridges was born at Walmer on 23 October 1844. He died at Boars Hill, Oxford on 21 April 1930.

ROBERT BRIDGES
from a photograph by Mrs. M. G. Perkins

ROBERT BRIDGES

by JOHN SPARROW

PUBLISHED FOR
THE BRITISH COUNCIL
and the NATIONAL BOOK LEAGUE
by LONGMANS, GREEN & CO.

LONGMANS, GREEN & CO. LTD.
48 Grosvenor Street, London, W.1
Railway Crescent, Croydon, Victoria, Australia
Auckland, Kingston (Jamaica), Lahore, Nairobi
LONGMANS SOUTHERN AFRICA (PTY) LTD.
Thibault House, Thibault Square, Cape Town
Johannesburg, Salisbury
LONGMANS OF NIGERIA LTD.
W.R. Industrial Estate, Ikeja
LONGMANS OF GHANA LTD.
Industrial Estate, Ring Road South, Accra
LONGMANS, GREEN (FAR EAST) LTD.
443 Lockhart Road, Hong Kong
LONGMANS OF MALAYA LTD.
44 Jalan Ampang, Kuala Lumpur
ORIENT LONGMANS LTD.
Calcutta, Bombay, Madras
Delhi, Hyderabad, Dacca
LONGMANS CANADA LTD.
137 Bond Street, Toronto 2

First published in 1962
© John Sparrow 1962

Printed in Great Britain by
F. Mildner & Sons, London, E.C.1

ROBERT BRIDGES

I

ROBERT BRIDGES can claim one title to pre-eminence among English poets: he is surely the author of the largest body of entirely beautiful poetry in the language.

What do we mean when we call a poem beautiful? First, and most obviously, we may have in mind its formal beauty; we may mean that its sounds and rhythms, its audible colours and patterns, satisfy our ear and that its language and diction give us pleasure by the way in which they express and enforce its meaning. Or we may have in mind the theme and substance of the poem, and mean that we find beauty in the images and ideas that compose it and the thoughts and feelings that it expresses and evokes—leaving unanswered, at least for the moment, the question what is meant by the 'beauty' of a thought, an emotion, or an image.

Whatever the sense or faculty to which the beauty of a poem makes its appeal, if it is to be entirely beautiful there must be nothing in it—no cacophony, no harshness or infelicity of expression, no disharmony in the theme or imagery or in the tone and spirit of the composition—that mars the complex total effect.

To produce a work that is entirely beautiful is far from being the highest aim of the creative writer, but it is one that is rarely achieved. The novelist, the epic poet, the tragedian, work on too large a scale, and to their kinds of work the concept really has no application; a sonnet of Shakespeare may be entirely beautiful, but it makes no sense to apply the phrase to *Hamlet*. Entire beauty can hardly be achieved by a writer whose aim is to convey or reproduce the effect of an extended segment of human experience, actual or imagined; for an entirely beautiful poem we turn rather to the lyrical writer, and to such short pieces as we

find in the Greek Anthology or the Elizabethan song-books—
and even in those collections the entirely beautiful poem is
rare enough. It is still a rarer thing for a writer (though less so
for a painter or the composer of music) to be so enamoured
of beauty and so desirous of creating it that it pervades and
characterizes the whole body of his work. Prose writers,
after all, have many other things to do: even among poets
there are few of whom it can be said that their work is
consistently beautiful: Pindar, perhaps, was such a poet, and
so were Spenser and Keats, and it was to 'Intellectual
Beauty' that Shelley 'dedicated' his powers: the list is not a
long one, but in it Bridges undoubtedly has a place.

Bridges believed quite simply that the poet's task was to
create Beauty in the medium of words. 'The Artist', he
said, in a broadcast address on 'Poetry', 'and the Poet as
such, is the man who is possessed by the idea of Beauty.'
And it was his belief that the beauty of poetry (as of all
Art) lies primarily in the theme, the thing expressed, and
only secondarily in the expression, and that beauty of theme
is ultimately and essentially ethical, and it is our moral
sense that it appeals to. Art is 'non-moral' he declared,
'only in so far as we take Morals to mean the conventional
code of conduct recognised by the society to which we
happen to belong. Art, it is true', he continued, 'has very
little to do with that. But pure Ethics is man's moral beauty
and can no more be dissociated from Art than any other
kind of beauty, and, being man's highest beauty, it has the
very first claim to recognition.'[1]

It was to this doctrine—that Art is the creation of beauty
and that beauty can be explained only as a form of goodness

[1] "It must be admitted" he says, a little further on, "that no strict line
of distinction [between the ugly and the beautiful] can be drawn, and that the
average man's conception of beauty is absurdly limited and conventional;
also that as much admirable skill may be used in the expression of crime
as of virtue and so on; the portrait of a man suffering from confluent
small-pox might thus be a masterpiece." But to those who argue from
this that all these things are equally beautiful, or can be made so by
competent expression, his scornful answer was: "We live in a free
country where everyone may think and say what he pleases."

—that Bridges dedicated his career as a creative artist, and the last and most self-revealing of his poems, *The Testament of Beauty*, was devoted to the exposition of it. 'Beauty', he said in one of his Sonnets, is 'the best of all we know', and to Marlowe's question 'What is Beauty then?' he answered, in his 'loose Alexandrines',

> Beauty is the highest of all those occult influences
> the quality of appearance that thru' the sense
> wakeneth spiritual emotion in the mind of man.

Nothing could be well further from the aims of most English poets than the creation of beauty in this sense; no room here for Donne the sensualist or Pope the satirist, for a man of the world like Byron or a scavenger like Swift. Poets for whom poetry is primarily a deliverance of self, or whose aim is to reproduce some aspect of the world around them, will outlaw nothing that comes within the range of their experience; 'Beauty' is not a criterion that they apply, consciously or unconsciously, in editing their raw material; it is epiphenomenal—something that may come into being if they hit the mark. But a devotion to Beauty in Bridges's sense cuts off the poet from an immense range of human experience; and this was a sacrifice that Bridges was very ready to make in the interests of his art.

Bridges differs from most poets of today also in his attitude towards his calling. For him, poetry was essentially an affair of making rather than expressing, an art rather than an outlet. The craft of writing was an exacting one, demanding a concentrated discipline, and he gave so much time and thought to questions of technique that superficial and unsympathetic readers are inclined to think of him as a 'mere' craftsman—nothing more than a poetical Fabergé, intent on manufacturing, for the delight of his customers, well-cut or well-set jewels and toys of ingenious design. And indeed some of his poetical exercises may encourage, though they do not justify, this opinion.

Bridges himself described, both in prose and in verse, his attitude towards the art of poetry. In his Memoir of his school-fellow Digby Mackworth Dolben, after telling of the 'equal enthusiasm' for poetry that the two friends shared at Eton, and of the 'mutual divergence' of their tastes, he continued: 'Our instinctive attitudes towards poetry were very dissimilar, he regarded it from the emotional, I from the artistic side; and he was thus of a much intenser poetic temperament than I, for when he began to write poetry he would never have written on any subject that did not deeply move him, nor would he attend to poetry unless it expressed his own emotion; and I should say that he liked poetry on account of the power it had of exciting his valued emotions, and he may perhaps have recognised it as the language of faith. What had led me to poetry was the inexhaustible satisfaction of form, the magic of speech, lying as it seemed to me in the masterly control of the material; it was an art which I hoped to learn. An instinctive rightness was essential, but, given that, I did not suppose that the poet's emotions were in any way better than mine, nor mine than another's. There is a point in art where these two ways merge and unite, but in apprenticehood they are opposite approaches.'

The ways do meet, and much of Bridges's best poetry, as we shall see, is born of their union. His intense desire to achieve 'a masterly control of the material' was not due only to his sense of 'the fascination of what's difficult' in the art of expression, to his love of words for their own sake; it sprang also from his hieratic, almost sacramental, view of the function of poetry, his feeling that the vehicle of spiritual beauty must be worthy of its content. Both aspects of his creed are revealed in one of his best known lyrics:

> I love all beauteous things,
> I seek and adore them;
> God hath no better praise,

> And man in his hasty days
> Is honoured for them.
>
> I too will something make
> And joy in the making:
> Altho' to-morrow it seem
> Like the empty words of a dream
> Remembered on waking.

Here the second stanza testifies to Bridges's 'joy in the making'; the first reveals what I have called his hieratic view of the poet's function.

There is another characteristic that distinguishes Bridges's verse from most modern poetry and may make it more difficult for present-day readers to appreciate—his free use of poetic diction, of archaic and 'literary' forms and words. *Ye* and *thee*; *singest*; *looketh*; *bedight*; *beauteous*; *bower*; *wanhope*; *jocund*; *stell'd*; *orb'd in the eterne*—such words crop up on every page, and he regularly employs what he himself calls 'properties': he is lavish, for instance, of personifications and invocations of 'the Muse'. This was not due to unthinking acceptance of an inherited 'poetic' jargon; his use of archaic forms for instance, had a strictly practical purpose: 'The author would explain' (he says in a note to *The Testament of Beauty*) 'that the use of *eth* for the 3rd per. sing. of verbs is not an archaic fancy, but a practical advantage indispensable to him, not only for its syllabic lightness, but because by distinguishing verbs from the identical substantives, it sharpens the rhetoric and liberates the syntax.'

Those who contend that poetry should always and only make use of the forms and vocabulary of common con-temporary speech, and eschew 'poetic' images and properties, have to reckon with the practice of Shakespeare and Shelley just as much as with that of Bridges; indeed there is hardly a serious poet in English who does not invite their attack. Bridges himself met this line of criticism in a paper on 'Poetic Diction in English'. He admitted that 'the revolt against the old diction is a reaction which in its general attitude is rational' and in line with the reaction of the Lake Poets. He answered it by contrasting *Lycidas* and *Adonais*, in which the poetic convention is seen at its most extreme, with *Thyrsis*, in which the diction is Words-worthian in its plainness and the poetic convention ('Alas for Corydon!' and so on) merely ornamental and not organic: of the three Elegies, he says, it is *Thyrsis* with its rational attitude and simple diction, 'that lacks in passion, as if it were a handling of emotions rather than the compelling utterance of them'; in it 'the sorrow and the friendship seem least profound', and 'though it is agreeable reading, it leaves one cold at the end'. How far this is actually due (as he suggests) to the rational, prosaic treatment and how far to other factors ('its fanciful argument and the poet's mentality') cannot, he admits, be demonstrated, and his answer to the 'rationalists' in the matter of diction rests ultimately upon his assertion that 'Since poetic language is essentially a rarity of expression of one sort or another it is unreasonable to forbid apt and desirable grammatical forms' —and he might have included words and images—'merely because they are not read in the newspapers or heard at the dinner-table'. The premise that 'poetic language is essentially a rarity of expression' begs the question; the truth is, as he says later in his paper, that diction cannot be considered apart from what he calls 'keeping', that is, 'the harmonizing of the artistic medium', so that diction, image, and theme all assist each other. Any diction is good that is effective in the given case.

There are moments in Bridges when his poetic diction rings hollow:

> The making mind, that must untimely perish
> Amidst its work which time may not destroy,
> The beauteous forms which man shall love to cherish,
> The glorious songs that combat earth's annoy—

there is no need to point out the faults in those four lines:

'poetic' words have been called in to clothe banality of thought and swollen phrases to sustain a halting metre.

Bridges is not often guilty of such lapses; where they occur, the diction is not itself at fault; its incongruity is the symptom of a deeper trouble, revealing the momentary lack of poetic inspiration, a failure of the power to fuse feeling and image in speech. For contrast, take another stanza:

> I will not let thee go.
> I hold thee by too many bands:
> Thou sayest farewell, and lo!
> I have thee by the hands,
> And will not let thee go—

there, the archaic and 'poetic' diction is the natural and genuine language of passion, and no unprejudiced critic would complain of it.

It is not only his meticulous craftsmanship and his conscious use of 'poetic diction' that have led critics to overlook, or to under-estimate, the emotional element in Bridges's work; their mistake is due also to something in the nature of the emotion itself, something that for want of a better word one may call its impersonality. Strictly, 'impersonal emotion' is a meaningless pair of words, and the phrase might be taken to suggest an absence of real feeling; but that is not what I mean. Many of Bridges's poems express passionate love or joy or delight in the world around him; one cannot doubt that they were *felt*. But, reading them, while one is made aware of the emotion experienced, one is somehow unaware of the person who is experiencing it—which is very far from being the case when one reads Hopkins, or Yeats, or Donne, or almost any poet who has left a large body of passionate work. This impersonality in Bridges's work is not due to a deliberate abnegation of self or a conscious generalizing of emotion (if, indeed, those phrases have any real meaning); nor is it that his care for his craft has stifled or frozen the feeling that made him write. His most passionate poems—'Awake my heart to be loved', 'I will not let thee go', 'Since thou O fondest and truest', for example—for all the art that went to the shaping of them, impress one as absolutely spontaneous. His 'impersonality' is no more than the normality, the simplicity, the sanity of his nature. Though he has an easily recognisable style, and the whole body of his work carries the impress of a strong personality, his emotions are devoid of idiosyncrasy, even of individuality; in his love-poems, though he is speaking for himself, he speaks also for every lover; his utterance has the transparency and, in a good sense, the tastelessness of pure water. *Fieri non potest ut idem sentiant* (as Hopkins more than once reminded his friend) *qui aquam et qui vinum bibunt*, and one may well ask, at times, for a more strongly flavoured or a more intoxicating draught—in the words of Dowden, 'some dominant note, some fine extravagance, even some splendid sins'. But Bridges would not have been true to his poetic creed or to his own nature had he attempted to give us that.

II

Bridges was born on 23 October, 1844 at Walmer in Kent. His father's family were 'substantial Kentish yeomen', and his mother was the daughter of a baronet in Holy Orders. In two long Elegies—*Recollections of Solitude* and *The Summerhouse on the Mound*—the poet himself described the beauties of the home of his childhood, with its garden looking out upon the Channel; and he recalled in prose the tradition of a family 'that seemed to the younger generation to have been unusually supplied with a dignified and long lived aristocracy of generals, baronets and divines, whose features (he said) were familiar to me among the many miniatures, silhouettes and other little portraits, mementos of personal affection, that hung in my mother's rooms, and in their eighteenth century fashions, kindled our imaginations of a strange and remote world'. His father died when he was barely ten years old, leaving his future well provided for. At Eton, where he was sent before his tenth birthday, he was happy and successful, making many friends and becoming captain of his house; at Oxford he rowed for his college, Corpus Christi, and took Honours in the Schools. Leaving the University, he spent two years (1867-9) in foreign travel and, returning home, made his plans for life. His was an unusual ambition; he wished to be a poet. More unusual still, he intended first to embark upon an active profession in order to equip himself for fulfilling his ultimate purpose: he resolved to practise medicine until he was forty and then to retire and devote himself to the writing of poetry. So, in 1869, Bridges entered himself at St. Bartholomew's where he worked for five years (with intervals of foreign travel) as a medical student. After taking his M.B. in 1874 he held a series of appointments as physician at several London hospitals, until in 1881 a serious illness forced him to abandon medical practice and, after a short spell abroad, he retired with his mother (now widowed a second time) to live in the country at the Manor House at Yattendon in Berkshire.[1] Two years later, in 1884, he married Mary Monica, daughter of Alfred Waterhouse, R.A., a successful architect, and with her he shared a happy married life—he was fortunate also in his children—until the end of his days.

In 1907 Bridges moved to Chilswell, a house he had built for himself on Boar's Hill, near Oxford, and there he passed the remainder of a life that was devoid of outward incident. He was made Poet Laureate in 1913, and he received the Order of Merit on the publication of *The Testament of Beauty* in 1929, a few months before his death on 23 April 1930.

From this short sketch it will be seen that Bridges was able for nearly half a century to devote himself to practising

[1] She had married as her second husband, the Rev. J. E. N. Molesworth, Vicar of Rochdale in Lancashire, which thus became the poet's second home—a striking contrast, one may suppose, to his Kentish birthplace.

the art of poetry, while he lived the life of a cultured
country gentleman, in a comfortable and happy home set
in the pastoral landscape that he loved, and within easy
reach of his Oxford friends. He was speaking for himself
when he said:

> And country life I praise
> And lead, because I find
> The philosophic mind
> Can take no middle ways;
> She will not leave her love
> To mix with men, her art
> Is all to strive above
> The crowd, or stand apart.

Bridges never wavered from his choice to stand apart
from the crowd and not to "strive above" it.

None the less, his earlier life had not been entirely
sheltered: he had travelled; his home had been for a time
in the industrial north; he had worked for ten years in
busy London hospitals. And his sensitive and emotional
nature had had its share of grief; the death of his younger
brother Edward, in 1866, plunged him, he said in after
years, 'into deep sorrow at the time, and considerably
altered the prospects of [his] life', and little more than a
year later his cousin and school friend Digby Dolben was
accidentally drowned when almost on the point of joining
Bridges at the University. How deeply Bridges was shaken
by this loss can be gathered from the sketch of Dolben's
life that he wrote nearly half a century later. Plainly, his
friendships in youth and early manhood were deeply tinged
with emotion, and the happiness they brought him was not
unalloyed. His dearest friend at Oxford was Gerard Manley
Hopkins, and though the difference in their outlooks upon
life did not lessen their mutual affection, it precluded
perfect sympathy and necessitated a parting of their ways;
Hopkins's allegiance to the Jesuit discipline prevented them

from meeting except on rare occasions during the twenty years that preceded his early death in 1889. None the less the two friends kept up, with few breaks, a correspondence (of which Hopkins's side alone survives) that shows how devoted each was to the other and how deeply each was interested in and admired the other's poetry.

There are in Bridges's poems echoes of these personal sorrows, and they reveal here and there a vein of unsuspected melancholy. But that vein, if deep, was a thin one; his temperament was sanguine, circumstances allowed him a happy life, and—in his own words—'the best of his art' was 'gay'.

If he was favoured by circumstances, he was also richly endowed by nature. Lovers of beauty—one thinks of Pater, of Socrates, of Matthew Arnold—have not always been beautiful themselves; but Bridges, in youth and in age, was, in the words of W. B. Yeats, 'an image of mental and physical perfection'.

'In presence', said his friend Henry Newbolt, 'Bridges was one of the most remarkable figures of his time; there is no company in which he would not have been distinguished. He had great stature and fine proportions, a leonine head, deep eyes, expressive lips, and a full-toned voice, made more effective by a slight occasional hesitation in his speech. His extraordinary personal charm was, however, due to something deeper than these; it lay in the transparent sincerity with which every word and motion expressed the whole of his character, its greatness and its scarcely less memorable littlenesses . . . none would have wished these away; they were not the flaws but the 'grotesque' ornaments of his character. Behind him there was always visible the strength of a towering and many sided nature, at once aristocratic and unconventional, virile and affectionate, fearlessly inquiring and profoundly religious.' The fineness of his instincts, it may be added, showed itself in the 'properties' of his life, in the beauty of his handwriting, for instance, and the careless elegance of his dress.

Bridges was a natural aristocrat not only in physique; he was aloof and independent in his attitude of mind, an eclectic in philosophy, in religion, and in literature. *The Testament of Beauty*, with its swarm of illustrations drawn from art and archaeology, from the historians and the philosophers, reveals both the range and the independence of his questing intellect; he drew upon Plato and Aristotle indifferently, and if the poem is suffused with Christian feeling it is also, as he once said in conversation, 'all against the clergy'. Religious by temperament, he had been led at school, together with his friends Dolben and V. S. S. Coles, far along the High Anglican paths of the Oxford Movement. He had even intended, it is said, when he came up to Oxford, to take Holy Orders. But a natural paganism soon asserted itself, and orthodoxy was not the leading characteristic of one who could write: "The Christian churches will not leave the old ruts. The Pope still hankers after temporal power, and to get it would crown Tiglath-Pileser in St. Peter's while our Protestant church still begins its morning devotions by singing of 'God swearing in his wrath that his people should not enter into his rest'." In literature too Bridges was immune from the impact of authority: by date a Victorian, he was unmoved by the 'movements' and uninfluenced by the 'influences' of that age; echoes of his distaste for its leading poets—Tennyson, Browning, Matthew Arnold—make themselves heard in his correspondence with Gerard Hopkins, and among his contemporaries the poets who most influenced him were two isolated figures—Hopkins himself and Canon Dixon. If one asks what earlier writers he looked upon as masters, the Index to *The Spirit of Man* (1916), his wartime anthology, gives the key: the authors he draws upon far more freely than any others are Shakespeare, Milton, Shelley and Keats.[1]

[1] Wordsworth, Blake and Amiel (and also Dixon, in regard to whom he was no doubt influenced by personal predilection) come next, and in their cases the choice is accounted for by the avowed purpose of the anthology, which was to illustrate the belief that "spirituality is the basis and foundation of human life".

Bridges was not interested in 'literature' or literary history; gossip about dead men of letters and scholarly studies of second-rate performers bored him, and he would not waste his time on what he found uncongenial. But he was passionately devoted (the *cliché* expresses a literal truth) to the art of poetry and intensely concerned about the secret springs of the delight it gave him. The problems that intrigued him were philosophical and technical: what is it in the work that appeals to our sense of beauty, and what is it in us that responds to the appeal?

The circumstances of his life at Yattendon and Chilswell enabled him to spend years in pondering these questions and pursuing the answers to them down to the remotest detail—the setting of words to music; the parts played by accent, by quantity, by rhythm, in metrical composition; the proper pronunciation of English, and the best way of expressing that pronunciation, and safeguarding it from corruption, by phonetic spellings and specially devised alphabets. The work that he did in these fields does not lend itself to summary treatment or to quotation; some indication of his activities will be gathered from the Bibliography on p.34, but special mention must be made of his connection with the Society for Pure English. This Society was formed by Bridges, together with his friends Henry Bradley, Sir Walter Raleigh and Logan Pearsall Smith, in 1913; but owing to the intervention of the first Great War it did not get going until six years later. Its objects were, in the words of Pearsall Smith, its first secretary, 'to safeguard our inherited form of speech from the dangers threatening it under modern conditions, to help defend its integrity and beauty, and make it, perhaps, into an even more adequate means of expression for modern ideas'. So far as the aim of the Society was to influence the public at large, it was (in the words of Raleigh) 'rather like proposing that everyone shall dress well and move gracefully'; but its publications provided an excellent vehicle for Bridges and fellow-enthusiasts (including the authors of *Modern English Usage*) to expound and urge their views on linguistic topics of general interest. Between 1919 and 1931 there appeared a stream of 'S.P.E.' pamphlets, under Bridges's editorship, of several of which he was himself the author, on linguistic usage, idiom, vocabulary, pronunciation, spelling, handwriting, and kindred topics. In all these matters, his general attitude was (in the words of his daughter, who inherited her father's poetic gift) 'at once conservative and democratic, aesthetic and rational. Besides fighting to preserve the traditional and characteristic beauties of our language from the dangers of slovenly and meaningless degradation, and from all confusion and ugliness, whether of thought or sound, he was at the same time a keen experimenter, and no one was more ready to appreciate and encourage all natural and healthy developments of the national genius.'

Bridges once told Pearsall Smith that his poetical inspiration came to him at intervals—'there would be periods, sometimes long periods, in which he felt no impulse to create; he could, indeed, write verses if he wished in these periods, but such verses he said would have no poetic value. Then, one auspicious morning the world would take on a new appearance; everything would be full of poetic interest, and the sight of a tree, a picture on the wall of his bedroom, would suggest subjects in such abundance that he was almost embarrassed by them. Then, after a few weeks or months or even longer periods, he would find that the capricious Muses had taken their departure.' The study of the technical problems that fascinated him served to occupy these periods of vacancy; but the business of his life was Poetry.

III

It is difficult to praise, to criticize, even to describe except in the most general terms, work so impersonal, so uniform, so lacking, as it were, in incident as are the lyrics of Bridges; there are no obscurities to explain, few allusions to identify, no 'developments' to trace; the only way to convey its quality is to quote. But the attempt to detach a stanza from almost any of his poems reveals how closely woven is its texture, and if one quotes, one must, to do him justice, quote in full.

Bridges's lyrical and shorter poems are not, in fact, as uniform in kind as they might at first sight seem to be: they fall into several categories. The poems that one naturally thinks of first, and thinks of as being most characteristic, are those pure lyrics in which he expresses strong and spontaneous feeling—almost all of them poems of happy, even triumphantly happy, love:

> My delight and thy delight
> Walking, like two angels white,
> In the gardens of the night:
>
> My desire and thy desire
> Twining to a tongue of fire,
> Leaping live, and laughing higher;
> Thro' the everlasting strife
> In the mystery of life.
>
> Love, from whom the world begun,
> Hath the secret of the sun.
>
> Love can tell, and love alone,
> Whence the million stars were strewn,
> Why each atom knows its own,
> How, in spite of woe and death,
> Gay is life, and sweet is breath:
>
> This he taught us, this we know,
> Happy in his science true,
> Hand in hand as we stood
> Neath the shadows of the wood,
> Heart to heart as we lay
> In the dawning of the day.

That is not absolutely without blemish: the seventh and

eighth lines, though high-sounding, are empty, and 'in his science true' adds nothing to its context beyond a touch of incongruity. But surely the whole lyric conveys, with Blake-like simplicity and exaltation, the ecstasy that inspired it? By its side one may set a dozen others, for instance, 'I will not let thee go' (SP I 7); 'Awake, my heart, to be loved' (SP III 15); 'Since thou, O fondest and truest' (SP III 17); 'My spirit kisseth thine' (SP IV 28) and 'So sweet love seemed that April morn' (SP V 5):

> So sweet love seemed that April morn,
> When first we kissed beside the thorn,
> So strangely sweet, it was not strange
> We thought that love could never change.
>
> But I can tell—let truth be told—
> That love will change in growing old;
> Though day by day is nought to see,
> So delicate his motions be.
>
> And in the end 'twill come to pass
> Quite to forget what once he was,
> Nor even in fancy to recall
> The pleasure that was all in all.
>
> His little spring, that sweet we found,
> So deep in summer floods is drowned,
> I wonder, bathed in joy complete,
> How love so young could be so sweet.

Two of Bridges's best known and most moving poems were inspired not by the passion of love but by the thought of another's death—the simple lines 'I never shall love the snow again' (SP V 11), commemorating his wife's brother, Maurice Waterhouse, and the reflective stanzas *On a Dead Child* (SP III 4), evidently the fruit of experience at St. Bartholomew's. The last two stanzas from the latter poem may be quoted to show the mastery with which Bridges manipulates a difficult metre and the depth of feeling with which he conveys 'the last curiosity':

> So quiet! Doth the change content thee?—Death, whither
> hath he taken thee?
> To a world, do I think, that rights the disaster of this?
> The vision of which I miss,
> Who weep for the body, and wish but to warm thee
> and awaken thee?
> Ah! little at best can all our hopes avail us
> To lift this sorrow, or cheer us, when in the dark,
> Unwilling, alone we embark,
> And the things we have seen and have known and
> have heard of, fail us.

Another poem that expresses feeling arising from a human relationship is the little known *The Portrait of a Grandfather* (LP 13):

> With mild eyes agaze, and lips ready to speak,
> Whereon the yearning of love, the warning of wisdom plays,
> One portrait ever charms me and teaches me when I seek:
> It is of him whom I, remembering my young days,
> Imagine fathering my father; when he, in sonship afore,
> Liv'd honouring and obeying the eyes now pictur'd agaze,
> The lips ready to speak, that promise but speak no more.
>
> O high parental claim, that were not but for the knowing,
> O fateful bond of duty, O more than body that bore,
> The smile that guides me to right, the gaze that follows my
> going,
> How had I stray'd without thee! and yet how few will seek
> The spirit-hands, that heaven, in tender-free bestowing,
> Holds to her children, to guide the wandering and aid the
> weak.
>
> And Thee! ah what of thee, thou lover of men? if truly
> A painter had stell'd thee there, with thy lips ready to speak,
> In all-fathering passion to souls enchanted newly,
> —Tenderer call than of sire to son, or of lover to maiden,—
> Ever ready to speak to us, if we will hearken duly,
> 'Come, O come unto me, ye weary and heavy-laden!'

That is a poem about the filial relationship, manifested in three generations, the theme being translated from the human plane to the Divine, and there too repeated, for the Son is thought of as fathering his human children. It is also about two pictures—an actual picture in the first stanza and an imagined picture in the third. The whole poem turns, as on a pivot, upon the mid-line of the second stanza—'How had I strayed without thee! and yet how few will seek . . .', and the second portrait is suggested by the opening words of the stanza 3—'And Thee! ah what of thee, thou lover of men?'—and completed by the familiar quotation in the last line, a subtle touch that sets vividly before our eyes the image of the Man of Sorrows.[1]

Bridges's best known poems are those in which he describes the visible world—the beauties of flower and field, of sky and sea; the best example of such sheerly descriptive writing is the miraculous *London Snow* (S.P. III 2):

> When men were all asleep the snow came flying,
> In large white flakes falling on the city brown,
> Stealthily and perpetually settling and loosely lying,
>   Hushing the latest traffic of the drowsy town;
> Deadening, muffling, stifling its murmurs failing;
> Lazily and incessantly floating down and down:
>   Silently sifting and veiling road, roof and railing;
> Hiding difference, making unevenness even,
> Into angles and crevices softly drifting and sailing.
>   All night it fell, and when full inches seven
> It lay in the depth of its uncompacted lightness,
> The clouds blew off from a high and frosty heaven;
>   And all woke earlier for the unaccustomed brightness
> Of the winter dawning, the strange unheavenly glare:
> The eye marvelled—marvelled at the dazzling whiteness;
>   The ear hearkened to the stillness of the solemn air . . .

The anthologists have made that poem so familiar that there is no need to quote further. They have done as much

[1] The only blemish in this strange and moving poem is the obscurity of 'that were not but for the knowing' in l.8 and of the word 'fateful' in the next line.

for another remarkable word-picture, *A Passer-by* (S.P. II 2); and to the same class of pictorial writing belong a whole gallery of landscape poems, for instance: 'There is a hill beside the silver Thames' (S P II 5); *The Downs* (S P II 7); *The Winnowers* (S P V 1), and *The Garden in September* (S P V 4). The following (S P I 9) shows the poet's minute and sympathetic observation:

> A poppy grows upon the shore,
> Bursts her twin cup in summer late:
> Her leaves are glaucous-green and hoar,
> Her petals yellow, delicate.
>
> Oft to her cousins turns her thought,
> In wonder if they care that she
> Is fed with spray for dew, and caught
> By every gale that sweeps the sea.
>
> She has no lovers like the red,
> That dances with the noble corn:
> Her blossoms on the waves are shed,
> Where she stands shivering and forlorn.

'Her pétals yéllow, délicate': 'no lóvers like the réd That dánces with the nóble córn'—the accented syllables, both by their sound and by what they signify, enforce the contrast between the frail lemon-coloured flower and its proud crimson cousin.

Not all Bridges's descriptive poems, however, consist only of description; sometimes the scene portrayed evokes or recalls a personal emotion, and the picture is charged with human feeling. Sometimes, as in *The Voice of Nature* (S P III 3), he draws an explicit lesson from what he sees; and sometimes (N P 11) the natural scene prompts a comparison with the human condition or with human art:

> The sea keeps not the Sabbath day,
> His waves come rolling evermore;
> His noisy toil grindeth the shore,
> And all the cliff is drencht with spray.

Here as we sit, my love and I,
Under the pine upon the hill,
The sadness of the clouded sky,
The bitter wind, the gloomy roar,
The seamew's melancholy cry
With loving fancy suit but ill.

We talk of moons and cooling suns,
Of geologic time and tide,
The eternal sluggards that abide,
While our fair love so swiftly runs,

Of nature that doth half consent
That men should guess her dreary scheme
Lest he should live too well content
In his fair house of mirth and dream:

Whose labour irks his ageing heart,
His heart that wearies of desire,
Being so fugitive a part
Of what so slowly must expire.

She in her agelong toil and care
Persistent, wearies not nor stays,
Mocking alike hope and despair.

—Ah, but she too can mock our praise,
Enchanted on her brighter days,

Days, that the thought of grief refuse,
Days that are one with human art,
Worthy of the Virgilian muse,
Fit for the gaiety of Mozart.

Bridges possesses the gift of persuading us of the truth of the 'pathetic fallacy': he can make us feel, simply by describing a natural scene, that Nature is an organism with emotions of its own. Take, for instance, the closing lines of 'The storm is over, the land hushes to rest' (S P IV 23):

The day is done: the tired land looks for night:
She prays to the night to keep
In peace her nerves of delight:
While silver mist upstealeth silently,
And the broad cloud-driving moon in the clear sky
Lifts o'er the firs her shining shield,
And in her tranquil light
Sleep falls on forest and field.
Sée! sléep hath fallen: the trees are asleep:
The night is come. The land is wrapt in sleep.

The personification here is not simply 'poetic', a literary device; it expresses quite naturally the completeness with which the poet enters into and identifies himself with what he sees.

These lines are taken from one of several pieces in which Bridges eschews the stanza and lets the matter dictate the form, so that the metre follows, with the exactness of a draughtsman's pencil, the lineaments of the thing described. *November* (N P 14) is another such poem, and here too, in its last lines, he makes us feel, with him, that Nature is a sentient organism:

And now, if the night shall be cold, across the sky
Linnets and twites, in small flocks helter-skelter,
All the afternoon to the gardens fly,
From thistle-pastures hurrying to gain the shelter,
Of American rhododendron or cherry-laurel;
And here and there, near chilly setting of sun,
In an isolated tree a congregation
Of starlings chatter and chide,
Thickset as summer leaves, in garrulous quarrel:
Suddenly they hush as one,—
The tree top springs,—
And off, with a whirr of wings,
They fly by the score
To the holly-thicket, and there with myriads more
Dispute for the roosts; and from the unseen nation
A babel of tongues, like running water unceasing,
Makes live the wood, the flocking cries increasing,

Wrangling discordantly, incessantly,
While falls the night on them self-occupied;
The long dark night, that lengthens slow,
Deepening with Winter to starve grass and tree,
And soon to bury in snow
The Earth, that, sleeping 'neath her frozen stole,
Shall dream a dream crept from the sunless pole
Of how her end shall be.

For virtuosity, the opening passage matches *London Snow*: every line, almost every phrase, brings vividly before the eye and ear the object or sound that it describes:

In an isolated tree a congregation
Of starlings chatter and chide,
Thickset as summer leaves, in garrulous quarrel—

one *sees* the 'isolated tree', the long vowels and the final monosyllable making an island of the phrase itself; one *hears* the chatter of the birds; one *feels* the thickset clustering of the leaves to which their 'congregation' is compared. These effects are achieved by manipulating sounds; of course they are not due to sound alone, and a listener who knew no English would get no inkling of what was being described; but once the meaning has given the key, one appreciates the miraculous appropriateness of sound to subject. There is a touch of deeper magic in the last six lines:

The long dark night, that lengthens slow

changes at once the pace and the tone of the poem, and we pass from the visible and audible world to a realm of pure imagination.

The vision in *November* is apocalyptic and frightening; such glimpses—'Dim indications of the power That doometh man to woe'—are rare in Bridges' work; they seem to come to him against his will and were perhaps a part of his experience not fully represented in his poetry. 'Ah, many have my visions been', he says in *The North Wind* (S P V 15),

> And some I know full well:
> I would that all that I have seen
> Were fit for speech to tell.

That poem is too long to quote in full, and impossible to convey by extracts. Another midnight vision is described in *Melancholy* (N V 9), a poem of the Great War of 1914:

> 'Twas mid of the moon but the night was dark with rain,
> Drops lashed the pane, the wind howl'd under the door,
> For me, my heart heard nought but the cannon-roar
> On the fields of war, where Hell was raging amain:
> My heart was sore for the slain:—
> As when on an Autumn plain the storm lays low the wheat,
> So fell the flower of England, her golden grain,
> Her harvesting hope trodden under the feet
> Of Moloch, Woden and Thor,
> And the loving kindness of Christ held in disdain.
> My heart gave way to the strain, renouncing more and
> more;
> Its bloodstream fainted down to the slothful weary beat
> Of the age-long moment, that swelleth where ages meet,
> Marking time 'twixt dark Hereafter and Long-before;
> Which greet awhile and awhile, again to retreat;
> The Never-the-same repeating again and again,
> Completing itself in monotony incomplete,
> A wash of beauty and horror in shadows that fleet,
> Always the Never-the-same still to repeat,
> The devouring glide of a dream that keepeth no store.
> Meseem'd I stood on the flats of a waveless shore,
> Where MELANCHOLY unrobed of her earthly weeds,
> Haunteth in naked beauty without stain;
> In reconcilement of Death, and Vanity of all needs;
> A melting of life in oblivion of all deeds;
> No other beauty nor passion nor love nor lore;
> No other goddess abideth for man to adore;
> All things remaining nowhere with nought to remain;

The consummation of thought in nought to attain.
  I had come myself to that ultimate Ocean-shore,
Like labourer Love when his life-day is o'er,
Who home returning fatigued is fain to regain
The house where he was unconsciously born of yore;
Stumbling on the threshold he sinketh down on the floor;
Half-hearteth a prayer as he lieth, and nothing heeds,
If only he sleep and sleep have rest for evermore.

It is difficult to know which to praise most in this wonderful poem, the imaginative power that communicates feeling through vision, or the art that intensifies the emotion by means of word-pattern—a heavily recurring accent and changes rung through the whole length of the piece on three main vowel-sounds, used both as final and as internal rhymes.

I have quoted these powerful, grim, and visionary poems partly for their quality, and partly because this sombre element in Bridges's work—other examples are *Low Barometer* (N V 16) and *Melancholia* (L P 7)—has been lost sight of in the dazzling sunlight of so much happy extroverted verse.

Having praised the high level of his performance, it is right that I should mention his failures. In his longer formal poems, his Masks and Odes and Dramas, the characters do not come to life, the situations lack dramatic effect, and inspiration—except in interspersed lyrics and occasional passages of descriptive beauty—is sadly deficient: we feel that we are reading a poetical exercise. In his lyrics there are two veins that he explored on occasion with unfortunate effect: the humorous and the patriotic. He rightly excluded from his own final selection of Shorter Poems (published in 1931) a handful of facetious and colloquial verses that had appeared in earlier collections; though his gay and mordant humour appeared to good effect in his prose criticism, he could not, evidently, marry it to verse; and he was right also in excluding such poems as *Regina Cara*, a celebration of the Diamond Jubilee, *Matres Dolorosae*, an elegy on the conclusion of the South African War, and *Britannia Victrix*, published on the occasion of the Armistice in 1918, and several other poems of the 1914 war, included in *October*. These suggest too much the patriotic cartoons of Bernard Partridge, and they prove how wise he was—in spite of popular complaints that he was not doing his duty by the office—to restrict his utterances as Laureate.

If in his Odes for music Bridges is inclined to indulge in too grandiose an organ-swell of poetic diction, they contain none the less some beautiful lyrical passages, for he can pull out the *vox caelestis* with an effect sometimes reminiscent of Blake:

> Open for me the gates of delight,
> The gates of the garden of man's desire;
> Where spirits touched by heavenly fire
> Have planted the trees of life—[1]

and sometimes he produces a music that is entirely his own:

> Sweet compassionate tears
> Have dimm'd my earthly sight,
> Tears of love, the showers wherewith
> The eternal morn is bright:
> Dews of the heav'nly spheres.
> With tears my eyes are wet,
> Tears not of vain regret,
> Tears of no lost delight,
> Dews of the heav'nly spheres
> Have dimm'd my earthly sight,
> Sweet compassionate tears.[2]

I must touch on one other verse-form, the sonnet, before turning to the latest development of Bridges's verse-technique. Bridges published something like a hundred sonnets; by 1890 he had swollen the series in *The Growth*

[1] From the *Purcell Commemoration Ode*, 1895.
[2] From *A Hymn of Nature*, 1898.

of Love (1876) to three times its original size by the addition
of more than fifty pieces. After that, he practically abandoned
the sonnet-form, being increasingly preoccupied with experiments in quantitative, accentual, and syllabic unrhymed
metres. But in that form he had achieved some of the most
striking of his effects. Take for instance, the sestet of the
sonnet 'I care not if I live':

> I have no care for what was most my care,
> But all around me see fresh beauty born,
> And common sights grown lovelier than they were:
> I dream of love, and in the light of morn
> Tremble, beholding all things very fair
> And strong with strength that puts my strength to scorn.

Or take the opening of the sonnet, praised especially by
Hopkins, on a portrait of his mother:

> Tears of love, tears of joy and tears of care,
> Comforting tears that fell uncomforted,
> Tears o'er the new-born, tears beside the dead,
> Tears of hope, pride and pity, trust and prayer,
> Tears of contrition; all tears whatsoe'er
> Of tenderness or kindness had she shed
> Who here is pictured, ere upon her head
> The fine gold might be turn'd to silver there.

It is not easy to explain why these lines are so very moving.
Their peculiar effectiveness is due, it seems, not only to the
ideas themselves, but to their successive presentation—itself
somehow suggestive of a shower of tears—and to the falling
rhythm, beside which the cadence of 'Drop, drop, slow tears'
sounds almost crude.

In the following poem, which also won praise from
Gerard Hopkins, Bridges again bends the sonnet form to
unexpected uses:

I would be a bird, and straight on wings I arise,
And carry purpose up to the ends of the air:
In calm and storm my sails I feather, and where
By freezing cliffs the unransom'd wreckage lies:
Or, strutting on hot meridian banks, surprise
The silence: over plains in the moonlight bare
I chase my shadow and, perch where no bird dare
In treetops torn by fiercest winds of the skies.

   Poor simple birds, foolish birds! then I cry,
Ye pretty pictures of delight, unstirr'd
By the only joy of knowing that ye fly,
Ye are nót what ye are, but rather, sum'd in a word,
The alphabet of a god's idea, and I
Who master it, I am the only bird.

Who, in the year 1876, except perhaps Hopkins himself, had written a sonnet even remotely resembling that?

During the quarter of a century when he lived at Yattendon, Bridges composed a number of poetical exercises, including eight verse dramas, a 'Mask' and several formal Odes for music; but his most memorable work—apart from *The Testament of Beauty*—is to be found among his sonnets and shorter lyrical pieces.

Bridges also published criticism, which was collected after his death in ten small volumes containing thirty essays, reviews and lectures; their subjects range from Bunyan to Kipling, and they include a famous paper, *The Necessity of Poetry*, in which he stated his faith as a creative artist. In 1893 he published a study expounding his own original theories about the prosody of Milton's later works, and (two years later) a critical essay on Keats. His views are always his own, uninfluenced by the reputation of the author he is discussing or by the authority of previous critics, and they are set forth in a language that conveys the spoken word.

These critical essays, and his growing celebrity as a poet, explain why he was pressed to stand for the Professorship

of Poetry at Oxford in 1895. He refused to allow his name
to go forward, for he was not in any sense an 'academic', and
he never had the slightest desire to become a public figure;
and it was with reluctance probably, and certainly without
eagerness, that he accepted the Laureateship in 1913.

His critical studies influenced his own poetry; they
persuaded him to experiment with verses in classical prosody
and they opened his eyes to the existence of the 'neo-
Miltonic syllabics' in which much of his later work was
composed. 'Anyone may see', he wrote in 1912, 'that
serious rhyme is now exhausted in English verse'; and he
developed, in accordance with the principles he detected in
Milton, an unrhymed Alexandrine, to be measured by
numbering not accents but syllables. Here is a specimen,
the last lines of *The College Garden*, written in 1917:

> Thus hour draggeth on hour, and I feel every thrill
> of time's eternal stream that passeth over me
> the dream-stream of God's Will that made things as they be
> and me as I am, as unreluctant in the stream
> I lie, like one who hath wander'd all his summer morn
> among the heathery hills and hath come down at noon
> in a breathless valley upon a mountain-brook
> and for animal recreation of hot fatigue
> hath stripp'd his body naked to lie down and taste
> the play of the cool water on all his limbs and flesh
> and lying in a pebbly shallow beneath the sky
> supine and motionless feeleth each ripple pass
> until his thought is merged in the flow of the stream
> as it cometh upon him and lappeth him there
> stark as a white corpse that stranded upon the stones
> blocketh and for a moment delayeth the current
> ere it can pass to pay its thin tribute of salt
> into the choking storage of the quenchless sea.

It was in this metre that his last poem, *The Testament of
Beauty*, was composed. Through four long books Bridges
sustains a philosophical argument, designed to show

how the mind of man from inconscient existence
cometh thru' the animal by growth of reasoning
towards spiritual conscience—

and to make plain the relation of Beauty to Reason:

by Beauty (he says) it is that we come at Wisdom,
but not by Reason at Beauty.

Like all philosophical poems, *The Testament of Beauty* will
be read for its poetry, not for its philosophy; it is full of
memorable passages, reflective, descriptive, illustrative;
they grow naturally out of their context, but lose little by
being detached from it; and it is these, and its reflection of
the many-sided mind and the noble nature of the poet,
that will keep it alive.

ROBERT BRIDGES
A Select Bibliography
(Place of publication London, unless stated otherwise)

Note: Bridges lived long and published much: many of his works first appeared in privately printed and severely limited editions and were reprinted in collections the texts of which were repeatedly revised. Some of these, not listed here separately, are recorded below in the note to *Poetical Works*, 1898-1905.

Bibliography:
A BIBLIOGRAPHY OF ROBERT BRIDGES, by G. L. Mackay. New York (1933).

Collected Works:
POETICAL WORKS, 6 vols. (1898-1905)
—Vol. I (1898) *Prometheus the Firegiver* (first published, 1883); *Eros and Psyche* (1885); *The Growth of Love*; Vol. II (1899) *Shorter Poems*, with an additional section of "New Poems"; Vols. III-VI (1900-1905) Verse-dramas: *Nero Part I* (1885), *Achilles in Scyros* (1890), *Palicio* (1890), *The Return of Ulysses* (1890), *The Christian Captives* (1890), *Humours of the Court* (1893), *The Feast of Bacchus* (1889), *Nero Part II* (1894).

POETICAL WORKS. Oxford (1912)
—excludes the eight verse-dramas, but includes new poems published between 1900 and 1912. Re-issued with poems from *October, New Verse*, and *The Testament of Beauty*, in the Oxford Standard Authors, 1953.

COLLECTED ESSAYS, PAPERS ETC. 10 vols. Oxford (1927-1937)
—this series, which contains thirty essays, lectures etc., was published in ten small volumes, the editing after Bridges's death being undertaken by his widow. Special letters were cut for the text, which exhibits with increasing thoroughness as the series proceeds Bridges's suggested improvements in the alphabet and in phonetic spelling.

Selected Works:
POETRY AND PROSE, edited by J. Sparrow. Oxford (1955)
—in the Clarendon English Series. Contains selections from Bridges's poetry and prose and from critical estimates of his work.

Separate Works in Verse:

POEMS (1873)

—the author is said to have suppressed the unsold copies of this book, and he discouraged the reprinting of such of its contents as he did not himself include in subsequent collections.

THE GROWTH OF LOVE (1876)

—anonymous. Twenty-four sonnets; the series was enlarged to seventy-nine sonnets and published under the same title by C. H. O. Daniel at his press in Oxford, 1889.

POEMS BY THE AUTHOR OF THE GROWTH OF LOVE (1879)
—anonymous.

POEMS BY THE AUTHOR OF THE GROWTH OF LOVE. Third Series. (1880)
—anonymous.

POEMS. Daniel Press, Oxford (1884)

—anonymous. Selections from the collections of 1873, 1879, and 1880 above, with additions.

SHORTER POEMS. (Books I–IV, 1890; Book V, 1893)

—in Books I–III Bridges included such poems as he wished to preserve from the collections of 1873, 1870, 1880, and 1884, above, (all of which were published in limited editions); the poems in Books IV and V were new.

OCTOBER AND OTHER POEMS (1920).

NEW VERSE. Oxford (1925)

—contains Bridges's first experiments in "Neo-Miltonic Syllabics".

THE TESTAMENT OF BEAUTY. Oxford (1929).

Separate Works in Prose:

'Milton's Blank Verse in Paradise Lost', in H. C. Beeching's edition of Book I of *Paradise Lost*, Oxford. 1887.

THE PROSODY OF PARADISE LOST AND SAMSON AGONISTES. Blackwell, Oxford (1889)

—revised and reprinted as *Milton's Prosody*, 1893; final revised edition, 1921.

JOHN KEATS, A CRITICAL ESSAY (1895)

—privately printed. Published as the Introduction to the Muses' Library edition of Keats, 1896. Reprinted in *Collected Essays*.

'On the Influence of the Audience': Preface to Vol. X of the Shakespeare Head edition of Shakespeare's *Works*, 1907. Reprinted in *Collected Essays*.

SOCIETY FOR PURE ENGLISH TRACTS

—the original prospectus, largely the work of Bridges, appeared in 1913; Bridges contributed much, on pronunciation and philological questions, to the S.P.E. series of tracts between 1921 and 1929.

ADDRESS TO THE SWINDON BRANCH OF THE WORKERS EDUCATIONAL ASSOCIATION. Oxford (1916)

—on the improvement of popular education. Reprinted in *Collected Essays*.

THE NECESSITY OF POETRY. An Address to the Tredegar and District Co-operative Society. Oxford (1918). Reprinted in *Collected Essays*.

POETRY. (A broadcast delivered 28 February 1929 and printed in *The Listener*, March 1929)

—reprinted in *Collected Essays*.

THREE FRIENDS. Oxford (1932)

—Bridges's prose is seen at its best in this reprint of his Memoirs of Digby Mackworth Dolben (originally prefixed to Bridges's edition of Dolben's *Poems*, Oxford, 1911); Richard Watson Dixon (originally prefixed to Bridges's *Selection* from Dixon's *Poems* 1909); and Henry Bradley (printed privately, 1926; prefixed to Bradley's *Collected Papers*, Oxford, 1928).

THE CORRESPONDENCE OF BRIDGES AND BRADLEY, 1900-1923. Oxford (1940)

—Bridges destroyed his letters to Gerard Manley Hopkins, whose *Poems* (Oxford, 1918) he edited; Hopkins's side of the correspondence edited by C. C. Abbott, was published in 1935.

Some Critical and Biographical Studies:

ROBERT BRIDGES, by R. Brett Young (1914).

ROBERT BRIDGES 1844-1930, by E. Thompson. Oxford (1931)

—includes some personal reminiscences.

NOTES ON 'THE TESTAMENT OF BEAUTY', by N. C. Smith. Oxford (1931)

—an excellent guide to the understanding and appreciation of the poem.

ROBERT BRIDGES AND GERARD HOPKINS 1863-1889. A Literary Friendship, by J.-G. Ritz. Oxford (1960)

—a full and sympathetic story.

Arthur Hugh Clough

by ISOBEL ARMSTRONG

Published for The British Council
and The National Book League
by Longmans, Green & Co.

Two shillings and sixpence net

Mrs. Isobel Armstrong has as her subject one of the less well-known but very significant Victorian poets, Arthur Hugh Clough (1819-1861). Clough, a product of Arnold of Rugby and of Balliol College, Oxford, became a Fellow of Oriel, then, after throwing up his Fellowship, was offered the Principalship of University Hall, London. He was later an examiner in the Education Office, and died, very young, at Florence. His fine lyrics include the very well-known 'Say not the struggle nought availeth' and Matthew Arnold's 'Thyrsis' was written to commemorate his death.

Mrs. Armstrong's is a very full survey of every aspect of Clough's work, and her bibliography is even more detailed than is usual in this series. She is a graduate of the University of Leicester and is working at present on nineteenth century poetry.

Bibliographical Series
of Supplements to 'British Book News'
on Writers and their Work

★

GENERAL EDITOR
Bonamy Dobrée

Arthur Hugh Clough

*From a chalk drawing of about 1860 by S. Rowse in the
National Portrait Gallery*

ARTHUR HUGH CLOUGH

by

ISOBEL ARMSTRONG

Published for the British Council and
The National Book League by
LONGMANS GREEN & CO.

LONGMANS, GREEN & CO. LTD.,
48 Grosvenor Street, London, W.1.
Railway Crescent, Croydon, Victoria, Australia
Auckland, Kingston (Jamaica), Lahore, Nairobi

LONGMANS SOUTHERN AFRICA (PTY) LTD.
Thibault House, Thibault Square, Cape Town,
Johannesburg, Salisbury

LONGMANS OF NIGERIA LTD.
W.R. Industrial Estate, Ikeja

LONGMANS OF GHANA LTD.
Industrial Estate, Ring Road South, Accra

LONGMANS GREEN (FAR EAST) LTD.
443 Lockhart Road, Hong Kong

LONGMANS OF MALAYA LTD.
44 Jalan Ampang, Kuala Lumpur

ORIENT LONGMANS LTD.
Calcutta, Bombay, Madras
Delhi, Hyderabad, Dacca

LONGMANS CANADA LTD.
137 Bond Street, Toronto 2

First published in 1962
© Isobel Armstrong, 1962

Printed in Great Britain by
*F. Mildner & Sons, London, E.C.*1

Contents

I. INTRODUCTION   *page* 7
  (i) Life   7
  (ii) Two Poems   13

II. AMBARVALIA, 1849   17

III. THE LONGER POEMS   20
  'The Bothie of Tober-na-Vuolich';
  'Amours de Voyage'; 'Dipsychus'
  (i) 'Myself my own experiment'   20
  (ii) Intellectuals ebullient—'The Bothie of Tober-na-Vuolich'; 'Amours de Voyage'   22
  (iii) 'Dipsychus'—The intellectual Agonistes   27
  (iv) Clough's allegory of the commonplace in the long poems   32
  (v) 'Grotesque' style and 'hurry scurry anapaests'   35

IV. MARI MAGNO—'On the great sea'   37

V. CONCLUSION: The Janus-poet   39

A Select Bibliography   42

¶ Arthur Hugh Clough was born on 1 Jan. 1819 and died on 13 Nov., 1861. He is buried in the Protestant cemetary at Florence.

A. H. CLOUGH

I. INTRODUCTION

(i) Life

CLOUGH has until recently been regarded as a marginal
and eccentric poet. Yet he is in no sense a peripheral
writer. His work is unique in Victorian poetry, and
he developed a remarkably individual idiom.

Even a new reader of Clough soon learns to recognise his
characteristic tones and manners of approach:

> So that the whole great wicked artificial civilised fabric—
> All its unfinished houses, lots for sale, and railway outworks
> Seems re-accepted, resumed . . .
>> ('The Bothie of Tober-na-Vuolich')

> Thou shalt have one God only; who
> Would be at the expense of two? . . .
> Thou shalt not kill; but needst not strive
> Officiously to keep alive.
>> ('The Latest Decalogue')

> Tibur is beautiful too, and the orchard slopes, and the Anio
> Falling, falling yet, to the ancient lyrical cadence.
>> ('Amours de Voyage')

Many of the qualities most distinctive of Clough's work are
suggested here: he assumed that the familiar details of
Victorian daily life could be valid material for poetry; he
used ironic wit and epigram for his most serious purposes,
and managed it with adroit sharpness; he extracted lyricism
from the sober ordinariness of language, and manipulated
the cadences of conversational speech so as to achieve an
apparently casual, understated eloquence. All these qualities
are typical of Clough, but hardly typical of Victorian poetry.

They make his work unorthodox, inventive, sophisticated and self-conscious. Experiment and strong intelligence mark all that he wrote. One cannot claim that he is a major poet; but his unusual and individual achievement makes him among the most exciting and rewarding of Victorian minor poets.

The 1869 volume of Clough's poetry was reprinted fourteen times before the end of Victoria's reign; but in the twentieth century interest in his work declined. Perhaps Clough did not live long enough to achieve the status of a Great Victorian: he was born in 1819 and died in 1861, when he was only 42. He achieved little in public life, a failure constantly regretted by his friends, who had expected much. His life is nevertheless full of interest. His formative experiences were those of many mid-nineteenth century intellectuals, but he responded to them with exceptional sensitivity. These experiences are germane to an understanding of his poetry and of his surprising eclipse.

The first important phase in Clough's life began in 1829, when he went to Rugby School. Until this time his life had been unusual; his father, a moderately wealthy middle class cotton merchant, had moved from Liverpool to Charleston in the United States when Clough was only four, and Clough did not return to England until 1828. Yet neither Charleston nor his family were important influences; from the time he went to Rugby until his entry to Balliol College, Oxford, in 1837, he was dominated by Dr. Thomas Arnold, the Headmaster. 'This was practically the end of Arthur's childhood', his sister said, of Clough's return to England; justifiably, for after this he was forced to develop precociously under the pressure of the moral and intellectual responsibilities Rugby imposed on him. The discipline of his Rugby training, and the strain he experienced in acquiring it, affected him throughout his life.

Dr. Arnold, whose ideas were to revolutionise the English public school system, found Clough an ideal pupil not only for his academic brilliance, but because he was responsive to the new concepts of boarding-school life which Arnold introduced at Rugby. Clough, with his almost obsessive loyalty to the place, and his efforts, especially in the senior form, to be a moral example to the rest of the school, was an illustration of Arnold's belief that education and moral training were inseparable. Even Clough's early letters are full of self-important piety redolent of Rugby's earnestness—'Here is a bit of a hymn for you Georgy', he wrote in a P.S. to his younger brother. By the time he was in the senior form he spoke about the school with intense reverence.

'I verily believe my whole being is regularly soaked through with the wishing and hoping and striving to do the school good . . .' (20 January, 1836. *Correspondence of A. H. Clough*, Vol. I, p. 35).

Clough never lost the moral scrupulousness fundamental to a Rugby training, even though in the ten years after leaving the school he rejected almost all the particular intellectual positions he had held so unquestioningly while there. Like so many mid-nineteenth century intellectuals, he went through a crisis in religious belief and a period of intense disillusionment with the values of his society. In the long poems written during this time, *The Bothie of Tober-na-Vuolich* (1848), *Amours de Voyage* (1849) and *Dipsychus* (1849–50), the evidence of mental and emotional strain is increasingly obvious.

Clough's period of anxiety began when he was plunged into the theological controversy of the Oxford or Tractarian Movement which was at its height at the time he went up to Oxford in 1837. Dr. Arnold was bitterly opposed to the ideas of John Henry Newman, the leader of the Oxford Movement (which attempted to bring the Anglican Church closer to the Catholic tradition, emphasising accordingly the authority of the Church and the importance of dogma, rather than the Protestant ideas of the responsibility of the individual conscience and private judgement in spiritual matters), and Clough was drawn into the controversy 'like a straw drawn up the draught of a chimney'. The effect of this intensive intellectual upheaval and preoccupation with fundamental religious questions was eventually to undermine *all* his beliefs. To the end of his life Clough felt the need, a need made more acute by his sensitive Rugby conscience, to analyse and re-think every position, in any sphere, religious, political or social. In religion this habit was particularly strong. In his essay on Clough, Walter Bagehot, who knew him, described his temperament in this way: 'If you offer them any known religion they 'won't have that'; if you offer them no religion they will not have that either; if you ask them to accept a new and as yet unrecognised religion, they altogether refuse to do so. They seem not only to believe in an 'unknown God', but in a God whom no man can ever know.' (*Literary Studies*, 1879, Vol. II). Clough's academic achievement also suffered from the distractions of theology, and he did not get the First Class degree expected of him. ('I have failed', he said dramatically to Dr. Arnold after walking from Oxford to Rugby on this occasion). He redeemed himself, however, by winning a fellowship to Oriel College in 1842.

Clough's time at Oxford was not happy; towards the end of his undergraduate career, his father's business began to fail; in June, 1842, Dr. Arnold died; his brother George and his father died shortly afterwards, and in October, 1848, he voluntarily ended his term at Oxford by resigning his fellowship on the grounds that he could no longer make the subscription to the Thirty Nine Articles required by University Statutes. Oxford, nevertheless, was a time of freedom in comparison with his later experiences. At Oxford, he consolidated a lasting friendship with Thomas and Matthew Arnold (particularly with Matthew, the poet), sons of Dr. Arnold. He was an active member of the Decade, an intimate debating club, and in the long vacations went on reading parties to the Lake District or Scotland. These carefree occasions gave him material for his first long poem, *The Bothie of Tober-na-Vuolich* (1848).

After he left Oxford, Clough's life was unsettled until he

married Blanche Smith, a cousin of Florence Nightingale, in 1854. He spent a brief and lonely time in London from 1849 to 1852 where he was in charge of University Hall, a residential Hall for students of University College, London. This period was the nadir of his life. 'He shut himself up and went through his life in silence', his wife wrote of him. Finally, he left University Hall because of difficulties with the authorities over religious observance there, and emigrated to America in 1852, intending to live by writing and teaching at Cambridge, Massachusetts. This was not easy (his largest commission was the drudging task of revising that translation of Plutarch's 'Lives', known as Dryden's) so he returned to England in 1853, and his friends found him a minor post in the Education Office. This post enabled him to marry, but even now he was overwhelmed by work, and with astonishing selflessness he voluntarily increased the strain on his health by assisting his exacting cousin, Florence Nightingale, in her charitable work. Travel abroad in the last year of his life did not restore his health, and he died in Florence in 1861.

The detailed record of Clough's life might at first suggest that he was dogged by misfortune. Yet in spite of the considerable information that exists, and Clough's extensive correspondence, it is difficult to be certain that he was radically damaged by his misfortunes, for his personality is an enigma. His letters, for instance, are in the main so impersonal and toneless that disappointingly little emerges from them (he is exceptionally evasive, for example, about the true nature of his religious problems, and even his love letters are outstanding only for their uncompromising reserve). Though there are letters to a great number of important literary and intellectual figures—Matthew Arnold, Carlyle, Emerson, Froude, Charles Eliot Norton, Jowett, Kingsley—it is difficult to deduce from them why he should have been so highly respected by these men. Even his contemporaries were puzzled by him. This description by Thomas Arnold is hardly informative. It is hesitant, as if

Arnold were aware that he had not completely understood Clough's personality:

> His clear black eyes, under a broad, full and lofty forehead, were often partly closed as if through the pressure of thought; but when the problem occupying him was solved a glorious flash would break from his eyes, expressive of an inner joy and sudden illumination . . . His mouth was beautifully formed, but both it and the chin were characterised by some lack of determination and firmness. This deficiency, however, so far as it existed, was harmful only to himself; those who sought his counsel or help found him the wisest of advisers, the steadiest and kindest of friends.
>
> (Thomas Arnold, *The Nineteenth Century*, 1898).

In the absence of convincing accounts of Clough's personality, conjecture is inevitable. Until recently, the picture of him has been unfortunate and over-simplified, and this may well have discouraged the reading of his poetry. He has been caricatured as the first and quint-essential product of the English public school system (for example, by Lytton Strachey in *Eminent Victorians*); certainly to be mentioned in *Tom Brown's Schooldays*, that naively pious schoolboys' epic of Rugby life under Dr. Arnold, as 'our own Rugby poet', is almost enough to justify such a picture. Alternatively, critics have followed the account of Clough presented in 'Thyrsis', Matthew Arnold's elegy on him. 'Thyrsis', while epitomising Clough as the Victorian intellectual defeated by the dilemmas of his generation, has been far too influential:

> Some life of men unblest
> He knew, which made him droop, and fill'd his head.
> He went; his piping took a troubled sound
> Of storms that rage outside our happy ground;
> He could not wait their passing, he is dead.

'Thyrsis', as even Arnold admitted, is a highly selective account of Clough. Yet his portrait of Clough as the poet of a kind of low seriousness, radically unsettled by anxiety, nagging inconclusively at intellectual problems, has prevailed. Arnold's criticisms have some relevance but they are exaggerated; the neurotic Clough of 'Thyrsis' needs to be modified. Fortunately, this corrective is to be found in an analysis of Clough's poetry by his contemporary, R. H. Hutton. Hutton usefully compares Clough's poetry with that of Matthew Arnold. He recognises that Clough could be over-introspective, but:

> With all his intellectual precision, there is a something of the boyishness, of the simplicity, of the vascular Saxon breadth of Chaucer's poetry in Clough . . . There are both flesh and spirit, as well as emotion and speculation . . . Clough's is the tenderness of earthly sympathy . . . Both [Arnold and Clough] fill half their poems with the most subtle intellectual meditations; but Clough leaves the problems he touches on all but where they were, re-proaching himself for mooning over them so long . . . Finally, when they both reach their highest poetical point, Mr. Arnold is found painting lucidly in a region of pure and exquisite sentiment, Clough singing a sort of paean of buoyant and exultant strength.
>
> (*Theological and Literary Essays* (1877), Vol. II, p. 256.)

The 'buoyant and exultant strength' described by Hutton has to be constantly invoked to balance the melancholy threnody of *Thyrsis*, for Clough's poetry has firmly positive qualities; it is at once sensitive and sturdy; a strong poetry, permeated with humane objectivity and realism. It is often broadly humorous, brilliantly witty and ironic.

An examination of two of Clough's poems, 'O Land of Empire, art and love!' and 'Say not the struggle nought availeth' will show how assessments of Clough's work as widely apart as those of Arnold and Hutton were possible. It will also serve as an introduction to a general discussion of his work.

(ii) TWO POEMS

'O land of Empire, art and love!' is ostensibly a satire on over-delicacy, but the purpose of the satire is to develop by implication a social theory of art which is deliberately unsentimental and anti-romantic, and which, as will become clear, defends the whole range and subject matter of Clough's poetry. The opening at once establishes the poet's firm common sense and lack of squeamishness. With uninhibited irony, it satirises the uneasy English tourist in Italy, who is alarmed to find that his aesthetic enjoyment of Italian art and culture is spoiled by the squalor of their setting. Clough mocks the tourist's accents:

> Yet, boy, that nuisance why commit
>   On this Corinthian column? . . .
> . . . Are these the fixed condition
> On which may Northern pilgrim come
> To imbibe thine ether-air, and sum
>   Thy store of old tradition?
> Must we be chill, if clean, and stand
> Foot-deep in dirt in classic land?

As the poem proceeds, the Corinthian column described in the introduction is seen to be the symbol for a work of art, and the physical squalor represents the whole life— sordid and crude as well as refined—of the society which produces a work of art. By using a further analogy between art and a growing flower (thereby bringing in the ideas of vitality and nourishment), Clough makes it clear that art and society must have a symbiotic relation one with another. A healthy art can develop only when it draws upon the whole life of its environment, just as a flower draws upon the earth.

> From homely roots unseen below . . .
> The stem that bears the etherial flower
> Derives that emanative power;
> From mixtures fetid foul and sour
> Draws juices that those petals fill.

Matthew Arnold was to say that poetry is 'at bottom a criticism of life'. In this poem Clough forestalled him and went even further by saying that poetry is primarily a criticism of *everyday* life and society also. It must accept the whole of life, and be firmly related to the solid facts of day-to-day existence. When in 1853 he wrote his *Review of some poems by Alexander Smith and Matthew Arnold*, Clough urgently demanded a new realism, a poetry dealing 'with general wants, ordinary feelings, the obvious rather than the rare facts of human nature', and with 'positive matters of fact'. His own poetry fulfils these demands. In the poetic form particularly suited to describing the domestic affairs of everyday life, the verse novel, he dealt sanely and frankly with love, sex, personal relations. In his poems appear the 'obvious' surroundings and situations of contemporary life: reading parties in Scotland (*The Bothie*), tourism in Europe (*Amours de Voyage*). His theory plainly committed him to write of contemporary problems—social, political and religious—and accordingly he wrote of the siege of Rome in 1849, Chartist ideas, equality, the relation of rich and poor, Strauss and German Biblical criticism. Arnold was particularly disturbed by Clough's willingness to discuss contemporary problems because he felt that it would increase the tendency to morbid intellectuality which, as 'Thyrsis' shows, he considered the flaw of his poetry; but Clough's theory was based on a firm and realistic acceptance of things. It is not surprising that in the review just quoted, he stated a preference for the 'real flesh and blood' of the minor poet, Alexander Smith, in comparison with the fastidiousnes of his friend Matthew Arnold.

'Say not the struggle nought availeth' is Clough's most famous poem.

> Say not the struggle nought availeth,
>   The labour and the wounds are vain,
> The enemy faints not, nor faileth,
>   And as things have been, things remain.
>
> If hopes were dupes, fears may be liars;
>   It may be, in yon smoke concealed,
> Your comrades chase e'en now the fliers,
>   And, but for you, possess the field.

For while the tired waves, vainly breaking,
    Seem here no painful inch to gain,
Far back through creeks and inlets making
    Came, silent, flooding in, the main,

And not by eastern windows only,
    When daylight comes, comes in the light,
In front the sun climbs slow, how slowly,
    But westward, look, the land is bright.

The rejection of defeatism is Clough's most insistent theme. For all his commitment to facts, he was determined never to be defeated by them. The old, well-worn metaphor of battle could easily lead to facile optimism and superficial heroics, but there are none here. Instead, with a peculiarly firm diffidence, he states that fear, just as much as hope, can be deceptive. The very structure of the lines reflects an empirical balance in the thought and precludes attitudinising—'If hopes were dupes, fears may be liars'. 'Say not' is Clough's celebration of a heroic ideal, and yet is rooted in common sense reality. Its strength is that it holds the two moods in equipoise. There is a tension between the sense of achievement, and certain triumph, and the weariness, of dogged, tired effort—'For while the tired waves, vainly breaking . . .' The emotional force of this image is just prevented from dominating the whole poem. It does not counteract the equally powerful rejection of defeat.

This finely adjusted balance is not always achieved in Clough's poetry, and therefore the criticisms in 'Thyrsis', over-stated as they are, cannot altogether be displaced by Hutton's 'buoyant and exultant strength'. Bagehot felt that Dr. Arnold's pupils suffered from 'a fatigued way of looking at great subjects'; certainly, some poems ('Easter Day II' among the short poems, and *Dipsychus* among the long poems), state the intellectual meaning that it is worth 'going on', and yet the general mood of the poem suggests that it is not.

The order in which Clough wrote his poems is not the

order in which they were published. Therefore, before discussing *Ambarvalia*, his earliest work, it is convenient to give a brief chronology in order of publication (omitting the occasional prose pieces, the most important of which were published in *Poems and Prose Remains of A. H. Clough*, 1869, and which are only of relevance in so far as they bear upon his poetry). *The Bothie of Tober-na-Vuolich* appeared in 1848. *Ambarvalia*, a joint production of Clough and Thomas Burbidge*, was published in 1849, though the poems in it were written before *The Bothie*. *Amours de Voyage* first appeared in *The Boston Atlantic Monthly* in 1858, though it was written during 1849. *Dispychus*, published posthumously in 1865, belongs to the same period of composition as *Amours de Voyage*. *Mari Magno*, Clough's last poem, a succession of brief, linked narratives, was composed in 1861 and first appeared in a cut version in 1862. There are a number of shorter poems, and the unfinished *Mystery of the Fall*, belonging to the same period as *Amours de Voyage* and *Dipsychus*.

II AMBARVALIA, 1849

'Why should I say I see the things I see not?'

The title of this volume of poems, *Ambarvalia*, refers to the annual festival in ancient Rome during which the fields and boundaries were purified. It seems to have been chosen as a gesture of modesty, for the festival had homely, agricultural associations. Yet Clough's contributions to the volume have none of the parochialism the title was meant to imply. In comparison with Burbidge's poems, Clough's (written for the most part during his time at Oxford) have an intellectual grip and maturity which are unusual. Burbidge's pieces are capable enough—mild, gentlemanly productions, carefully worked out and sincerely felt—but

---

* Thomas Burbidge (1816-92), was a poet and clergyman. Clough's friendship with him began at Rugby School.

Clough's are imaginatively and intellectually superior because they possess that 'buoyant and exultant strength' which was with him from the beginning.

> Beside me—in the car—she sat,
>   She spake not, no, nor looked at me:
> From her to me, from me to her,
>   What passed so subtly stealthily? . . .
>
>   Yet owned we, fused in one,
>   The Power which e'en in stones and earths
> By blind elections felt, in forms
>   Organic breeds to myriad births;
> By lichen small on granite wall
>   Approved, its faintest feeblest stir
> Slow-spreading, strengthening long, at last
>   Vibrated full in me and her.
>
> ('Natura Naturans')

There is an exhilarating response here to those ordinary facts of human life which were already important to Clough. The poet simply meets a girl on a train. With joyful frankness Clough celebrates the physical awareness between them, and then, in a sudden and imaginative enlargement of vision, he shows that the experience gave him insight into the significance of evolution. The slow generation of species culminated in human love and love is the energy working in creation. The muscular strength of the alliteration conveys a sense of fecundity.

> Flashed flickering forth fantastic flies,
>   Big bees their burly bodies swung . . .
>   The leopard lithe in Indian glade,
> And dolphin, brightening tropic seas,
>   In us were living, leapt and played.

All the poems in *Ambarvalia* manifest Clough's strength; his expressions of moral responsibility have a firmness, a quiet integrity and eloquence. There is the sober, urgent dignity of 'Qui laborat orat', in which Clough says that genuine prayer expresses itself as action in practical life, an early statement of an habitual theme. Or there is the poised gravity of 'Qua cursum ventus':

> To veer, how vain! On, onward strain,
>   Brave barks! In light, in darkness too,
> Through winds and tides one compass guides—
>   To that, and your own selves, be true.

Something more distinguishes Clough's poems—a theme. The aggressive 'Why should I say I see the things I see not?' is a key line. The poems defend intellectual honesty; implicitly or explicitly they claim the right to question, the right to be sceptical, demanding enquiry and analysis in every sphere. There is the iconoclastic poem on duty, where Clough attacks social convention because it restricts intellectual and moral freedom:

> Ready money of affection
>   Pay, whoever drew the bill.
> With the form conforming duly,
> Senseless what it meaneth truly,
> Go to church—the world require you,
>   To balls—the world require you too . . .
> Duty—'tis to take on trust
>   What things are good, and right, and just.
>   ('Duty—that's to say complying')

In another poem on religion he examines the possibility of belief or non-belief alike with conscientious distrust, and reiterates an honest scepticism rather than the honest doubt which Tennyson later professed in *In Memoriam*:

> Receive it not, but leave it not,
>   And wait it out, O Man!
>
>   ('When Israel came out of Egypt')

In this constant intellectual analysis, Clough transferred his Rugby scrupulousness to all areas of experience. He once wrote that he wanted to escape 'the vortex of Philosophism' at Oxford, yet 'Philosophism' is germane to these poems. In the more mature longer poems he turned it to further artistic advantage, and evolved a highly successful technique for presenting 'Philosophism' in verse.

III THE LONGER POEMS:

The Bothie of Tober-na-Vuolich
Amours de Voyage
Dipsychus

(i) 'Myself my own experiment'

'. . . but you know you are a mere d — d depth hunter in poetry', Arnold wrote to Clough in a letter of 24 May 1848, shortly before the publication of *The Bothie*. He was objecting to the predominance of 'thinking aloud' in Clough's poetry, but in accusing him of trying to 'solve the universe', and in interpreting this as a sign of weakness, Arnold underrated Clough's self-consciousness and intelligence, failing to grasp that in these poems, reasoning is not only a procedure but a theme. All these poems, though they otherwise differ, have a common theme—that of the intellectual temperament itself.

In *Ambarvalia* Clough insisted on the primacy of analysis and enquiry but he understood its dangers. He early recognised his own tendency to what he called in a letter of 26 August, 1837, 'double-mindedness', a faculty for analysing problems so minutely and fairly that what started as a discipline in empirical honesty ended as vacillating inconclusiveness. Asserting his pragmatic commitment to 'positive matters of fact' in the long poems, he satirised any kind of gratuitous theorising (whether it took the form of abstract speculation or introspection). The long poems are brilliant studies in the psychology of intellectuals.

Clough regarded the over-analytic temperament seriously

enough to make it the crux of the unfinished *Mystery of the Fall* where it is the salient characteristic of fallen man. Adam exults in reasoning and self-analysis because the 'curious seething process' of introspection makes him intellectually autonomous—'myself my own experiment'. But Eve condemns the interminable 'thinkings and cross-thinkings' which began with self-consciousness. These 'thinkings and cross-thinkings' are dramatised in the long poems. The hero of *The Bothie*, Philip, is the victim of his own over-impulsive theorising. Claude, the hero of *Amours de Voyage*, is betrayed by his fastidious introspections, and the hero of *Dipsychus* has an almost pathological conscientiousness.

Though Arnold and Clough seem to be diametrically opposed as to poetic principles, their diagnosis of the vitiating intellectual habit of the nineteenth century was the same; they agree that this habit was a morbid 'dialogue of the mind with itself', as Arnold called it in the preface to his own poems of 1853. Arnold tried to eradicate it altogether from his poetry; Clough deliberately explored it. In doing so he avoided morbidity (two of the poems are straightforward comedies) by means of presenting the psychology of the analytic mind dramatically; '. . . it is both critically best and morally safest to dramaticize [sic] your feelings where they are of private personal character', he wrote in a letter of 7 July, 1838, early in his poetic career. In the three long poems, Clough greatly developed the 'dramaticizing' method, and the dramaticizing technique creates the effect of impersonal, objective presentation. Further, the dramatic presentation allows him to pack these poems with energy and life because his intellectuals soliloquise in a concrete, vividly delineated environment, surrounded by characters as much individualised as themselves. The sense of locality is so strong that the characters never become detached from their contexts. In *Amours de Voyage* ,which is set in Rome, the topography of Rome and its surroundings is never allowed to become indistinct:

Ye, too, Ye marvellous Twain, that erect on Monte Cavallo
Stand by your rearing steeds in the grace of your
motionless movement,
Stand with your upstretched arms and tranquil
regardant faces,
Stand as instinct with life in the might of immutable
manhood,—

These long poems are Clough's major achievement and
culminate in the *tour de force* of *Dipsychus*, where Clough
treated the theme of the intellectual with more seriousness,
if with more pessimism, than in the other poems.

(ii)   *Intellectuals ebullient*

The Bothie of Tober-na-Vuolich and *Amours de Voyage*

These two poems, both verse novels written in hexameters, are predominantly comic studies of intellectuals.
The Bothie is a mock heroic account of an undergraduate
reading party or vacation study group in Scotland. Philip,
the hero, is full of unrealistic radical and egalitarian ideas
which lead him particularly to sentimentalise working class
women. Slipping away from his companions while on a
walking tour, he has an eminently rash flirtation with a
servant girl, Katie. His disappointment over this affair
drives him to the other extreme, and he has an equally
unsuccessful flirtation with an heiress, Lady Maria. His
friends and tutor hear rumours of his activities with suspense
and puzzlement shared by the reader. Finally, he falls
genuinely in love with Elspie, a poor Highland girl, daughter
of the owner of the 'bothie' or hut, named in the title of
the poem. As he achieves emotional maturity and a sense
of responsibility in personal relationships, so he begins to
hold his political ideas with more realism. The two processes
are interdependent.

Amours de Voyage is in letter form. Claude, the hero,
happens to visit Rome during Mazzini's defence of the

Roman republic when the French besieged Rome in 1849. He is thrown into the company of the Trevellyns, an English family also travelling. He loses the opportunity to propose to their daughter, Mary, who loves him, by examining his state of mind so lengthily that she leaves Rome before he has completed his self-analysis. Claude can make up his mind about nothing; 'Il doutait de tout, même de l'amour', runs one of the epigraphs to the poem.

In each poem the intellectual and his characteristics emerge fully from the narrative. Wit is an almost obligatory part of the intellectual's equipment, and Clough exploited the intellectual's wit and wrote from within its own terms—its jokes, epigrams, aphorisms, its ebullient delight in sheer sophisticated cleverness, or its effervescent, extravagant indulgence in undergraduate humour. The humour of these poems is always the humour of the educated. Clough understood the humour of the intellectual mentality so well that he reproduced with remarkable authenticity the educated voice, speaking from the intellectual's exclusive world of assured knowledge, and easy, almost negligent intelligence. When the undergraduates of *The Bothie* decide to abandon their studies temporarily, they dismiss the classics with an absurd, exhilarated mock-rhetorical apostrophe which only a knowledge of the classics could have allowed them to make:

> Slumber in Liddell-and-Scott, O musical chaff
> of old Athens,
> Dishes, and fishes, bird, beast, and sesquipedalian
> blackguard!
> Sleep, weary ghosts, be at peace and abide in your lexicon-
> limbo!

Claude, the hero of *Amours de Voyage*, analyses Italian art and culture in knowledgeable, elegant arabesques of wit as he wanders in Rome. 'Rome disappoints me much', he says. '*Rubbishy* seems the word that most exactly would suit it.'

What do I find in the Forum? An archway and
                two or three pillars.
Well, but St. Peter's? Alas, Bernini has filled
                it with sculpture!
... Yet of solidity much, but of splendour little is
                extant:
'Brickwork I found thee, and marble I left thee!'
                their Emperor vaunted:
'Marble I thought thee, and brickwork I find thee!'
                the Tourist may answer.

All the freedom of comment, irreverence and iconoclastic allusion in these poems is achieved by exploiting the voice of the intellectual.

The dramatic situations of *The Bothie* and *Amours de Voyage* are the same—the intellectual in love—and yet the two poems are very different. *The Bothie*, despite its searching criticism of Philip's ideals, is a young man's idyll, while *Amours de Voyage* is a mature and highly finished satire. Accordingly, in *Amours de Voyage* elegant verbal sharpness supersedes the boisterous mock-heroic verse of *The Bothie*. Yet the boisterousness of *The Bothie* gives the poem its distinctive 'buoyant and exultant' energy. Clough parodies epic description with exuberance; he makes one young man dress for dinner in the 'waistcoat work of a lady', and another in a 'shirt as of crochet of women' as if they were elaborately arming for battle. The best swimmer in the company becomes heroically 'the Glory of Headers'. And yet this mocking syntax, which sounds like a pedantically literal translation, moves easily into the lyrical phrasing of 'perfection of water' when Clough describes the pool used by the group for bathing:

> where beads of foam uprising
> Mingle their clouds of white with the delicate hue of the
>   stillness.

Clough never allows the poem to lose buoyancy. The

grave advice of the young man's tutor, Adam, is juxtaposed with a flippant discussion of women put into the terminology of Gothic architecture—the 'sculliony stumpy-columnar', the 'Modern-Florid, modern-fine-lady'. When Philip laments over Katie, feeling that he has deserted her too brutally, his sad reiterations—'Would I were dead, I keep saying, that so I could go and uphold her!'—are followed immediately by a gay account of a Highland reel, 'swinging and flinging, and stamping and tramping, and grasping and clasping'.

The gaiety of *The Bothie*, is mitigated in *Amours de Voyage*; here Clough presents the fastidious introspections of Claude, the over-selfconscious intellectual, with particularly cutting satire. Claude is so intellectually scrupulous, witty, sensitive, cleverly cruel, that he reduces all experience to bathos. When he exclaims 'Hang this thinking!', he inadvertently defines his own weakness. His habit of analysis is a defence against what he calls 'the factitious'. He is so afraid of the factitious that he cannot believe even in his own emotion.

'I am in love, you say: I do not think so, exactly.'

The line—a lingering half-denial followed by a half-retraction—is the epitome of equivocation. In the comedy of the statement, with its scrupulous phraseology, and the final outrageous pseudo-precision of 'exactly', Clough does not disguise Claude's chronic inability to commit himself.

As a self-conscious study in self-consciousness, *Amours de Voyage* is a kind of nineteenth century '*Love song of J. Alfred Prufrock*'. In both poems, the mixture of wit and poignancy, comedy and pain, comes from the protagonist's never quite successful attempt to control emotions by reducing their importance. Claude's intellectual posturings and defensive detachment are shared by Eliot's hero. The protagonists of both poems have a faculty for dismissing themselves with self-deprecating irony, a sort of supercilious verbal shrug.

I grow old . . . I grow old . . .
I shall wear the bottoms of my trousers rolled.

('Prufrock')

After all, perhaps there was something factitious about it;
I have had pain, it is true; have wept; and so have the actors.

Amours de Voyage, however cutting its satire, is not a harsh poem. It is constantly lightened by the brilliant verbal extravagance of Claude himself: 'After endeavouring idly to minister balm to the trembling Quinquagenarian fears of two lone British spinsters'—thus he describes his gallantry during the siege. Clough broadens the poem by presenting other characters beside Claude, and by treating Mary's feelings with genuine sympathy. Mary's typically Victorian family, naive middle class tourists who create their unmistakeably British ethos with complete assurance wherever they go, are refreshingly normal. Her sister, Georgina, engaged to the 'tender domestic' Vernon, is particularly appealing, chattering her way through Rome with artless superficiality:

Rome is a wonderful place . . .
Not very gay, however; the English are mostly
at Naples;
There are the A.'s, we hear, and most of the W. party.

Mary herself ends the poem, determining to forget Claude in sad but sane resignation. 'You have heard nothing [of Claude]; of course, I know you can have heard nothing', she writes to a friend. Her resignation puts the action of the poem in proportion, a proportion provided also by the short lyrics which head each canto. These, recalling in warm and tender lyricism the ancient Rome of gods and heroes which 'Lives in the exquisite grace of column disjointed and single', are set against the tensions of the siege, and the emotional problems of the central characters.

Over the great windy waters, and over the clear-crested
summits,
Unto the sun and the sky, and unto the perfecter
earth,
Come, let us go,—to a land wherein gods of the old time
wandered,
Where every breath even now changes to ether
divine.

(iii) Dipsychus—The intellectual agonistes

Dipsychus is set in Venice, and consists of a series of soliloquies and dialogues between Dipsychus and a character designated as 'Spirit', as they wander through Venice. 'Dipsychus' translated means 'double-minded', and the double-mindedness of Dipsychus is of the moral sort. 'Now the over-tender conscience will, of course, exaggerate the wickedness of the world', Clough wrote in the Epilogue to *Dipsychus*. Dipsychus is divided against himself because his moral scruples prevent him from deciding on any course of action in the morally degenerate society (as he interprets it) in which he lives. The Spirit, always in opposition to Dipsychus, represents this materialist society, the society of mid-nineteenth century Europe.

'I could have gone cracked . . .' was Clough's comment on his state of mind during the time he composed *Dipsychus*, and the poem has none of the free assurance behind *The Bothie* and *Amours de Voyage*. Its equivalent to their wit is a tone of corroding mockery and tragic cynicism:

I dreamt a dream; till morning light
A bell rang in my head all night,
Tinkling and tinkling first, and then
Tolling; and tinkling; tolling again.
So brisk and gay, and then so slow!
O joy, and terror! mirth, and woe!
Ting, ting, there is no God; ting, ting—
Dong, there is no God; dong,
There is no God; dong, dong!

Dipsychus is a study of the mental and spiritual crisis of the contemporary Victorian intellectual, and voices the sense of loss—loss of belief, loss of confidence in the values of society—which fills so much of Victorian poetry. The intellectual's dilemma in *Dipsychus* is that his values run counter to the values of society so that he is in moral isolation. He is able to diagnose but not to remedy the limitations of his society and the predicament is demoralising. Since it has this wide reference, *Dipsychus* is more ambitious than the other long poems, though it was never finished.

The opposition between the intellectual and his society is displayed by means of counterpoint. Throughout the poem Dipsychus's despair of society and the Spirit's cynical acceptance of it create a counterpoint of moods and attitudes. Deep emotion alternates with callousness, just as in the elegy quoted above, which alternates lightness and resonance

> 'Ting, ting, there is no God; ting, ting—
> Dong, there is no God, dong . . .'

Clough allows the Spirit to voice among other things the materialist attitudes which he particularly wanted to attack; and the Spirit, a cheerfully insensitive philistine, subjects all major questions—sex, class, religion—to a coarse irony:

> . . . Once in a fortnight say, by lucky chance
> Of happier-tempered coffee, gain (Great Heaven!)
> A pious rapture.
>
> Why as to feelings of devotion—
> I interdict all vague emotion.
>
> They may talk as they please about what they call pelf,
> And how one ought never to think of one's self,
> And how pleasures of thought surpass eating and drinking—
> My pleasure of thought is the pleasure of thinking
>   How pleasant it is to have money, heigh ho!
>   How pleasant it is to have money.

This satire is a continuation of Clough's attacks on commercial values begun in *The Bothie* and extended in short poems such as 'In the Great Metropolis', with its savage jig-like refrain 'The devil take the hind most, O!' (Clough was radical enough to be addressed by his friends as 'Citizen Clough'). In *Dipsychus* the satire is deepened and supplemented by the profounder despairing commentary of Dipsychus himself. He cannot share the common sense of the Spirit who will recognize a vague and ill-defined God when distress or trouble force him to take refuge in belief.

> And almost every one when age,
> Disease, or sorrows strike him,
> Inclines to think there is a God,
> Or something very like Him.

Dipsychus feels too intensely the loss of firm Christian morality and religious feeling.

> O pretty girl who trippest along,
> Come to my bed—it isn't wrong.
> Uncork the bottle, sing the song!
> Ting, ting a ding: dong, dong.
> Wine has dregs; the song an end;
> A silly girl is a poor friend
> And age and weakness who shall mend?
> Dong, there is no God; Dong!

Dipsychus's statements have a dramatic immediacy because of their directly topical implications, yet their seriousness gives the poem more than topical relevance.

The antagonism between Dipsychus and the Spirit represents more than the antagonism between the intellectual and his society. The satire in the poem has a double focus, and the opposition between the two characters serves a further purpose. It represents the conflict of an over-sensitive conscience (Dipsychus might have been a product of Dr. Arnold's Rugby) with instinct and impulse, the animal side of man which Dipsychus regards with unnecessary dread and timidity. In this sense the poem is a dialogue between soul and body, taking place within Dipsychus himself. However superficial the Spirit's morality, he has the reasonableness of the natural man eminently lacking in Dipsychus. His flippant Gilbertian rhymes and neat satiric couplets embody some precise and acute comment, and he speaks the most energetic verse in the poem:

> These juicy meats, this flashing wine,
> May be an unreal mere appearance;
> Only—for my inside, in fine,
> They have a singular coherence.
>
> This lovely creature's glowing charms
> Are gross illusion, I don't doubt that;
> But when I pressed her in my arms
> I somehow didn't think about that.
>
> * * *
>
> Thus life we see is wondrous odd,
> And so, we argue, may be God.
> At any rate, this rationalistic
> Half-puritano—semitheistic
> Cross of Neologist and mystic
> Is, of all doctrines, the least reasonable.

The spirit emphasises that Dipsychus makes his problems more acute by being intellectually and morally effete. Fastidiously afraid of being contaminated by the vices of 'the world', he is too much inhibited by moral scruples, as Claude was by intellectual scruples. 'It's all Arnold's doing; he spoilt the public schools', grumbles the supposed uncle of the author who discusses the poem with him in the engaging epilogue to *Dipsychus*. He echoes a friend's criticism of Rugby boys—'They're all so pious'; the situation of Dipsychus makes his comment almost justifiable.

Dipsychus is the only one of Clough's poems to which the criticisms in 'Thyrsis' are applicable. The 'feeling of depression, the feeling of ennui', which Arnold described as the dominating mood of his generation are to be found in *Dipsychus* because it is infused with the self-pity it tries to objectify. *Dipsychus* opens with a specific reference to an earlier poem, 'Easter Day', an elegy on the general loss of Christian morality and religious feeling. The literal occurrence of the Resurrection in the past, Clough says there, is of minor importance compared with the necessity to practise Christian morality in the present:

> Weep not beside the Tomb
> Ye women ...
> Go to your homes, your living children tend,
> Your earthly spouses love;
> Set your affections *not* on things above ...

This shows signs of the influence of Carlyle, whose early essays, with their doctrine of work ('Do the Duty which lies nearest to thee.') Clough read enthusiastically as an undergraduate. Clough's confidence in these ideas had lessened by the time he wrote *Dipsychus*. Perhaps, as Bagehot suggests, those 'terrible notions of duty' (*Amours de Voyage*) instilled by Dr. Arnold proved too exhausting. The poem has some of that drudging weariness which is just controlled in 'Say not'. Though Dipsychus takes up the words of 'Easter Day' in the opening elegy—'Christ is not risen'—it has none of the implicit confidence asserted by the resonant phrasing of 'Easter Day'. In 'Easter Day' Clough rejected Christian myth but maintained hope in Christian morality and therefore there is a certain stoical grandeur in his rejection of the Resurrection, a grandeur lacking in *Dipsychus*, in spite of the profoundly elegiac quality of Dipsychus's laments, and the vigour of the Spirit's verse:

> Through the great sinful streets of Naples as I past,
> With fiercer heat than flamed above my head
> My heart was hot within me; till at last
> My brain was lightened, when my tongue had said

Christ is not risen!

Christ is not risen, no,
He lies and moulders low;
Christ is not risen.
     ('Easter Day').

(iv) *Clough's allegory of the commonplace in the long poems*

Arnold was too much of a purist fully to appreciate Clough's work. He wished to remove poetry as far as possible from the commonplace—a position exactly the opposite of Clough's. The essentials of poetry, Arnold wrote in 1853 (in the Preface to his own volume of poetry), were 'great actions, calculated powerfully and delightfully to affect what is permanent in the human soul'. The actions of Clough's poems—all local, topical and domestic— seemed to him to fall far short of these essentials. Yet Arnold was led to misread Clough. All Clough's long poems transcend a narrowly contemporary significance. To understand why it is necessary to return again to his emphasis on 'positive matters of fact'; the reiterated theme of those long poems is the importance of the commonplace. They all assert that life has to be lived actively and creatively in and through the commonplace. This is the equivalent of the 'great actions' proposed by Arnold. In Clough's poems the 'permanent' things are the commonplace emotions and activities of ordinary experience and practical life. Taken together, these poems are a protest against the devaluation of ordinary experience and this is the permanently relevant theme of Clough's poetry.

The long poems repeatedly show the fallacy of departing from 'positive matters of fact' (fact is a key word in them), and whatever the subject under discussion—love, religion, social criticism, politics—it is always checked against solid reality. Clough's imaginative perception of the possibilities of ordinary experience shows itself particularly when he uses a group of symbolic situations and images which he relates firmly to the commonplace facts of everyday life—battle, marriage, building, growing things. These gather significance as they are explored in the poems, sometimes appearing as metaphors, or literal situations in the poems may be simultaneously real and allegorical. Battle is one of the most significant symbols, and as in 'Say Not', Clough revivifies this well-worn image by giving it a precise application, particularly in *The Bothie* and *Amours de Voyage*, and exploring it with his customary sanity.

The battle symbol was particularly suitable for Clough's purpose; it implies a practical struggle in exacting circumstances, and he used it to show that the actuality of the commonplace must be accepted with similar action and vigour. Such an acceptance of the facts was to him a great and demanding exercise, and the heroic associations of battle endorse this idea—an idea condensed in 'Say not the struggle nought availeth'. In *The Bothie*, just as in 'Say not', the battle image is used to renounce defeatism. At the end of *The Bothie*, Philip, whose love for Elspie has given him new hopes and a new sense of responsibility, decides to give his social ideals a practical application. He regains vigour and energy, asking 'Where is the battle!'

> O where is the battle!
> Neither battle I see, nor arraying, nor king in Israel,
> Only infinite jumble and mess and dislocation,
> Backed by a solemn appeal, 'For God's sake do
> not stir, there!'

The decision to fight the 'infinite jumble' of society is supported by two metaphors of hope, the tide turning, and daylight gradually illuminating a drab town.

> As at return of tide the total weight of ocean,
> Drawn by moon and sun from Labrador and Greenland,
> Sets-in amain, in the open space betwixt Mull and Scarba,

Heaving, swelling, spreading, the might of the mighty
                Atlantic;
There into cranny and slit of the rocky, cavernous bottom
Settles down, and with dimples huge the smooth sea-surface
Eddies, coils, and whirls; by dangerous Corryvreckan:
So in my soul of souls through its cells and secret recesses,
Comes back, swelling and spreading, the old democratic
                fervour.

But as the light of day enters some populous city,
Shaming away, ere it come, by the chilly day-streak signal,
High and low, the misusers of night, shaming out the
                gas lamps—
All the great empty streets are flooded with broadening
                clearness,
Which, withal, by inscrutable simultaneous access
Permeates far and pierces to the very cellars lying in
Narrow high back-lane, and court, and alley of alleys . . .
—Such—in me, and to me, and on me the love of Elspie!

This passage, where the hexameters gather a magnificent
energy, is one of the finest sustained pieces Clough ever
wrote. The images of battle, sea and daylight are parallel
with those used in 'Say not', and they have identical
implications.

In *Amours de Voyage* the actual battle during the siege of
Rome takes on a symbolic meaning, and it is used to expose
Claude's habit of devaluating all important experience,
particularly the common experience of falling in love. When
Rome is besieged by the French, he asks of the Italians 'Will
they fight?' Will he himself fight? 'Am I prepared to lay
down my life for the British female?' he asks, wondering
whether he will assist the English women during the siege,
and the parodying tone immediately reduces an ethical
question to one of ironic good manners. By fighting against
the French in an unequal struggle, the Italians attempt on
the public, social level what Claude fails to attempt on the
personal level when he retreats from the responsibilities of
his love affair. Claude's literal refusal 'to lay down my life
for the British female' is also a metaphorical rejection of effort

and action not only in the sphere of personal relationships but in all spheres of experience, a refusal to fight the symbolic battle of *The Bothie* and 'Say not'. The battle in Clough's poetry always stands for commitment to experience and actuality. Clough's battle symbol contrasts sharply with Arnold's. His armies are not the 'ignorant armies' which 'clash by night' of Arnold's 'Dover Beach'.

(v) *'Grotesque'* style and *'hurry scurry anapaests'*

Arnold wrote, complaining of Clough's style, of 'A growing sense of the deficiency of the beautiful in your poems' (24 Feb., 1848). He complained thus well before the publication of *Ambarvalia*; when Clough adopted the hexameter he was generally unsympathetic. Much later he described elements of Clough's style as 'grotesque', and Clough's use of the hexameter must have seemed to him gratuitously inelegant.

> On the whole, we conclude the Romans won't do it,
> and I shan't.
> (*Amours de Voyage*)

Certainly, on first inspection the elements of Clough's style seem unpromising; the lines are built up by a simple grammar full of slack construction, relying on long series of unconnected adjectives, and on the simple connective expedient of 'and'; this ramifying grammar supports cumbersome words; the lines abound in repetition. Clough had his own conception of 'the beautiful', resting on the axiom that almost any word or expression, however ordinary or however grotesque, has potential poetic value, just as he recognised that almost any situation is capable of poetic treatment. From this basis he created an idiom of extraordinary sensitivity and expressiveness.

By far his most frequent poetic device is repetition—repetition of words, of phrases, repetition in the form of synonymous expressions. Yet it never becomes monotonous. In the following passage it creates a literal, understated lyricism, emerging unassumingly with sober beauty from the most ordinary details of description and from the most ordinary words:

> . . . where over a ledge of granite
> Into a granite basin the amber torrent descended;
> Beautiful, very, to gaze-in ere plunging; beautiful also,
> Perfect as picture, as vision entrancing that comes to the
> sightless,
> Through the great granite jambs the stream, the glen,
> and the mountain,
> Beautiful, seen by snatches at intervals of dressing,
> Morn after morn, unsought for, recurring;
> (*The Bothie of Tober-na-Vuolich*)

The most controversial element in Clough's poetry is his hexameter. The hexameter is a six stress line which, when it is unrhymed, can be used even more freely than blank verse, and Clough realised that he could create with it a supple line, full of modulations of phrasing. His hexameters are used to achieve informal, naturalistic speech rhythms. They sound casual, yet they demand as much technical skill as the disciplined satiric couplets spoken by the Spirit in *Dipsychus*. In the Prologue to *Dipsychus*, the supposed uncle of the author attacks his nephew's 'hurry scurry anapaests', and objects that there can be 'three or four ways of reading' every line, 'each as good and as much intended as the other'. But the author defends his refusal to keep to the metrical stress of the line and shows that the deviation is deliberate. And this calculated deviation is justified by the verse, for by it Clough achieved subtle shifts of emphasis, pauses, and delicate rhythmic effects. Such flexible irregularities make his hexameter a precise instrument. It can record the fussy volubility of Georgina, Mary Trevellyn's sister, in *Amours de Voyage*:

> Dear, I must really stop, for the carriage, they
> tell me, is waiting.

Or it can realise the slow movement of pauses and re-commencements as in the cadences of the following line. By its sheer phrasing, lyrically embodying Claude's involuntary enchantment with Mary Trevellyn, it achieves 'the beautiful':

> She goes,—therefore I go; she moves,—I move, not
> to lose her.

IV. MARI MAGNO—'On the great sea'

Mari Magno, resembling in structure Chaucer's *Canterbury Tales*, is a series of tales told by strangers travelling to America on a liner. The tales themselves are all of travel—in England and Scotland, on the continent, to the colonies. Travel is indeed related to the main theme of *Mari Magno*. All the stories are about love and marriage: the success or failure of personal relations; the physical travel and movement which the characters have to undertake represents the demands of changing experience. Clough used the tales in *Mari Magno* to ask: What is love? Does it work out in experience? How far is it dependent on circumstances? These are the questions behind his examination of adolescent love (The Lawyer's First Tale, The Clergyman's First Tale), love, marriage and sexual infidelity (The Clergyman's Second Tale), love, marriage and class (The Lawyer's Second Tale), love and chance, love and expedience (The American's Tale, The Mate's Story). Clough had also used travel with a semi-symbolic sense in the other poems; in *Amours de Voyage*, for instance, Claude decides to travel to Egypt, and his aimless travel reflects his vacillating temperament. Yet the travel motif is more dominant in *Mari Magno* because the poem is particularly concerned with the challenge of change.

Hutton's remark, 'Clough's is the tenderness of earthly sympathy' is particularly relevant to *Mari Magno*. A realistic tenderness and a kind of humane poignancy are the poem's shaping moods. These moods are not common in the long poems, though they emerge in short lyrics such as 'Les Vaches', a poem at once exquisite and sturdy, the reverie of a peasant girl as she drives the cows home and wonders how she and her lover will stand the test of time:

> Ah dear, and where is he, a year agone
> Who stepped beside and cheered us on and on?
> My sweetheart wanders far away from me,
> In foreign land or o'er a foreign sea.
> Home, Rose, and home, Provence and La Palie.
>
> . . . Or shall he find before his term be sped,
> Some comelier maid that he shall wish to wed?
> (Home, Rose, and home, Provence and La Palie,)
> For weary is work, and weary day by day
> To have your comfort miles on miles away.

With the same sensitive realism that underlies 'Les Vaches', Clough writes in *Mari Magno* of adultery, seduction, illegitimacy, the force of sexual desire. *Mari Magno* is distinguished from the other long poems by its subtle treatment of the emotions. This passage in the Clergyman's First Tale, where an adolescent boy first becomes aware of adult feeling, is characteristic of the poem:

> 'Emma', he called,—then knew that he was wrong,
> Knew that her name to him did not belong.
> Half was the colour mounted on her face,
> Her tardy movement had an adult grace.
> Her look and manner proved his feeling true,—
> A child no more, her womanhood she knew.
> Vexed with himself, and shamed, he felt . . .
> Something there was that from this date began,
> Within their bloods a common feeling ran.

The new tenderness in *Mari Magno* does not entirely compensate for the loss of other qualities. It is a retrospective poem. Habitual themes and situations reappear—an Oxford don falls in love with a Highland girl, a young man is unable to make up his mind about his feelings—and there is a loss of immediacy in the repetition. *Mari Magno* is deficient in comedy; though the lyric of the *Conducteur* (who cannot put love behind him in spite of middle age) in 'My Tale' is wryly humorous, the ebullient wit and iconoclasm of the early poems is absent. All in all, *Mari Magno* does not equal the achievement of the earlier long poems. Clough abandoned the 'dramaticizing' technique, and the poem lacks the vitality of the other poems because the characters no longer speak for themselves. He replaced the hexameter either with octosyllabic or heroic couplets, and by keeping strictly to the metrical stress he eliminated some of the elements which give life to his verse—variety of cadence, idiomatic tones. The plainness of the language is often flat, without its customary succinctness. It was as if he were determined that no device of style, no image or linguistic detail, should get between the reader and the reality of the human situations he describes. His desire for 'positive matters of fact' defeats the poetry in *Mari Magno* by making it factual.

V. CONCLUSION: *The Janus-poet*

It is difficult to assess Clough's work with any finality because of the paradoxes within it. He is in some ways a precursor of twentieth century poetry, yet some aspects of his work make it possible to discuss him as a poet within the eighteenth century tradition who found himself living in the nineteenth century. He has a special minor place in English poetry since he is a Janus-like poet, both retrospective and revolutionary.

By temperament empirical and pragmatic, eminently concerned with fact, objectivity and common sense,

Clough might seem emotionally and intellectually of the eighteenth century. His poetry is intelligent, witty and satiric; it is concerned with society as well as the poet's individual imagination; it has formal and verbal affinities with eighteenth century poetry. On the other hand, Clough was disturbed by a consciousness of disequilibrium and instability, and these have to be emphasised when he is considered as a precursor of modern poetry.

> . . . I see . . .
> Only infinite jumble and mess and dislocation.

The frustration with which the isolated intellectual views his society is the phenomenon of modern poetry; so is his response to this condition—analysis, the 'dialogue of the mind with itself'—and Clough acknowledged and responded to the modern situation in this way. In content, the inclusiveness and realism he demanded anticipated the modern poetry of the city, the urban and industrial environment; in technique, his hexameter achieved some of the rhythmical freedom of modern verse.

That Clough's poetry can be analysed in two ways points to the complexities of his work, its peculiar blend of sensitive commonsense, sturdiness and sophistication. If these qualities are puzzling, they make for endurance. Clough's work is still important and relevant. He was one of the first poets to write about the intellectual; the searching, buoyant sanity he brought to problems still familiar will always be refreshing. He was one of the few Victorian poets to be witty without writing 'comic' verse, and he is not witty alone but serious without being heavy, moving without being melodramatic. His most enduring quality proves to be what his wife called, rather anxiously, 'honest coarse strength and perception'. Though she added, 'can there not be strength without losing delicacy?', Clough's 'coarse strength' vindicates his poetry by giving it energy. Even Arnold, always Clough's most persistent critic, allowed him on this account the finest praise. Though he was writing about *The Bothie*, his remark applies to a great deal in Clough's work as a whole; it gives the reader, he said, 'the sense of having, within short limits of time, a large portion of human life presented to him, instead of a small portion'.

ARTHUR HUGH CLOUGH

A Select Bibliography

(Place of publication London, unless stated otherwise)

Note:

The bulk of the Clough MSS are in the Bodleian Library, Oxford. They were presented in 1959 by Miss Blanche Athena Clough and Miss Katherine Duff. Other documents are at Balliol College, Oxford, Oriel College, Oxford, and Dr. Williams Library, London. In America there are MSS in the Houghton Library, Harvard University, and some journals deposited with the Honnold Library, University of California. Particulars of Clough's MS notebooks and papers are given in the definitive edition of his POEMS (1951).

Bibliographies:

BIBLIOGRAPHIES OF TWELVE VICTORIAN AUTHORS, by T. G. Ehrsam and R. H. Deily. New York (1936)
—records only books and articles about Clough.
    A Supplement by J. G. Fucilla appeared in *Modern Philology*, XXXVII, 1939.
THE VICTORIAN POETS, A Guide to Research: edited by F. E. Faverty. Cambridge, Mass. (1956).
'Prose Works of Clough: A Check List and Calendar.' by W. E. Houghton in the *Bulletin of the New York Public Library*, 64. 1960
—this check-list will form Part 2 of a general bibliography on Clough which is to appear in 1963.

Collected Works:

THE RUGBY MAGAZINE, 2 vols. (1835-7)
—Clough edited six out of the eight issues of the Rugby School magazine. 17 poems and 13 articles by him are signed variously "T.Y.C.", "Z" and "A.V.".

Poems in the *Rugby Magazine* assumed to be Clough's:
'The Poacher of Dead Man's Corner, vol. 1, p.35 (July 1835); 'The Warrior's Last Fight, vol. 1, p.62(July 1835); 'Count Egmont', vol. 1, p. 160(October 1835); 'Sonnet I', 'Sonnet 4', vol. 1, p. 173, 175

(October 1835); 'I watched them from the Window', vol. 1, p. 308 (Jan. 1836); 'Song of the Hyperborean Maidens', vol. 1, p. 309 (Jan. 1836); 'To ———, on going to India', vol. 1, p. 320 (April 1836); 'The old man of Athens', vol. 1, p. 399 (April 1836); 'The Exordium of a very long Poem', vol. 1, p. 404 (April 1836); 'Lines', vol. 2, p. 74 (July 1836); 'An Answer to Memory', vol. 2, p. 132 (December 1836); 'An Incident', vol. 2, p. 135 (December 1836); 'Epilogue to the Sonnets' vol. 2, p. 284 (July 1837); 'Verses from the School House', vol. 2, p. 346 (November 1837); 'Rosabel's Dream', vol. 2, p. 361 (November 1837); 'To a Crab Tree', vol. 2, p. 397 (November 1837).

Prose in the *Rugby Magazine* assumed to be Clough's:
'Introductory', vol. 1, pp. 9-14 (July 1835); 'Ten Minutes before Locking Up', vol. 1, pp. 91-95 (July 1835); 'Macaulay's Battle of Ivry', vol. 1, pp. 123-132 (October 1835); 'October', vol. 1, pp. 199-205 (October 1835); 'School Society', vol. 1, pp. 207-215 (January 1836); 'A Long Talk', vol. 1, pp. 311-319 (April 1836); 'Henry Sinclair or, 'Tis Six Years Ago', vol. 2, pp. 56-61 (July 1836); 'May it please Your Royal Majesty', vol. 2, pp. 103-104 (July 1836); 'The Rugby Register', vol. 2, pp. 105-111 (December 1836); 'A Peripateticographical Article', vol. 2, pp. 223-234 (July 1837); 'Sonnets in the Abstract', vol. 2, pp. 270-274 (July 1837); 'Two Autumn Days in Athens', vol. 2, pp. 345-358 (November 1837); 'Address of Leave-Taking', vol. 2, pp. 398-400 (November 1837).

Collected Editions, Poetry and Prose (a selection):

POEMS, with a Memoir by F. T. Palgrave (1862)
—edited by the poet's wife. Second edition, enlarged, 1863; edited by C. Whibley, 1913.

LETTERS AND REMAINS (1865)
—privately printed. Contains the first complete version of 'Dipsychus'.

THE POEMS AND PROSE REMAINS, 2 vols. with a selection from his Letters and a Memoir, edited by his wife with J. A. Symonds (1869)
—reprinted 14 times before 1902. The Prose Remains were reprinted separately in 1888.

THE POETICAL WORKS: With a Memoir by F. T. Palgrave (1906)
—in the Muses' Library.

THE POEMS, edited by H. F. Lowry, A. L. P. Norrington, and F. L. Mulhauser, Oxford (1951)

—the definitive edition with Oxford English Texts from which all titles and quotations in the present essay have been taken.

Collected Prose (a selection):

PROSE REMAINS OF A. H. CLOUGH, with a selection from his letters and a memoir: edited by his wife (1888).

EMERSON–CLOUGH LETTERS, edited by H. F. Lowry and R. L. Rusk. Cleveland (1932).

CORRESPONDENCE, edited by F. L. Mulhauser, 2 vols., (1957).

Selected Works:

SELECTIONS FROM THE POEMS OF A. H. CLOUGH (1894)
—in the Golden Treasury Series.

THE BOTHIE AND OTHER POEMS, edited by E. Rhys (1896).

POEMS, including 'Ambarvalia', both versions of 'The Bothie', 'Amours de Voyage' etc., edited by H. S. Milford (1910)
—contains, in the editor's Preface, the best account of Clough's hexameters.

Separate Works:

THE LONGEST DAY: A Poem written at Rugby School (1836).

THE BOTHIE OF TOPER-NA-FUOSICH: A Long-Vacation Pastoral, Oxford (1848)
—Clough subsequently changed the title to "Tober-na-Vuolich" and a revised version of the poem appeared in Poems 1863.

AMBARVALIA: Poems by T. Burbidge and A. H. Clough (1849)
—Clough's contributions were re-issued as a separate volume (without a title leaf) in 1850.

AMOURS DE VOYAGE [first published serially in The Atlantic Monthly Boston, Mass., Feb.-May, 1858, and first printed as a whole in Poems, 1862.]

DICTIONARY OF GREEK AND ROMAN BIOGRAPHY AND MYTH, edited by W. Smith, 3 vols. (1844-49)
—Clough contributed seventy seven short biographies to the first two volumes. Each article is signed "A.H.C.".

ILLUSTRATIONS OF LATIN LYRICAL METRES. (Classical Museum, IV 1846). See "New Verses by Clough", by G. Tillotson (The Times Literary Supplement, June 18th, 1954).

POEMS AND BALLADS OF GOETHE. *Fraser's Magazine* LIX (1859). Review of "Poems and Ballads of Goethe", translated by W. E. Aytoun, D.C.L., and T. Martin (1859).

GREEK HISTORY FROM THEMISTOCLES TO ALEXANDER in a series of Lives from Plutarch. Revised and arranged (with a Preface) by A. H. Clough (1860).

PLUTARCH'S LIVES. The translation called Dryden's, corrected from the Greek and revised (with an introduction) by A. H. Clough, 5 vols. Boston (1864, 1874, 1876, 1902): edited by E. Rhys, 3 vols. Everyman's Library (1910).

Some Critical and Biographical Studies:

ON TRANSLATING HOMER, by M. Arnold (1861)
—contains some illuminating asides on *The Bothie.*

ESSAYS, THEOLOGICAL AND LITERARY II, by R. H. Hutton (1877)
—contains commentary on Clough.

LITERARY STUDIES II, by W. Bagehot (1879)
—contains a perceptive and sympathetic study of Clough.

ARTHUR HUGH CLOUGH: A MONOGRAPH, by S. Waddington (1883)
—the first full-length study.

LITERARY ESSAYS, by R. H. Hutton (1888).

PORTRAITS OF FRIENDS, by J. C. Shairp (1889)
—contains Shairp's contribution to the Memoir, prefixed to Poems and Prose Remains.

STUDIES IN INTERPRETATION, by W. H. Hudson (1896).

NEW ESSAYS TOWARDS A CRITICAL METHOD, by J. M. Robertson (1897).

FAITH AND DOUBT IN THE CENTURY'S POETS, by R. A. Armstrong (1898).

ENGLISH TALES IN VERSE, by C. H. Herford (1902).

MISCELLANEOUS ESSAYS AND ADDRESSES, by H. Sidgwick (1904).

BRIEF LITERARY CRITICISMS, by R. H. Hutton (1906).

ENGLISH LITERATURE IN ACCOUNT WITH RELIGION, by E. M. Chapman (1910).

FOUR POETS: Clough, Arnold, Rossetti, Morris, by S. A. Brooke (1913).

ESSAI SUR LA FORMATION PHISOSOPHIQUE DU POETE CLOUGH: Pragmatisme et Intellectualisme, par E. Guyot. Paris (1913).

ARTHUR HUGH CLOUGH, by J. I. Osborne (1920).

STUDIES IN VICTORIAN LITERATURE, by S. T. Williams. New York (1923).

EIGHT VICTORIAN POETS, by F. L. Lucas (1930).

POETRY AND THE CRITICISM OF LIFE, by W. H. Garrod (1931).

PORTRAITS, by D. MacCarthy (1931).

THE EIGHTEEN SIXTIES, edited by J. Drinkwater (1932)

—contains an essay on Clough by H. Wolfe. Wolfe develops a new approach to Clough and interprets him as outstandingly a satirical poet.

THE LONELY WAYFARING MAN, by T. Scudder (1836).

ARTHUR HUGH CLOUGH, by G. Levy (1938).

THE DARKLING PLAIN, by J. Heath-Stubbs (1950).

BOOKS IN GENERAL, by V. S. Pritchett (1953).

THE DOCTOR'S DISCIPLES, by F. J. Woodward (1954).

ARTHUR HUGH CLOUGH: The Uncommitted Mind, by K. Chorley. Oxford (1962)

—an authoritative biography. The most sensitive and sympathetic discussion of Clough's work yet to appear.

Critical and Biographical Essays in Periodicals (a selection):

Nineteenth Century Periodicals:

'Review of the Bothie of Toper-na-Fuosich' (i.e. Tober-na-Vuolich), by C. Kingsley. (*Fraser's Magazine*, 1849).

'Review of the Bothie of Toper-na-Fuosich' (i.e. Tober-na-Vuolich), by W. M. Rossetti. (*The Germ*, I, 1850).

'Clough's Poems', by D. Masson (*Macmillan's Magazine*, 1862).

'Arthur Hugh Clough', by F. T. Palgrave. (*Fraser's Magazine*, 1862).

'Arthur Hugh Clough', by J. A. Symonds. (*Fortnightly Review*, 1868)

—a particularly penetrating discussion of Clough's work.

'Arthur Hugh Clough', by J. Dowden. (*Contemporary Review*, 1869).

'Balliol Scholars: A Remembrance', by J. C. Shairp. (*Macmillan's Magazine*, 1873)

—a poem which begins with a description of Clough very like Matthew Arnold's 'Thyrsis' in tone.

'Arthur Hugh Clough: A Sketch', by T. Arnold. (*Nineteenth Century*, 1898).

Twentieth Century Periodicals:

'A Study of Clough's Mari Magno', by A. M. Turner. (*Publications of the Modern Language Association*, XCIV, 1929).

'A Balliol Scholar', by M. Kent (*Criterion*, July 1830).

'Was Clough a Failure?', by F. W. Palmer. (*Philological Quarterly*, XXII, 1943).

'The Bearing of Science on the Thought of Arthur Hugh Clough', by F. W. Palmer. (*Publications of the Modern Language Association*, LIX, 1944).

'Clough's Love and Reason', by F. L. Mulhauser. (*Modern Philology* XLII, 1954).

'A. H. Clough', by E. Underwood. (*Times Literary Supplement*, 8th September 1945).

'Victorian Verse Novels', by I. Macdonald. (*The Listener*, 16th March 1950).

'Clough as Dipsychus', by K. Badger. (*Modern Language Quarterly* XII, 1951).

'Clough at Oriel and at University Hall', by G. P. Johari. (*Publications of the Modern Language Association* LXVI, 1951).

'Clough: The Shorter Poems', by D. N. Dalglish. (*Essays in Criticism* II, 1952)

—a demonstration of the vigour and energy of Clough's shorter poems. Clough's reputation improved after the authoritative edition of his poetry appeared in 1951. There was a renewal of scholarly and critical interest in his work, and the following essays attempt to reach a closer understanding of his life and poetry.

'Clough's Amours de Voyage', by J. D. Jump. (*English* IX, 1953).

'Un Regain d'interest pour Arthur Hugh Clough', par P.Veyriras. (*Etudes Anglaises* XI, 1958).

'Arthur Hugh Clough's Formative Years: 1819-1841', by R. Gollin. (*Dissertation Abstracts XX*, 1959).

'Arthur Hugh Clough: A Portrait Retouched', by M. Timko. (*Victorian News Letter* XV, 1959).

'The 'True Creed' of Arthur Hugh Clough', by M. Timko. (*Modern Language Quarterly* XXI, 1960).

'Amours de Voyage: Substance or Smoke?', by M. Timko. (*English* XIII, 1960).

'Arthur Hugh Clough: A Hundred Years of Disparagement', by W. E. Houghton. (*English Studies* I, 1961).

Miscellaneous Works relevant to Clough and his circle:

Clough's Family:

A MEMOIR OF ANNE JEMIMA CLOUGH, by B. A. Clough (1897)

—Anne Clough was Clough's only sister. This biography contains extracts from Anne's early journal, many concerned with Arthur Hugh.

The Arnolds:

THE LIFE AND CORRESPONDENCE OF THOMAS ARNOLD, D.D., late
 Headmaster of Rugby School, by A. P. Stanley, 2 vols. (1844).

TOM BROWN'S SCHOOLDAYS, by T. Hughes (1857)

—its naive view of Dr. Arnold's aims fostered the belief that Arnold
 represented nothing but a complacent moral earnestness.

EMINENT VICTORIANS, by L. Strachey (1918)

—an iconoclastic attack on Dr. Arnold and his influence, contains
 some satirical remarks on Clough.

Matthew Arnold:

THE LETTERS OF MATTHEW ARNOLD TO ARTHUR HUGH CLOUGH, edited
 by H. F. Lowry (1932)

—invaluable for Arnold's view of Clough's poetry. Arnold's criticisms
 still remain the best case against Clough.

MATTHEW ARNOLD, by L. Trilling (1939).

THE POETRY OF MATTHEW ARNOLD, edited by C. B. Tinker and H. F.
 Lowry (1950).

J. M. Synge

and

Lady Gregory

by

ELIZABETH COXHEAD

Published for The British Council
and The National Book League
by Longmans, Green & Co.

Two shillings and sixpence net

Miss Elizabeth Coxhead published last year an attractive portrait of Lady Gregory (1852-1932), the mainspring of the Abbey Theatre, Dublin. In this essay she gives an account of Lady Gregory's work, and she also considers the work of J. M. Synge (1871-1909) whose plays, *Riders to the Sea* and *The Playboy of the Western World*, have won world renown.

The old Abbey Theatre was destroyed by fire in 1951: last year rebuilding began. Meanwhile, interest continues in the flowering of literature and drama which has taken place in Ireland during the last seventy years. Miss Coxhead's booklet will help towards understanding the nature and achievement of dramatists and actors of the great years in Dublin.

Bibliographical Series

of Supplements to 'British Book News'

GENERAL EDITOR
Bonamy Dobrée

J. M. SYNGE
*from a drawing
of 1906
by James Paterson*

LADY
GREGORY
*from a bust
by Epstein*

J. M. SYNGE
and
LADY GREGORY

by

Elizabeth Coxhead

PUBLISHED FOR
THE BRITISH COUNCIL
and the NATIONAL BOOK LEAGUE
by LONGMANS, GREEN & CO.

LONGMANS, GREEN & CO. LTD.
48 Grosvenor Street, London, W.1
Railway Crescent, Croydon, Victoria, Australia
Auckland, Kingston (Jamaica), Lahore, Nairobi

LONGMANS SOUTHERN AFRICA (PTY) LTD.
Thibault House, Thibault Square, Cape Town
Johannesburg, Salisbury

LONGMANS OF NIGERIA LTD.
W.R. Industrial Estate, Ikeja

LONGMANS OF GHANA LTD.
Industrial Estate, Ring Road South, Accra

LONGMANS, GREEN (FAR EAST) LTD.
443 Lockhart Road, Hong Kong

LONGMANS OF MALAYA LTD.
44 Jalan Ampang, Kuala Lumpur

ORIENT LONGMANS LTD.
Calcutta, Bombay, Madras
Delhi, Hyberadad, Dacca

LONGMANS CANADA LTD.
137 Bond Street, Toronto 2

Printed in Great Britain by
F. Mildner & Sons, London, E.C.1

Dates

1852   15 March. Augusta Persse born at Roxborough House, Co. Galway. Marries Sir William Gregory, 1880. Widowed, 1892.

1871   16 April. J. M. Synge born at Rathfarnham, Dublin.

1896   Yeats and Synge meet in Paris.

1897   Yeats, Lady Gregory and Edward Martyn plan an Irish theatre.

1898   First visits of Synge and of Lady Gregory to the Aran Islands.

1903   March, Lady Gregory's first play, *Twenty-five*, given by the Fay's Company at the Molesworth Hall in Dublin.

October, First production of *The Shadow of the Glen* at the Molesworth Hall.

1904   First production of *Riders to the Sea* at the Molesworth Hall. 27 December opening night of the Abbey Theatre, and first production of Lady Gregory's *Spreading the News*.

1905   First production of *The Well of the Saints* at the Abbey.

1907   January—first production of *The Playboy of the Western World* at the Abbey; a week of riots. Summer—given successfully in Oxford and London.

Synge's book *The Aran Islands* published.

1909   24 March. Synge dies in Dublin.

First production of *The Tinker's Wedding* in London.

Lady Gregory's *Seven Short Plays* published.

1910   First production of *Deirdre of the Sorrows* at the Abbey. First collected edition of Synge's plays published.

1911   Lady Gregory and the Abbey Company tour America, with *Playboy;* more riots.

1913   Lady Gregory's *Our Irish Theatre* published.

1921   Lady Gregory 'discovers' Sean O'Casey.

1925   Abbey Theatre becomes the first state-subsidised theatre in the English-speaking world.

1932   22 May. Lady Gregory dies at Coole.

1951   Abbey Theatre gutted by fire.

1961   Building of new Abbey Theatre begins.

J. M. SYNGE and LADY GREGORY

I.

IN the 1890s, in an Ireland still firmly under English rule, there occurred a quite remarkable upsurge of creative interest in literature and the arts. Temporarily frustrated in their struggle for political independence by the fall of the great nationalist leader Parnell, Irishmen of the middle and upper classes (mainly from the Protestant 'Ascendancy', which had all the educational advantages) turned for consolation to the epics of Ireland's ancient heroic past, recently translated by Celtic scholars. Folklorists like Douglas Hyde taught themselves the Irish language still spoken by the peasantry along the western seaboard, and made the exciting discovery that these same stories were still a living part of the folk consciousness, along with a vernacular poetry composed and handed down by wandering bards.

They also discovered that people whose first language was Irish Gaelic spoke an uncommonly musical and vivid English, partly based on mental translation from the Gaelic, but also filled with rich Elizabethan turns of phrase.

Plainly, there was a wealth of poetic material here. But it might never have got beyond the cottage hearth and the folklore conference, had there not coincided, in space and time, a handful of men and one woman with the gifts that could transmute it into a literature of universal appeal.

The leader was W. B. Yeats, already famous as a lyric poet, and hankering, as Shelley, Tennyson and Browning had done before him, after some means of reviving the poetic drama of the Elizabethans. The worst of artistic forms, he pronounced, was the play about modern educated people, with its meagre language and its action crushed into the narrow limits of possibility. 'Educated and well-bred people do not wear their hearts upon their sleeves, and they have no artistic and charming language except light persiflage, and no powerful language at all, and when they are deeply moved they look silently into the fireplace.' He was equally repelled by Ibsen's didactic 'drama of ideas', the later plays of Ibsen being then unknown to him. The London stage seemed to him to be dominated and vulgarised by powerful actor-managers; and Ireland had no native drama, but depended entirely on visiting English companies, who, if they brought Irish characters on to the stage, presented them as figures of farce.

A richer dramatic language was needed, an escape from realism, to heroic and universal themes: 'it is only by extravagance, by an emphasis far greater than that of life as we observe it, that we can crowd into a few minutes the knowledge of years', as Shakespeare or as Sophocles had been able to do.

But Yeats was primarily a lyric poet, not a dramatic one. His early verse dramas have great verbal beauty, but they lack the spark of dramatic life. The whole play-writing movement, and the very existence of the Abbey Theatre, are due to his inspiration and leadership; but ironically enough, the drama he envisaged was not to be written by him. It was created on the lesser scale of talent by his friend Augusta Gregory, and on the greater scale of genius by his protégé, J. M. Synge.

II.

Their origins were similar. Augusta Persse was born in 1852 of a Galway landowning family, and as a child heard folk-tales and 'rebel' talk from her Irish nurse, and longed in vain to learn the mysterious language spoken all around her. She grew up into a sort of unpaid social worker on her father's enormous estate, visiting the peasants, and helping those who could scarcely read and write with their letters to children in America, and thus she gained her unrivalled insight into the Irish peasant character. At the age of twenty-eight she married a much older neighbour, Sir William

Gregory of Coole, a delightful and distinguished man who had been Governor of Ceylon, and with him she travelled widely and came to know the great world of London politics and art. But sketches of Irish peasant life written during her married years show that she always knew this was to be her literary material, and when after twelve years Sir William died, leaving the house and estate of Coole to her in trust for their son, she flung herself into the new literary movement, learnt Irish, took up the collecting of folklore, and in the years 1895-6 got to know Yeats.

John Millington Synge[1] was born in 1871 at Rathfarnham, a Dublin suburb, of a family which had been important but had lost most of its wealth and land. His father died the next year, and he was brought up by his mother, a woman of narrow Protestant piety, to whom he was closely bound by an exasperated and rebellious affection. His holidays were spent among the peasantry of Wicklow, though because of his mother's prejudices he could never know them as closely as Augusta Persse did her Galway tenants.

He took a desultory degree at Trinity College, Dublin, then drifted into the apparently unprofitable life of a perpetual student, first in Germany, then at the Sorbonne in Paris, studying music and the Celtic languages. In fact these were years of slow ripening, as he became acquainted with European literature, and with all sorts and conditions of men—and women. With men he was shy, and could appear morose, but although an unsuccessful lover—twice his proposals of marriage were refused by girls who could not see that he had any material prospects and Molly Allgood, the beautiful young actress to whom he was engaged when he died, was rather a receiver than a giver of adoration—he had a natural gift for securing the friendship and the confidence of women, and this helped his imagination to create the brilliant galaxy of feminine portraits in his plays.

[1]Pronounced 'Sing', and by a charming family legend, bestowed by Henry VIII on an uncommonly sweet-voiced ancestor.

In 1896, Yeats took a walking-tour in the west of Ireland which cemented his friendship with Lady Gregory, and also carried him out on a brief trip to the Aran Islands, three bare limestone plateaux which lie in the Atlantic across the mouth of Galway Bay. Later that year, Yeats met Synge in a students' boarding-house in Paris, recognised the latent talent in this shabby dilettante who had so far failed to publish a line, and told him roundly that he was wasting his time in an alien culture and should go back to Ireland and out to Aran: a quite uncanny instance of one genius sensing another's spiritual need.

Synge's first visit to Aran in 1898 was a true Renascence, a spiritual rebirth. The knowledge he had been subconsciously acquiring during his fallow years suddenly came into focus; he looked at these primitive people, and through them, into the heart of humanity. He found an almost untouched peasant culture, with Irish as the universal language, and with an extraordinary beauty and dignity in the bare cottages, the women's red dresses and the men's grey homespuns against the creamy limestone, the treasure of poems and stories that beguiled the evenings by the light of tiny cod-oil lamps. The chief industry was fishing from *curraghs*, or canoes of lath and canvas, and in the wild seas fatalities were frequent, so that men lived under the shadow of death, and women of bereavement; this bred in the people the passionate intensity of feeling for which the dramatist in Synge instinctively longed.

For five summers in succession he returned to the islands, living among the people as one of themselves, amusing them with conjuring tricks, absorbing their wildness and their strength—though there was one aspect of their lives, their fervent Roman Catholicism, which as an agnostic he could never reach; and a girl with whom he had made friends told him with something like revulsion that she was sure he would 'go to hell by and by'.

Four of the themes of his plays were taken directly from the islands, those of *Playboy* and *Riders to the Sea* from actual happenings, those of *Shadow of the Glen* and *The Well of the Saints* from folk-tales; but before he produced any plays, he had written as his first successful piece of prose a descriptive book on *The Aran Islands*, still remarkably evocative of their atmosphere today. In it, and in the posthumously published *In Wicklow and West Kerry*, can be traced much of the material he wove into the plays, and it enshrines his continued delight in strong character and vivid personality. 'These strange men with receding foreheads, high cheekbones and ungovernable eyes seem to represent some old type found on these few acres at the extreme border of Europe, where it is only in wild jests and laughter that they can express their loneliness and desolation.' There we have the essence of Synge: laughter interpenetrated with desolation, 'man as an angel inhabiting the body of a beast'.

But he could not turn to the writing of plays about these people until a theatre had been created, and actors found, capable of interpreting them; and this meanwhile was the principal labour of his new friends, Lady Gregory and Yeats.

III

When Yeats confided to Lady Gregory that he had written a poetic play on an Irish subject and failed to get it produced in London, she replied that the proper place to put on Irish plays was Dublin; and with the help of a wealthy neighbour, Edward Martyn, who was another aspiring playwright, funds were raised to bring over English companies for three years in succession. But it was not a very happy compromise, as the English actors could not even pronounce the Irish names aright. Then Yeats discovered that a body of Dublin amateurs, mainly working-class, were putting on little sketches in temperance clubs, under the direction of the brothers Frank and Willie Fay, who had had some technical training and were passionate enthusiasts; they knew, in fact, a good deal more about the new continental production methods than he did himself. Finding them changed everything, for now the Irish dramatist could create in genuinely native terms. The Fays and their devoted, hard-schooled actors (who continued as unpaid amateurs right through till 1905) made possible the writing of Synge's and Lady Gregory's plays.

The performances were given on a shoe-string in make-shift concert halls, and one of these, the Molesworth, saw in 1903 the production of Lady Gregory's first play *Twenty-Five*, a touching little piece which promised great talent to come.

That year and next came Synge's *Shadow of the Glen* and *Riders to the Sea*, and Dublin uneasily recognised that this was more than promise, it was a new and discon-certing form of achievement. Then Miss Horniman, a well-to-do Englishwoman who was a fervent admirer of Yeat's poetic plays, offered to give the movement a proper home, and a former mechanics' institute in Abbey Street was converted into a simple but adequate little playhouse; and thus, what future historians will probably recognise as the most vital theatre of the early twentieth century was born. The Abbey Theatre opened its doors on 27 December, 1904, with a double bill comprising Yeats's Cuchulain play *On Baile's Strand* and Lady Gregory's brilliant little Russian scandal comedy *Spreading the News*.

The audience at the Abbey was to show itself highly individualistic, and capable on occasion of quite as much violence and passion as the Aran islanders. The opposition was mainly political, and chiefly to the plays of Synge. At first, relations between the movement and the political Nationalists had been friendly, and they regarded *Kathleen ni Houlihan*, the famous propaganda playlet written jointly by Yeats and Lady Gregory, as ammunition in their cause. But then came Synge, presenting an Ireland in which wives could be unfaithful, priests unworthy, and sons capable of harbouring a death-wish against their fathers; and many felt that he was deliberately defacing the image so earnestly built up of a country wise, mature, and ready for self-government. Nationalist indignation culminated when *The Playboy of the Western World* was given its first week of performances in January of 1907, and shouted down every night. Lady Gregory and Yeats held firm and fought for it valiantly, which they were now in a position to do, since the little amateur society had been re-formed as a professional company, with themselves and Synge as unpaid directors. The authority was now theirs—and also the strenuous labour of discovering new playwrights, and reading scripts.

But not till the company made their summer tour of Oxford and London was *The Playboy* properly heard; then its immense originality was appreciated, and recognition came to Synge at last. It was just in time, for already the doctors knew that he was suffering from a malignant growth and could not live much more than a year. His last play, *Deirdre of the Sorrows*, was written under the shadow of death, chiefly at his mother's suburban house, where Molly Allgood would visit him and read scenes as he wrote them, and the possibility of happiness with her gradually and bitterly receded. He was never to see her create the part.

He entered a Dublin hospital in January of 1909, and on 24 March said 'It's no use fighting death any longer' and turned his face to the wall. Remarkable as his six plays are, it is possible to hold that he had only begun to do justice to his talent, and that his death was a loss to English literature comparable with the early death of Keats.

IV

The plays of Synge and Lady Gregory are often described as 'dialect', but their language does not present much serious difficulty to anyone reasonably conversant with standard English. There are not many unfamiliar words; it is rather a question of construction and usage; and though there are constructions based on Gaelic syntax (i.e. the infinitive used as subjunctive: 'It is a pity the banshee not to be crying for yourself'), the context makes the sense plain. 'Himself' and 'herself' used as nouns are the polite peasant way of referring to the man or woman of the house. 'You'd have a right to' has the force of 'you ought to', and 'dark' applied to a person usually means 'blind'. 'Itself' sprinkled liberally through Synge's dialogue equals 'actually' or 'even'. One soon becomes used to these and similar turns of phrase.

Synge's first play, the one-act *Shadow of the Glen*, shows his dialogue and method already mature; if it can be considered a comedy, and the figures of husband and lover are almost farcical, at any rate it is comedy shot through with feeling and pathos. He has transposed to Wicklow the very ancient folk-tale, first heard by him in Aran, of the husband shamming death in order to trap the wife suspected of infidelity. But the change is more than geographical. To the folk-teller, the wife was a villainess to be exposed, but the humane and sophisticated Synge with his background of European culture is entirely on the side of the wife, bound in the all-too-common Irish peasant institution of a loveless marriage, and stifled by the mists and dreariness of the lonely glen. His Nora is a free spirit, sensitive to beauty, and his moral is the wickedness of trying to keep such a one caged.

In fact, though he objected to Ibsen's 'pallid and joyless words', his Nora and the Nora of *A Doll's House* have much in common. Both slam the door on the loveless marriage, and take to the hard life of the outcast. Ibsen is closer to reality, however, in making Nora take it alone. If Synge's play has a weakness, it is in the not quite realised figure of the Tramp who leads her to freedom. As with all great dramatists, many of Synge's figures carry symbolic overtones. But henceforward, they will all be firmly grounded in human reality first.

His second play, *Riders to the Sea*, has been called the finest one-act tragedy in the English language, and its overtones are tremendous. Synge had noted of Aran that 'the maternal feeling is so powerful on these islands that it gives a life of torment to the women. Their sons grow up to be banished as soon as they are of age, or to live here in continual danger on the sea.' Accordingly, old Maurya, who has already lost five sons to the sea and is about to lose the sixth, becomes a universal symbol of maternal grief. But she is none the less a real old woman in a white-washed Aran cottage, with nets and a spinning-wheel, and white boards against the wall that are to be used as coffin for Michael's body when it is washed up—though we realise with a shudder that instead they will make the coffin for Bartley, the last surviving son, whom we see taking leave of his mother as he, too, rides off to the sea. Maurya foresees his death in a vision, and then her vision takes shape; her tragedy is complete.

"They're all gone now, and there isn't anything more the sea can do to me. I'll have no call now to be up crying and praying when the wind breaks from the south, and you can hear the surf is in the east, and the surf is in the west, making a great stir with the two noises, and they hitting one on the other. . . . It isn't that I haven't prayed for you, Bartley, to the Almighty God. It isn't that I haven't said prayers in the dark nights till you wouldn't know what I'd be saying; but it's a great rest I'll have now, and it's time, surely. It's a great rest I'll have now, and great sleeping in the long nights after Samhain,[1] if it's only a bit of wet flour we do have to eat, and maybe a fish that would be stinking. . . . They're all together this time, and the end is come. May the Almighty God have mercy on Bartley's soul, and on Michael's soul, and on the souls of Sheamus and Patch and Stephen and Shawn; and may He have mercy on my soul, Nora, and on the soul of every one is left living in the world. Michael has a clean burial in the far north, by the grace of Almighty God. Bartley will have a fine coffin out of the white boards, and a deep grave surely. What more can we want than that? No man at all can be living for ever, and we must be satisfied."

But although she calls on the Christian God, Maurya is

[1] Samhain: November.

not a straight portrait of an Aran woman, who would have found more direct comfort in her religion. The forces which have brought her beyond despair are those which bludgeon the protagonists in a Greek tragedy. I am told that *Riders to the Sea* is a favourite with student drama groups in Asian universities, remote indeed from Aran, because it transcends the way of life in an obscure Atlantic island, and summarises the universal predicament.

In strong contrast is the riotous two-act comedy of *The Tinker's Wedding*. The lawless bands of tinkers and gypsies who carried wildness the length and breadth of Ireland's roads always fascinated Synge, and here he takes a couple who have been living together, tinker-fashion, without benefit of wedding ring, and starts the girl hankering after respectability. A priest reluctantly agrees to marry them for a bit of gold and a tin can, but old Mary, Michael's mother, who regards the whole affair as a sad waste of time and tin, steals the can and pawns it for drink. The priest backs out and threatens to call the police, and the tinkers bundle him into a sack and make their escape. The piece is still not acted in Ireland, being considered an affront to the cloth, though it is this particular priest's unworthiness that Synge is exposing, and not altogether unkindly.

The play is merry, yet full of feeling, as comedy always is with Synge, particularly in the richly Falstaffian character of old Mary, with her relish for life, her pride in her daughter-in-law's beauty and ferocity, her moments of self-pity alternating with a fierce determination not to be left out of any fun:

> What good am I this night, God help me? What good are the grand stories I have when it's few would listen to an old woman, few but a girl maybe would be in great fear the time her hour was come, or a little child wouldn't be sleeping with the hunger on a cold night? Maybe the two of them have a good right to be walking out the little short while they'd be young; but if they have itself, they'll not keep Mary Byrne from her full pint when the night's fine, and there's a dry moon in the sky. Jemmy Neill's

a decent lad, and he'll give me a good drop for the can; and maybe if I keep near the peelers tomorrow for the first bit of the fair, herself won't strike me at all; and if she does itself, what's a little stroke on your head beside sitting lonesome on a fine night, hearing the dogs barking, and the bats squeaking, and you saying over, it's a short while only till you die.

The Well of the Saints is a three-act *comédie noire*, based on another widespread folktale of which Synge heard a version in Aran. Martin and Mary Doul are an elderly blind couple who have got on quite happily, begging at the crossroads and fancying themselves the handsomest pair in the country-side. A travelling Saint brings water from a holy well and restores their sight, so that they learn the truth about themselves and part with bitter recrimination. Martin's life is now desolate indeed; he must labour for Timmy the Smith instead of begging, and suffer an anguish of desire for Molly, Timmy's odious young fiancée. His sight begins to fade again, and so does Mary's; they come together, and grope towards a new illusion, that when her hair has turned white and he has grown a patriarchal beard they will be handsome after all. The Saint returns and offers to effect another cure, and Mary is tempted, but Martin will have none of it; he strikes the can and sends the holy water flying. The villagers, greatly shocked, drive the ungrateful pair away.

Synge is often accused of pessimism, and this play instanced as an example of it, but except in the sense that all agnostics must feel life and beauty to be ephemeral, I do not think it is an accusation he deserves. His characters are finally doomed, as we all are, but while they live, they relish life. There is nothing in them of our contemporary pessimism, which affects to regard life as boring and futile and death as a release. 'There's nothing more the sea can do to me', says Maurya, and Deirdre echoes it with 'In the grave we're safe surely', but only after they have put up a tremendous struggle to keep the life that is so rich and sweet. Here, the happiness of the blind couple is built on

illusion, but the illusion itself results from the divine gift
of imagination—the artist's faculty—and in possessing it,
Martin and Mary know a creative fulfilment forever
denied to Timmy and Molly, the materially successful pair.

V

Many critics have seen in this clash between illusion and
reality the main theme of Synge's work, but perhaps that
is to compress into the strait-jacket of a formula an approach
to life which was altogether more intuitive and complex.
Undeniably, however, both he and Lady Gregory were
fascinated by what she calls 'our incorrigible Irish talent
for myth-making', and derive from it their finest effects of
pathos, irony and fun. In *The Well of the Saints*, the myth is
preferred to the harshness of fact. Synge's next play, *The
Playboy of the Western World*,[1] is the triumph of a myth,
which, because it is believed in, becomes fact before our
eyes. The Playboy has felt himself to be a weakling, but
on falling in with a set of people who take him for a hero,
joyously discovers a hero's capacities.

Before Synge came to write *The Playboy*, he had abandoned Aran for West Kerry, where the people were bi-
lingual and still possessed a richly Elizabethan English
idiom; and this, as well as his increasing command of his
medium, may account for the firefly-brilliant, flickering,
gleaming dialogue of what is unquestionably his masterpiece. And only a masterpiece could fulfil the standard he
demands of drama in his Preface:

> On the stage one must have reality, and one must have joy;
> and that is why the intellectual modern drama has failed, and people
> have grown sick of the false joy of the musical comedy, that has
> been given them in place of the rich joy found only in what is

[1]'Western World' is Synge's translation of a Gaelic term for the western
seaboard of Ireland, as opposed to the 'Eastern World' of Dublin and St.
George's Channel.

superb and wild in reality. In a good play every speech should be as fully flavoured as a nut or apple, and such speeches cannot be written by anyone who works among people who have shut their lips on poetry. In Ireland, for a few years more, we have a popular imagination that is fiery, and magnificent, and tender; so that those of us who wish to write start with a chance that is not given to writers in places where the springtime of the local life has been forgotten, and the harvest is a memory only, and the straw has been turned into bricks.

Once again, an Aran story is given a radically different twist. The islanders had sheltered a real parricide, because they felt he was sincerely repentant and had suffered enough. But Christy Mahon, who creeps frightened and dirty into the public-house on the Mayo coast, has not really killed his father, he merely imagines he has; and Pegeen, the innkeeper's daughter, far from being shocked, welcomes so colourful a character into her life, as does her neighbour, the sardonic Widow Quin. 'It's great luck and company I've won me in the end of time', comments Christy as he settles into a comfortable bed: 'two fine women fighting for the likes of me—till I'm thinking this night wasn't I a foolish fellow not to kill my father in the years gone by.'

Under admiration, the poet in him flowers. He becomes a ready fellow with his fists, at the sports, and most of all with his tongue. The story of his crime, as he tells it to the village girls, brandishing a chicken-bone by way of illustration, grows in ferocity:

> *Christy:* With that the sun came out between the cloud and the hill, and it shining green in my face. "God have mercy on your soul", says he, lifting a scythe. "Or on your own", says I, raising the loy.[1]
>
> *Susan.* That's a grand story.
> *Honor.* He tells it lovely.
> *Christy.* He gave a drive with the scythe, and I gave a lep to the east. Then I turned around with my back to the north, and I

[1]loy: a square-sided spade for cutting peat, the common fuel in the west of Ireland.

hit a blow on the ridge of his skull, laid him stretched out, and he
split to the knob of his gullet.

Girls. Well, you're a marvel! Oh, God bless you! You're the
lad surely!

The arrival of Old Mahon with nothing worse than a
sore head momentarily shakes Christy's confidence, but
Widow Quin sends the old man off on a wild-goose chase,
and Christy plunges into a rapturous wooing of Pegeen,
carrying all before him:

> *Christy*. It's little you'll think if my love is a poacher's or an
> earl's itself, when you'll feel my two hands stretched around you,
> and I squeezing kisses on your puckered lips, till I'd feel a kind of
> pity for the Lord God is all ages sitting lonesome in His golden chair.
> *Pegeen:* That'll be right fun, Christy Mahon, and any girl would
> walk her heart out before she'd meet a young man was your like
> for eloquence, or talk at all.

Old Mahon discovers the trick, and returns. Pegeen's
illusion is shattered; she rounds on Christy with abuse, and
his attempt to make a proper job of his father's murder this
time only elicits from her the comment that 'there's a
great gap between a gallous [splendid] story and a dirty
deed.' But Christy is no longer a scared child. He has grown
into a man, able to defy Pegeen, father, villagers and all—
and none more delighted than Old Mahon, to find that he
has not fathered a weakling, and will be taking the orders
from now on. 'You've turned me a likely gaffer in the
end of all', says Christy, 'the way I'll go romancing through
a romping lifetime from this hour to the dawning of the
judgement day', and out he swaggers with his captive
parent. The comedy is his, and the tragedy Pegeen's, who
has failed to appreciate her handiwork, and is left to her
famous lamentation: 'Oh my grief, I've lost him surely.
I've lost the only Playboy of the Western World.'

Rebellion is built-in to *The Playboy*. It is an electric
play, tingling, dangerous; the riotous Dublin audiences

had some excuse, and for that matter, a good many people in Ireland dislike it to this day. For Synge has put his finger on something very deep in human nature, applicable everywhere, though particularly to Ireland: resentment at the dead hand of tradition and the tyranny of the older generation, the son's subconscious desire to be quit of his father and take his place. There is a truth here that few of us can face with complete equanimity, even while we laugh.

VI

Synge's dialogue, so easy and rippling to read, cost him an infinity of pains, and each play went through many drafts. *Deirdre of the Sorrows* was pieced together by Yeats and Lady Gregory after his death, and there are a few bare patches on which he would have done more work. Nevertheless, it is in all important respects the heroic tragedy on an ancient theme of which Yeats had dreamed. The peasant idiom shows itself, as it had already done in *Riders*, fully equal to the poetic expression of tragic feeling.

Deirdre's is the best-loved of the old stories, about the beautiful child of whom it was prophesied that she would bring doom on all who loved her, and the ageing King Conchubor, who had her brought up in mountain solitude, in order that she might escape the curse and safely become his wife. But you cannot play for safety in love, you cannot mate youth with age, you cannot cage beauty: those are lessons which run all through Synge's drama, and which came home to him most poignantly now that he was dying, and in love with a girl much younger than himself.

Deirdre is bound to meet with Naisi, the king's handsome nephew, and his two brothers. Inevitably, she forces them to flee with her to Alban (Scotland). There—and this is Synge's twist to the story—the same forces bend the fate of the lovers. They cannot play for safety either, or they will age and weary of each other, and their love will turn to recrimination. So when Conchubor invites them home, they return, though it is almost certain that his offer is treacherous.

And for a while, it seems that Conchubor will show himself generous. But he too is caught up in the web of his own weaving; the brothers are slain, and Deirdre, forever unattainable by him, makes her funeral oration before she stabs herself on the edge of their grave:

> "It's you three that will not see age or death coming—you that were my company when the fires on the hilltops were put out and the stars were our friends only. . . . Because of me there will be weasels and wild cats crying on a lonely wall where there were queens and armies and red gold, the way there will be a story told of a ruined city and a raving king and a woman will be young for ever. I see the trees naked and bare, and the moon shining. Little moon, little moon of Alban, it's lonesome you'll be this night, and tomorrow night, and long nights after, and you pacing the woods beyond Glen Laoi, looking every place for Deirdre and Naisi, the two lovers who slept so sweetly with each other. I have put away sorrow like a shoe that is worn out and muddy, for it is I have had a life that will be envied by great companies. It was not by a low birth that I made kings uneasy, and they sitting in the halls of Emain. It was not a low thing to be chosen by Conchubor, who was wise, and Naisi had no match for bravery. It is not a small thing to be rid of grey hairs, and the loosening of the teeth. It was the choice of lives we had in the clear woods, and in the grave we're safe, surely."

VII

Synge left behind him three short critical prefaces, to *The Tinker's Wedding*, *The Playboy* and his *Poems*, which contain more illumination than many a volume; and he left the *Poems* themselves, a handful composed at the end of his life out of his love for Molly and his rage against death. They have something of the clearness of vision, combined with roughness and even amateurishness of execution, which fascinate us in the poems of Emily Brontë. His prose style may be poetic, but his poetic style is stark, and in the Preface he underlines what seemed to him to be insincere in the 'beautiful' poetic diction of his contemporaries:

> Many of the older poets, such as Villon and Herrick and Burns, used the whole of their personal life as their material, and the verse written in this way was read by strong men, and thieves, and deacons, not by little cliques only. Then, in the town writing of the eighteenth century, ordinary life was put back into verse that was not poetry, and when poetry came back with Coleridge and Shelley, it went into verse that was not always human. In these days, poetry is usually a flower of evil or good; but it is the timber of poetry that wears most surely, and there is no timber that has not strong roots among the clay and worms. . . . It may almost be said that before verse can be human again it must learn to be brutal.

An astonishing statement for 1908, and one which foreshadows the whole of the modern movement. And the poems themselves bear it out. He rejects the faery world of the 'plumed yet skinny Shee' in which poets like Yeats and George Russell were still dwelling; instead:

> We'll stretch in Red Dan Sally's ditch
> And drink in Tubber fair,
> Or poach with Red Dan Philly's bitch
> The badger and the hare.

He tells Molly:

> I asked if I got sick and died, would you
> With my black funeral go walking too,
> If you'd stand close to hear them talk or pray
> While I'm let down in that steep bank of clay.
>
> And, No, you said, for if you saw a crew
> Of living idiots pressing round that new
> Oak coffin—they alive, I dead beneath
> That board—you'd rave and rend them with your teeth.

He contemplates sardonically his inevitable early death:

> I've thirty months, and that's my pride,
> Before my age's a double score,
> Though many lively men have died
> At twenty-nine or little more.
>
> I've left a long and famous set
> Behind some seven years or three
> But there are millions I'd forget
> Will have their laugh at passing me.

Synge's theory and practice had a profound effect on his champion Yeats, who presently learned to make his own verse 'brutal', and produced work of massive humanity. And Yeats's influence on all who have come after him is unquestioned. It has been justly claimed by Dr. Alan Price, latest and most perceptive of the Synge commentators, that 'Synge may be no more than a minor poet, but he is one of those minors who have played a part in the major changes of poetry'.

VIII

In the nature of things, Lady Gregory could not be so dedicated an artist as Synge. She did not write her first actable play till she was fifty, and she had much besides play-writing on her mind. She shouldered the chief responsibility for the Abbey, kept its precarious finances going after Miss Horniman had withdrawn her support in 1910, found producers, produced herself when none could be found, promoted new talent—and earned her richest reward in this direction by her discovery of Sean O'Casey in the early 1920's. She ran the house and estate of Coole, and made it Yeats's poetic sanctuary for every summer from the time of their meeting; in addition it gave holidays to those of the literary movement who needed them, and the most distinguished were invited to carve their initials on an immense copper-beech tree which is still an object of tourist pilgrimage. (The house itself, alas, was pulled down after her death.)

The last years of her life were embittered by a fruitless struggle to make the English Government restore to Ireland a group of Impressionist paintings, which her art-dealer nephew Hugh Lane had left to Dublin in an unluckily unwitnessed codicil to his will. (This injustice has now been righted by a compromise.) Altogether, she packed so much unselfish activity into her life—was so completely, as O'Casey said, 'a charwoman, but one with a star on her breast',—that much of her literary achievement was undervalued in her lifetime, and has been forgotten since.

It is an unjustified neglect. Hers is talent, not genius, but it is exquisitely satisfying of its kind, and her best things, notably her one-act plays, are minor classics. Her gentler domestic note is the natural complement to the wildness of Synge, though her temper and sympathies are heroic like his—she loves the generous gesture and the lost cause. Her dialect, 'Kiltartan' as her friends called it from the name of the district in which Coole stands, lacks his savagery and colour, but it has a delicious trot and lilt of its own, ideal for comedy, capable of pathos, but perhaps a trifle thin for tragic emotion. And her plays are models of neat, taut construction, much influenced by Molière, in whom she had steeped herself, and whose plays she regularly translated into 'Kiltartan' for performance at the Abbey.

The most successful, judging by the numbers of revivals, are the *Seven Short Plays*, published in one volume in 1909, with *The Rising of the Moon* leading the field by several lengths. It is an exciting little piece about a political prisoner trying to escape by night from the Galway quays, and a police sergeant wheedled into foregoing the £100 reward; in it one may see reflected the conflict in the mind of the child Augusta Persse during the Fenian rising, with sternly right-wing parents in the drawing-room, and a 'rebelly' nurse upstairs. Next in popularity comes *The Workhouse Ward*, where two ancient enemies are kept alive by their joy in their perpetual quarrel; listen to them boasting of their families, funeral glories, and of the attentions of the banshee, the spirit whose wailings were supposed to foretell death:

> *Michael Miskell.* I tell you but for the wheat that was to be sowed, there would be more side cars and more common cars at my father's funeral (God rest his soul!) than at any funeral ever left your own door.
>
> *Mike McInerney.* And what do you say to the banshee? Isn't she apt to have knowledge of the ancient race? Was she ever heard to cry for the Miskells?
>
> *Michael Miskell.* It is a pity the banshee not to be crying for yourself at this minute, and giving you a warning to quit your lies and your chat and your arguing and your contrary ways; for there is no one under the rising sun could stand you. I tell you you are not behaving as in the presence of the Lord!
>
> *Mike McInerney.* Is it wishful for my death you are? Let it come and meet me now and welcome so long as it will part from yourself! And I say, and I would kiss the book on it, I to have one request only to be granted, and I leaving it in my will, it is what I would request, nine furrows of the field, nine ridges of the hills, nine waves of the ocean to be put between your grave and my own grave the time we be laid in the ground!
>
> *Michael Miskell.* Amen to that!

Other gems are *Spreading the News*, baseless scandal growing at a fair; *The Jackdaw*, a benevolent deception which takes in even its perpetrators; *Hyacinth Halvey*, or 'how to give a dog a good name and refuse to hang him'. In every case she draws an accurate picture of Galway peasant life, and yet reaches down into the universal that lies beneath dialect and social class.

The volume also contains one moving miniature tragedy, *The Gaol Gate;* a peasant wife and mother learn that their man, falsely accused of murder, has been hanged because he would not inform on his friends. The young wife's lament shows Lady Gregory as a prose poet in her own right:

> What way will I be the Sunday, and I going up the hill to the Mass? Every woman with her own comrade, and Mary Cushin to be walking her lone!

What way will I be the Monday and the neighbours turning their heads from the house? The turf Denis cut lying on the bog, and no well-wisher to bring it to the hearth!

What way will I be in the night-time, and none but the dog calling after you? Two women to be mixing a cake, and not a man in the house to break it!

What way will I sow the field, and no man to drive the furrow? The sheaf to be scattered before spring time that was brought together at the harvest!

Lady Gregory's work in folklore opened up for her a new sort of historical drama, the 'folk-history', using for dialect the peasant idiom in a way that was neither anachronistic nor fancy-dress, and for theme, historical happenings as preserved in the folk memory, the Irish equivalent of 'Alfred and the cakes'. Thus, folk-history made James II escape in a barrel after the Battle of the Boyne, and declared of the greatest Tudor: 'Whatever man she had to do with, she would send him to the block in the morning, that he would be able to tell nothing.' The Queen Elizabeth theme makes the farce of *The Canavans*, and the James II theme the heroic comedy of *The White Cockade*. One-acters are *Dervorgilla*, a noble little tragedy of the woman whose faithlessness first brought the English into Ireland; and *The Wrens*, an ironic comedy of two strolling players whose quarrel is the means of losing Ireland her Parliament in 1799. Synge himself acknowledged that Lady Gregory's method 'had made the writing of historical plays again possible', and certainly it is the method adopted by most writers of costume-drama today.

And of plays based on the old legends, *Grania*, which has three acts and only three characters, makes a fascinating complement to the *Deirdre* of Synge. The themes are parallel; again a pair of lovers flee from the jealousy of an ageing king; but Lady Gregory finds a very different clue to the situation, in her experience of the 'loveless Irishman', with his preference for the company of his own sex and his habit of pushing his womenfolk into the background.

Grania is the member of the trio who has the real cause for jealousy; her lover Diarmuid has never ceased to hanker after the king's court and the warrior band, and his death brings the moment of truth. (At first glance Lady Gregory and James Joyce may appear poles apart, but compare the role allotted to Molly Bloom in *Ulysses* for confirmation.)

IX

Synge and Lady Gregory wrote for the stage, and for a specifically Irish stage, and this has militated against their wider acceptance, particularly as Ireland has an ungrateful habit of neglecting the talents she produces in such profusion. There is still real opposition to Synge, whom I have heard described as 'brutal and cruel', though *Playboy* and *Riders* get regular revivals. And till recently, the Abbey Theatre almost ignored the plays of its co-founder in the original, though they are frequently given in Irish as part of the policy of encouraging that language. They have always been, however, a standby of the amateur dramatic movement, both in Ireland and outside it, and every drama festival brings what has been unkindly dubbed 'the annual ritual murder of *The Rising of the Moon*'.

But there are signs of a change of professional attitude in Ireland, and of a welcome abroad. *The Playboy* has recently had triumphant runs in London and New York, playing to audiences larger and more intelligent than any Synge knew in his lifetime. The Abbey has already revived one Gregory play, and plans to put on more when it is re-housed in the new theatre now being built on the site of the old (for Miss Horniman's conversion was gutted by fire in 1951).

Both dramatists can stand the test of being read as literature; and indeed Synge was so studied from the first, particularly in France and Germany, where the European quality of his thinking was quickly recognised. The smallness of his output may prevent his being considered a figure of the first rank, but many have found his six plays a source of delight as inexhaustible as the six novels of Jane Austen.

It has been made a reproach that his language, and Lady Gregory's 'Kiltartan', proved dead-ends, founded no school, were impossible to copy and fatally easy to parody (Joyce puts a crude parody of Synge into the mouth of Buck Mulligan in *Ulysses*, having contrived to quarrel with Synge as he quarrelled with practically everyone). But what signifies, surely, is that their dialogue was right for their own purposes. We do not disparage Shakespeare and Webster because attempts to imitate them have produced intolerable pastiche.

Today especially, when much serious drama either consists still of 'pallid and joyless words' or is downright inarticulate, there is refreshment of the spirit to be found in these plays, allying Irish charm and a rich flow of language to a universal applicability. Some have seen Synge and Lady Gregory as the last of the romantics, the last to find an idiom both poetic and dramatic, and to use it for big themes. But I think that is to take a short-sighted view. Romance as they understood it, with its head in the stars but its feet firmly grounded in an affectionate knowledge of human nature, can never date or die. As we draw further away from them, and it is possible to put them into the perspective of literary history, they will appear as two honoured names in a splendid and continuous line.

JOHN MILLINGTON SYNGE —
AUGUSTA, LADY GREGORY

A Select Bibliography

(Place of publication London, unless stated otherwise)

I. General

OUR IRISH THEATRE, by [Lady] I. A. Gregory. New York (1913)
—the movement from within, by one of its originators; does not
set out to be a formal history, but is personal, discursive, and
indispensable.

IRELAND'S LITERARY RENAISSANCE, by E. A. Boyd (1916)
—an early historical survey. See also, the same author's *The Contemporary Drama of Ireland*, Dublin, 1918.

THE IRISH DRAMA, by A. E. Malone (1929)
—a competent historical account by one who never missed an Abbey
production; some critical assessments.

DRAMATIS PERSONAE, by W. B. Yeats (1936)
—an intensely subjective account of the movement's beginnings;
contains a great deal about Synge and Lady Gregory, but is not
always accurate or fair; primarily of importance for the light it
throws on Yeats's own personality and literary aims.

THE IRISH DRAMATIC MOVEMENT, by U. Ellis-Fermor (1939)
—still the best critical work on the whole subject; particularly
illuminating on Synge and Lady Gregory.

IRELAND'S ABBEY THEATRE: A HISTORY, 1899-1951, by L. Robinson
(1951)
—the Theatre's history up to 1950 by one who was its chief producer
as well as a leading dramatist; as sequel to Lady Gregory's book,
has the same merits and drawbacks; many gaps.

AUTOBIOGRAPHIES, by W. B. Yeats (1955)
—the definitive edition.

THE ABBEY THEATRE, CRADLE OF GENIUS, by G. Fay (1958)
—a detailed history for the years of the Fay's activities, 1899-1908.

31

THE IRISH WRITERS, 1880–1940, by H. Howarth (1958)
—relates the principal writers of the group to the political history of the time.

ESSAYS AND INTRODUCTIONS, by W. B. Yeats (1961)
—the definitive edition.

II.   J. M. Synge

Bibliography:

A BIBLIOGRAPHY, by M. J. McManus. Dublin (1930).
CATALOGUE OF EXHIBITION HELD IN TRINITY COLLEGE, DUBLIN, Dublin (1959).

Collected Works:

THE WORKS, 4 vols. Dublin (1910)
—Vols. I and II, *Plays, Poems and Translations;* Vol. III, *The Aran Islands;* Vol. IV, *In Wicklow, In West Kerry,* &c. A new Collected Edition including unpublished material is being prepared for the Oxford University Press.

THE DRAMATIC WORKS. Dublin (1915).

PLAYS, POEMS AND PROSE (1941)
—the Everyman's Library edition: reprinted with introduction by M. MacLiammoir, 1958. The most economical volume for the newcomer to Synge; contains all the plays and poems, and a selection from *The Aran Islands;* delightful short introduction by Ireland's most distinguished actor.

THE COLLECTED PLAYS, 2 vols. (1952)
—the Penguin edition.

FOUR PLAYS AND 'THE ARAN ISLANDS', edited with an introduction by R. Skelton (1962)
—in the World's Classics: the plays are *Riders to the Sea, The Shadow of the Glen, The Tinker's Wedding* and *The Playboy of the Western World.*

Separate Works:

THE WELL OF THE SAINTS. Dublin (1905).
THE SHADOW OF THE GLEN and RIDERS TO THE SEA (1905)
—an edition with notes by T. R. Henn, 1961.

THE PLAYBOY OF THE WESTERN WORLD. A Comedy in Three Acts. Dublin (1907)
—an edition with notes by E. R. Wood, 1961, includes *Riders to the Sea*.

THE TINKER'S WEDDING. A Comedy in Two Acts. Dublin (1907).

THE ARAN ISLANDS. Dublin (1907).

POEMS AND TRANSLATIONS. Dundrum (1909)
—printed at the Cuala Press. Enlarged edition, Dublin, 1910. The *Translations* including some unpublished, edited by R. Skelton, Dublin, 1961.

DEIRDRE OF THE SORROWS. Dundrum (1910)
—printed at the Cuala Press.

IN WICKLOW, WEST KERRY, AND CONNEMARA. Dublin (1911).

Some Critical and Biographical Studies:

SYNGE AND THE IRELAND OF HIS TIME, by W. B. Yeats. Dundrum (1911)
—printed at the Cuala Press. See also Yeats's *The Death of Synge and Other Passages from an old Diary*, Dublin, 1928.

J. M. SYNGE AND THE IRISH DRAMATIC MOVEMENT, by F. Bickley (1912).

J. M. SYNGE: A CRITICAL STUDY, by P. P. Howe (1912).

JOHN MILLINGTON SYNGE AND THE IRISH THEATRE, by M. Bourgeois (1913)
—the three books above did much for Synge's reputation but have been superseded by more recent critical studies.

JOHN M. SYNGE, by J. Masefield (1915)
—'a few personal recollections, with biographical notes'.

SYNGE AND ANGLO-IRISH LITERATURE, by D. Corkery. Cork (1931)
—Synge seen by an extreme Nationalist, with inevitable distortions.

LETTERS TO MY DAUGHTER. MEMORIES OF J. M. SYNGE, by S. Synge. Dublin [1932].

JOHN MILLINGTON SYNGE, by L. A. G. Strong (1941)
—a brief but sympathetic essay.

J. M. SYNGE, by D. H. Greene and E. M. Stephens. New York (1959)
—the indispensable fully-documented biography; attempts little in
the way of literary criticism.

SYNGE AND ANGLO-IRISH DRAMA, by A. Price (1961)
—the most thorough and perceptive critical assessment of Synge yet
published.

III.   Lady Gregory

Separate Works & Collections:

KINCORA. A Play in Three Acts. Dublin (1905)
—reprinted in *Irish Folk-History Plays*, I, 1912.

THE WHITE COCKADE. Dublin (1905)
—reprinted in *Irish Folk-History Plays*, II, 1912.

SPREADING THE NEWS: THE RISING OF THE MOON: THE POORHOUSE (with
Douglas Hyde). Dublin (1906)
—the first two plays reprinted, Dublin, 1909, and in *Seven Short
Plays*, Dublin, 1909.

THE UNICORN FROM THE STARS &c. Dublin (1908).

SEVEN SHORT PLAYS. Dublin (1909)
—contains *Spreading the News, Hyacinth Halvey, The Rising of the
Moon, The Jackdaw, The Workhouse Ward, The Travelling Man,
The Gaol Gate:* all reprinted separately, 1918, as *Lady Gregory's
Irish Plays.*

THE IMAGE. A Play in Three Acts. Dublin (1910)
—reprinted [1922] 'With Other Plays', namely *Hanrahan's Oath,
Shanwalla, The Wrens.*

NEW COMEDIES (1913)
—contains *The Bogie Men, Full Moon, Coats, Damer's Gold, McDonough's
Wife.*

OUR IRISH THEATRE: A CHAPTER OF AUTOBIOGRAPHY (1913).

THE GOLDEN APPLE. A Play for Kiltartan Children. (1916).

THE DRAGON. A Wonder Play in Three Acts. Dublin (1920).

THREE WONDER PLAYS (1923)
—contains *The Dragon, Aristotle's Bellows, The Jester.*

THE STORY BROUGHT BY BRIGIT. A Passion Play in Three Acts (1924).

ON THE RACECOURSE. New York (1925).

THREE LAST PLAYS (1928)
—contains *Sancho's Master, Dave, The Would-be Gentleman*.

MY FIRST PLAY [Colman and Guaire] (1930).

COOLE. Dundrum (1931)
—printed at the Cuala Press.

JOURNALS 1916–1930: A SELECTION EDITED WITH AN INTRODUCTION,
  by L. Robinson (1946)
—of value to her own and the Abbey Theatre's development, her
  experiences in the Civil War, and her struggle to retain the Lane
  Pictures, but the literary period covered is only from 1919 to 1930.

SELECTED PLAYS AND PROSE, chosen and introduced by E. Coxhead
  with a foreword by S. O'Casey (1962)
—includes *The Rising of the Moon, Spreading the News, Hyacinth
  Halvey, The Workhouse Ward, The Gaol Gate, Dervorgilla, The
  White Cockade, Grania, Dave*.

riticism:

LADY GREGORY, A LITERARY PORTRAIT, by E. Coxhead (1961)
—attempts an assessment of Lady Gregory as a writer and particularly
  as a dramatist, and gives some account of her life.

The Powys Brothers

by R. C. CHURCHILL

Published for The British Council
and The National Book League
by Longmans, Green & Co.

Two shillings and sixpence net

The 150th issue in the *Writers and Their Work* series, the first number of which appeared in June 1950, honours a remarkable contemporary family.

The three brothers Powys considered by Mr. Churchill are John Cowper Powys, who has just attained the age of ninety, an occasion which brought him world-wide congratulation; Theodore Powys, novelist and story-teller, who died nearly ten years ago; and Llewelyn Powys, a versatile writer who was the shortest lived of the three, though perhaps the widest in his interests. The bibliography contributed by Mr. Maurice Hussey includes books by brothers and sisters of the celebrated trio.

Mr. Churchill concurs with most critics that Theodore Powys was the most original of the brethren, but one of the merits of his essay is that he presents a balanced view of their diverse accomplishments.

Bibliographical Series
of Supplements to 'British Book News'
on Writers and Their Work

★

GENERAL EDITOR
Bonamy Dobrée

JOHN COWPER
POWYS

LLEWELLYN
POWYS

T. F. POWYS

THE POWYS BROTHERS

by

R. C. CHURCHILL

I well remember once hearing in a town in Iowa about a very philosophical, very gentlemanly, and very learned recluse, whose favourite writer was 'Powys'. I wonder if Theodore and Llewelyn have the same odd sensation when they hear or see the word 'Powys', and learn that it does not refer to themselves?

JOHN COWPER POWYS: *Autobiography.*

PUBLISHED FOR
THE BRITISH COUNCIL
and the NATIONAL BOOK LEAGUE
by LONGMANS, GREEN & CO.

LONGMANS, GREEN & CO. LTD.,
48 Grosvenor Street, London, W.1.
Railway Crescent, Croydon, Victoria, Australia
Auckland, Kingston (Jamaica), Lahore, Nairobi

LONGMANS SOUTHERN AFRICA (PTY) LTD.
Thibault House, Thibault Square, Cape Town,
Johannesburg, Salisbury

LONGMANS OF NIGERIA LTD.
W.R. Industrial Estate, Ikeja

LONGMANS OF GHANA LTD.
Industrial Estate, Ring Road, South Accra

LONGMANS GREEN (FAR EAST) LTD.
443 Lockhart Road, Hong Kong

LONGMANS OF MALAYA LTD.
44 Jalan Ampang, Kuala Lumpur

ORIENT LONGMANS LTD.
Calcutta, Bombay, Madras
Delhi, Hyderabad, Dacca

LONGMANS CANADA LTD.
137 Bond Street, Toronto 2

First Published in 1962
© R. C. Churchill 1962

Printed in Great Britain by
F. Mildner & Sons, London, E.C.1

CONTENTS

I THE BRONTËS AND THE POWYSES   *page* 7

II JOHN COWPER AND LLEWELYN POWYS   10

III T. F. POWYS: THE EARLY WORKS   18

IV *MR. WESTON* AND AFTER   23

V CONCLUSION   29

A Select Bibliography by Maurice Hussey   32

¶ JOHN COWPER POWYS was born at Shirley Vicarage, Shirley, near Ashbourne, Derbyshire, in 1872 and now lives in Merionethshire, North Wales; THEODORE FRANCIS POWYS was born at Shirley Vicarage in 1875 and died at Mappowder, near Sturminster Newton, Dorsetshire, in 1953; LLEWELYN POWYS was born at Rothesay House, Dorchester, Dorsetshire, in 1884 and died at Clavadel Sanatorium, Davos-Platz, Switzerland, in 1939.

THE POWYS BROTHERS

I

THE BRONTËS AND THE POWYSES

L ITERATURE, unlike music, does not often run in families.
There are many Bachs, but only one Dante; a whole
family of Strauss, but a single Shakespeare, a solitary
Voltaire. Among the English exceptions to this general rule,
the Brontë sisters and the Powys brothers are the most
remarkable; and it is natural to enquire whether the two
families have anything in common besides this.

The most obvious common factor leads to the chief
difference. Charlotte, Emily and Anne Brontë were the
daughters of the Rev. Patrick Brontë, a Church of England
clergyman of Evangelical outlook who was the son of an
Irish peasant farmer called Branty or Brunty; their mother
came from a Cornish Methodist family, so they had Celtic
ancestry on both sides. John Cowper, Theodore Francis
and Llewelyn Powys were of similar clerical origin, being
the sons of the Rev. Charles Francis Powys (1843-1923), a
Church of England clergyman of Evangelical views who
was descended from a branch of the ancient Welsh family
of Powys, intermarried in recent centuries with English and
Swiss stock; their mother, Mary Cowper Johnson (1849-
1914), was of part English, part Irish-German descent, on
her father's side related to that famous Norfolk family
which had given to literature the Jacobean poet John Donne,
Dean of St. Paul's, and William Cowper, the greatest
Evangelical poet of the eighteenth century. The Victorian
novelist sisters and the twentieth-century novelist brothers
have in common, therefore, a clerical, mainly Evangelical
background and a large measure of Celtic blood.

Of the value of the Celtic inheritance, crossed as it was
by English environment and upbringing—in Yorkshire in
the case of the Brontës, principally in Somerset and Dorset

in the case of the Powyses—there is ample evidence to be
found in their writings. The clerical and Evangelical
inheritance, however, worked in a contrary direction in the
Powys brothers to that which it took in the Brontës. John
Cowper Powys became a mystic philosopher, who rejects
conventional Christianity but nevertheless feels, like Bloody
Johnny in his *Glastonbury Romance*, that the material universe is not all; the philosophy which informs the novels
and stories of T. F. Powys may be briefly described as
pantheism with an heretical Christian accent; while
Llewelyn Powys, believing that 'Christianity teaches us to
despise life', became a militant Atheist whose book *The
Pathetic Fallacy* accuses the Church of distorting the simple
teachings of Jesus and who preached in *Damnable Opinions*,
'the hand-book of my beliefs', a gospel of happiness on
earth that rejects the Christian doctrine of immortality.
Some aspects of *Wuthering Heights* and *Jane Eyre* may not
have been altogether to the taste of the Rev. Patrick
Brontë, but his daughters lived and died in the Christian
faith in which they had been brought up. The Powys
brothers, by contrast, reveal an almost complete break
with their clerical inheritance. T. F. Powys, it is true, read
the lessons in East Chaldon church for nearly forty years,
but his acknowledged masterpieces in fiction—*Mr. Weston's
Good Wine*, the *Fables* and *Unclay*—reveal an attitude towards Christianity which no clergyman, however broad or
modern in outlook, could fully condone.

But this production of heretics from a clerical root had
nothing in common with the classic Victorian case of
Samuel Butler. (And the root had its revenge, the clerical
collar came full circle, when John Cowper's son became a
clergyman, like his grandfather, great-grandfather and
great-great-grandfather.) There was little repression, comparable to that recorded in Butler's *Way of All Flesh*, about
the childhood of the Powys brothers; on the contrary, the
happiness of the Powys family life, and the deep affection of
all its members for each other, is evident from John

Cowper's *Autobiography* and Llewelyn's *Skin for Skin*, confirmed by their brother Littleton Powys, when he writes that 'though in tastes and interests no two members of the family were alike, in affection for each other they were bound together by bonds which nothing in this world could ever loosen.'* We are reminded, not of the Butler background to *The Way of All Flesh*, but again of the Brontë sisters, not simply because of the similar close affection of the family life but because of the common urge in later years to look back upon their youth. The clannishness of the Powys brothers, which they themselves were the first to recognize, is similar at some points to the closed family circle of the Brontës.

But Charlotte and Anne Brontë are very different writers from Emily, and a gulf of somewhat the same kind separates the *Glastonbury Romance* from the *Fables, Love and Death* from *Mr. Weston's Good Wine*. It is the gulf, in simple terms, separating the romantic and subjective from the more classical, more impersonal. Both John Cowper and Llewelyn Powys are intensely autobiographical writers, whose virtues and faults spring alike from their obsession with their own feelings. They were, moreover, very close to each other in life, even by the remarkably close standards of the Powys family in general; whereas Theodore, by the same remarkably close standards, 'was the most original of the Powys family'—as an American friend once shrewdly put it—'and his originality was such that it inevitably isolated him even from his closest friends and relations.' I shall accordingly consider, together, the writings of the two brothers who were closest in life and in their work, before turning to T. F. Powys, who seems to me the greatest figure, though not all of his writing is on the high level of his comparatively few masterpieces.

* The Rev. C. F. Powys had eleven children in all, including the scholar and sportsman Littleton Charles Powys, the artist Gertrude Mary Powys, who illustrated some of Llewelyn's books, the architect Albert Reginald Powys, and the poet Philippa Powys.

II

JOHN COWPER AND LLEWELYN POWYS

Despite the closeness of the family tie, there is only one work of collaboration in the bibliography of the Powys family, and it seems natural that this should be the *Confessions of Two Brothers* (1916) by John Cowper and Llewelyn. This was Llewelyn's first book, but John Cowper, the eldest of the family, was known as a lecturer in England and America and had published poetry, stories, critical essays and his first novel *Wood and Stone* (1915), in which he mirrored the intimate relationship between himself and Llewelyn in the characters of the brothers Anderson.

The importance of the *Confessions* is twofold: first, that it gave Llewelyn—who had spent seventeen months in a Swiss sanatorium for consumptives from 1909 to 1911 and was now managing his brother William's farm in Kenya—the first sight of his writings in print, an encouragement he needed in order to persevere with his stories and sketches of England and Africa later collected in two of his best books, *Ebony and Ivory* (1923) and *Black Laughter* (1925); secondly, that John Cowper's contributions were a first version of chapters afterwards revised for his *Autobiography* (1934), one of the best and one of the most characteristic of his varied work.

Work varied, that is to say, in outward form. For, in a more inward sense, it is no great exaggeration to describe almost all J. C. Powys's creative work—and some of his critical work too—under the one heading of autobiography. It is not merely in the volume with that title that he reveals himself in all his paradoxical mixture of genuine insight and self-confessed charlatanry. There has always been, by his own admission, a touch of the theatrical about John Cowper Powys: 'There is no use trying to conceal the fact', he writes in the *Autobiography*, 'that Nature from the start had made me an actor.' From youth onward, he has relished his own performance, often observing it, however, with a satirical smile, not altogether taken in by the act but grateful, so to speak, for his privileged seat in the front row. His own complex personality, the various masks he has assumed at different periods of his life, his search for a coherent philosophy which would satisfy his soul, as orthodox Christianity satisfied his beloved father's: these have been the mainspring of his writing for over fifty years.

In the early part of his career, he was mainly known as a lecturer—and by all accounts he was a brilliant one. A protean figure on the platform, his native gifts of wit and eloquence enabled him to share with his audience the fruits of his remarkably wide reading. He tried to get *inside* the author he was discussing:

> In all these lectures . . . [he writes in the *Autobiography*] I worked myself up to such a pitch that I *became* the figure I was analysing . . . I gave myself up to the spirit of my particular man of genius. And it was with almost an erotic emotion, as if I were indulging myself in some kind of perverted love affair, that I entered the nerves of Dickens or Paul Verlaine or Henry James or Dostoievsky or Keats or Blake! . . . My whole idea of *criticism* was different from the academic idea. What I aimed at was a sort of transmigration of my soul, till, like a demon possessing a person, I serpentined myself into the skeleton of my author, and expounded his most eccentric reactions to life from the actual nerve-centres where these reactions originated.

The danger of such an undertaking is, of course, that no critic, however protean his nerve-centres, can be quite certain that in the transmigratory process he has not revealed more of himself than of his author. Dickens, Dostoievsky, Henry James . . . all have a distinct flavour of John Cowper Powys before he has done with them, as G. K. Chesterton imposed his own characteristics upon such varied figures as Cobbett, Browning and St. Thomas Aquinas. We can judge something of the effect of these lectures by reading Powys's published criticisms, such books as *Visions and Revisions* (1915), *Suspended Judgments: Essays on Books and*

Sensations (1916), *The Meaning of Culture* (1930) and *The Pleasures of Literature* (1938). Prolix and repetitive as they are, these books do reveal something of the genius that made the author such a stimulating figure on the platform and such a brilliant conversationalist in private life. The valuable insights are always there, if the reader has to quarry for them among much else.

The prodigal fluency and the genius for introspective digression are seen at their height in the *Autobiography*, but here they can be accepted without much reservation. It was part of Powys's purpose in this remarkable book to disarm criticism by making such a display of his own failings—'my naughty passion', he calls it, 'for tearing my own repute to tatters'—that the confession, like a modern Rousseau's, would be transformed into a virtue. Here the admitted theatricality comes perilously close to exhibitionism, the impulse to 'glory in the feminine aspects of my character' too much indulged in to make unembarrassed reading. Yet there is much to be said on the other side. Autobiography is a loose form of literature and can survive treatment that would be fatal elsewhere. To digress, to turn aside as a thought strikes one—as the memory of the American negro struck Powys while summing up his impressions of the United States:

> But I have not yet touched upon the most important blessing in this nomadic life of mine . . . I found myself in contact with a race of human beings who are as superior to the rest of humanity, in all the qualities that I, as a philosopher, have come most to admire, as moss is superior to lichen . . .
>
> Slavery, with its appalling slave-ships navigated by so many sea-dogs of English birth, has at least, this worst crime of our race, resulted in the emergence of a divine and incomparable breed of men and women . . . How this black race did redeem humanity for me as I moved about their adopted home! . . . I came to look forward to every 'Diner' because of its African waiter and to every night-coach because of its African porter. The mere sound of these people's voices . . .

—such digressions are no more a weakness here than to be conscious, as John Cowper Powys has always been, of the masks which a complicated, sensitive personality like himself has necessarily had to assume in order to face the world. The overall impression left by the *Autobiography* is one of respect for a soul seeking to come to terms with itself, if we can also see why the paradoxes in the author's nature have so irritated some of his closest friends.

He was affectionately caricatured as 'Jack Welsh' in Louis Wilkinson's novel *The Buffoon*, and in *Blasphemy and Religion* (1916) Wilkinson contrasted the 'sensationalism' of *Wood and Stone* with the 'valid experience' of Theodore's *Soliloquies of a Hermit*, maintaining that while John Cowper's novel is 'as sounding brass and tinkling cymbal', people would still be reading the *Soliloquies* in a hundred years' time. This is an over-kind judgement on the *Soliloquies* themselves, if an impressive forecast—made before most of them were written—of the abiding quality of Theodore's novels and stories. There is certainly a relevant distinction, in point of 'valid experience', between the best novels and stories of Theodore and the early romances of John. But 'sensationalism' is hardly the final word for John Cowper's fiction in its most striking development—as seen, for example, in *Wolf Solent* (1929), *A Glastonbury Romance* (1933), *Jobber Skald* (1935) and *Maiden Castle* (1936). Rather are we conscious, in these extraordinary—but also extraordinarily interesting—productions of the romantic, philosophical and humorous imagination, of a similar blend of strength and weakness to that we observed in the critical work and in the *Autobiography*. For most people's tastes, there is altogether too much talk of such metaphysical sensations as 'The Unpardonable Sin', as in the chapter of that name in the *Glastonbury Romance:*

> The three men had reached the Abbey Barn at the corner of Bere Lane when things came to the worst with Mr. Evans.
> The wild and desperate thought seized him . . . 'Why not fling away every scruple?'

His mind seemed at that second absolutely balanced on a taut and twanging wire between two terrible eternities, an eternity of wilful horror, and an eternity of bleached, arid futility, devoid of all life-sap. He could feel the path to the horror, shivering with deadly phosphorescent sweetness. He could feel the path to the renunciation filling his nostrils with acrid dust, parching his naked feet, withering every human sensation till it was hollow as the shard of a dead beetle! The nature of his temptation was such that it had nothing to redeem it. Such abominable wickedness came straight out of the evil in the heart of the First Cause, travelled through the interlunar spaces, and entered the particular nerve in the erotic organism of Mr. Evans which was predestined to respond to it.

For most people's tastes, too, there are altogether too many exclamation marks on nearly every page of these romances. The true value of an exclamation mark surely becomes weakened if it is placed almost automatically at the end of nearly every sentence, as it frequently is in *Wolf Solent*:

> The intense reality of Mr. Malakite's figure beneath those bed-clothes, of his beard above them, of his nostrils, his old-man's eyelids, his ugly beast-ears, narrowed the reality of his own life, with its gathered memories, into something as concrete, tangible, compact as the bony knuckles of his own gaunt hands now resting upon his protruding knees! Thought? It was 'thought', of course! But not thought in the abstract. It was the thought of a tree, of a snake, of an ox, of a man, a man begotten, a man conceived, a man like enough to die to-morrow! With what within him had he felt that shrewd thrust just now about his true-love Chris? Not with any 'glassy essence'. Simply with his vegetable-animal integrity, *with his life*, as a tree would feel the loss of its companion . . . as a beast the loss of its mate!

This breathless, feminine, introspective prose is typical of many chapters in the romances, as it is of many passages in the *Autobiography* and in the critical and philosophical works. But it has its more admirable side. Novelists who are as much interested in the darker and more eccentric 'countries of the mind' as in the normal actions and thoughts of their characters are not common in English literature; to find a parallel we must turn rather to some of the Russian novelists of the nineteenth century, particularly perhaps to Dostoievsky, whom Powys regards 'with Thomas Hardy and Sir Walter Scott as his sole rivals, as the greatest of all novelists in the world.' John Cowper's protean nature serves him well in the romances: the 'masks' and the 'feminine aspects' are here given a local habitation and a name—the locality being mainly the Somerset and Dorset of his own upbringing, the name being Wolf Solent, Christie Malakite, John Crow, Nell Zoyland, 'Bloody Johnny', Owen Evans or another. Every character shares in John Cowper's own introspective habits, even in the most private and intimate circumstances of life:

> And now, as their dalliance sank into quiescence, one of Wolf's final thoughts before he slept was of the vast tracts of unknown country that every human consciousness includes in its scope. Here, to the superficial eye, were two skulls, lying side by side; but, in reality, here were two far-extending continents, each with its own sky, its own land and water, its own strange-blowing winds. And it was only because his own soul had been, so to speak, washed clean of its body that day that he was able to feel as he felt at this moment. But—even so—what those thoughts of hers had been, that he had interrupted by his return, he knew no better now than when first he had entered her room and had blown out her candle.

When John Cowper's genuine insights are balanced against his 'sensationalism' it must be admitted that he has explored more than most novelists into those 'vast tracts of unknown country' which have always so fascinated him— even if, in the final analysis, he has only discovered himself. His most famous novel, *A Glastonbury Romance*, which is a modern interpretation or endorsement of the ancient legend about Joseph of Arimathaea and the Holy Grail:

> . . . what really allured me about the Holy Grail were the unholy elements in both its history and its mystery . . . the unquestionable fact that it was much older than Christianity itself . . .

even this novel, with its thousand pages and scores of individual characters, is no real exception to the general characteristic governing all Powys's work. 'Every face on the canvas', John Redwood Anderson has truly written, is 'an aspect of a multitudinous and all-embracing self-portrait.' Or, as John Cowper has himself put it, in a recent edition of an earlier novel: 'Writing a preface to this book entitled *Wolf Solent* is like writing a commentary on my whole life . . .'

Llewelyn Powys was at times John Cowper's severest critic—once accusing him of being 'spiritually insincere'—but to this brother, twelve years younger, 'Daddy Jack' was the supreme genius of the family, 'by far the most exciting and God-like figure I have ever had to do with'. He felt he owed nearly everything to his brother's stimulating talk and encouragement:

> Have I not for a quarter of a century [he wrote in 1926] followed in the wake of John Cowper? All that I am I owe to him. Like a sagacious Sancho Panza, I have ever kept close behind his great medieval wain full of the foison of I know not what rich harvest-field. And whatever out of its largess his ample wagon gave to the wayside hedge, that have I had the wit to garner and . . . carry shrewdly off to the nearest market. For let them say what they will, it is John alone of all of us who can be likened to the forked lightning, he alone has undisputed access to those deep, cool wells where the gods themselves let down their buckets.

The comparison of John Cowper to Don Quixote has an unintentional critical force, but Llewelyn was too modest in calling himself the Sancho Panza. To his brother's encouragement he certainly owed a good deal, and his work in general can be described as 'autobiography' with even greater truth than John Cowper's. To John's influence, too, can be traced those features of Llewelyn's prose style which their brother, the architect A. R. Powys, rightly called 'affected'. There is hardly an unusual word in the whole of Theodore's writings: 'unclay' in the novel of that name is the only instance that springs to mind. But both John Cowper and Llewelyn Powys, like their elder contemporary Frederick Rolfe ('Baron Corvo'), are very fond of the unusual, particularly the archaic, word. As John Cowper's romances are full of words like 'mal-ease', 'malcontent', 'deviltry', 'discomfortable', 'umbrageous', 'talismanic', 'wittol', 'pilgarlic', 'welkin', 'ichor', 'semi-cirque' and 'eidolon', so Llewelyn is fond of 'whoreson', 'benison', 'shotten', 'largess', 'foison' and 'wain'.

But when Llewelyn Powys was not trying to 'write choice periods of prose', as he himself put it, he could write as simply and effectively as Theodore. His gift for fiction was not great, compared with his brothers'; he lacked John's fertility of invention and Theodore's power for allegory and fable. His one real novel, *Apples Be Ripe* (1930), for all the charm of its best passages, is a lesser thing altogether than his 'imaginary autobiography' *Love and Death* (1939) and the half-fictional, half-reminiscent stories and sketches in *Ebony and Ivory* and *Black Laughter*. Where Llewelyn excels is in his evocative descriptions of place and of nature: the Palestine of *A Pagan's Pilgrimage* (1931), the England of *Earth Memories* (1934), the Africa of *Black Laughter*:

> And then darkness would fall and the air would become full of unexplained noises and strange unexpected smells, and the African wind would blow against our faces and set the long tufted branches of the forest trees tossing against each other, and we would stumble through the grass to the old familiar shamba-track and so come nearer and nearer to the small lamp-lit house, where . . . we would sit over a crackling wood fire and talk of old days in Somersetshire . . .
>
> Suddenly clear and unmistakable out of the darkness would come the heavy booming of a gun. I never heard one of those gun-traps go off without a curious shock. One felt as though oneself was present down there under the trees by the black flowing water in utter loneliness . . .
>
> Morning would come at last, and we would . . . set off through the damp scrub down to the trap, and . . . there before us, stretched

out upon the cool, shining, dewy grass, would lie the long snake-like body of a gilded ebon-spotted cat. The mere fact that such an animal should actually be abroad upon the earth used to seem to me amazing . . . What taut muscles! What a suggestion of lithe and dangerous strength knit together with elastic ligaments! And how heavy that limp skin was, that limp gorgeous skin that smelt of the fierce leopard sweat of a thousand jungle nights.

Llewelyn Powys travelled nearly as widely as D. H. Lawrence. Italy, Greece, Palestine, Kenya, the United States, the West Indies . . . were among the countries he saw and described so vividly in his books and letters. And a walk on the Dorset downs with Llewelyn Powys was as fruitful an experience for his companions as a walk with Lawrence through the Midland countryside. Both men had the same gift for seeing nature with fresh eyes, with the added intensity of vision that has so often been remarked of consumptives.

It was in Kenya that he first found himself as a writer, and *Ebony and Ivory* (begun in England in 1913) and *Black Laughter* remain two of the best of his books. They also gave him his first welcome taste of success, so much so indeed that John Cowper in the *Autobiography* reflects—wryly as a writer, proudly as a brother—that in the middle twenties Llewelyn's reputation in the United States as much surpassed his own as Theodore's did in England: 'They were both recognized authors while I was still "John, the Talker".' It was not till the publication of the *Glastonbury Romance* and the *Autobiography* in the thirties that the fame of 'Don John' exceeded that of the self-styled Sancho Panza.

III

T. F. POWYS: THE EARLY WORKS

Few writers of our time have had so outwardly uneventful a life as Theodore Francis Powys. Born, like his elder brothers John and Littleton, at Shirley in Derbyshire, in 1875, he did not follow them to Cambridge but after his schooldays became a farmer for a short while in Suffolk. Then, in the autumn of 1901, he moved to a labourer's cottage in the seaside village of Studland, Dorset, resolving to live a life of contemplation on his father's allowance of £60 a year. He left Studland for East Chaldon in 1904, and it was about this time that he began to write *An Interpretation of Genesis*, privately printed in 1908. He started his first novel, *Mr. Tasker's Gods*, in 1916, but he did not begin to be known till 1923, with the publication of *The Left Leg*. Thereafter his publication was constant till the early thirties, after which he wrote little of importance. He moved in 1940 to Mappowder, where he died in 1953.

He was late in finding his true path, but then comparatively prolific for about ten years, from 1921 to 1931. He blossomed in the late summer or early autumn of his life, his best work being accomplished in his late forties and fifties. But we must always bear in mind, when speaking of T. F. Powys, the often considerable gap between composition and publication. As his son has told us:

> For many years publishers and editors would have none of him, and he worked on without recognition. His cupboards became filled with manuscripts copied and recopied laboriously in long-hand. When finally he became known his books were published in quick succession, for he only needed to open one of those cupboards to produce a ready-made novel or a short story.

I shall treat of his early work in order of composition, the order being known in most cases on the authority of Powys himself; otherwise his progress towards mastery would appear haphazard.

The *Interpretation of Genesis* need not detain us. There is little in this dialogue between Moses the Lawgiver and the author's mouthpiece, Zetetes the Seeker, to suggest the great Powys of *Mr. Weston* and the *Fables*, unless we see a faint resemblance to the latter in the use of the dialogue form. *Soliloquies of a Hermit* (written 1915, published 1916) is much more interesting, for here we first come across some of his leading ideas. For Powys, death is the desired end; and it would appear from the *Soliloquies* that he was led to this glad acceptance by considering that the most beautiful things in life blossom and fade, while unlovely things, like the stones of the field and 'the everlasting mud', remain. 'The attributes of immortality' to Powys are 'greed, hardness of heart, cunning—all the biting instincts of the animal.' His reverence for Jesus stems from his appreciation of the way Christ preached and practised the opposite. 'It does not matter if He is true', he adds: 'He is beyond all Truth.' The *Soliloquies* are lay sermons; the clerical inheritance, though brought here to a most unorthodox pass, was not entirely revoked.

More important, from the point of view of Powys the literary artist, is the way this early book of sometimes undigested philosophy looks forward to his greater work. We see, for instance, the *Fables* in embryo when he confesses here that he wants:

> to cultivate the kind of mind that can turn . . . a dull hour into heavenly glory . . . For what we call dullness is really the best soil we can dig in, because the gold that it yields is very precious . . .

Powys, however, had some way to go before he could mine gold from the seemingly dull and ordinary things in life; and he was always liable to fall into his main weakness of whimsicality, which makes some of his work 'very precious' in a different sense. To begin with, he was not quite sure of his path, and—curious as it seems for the future author of *Mr. Weston* and *Unclay*—he started his career in fiction by trying to be a realistic novelist. Between the composition of the *Soliloquies* and their publication in England (they were published first in the United States through the recommendation of John Cowper) he wrote two novels—*Mr. Tasker's Gods* (1916-17, published 1924) and *Black Bryony* (1917, published 1923)—besides a *nouvelle*, *Hester Dominy*, and a number of short stories. There are some fine things in all these, but their most striking characteristic, compared with the majority of the later work, is their bitter irony, their refusal to find comfort or compensation. *Mr. Tasker* has ironic moments worthy of Swift, but in general—and the criticism is almost equally true of *Black Bryony* and *Hester*— the worldly characters like Tasker himself (whose 'gods' are his pigs) have it so much their own way, and the unworldly are so feeble and so clearly doomed to failure from the start, that the novel leaves an unbalanced impression. Powys at this period (which was also, of course, the period of the bloodiest fighting of the First World War) seems to have been so bitterly convinced of man's inhumanity to man that his feelings would not allow him the artistic freedom he desired. There is a parallel here with his eighteenth-century ancestor Cowper, whose poetry he so much admired.

The change comes with *The Left Leg*: written 1921, published 1923. Like another Christian, though an heretical one, Powys passed through the Slough of Despond and took at last the true, allegorical path that was to lead to his most inspiring work. The reference to the *Pilgrim's Progress* is not inapposite, for from *The Left Leg* onwards Bunyan is evidently very much in Powys's mind. Eschewing realism, as usually understood, Powys became an allegorist and a fabulist and in so doing achieved, in the poetic or dramatic sense, a more profound reality. The worldly and the vicious prosper in *The Left Leg* almost as much as in *Mr. Tasker*, and the innocents in Madder village come to grief; but a whole new dimension is introduced, symbolised by the travelling tinker Jar. 'Who be wold Jar?' Mad Tom Button asks, and he answers his own question:

> ' 'E be the leaf that do drift in the wind. 'E be the cloud that do cross the moon at night time. 'E be the stone that a poor man do take up in road to throw at 'is dog. 'E be the pond weeds where do bide the wold toad. 'E be the bastard child before 'tis born. Wold Jar be come.'

And with the coming of 'wold Jar', both to Madder village and to Powys's work, the road to *Mr. Weston*, the *Fables* and *Unclay* lies open. The name Jar probably comes from the Hebrew divine name YHWH, translated into English as Jahweh or Jehovah. But Powys's God is a pantheistic conception, whether symbolised by Tinker Jar, by Squire Jar in *The Key of the Field*, by the fisherman in *Mockery Gap*, by Mr. Weston in the *Good Wine* or by the vision of Christ the compassionate which appears to the good dog in the fable *The Dog and the Lantern:*

> 'The Saviour of the world', replied the Christ, 'can be every-thing. Little Betty may find a lucky stone by the seaside—that stone am I. Dig down into the clay where poor Tom, the madman, lies buried. His coffin-boards are rotted, his flesh is clay—I am he. The sexton stole the church oil—I was that too—and sold it to the shepherd, who filled me with it.'

Absolute consistency in philosophical ideas is not required of a novelist or a poet. It may be doubted, for example, whether Powys's idea of the grave as a place of rest is quite consistent with his denial of immortality. We only know we have been asleep when we wake up, and if we do not wake up the whole analogy of death with sleeping is logically false. It is a fair criticism of Powys to point out, too, that sometimes his Gods are too numerous for conviction: there does not seem to be any necessity for bringing Jar into *Mr. Weston* or Mr. Weston into *Unclay*. But what is import-ant is the undoubted fact that, with this whole new dimension added, the novels and stories become much more alive. There is a poetic reality in *The Left Leg* more impres-sive, on the whole, than the comparatively laboured realism of *Mr. Tasker, Black Bryony* or *Hester Dominy*. Farmer Mew, who 'do swallow all', is not a realistic figure, but he is a convincing personification of greed, a worthy adversary for Tinker Jar:

> The figure and the aspect of the man were terrible. He stood as though he were resisting to the uttermost a huge force. With every sinew he fought Jar.

He is as real to the reader as comparable characters in the plays of Ben Jonson and the novels of Dickens.

The success of *The Left Leg* must have shown Powys where his true strength lay, though for some time he was to dissipate it by his unfortunate taste for the fanciful. The succeeding novels of the early twenties—*Mark Only* (1922, published 1924) *Mockery Gap* (1923, published 1925) and *Innocent Birds* (1923-4, published 1926)—show a progressive mastery in control of the allegorical, the last-named in particular being one of Powys's most impressive early achievements. Dorset in these novels, like the Yorkshire moors in *Wuthering Heights*, is the world in miniature: 'a picture', as Mr. Solly puts it in *Innocent Birds*, 'that can show a vaster and a grander one behind it.' If Powys had ended his career here, however, he would not have been the great writer he so clearly is, for even the best of these early novels and stories can fairly be criticized for their weaknesses of whimsicality and melodrama. But the first masterpiece lay immediately ahead. Powys began *Mr. Weston's Good Wine* in January 1924 and completed it in the autumn of the following year; it was published in 1927 and has been the most widely read and the most frequently translated of all his work.

IV

MR. WESTON AND AFTER

The difference between *Mr. Weston's Good Wine* and the best of the early novels and stories is not one of kind—not the difference that separates *The Left Leg* from *Mr. Tasker's Gods*—but one of degree: this first masterpiece, completed when the author was fifty, is a triumph of tone and controlled energy, in which the incidental weaknesses of even the best of the early work are almost entirely overcome. It makes deceptively easy reading, but behind the apparent simplicity lay eighteen months' writing and rewriting, before the author was satisfied that he had the precise effect he desired. Mr. Weston himself is a creation who could easily have become spoilt for the reader at many delicate points, particularly in the early chapters. We can only admire the way Powys has succeeded in making the wine-merchant human and likeable and at the same time indubitably God, the creator of the village of Folly Down (there is an actual village of Folly, near Mappowder) and the town of Maidenbridge (Dorchester) which Hardy in the Wessex novels calls Casterbridge. Mr. Weston can move easily from the most familiar speech and all too human failings—he has an author's vanity about his own collected writings, the Bible—to the most profound and lofty utterance; he can discuss the poet Cowper with Luke Bird and also, like Jesus at Cana, turn the water into wine to facilitate Luke's marriage to Jenny Bunce; he can converse on equal and waggish terms with the landlord and customers of the Angel Inn, but when he hides his face in his mug and takes 'a very deep draught' the words (from *Isaiah* XLV, 7):

> 'I form the light, and create darkness: I make peace, and create evil: I, the Lord, do all these things . . .'

are heard by everyone in the room, though no one knows who said them. The triumph of the novel is partly a triumph of language.

Dorset is the epitome of the world, and the Dorset dialect is transformed into poetry without losing its characteristic local qualities. As early as *The Left Leg* Powys had been able to make this transformation; here it is the grave-digger Mr. Grunter who rises to the heights of simple eloquence when Mr. Weston confronts the Mumby brothers with the corrupted body of Ada Kiddle, who had drowned herself after being ravished by them:

> Though the worms had destroyed Ada's beauty, her shape was still there, and Mr. Grunter regarded her compassionately . . . 'When life bain't', said Mr. Grunter slowly, 'death be' . . .

A picture may move a man, and this picture affected Mr. Grunter . . . 'Ada', he said . . .' 'tain't I that have moulded 'ee, 'tain't I that have rotted thee's merry ways wi' wormy clay . . .'

. . . Mr. Weston had covered his face with his hands, as if he wept.

God as a tradesman, with a Ford car: it is an even more original conception than God as a travelling tinker, whose 'only garment is a thundercloud but he sometimes mends kettles'. Mr. Weston sells two kinds of wine: the Light Wine, which is Love, and for which the payment is Love returned; and the Dark Wine, which is Death, and for which the payment is Life. And these two wines, in the Powysian creed, are not two wines but one wine—an idea which Powys developed further in *Unclay*, where Death says to Priscilla Hayhoe:

'I kill, and Love gives life, but in reality we are one and the same. We often exchange our weapons. And then 'tis I that give life, and Love that kills . . .'

as Love kills Tamar in *Mr. Weston* after she has met her angel Michael 'in oak-tree bed'.

Another subtle point in *Mr. Weston*, that the wine-merchant himself longs to die but cannot—'I long to drink my own dark wine'—is developed further, not only in *Unclay* but in *The Only Penitent* and the *Fables*. This latter series of stories—written 1927, published 1929, republished 1934 under the title *No Painted Plumage*—is Powys's second masterpiece, as original in conception and as successful in execution as *Mr. Weston* itself. It owes part of its origin to a remark by Llewelyn Powys, who suggested to his brother that he should 'write about *anything*; write about that log of wood and that old boot.' Somewhat in the spirit of their ancestor Cowper's *Task*, Powys proceeded to do just that, in a series of stories whose principal feature is dialogue between such varied personalities as a clout and a pan, a donkey and a rabbit, a stone and a skull, a bucket and a rope, a spittoon and a slate. These stories—delightfully humorous and ironic, yet often the vehicle for the profoundest meditations upon life and death—rival *Mr. Weston* itself in their masterly simplicity, in their easy transition from the most familiar, everyday things to the most momentous. In the opening fable, for instance, the pan passes from talk of Mrs. Keddle's cracked bedroom basin to remark:

> 'Time goes on—'
> 'Alas! that is true,' murmured the clout, 'and I that am but a cotton rag, and all the Keddles upon the earth, together with the most huge and distant stars, must know of its going.'

The Dorset dialect is again transformed into poetry, as when the church clerk in the fable *Mr. Pim and the Holy Crumb* imagines God to resemble the landlord at the village inn:

> ' 'E did draw I out of 'Is great barrel into a little cup, and when I die 'E do but empty I again into the dirt from whence I came. They be 'Is notions . . . Some do fall of a sudden, some bent and tottering like wold Barker do tarry long, but all do go to dust.'

It is in this fable—perhaps the masterpiece of the whole series—that the Holy Crumb, dropped by Mr. Pim at his first Communion, repeats the lonely cry of Mr. Weston the wine-trader. 'But bain't 'E God?' demands Mr. Pim, puzzled. 'Yes, alas so!' replies the Crumb. . . . The awful loneliness of God, however many forms He may take in the pantheistic imagination, was a problem that never ceased to exercise Powys's mind.

The chief of the later works, in order of publication (the exact time of writing not being known here), are *Kindness in a Corner* (1930), a light, humorous novel with one magnificent chapter about a country churchyard entitled 'The Dirt of God'; the story *The Only Penitent* (1931), later included in the collection *Bottle's Path* (1946); his last full-length novel *Unclay* (1931); and the *nouvelle*, *The Two Thieves*, published with two other stories in

1932. Powys had written stories of varying length, collected at different times, from as early as 1917; and he continued to do so. At his best, he is equal to the most distinguished writers of the short story in our time; but it must be admitted that there are quite a number of his shorter pieces which are very feeble indeed in their forced whimsicality and stale repetition of effects.

His last full-length novel, *Unclay*, was a conscious attempt to sum up his life's work. He had always been fond of giving his characters in one story a new lease of life in another; such figures as Luke Bird, Miss Pettifer, Mr. Balliboy, Lord Bullman, 'wold Barker', Farmer Told . . . recur frequently. But the way characters and situations from earlier novels recur in *Unclay* is evidence of deliberate design. He could not resurrect Farmer Mew, because that personification of greed had blown himself up, his left leg falling from the sky 'according to the scriptures' of the English nursery rhyme; but the brutal Farmer Mere in *Unclay* is a deliberate reminder of him, as is Mere's victim Susie Dawe of Mew's victim Mary Gillet. Powys even goes back to the mood of the *Soliloquies*, for the meditations which are a feature of this last novel:

> In the common lives of people, one power is always waiting ready to drive out another, in order to rule in its place. There is always a stronger one coming. Each guardian of the temple is slain in his turn, then the victor becomes priest in his stead. Power that conquers power is the order of all our lives, but who is it that dare name the last power to kill? What will He do, when the fatal blow is struck, and He becomes lord of the temple, with no rival to challenge His victory? . . . Shall He hear again the many trampling feet of a new generation of men, or will the last enemy destroy Him too? Will God die? . . .
>
> All thought in Dodder was quieted. Still waters covered all motion, and no mental webs were being spun there that bring false hope to man. To grow like the field flowers, what else could man do? To bloom in the summer . . . and drink the dark wine of the sadness of the earth during the fall. To breathe deep again,

perhaps, when the winter's sleep is ended . . . To exist as a creature of the earth for a moment, what more should be needed?

The evening gnats quivered and danced in the warm air, unmindful of danger. The swallows caught them and they heeded not the act . . . So the evening is devoured by the night, and the dawn by the day.

Unclay is the complement to *Mr. Weston*: as time stops in that novel, so here Death loses his commission and is forced to give his scythe a rest. And Powys here tries to solve some of the philosophical problems raised by the earlier masterpiece. The attempt is not entirely successful; and while this last novel is Powys's most profound treatment of the themes of Love and Death, it is not so much of an artistic unity as *Mr. Weston*.

The Only Penitent, written about the same time as *Unclay*, sums up Powys's matured views in a smaller space. No one comes to Mr. Hayhoe to confess his sins till one sultry afternoon, culminating in a thunderstorm—the Powyses use weather for dramatic effect with Shakespearean assurance— a Person descends Madder Hill, enters the church, and kneels humbly before him:

'Who are you?' asked Mr. Hayhoe, whose own voice sounded strange to him.

'I am the Only Penitent', replied Jar. 'I have come to confess my sin to you . . . Only by the forgiveness of man can I be saved . . . By love, all is forgiven.'

'Dare I love you?' asked Mr. Hayhoe.

Jar bowed his head.

'I crucified my son', he said . . . ' 'Twas I who created every terror in the earth, the rack, the plague, all despair, all torment . . . Can you love me now?'

In earlier days, Powys would have had no answer; even Mr. Weston is silent when accused by Martin Mumby at the graveside of Ada Kiddle. But now, in an inspired moment, Mr. Hayhoe looks up from the kneeling Jar and sees his wife Priscilla waiting for him; and he knows that

Jar's bitterness—like the bitterness of *Mr. Tasker's Gods* and *Black Bryony*—is not the whole truth:

> 'You have not told all', he said. 'You have not spoken of the joy and love that a woman can give, you have not told of the great peace that you also can bestow upon those who desire it . . .'
>
> 'I destroy all men with a sword', said Jar. 'I cast them down into the pit, they become nothing.'
>
> 'Hold!' cried Mr. Hayhoe. 'Is that last word true?'
>
> 'It is', answered Jar.
>
> 'Then, in the name of Man,' said Mr. Hayhoe boldly, 'I forgive your sin; I pardon and deliver you from all your evil; confirm and strengthen you in all goodness, and bring you to everlasting death.'

Jar is forgiven by his creation; Mr. Weston can drink his own dark wine. . . . There is a perfection about the ending of this story that is not common in English literature. It did not come easily; all the bitter irony of *Mr. Tasker* and its successors had to be worked through first, the blind alleys of whimsicality had to be thoroughly explored, before Powys could attain these apparently simple heights. He was not often to attain them again, though *The Two Thieves* is a fine and assured allegory, in which John Roe—or Everyman—occupies much the same position in regard to Tinker Jar as Mr. Hayhoe in *The Only Penitent*.

V

CONCLUSION

It is an axiom in literary criticism that an author shall be judged by his best works, and fortunately in the case of the Powys brothers there has been little controversy as to which these are. The greatness of T. F. Powys is clearly in his *Fables* and in the more allegorical of his novels and stories, particularly perhaps *Mr. Weston's Good Wine*, *Unclay*, *The Left Leg*, *The Only Penitent* and *The Two Thieves*. Where he has attempted a more realistic path, as in *Mr. Tasker's Gods* and *Black Bryony*, or where his weakness for the whimsical has got the better of him, as in *Kindness in a Corner* and some of the shorter stories, he is not, on the whole, so convincing and cannot be called more than an interesting minor writer of our time.

Similarly, though John Cowper Powys has written a good deal in nearly every branch of literature except—curiously enough—the dramatic, he is clearly not one of our greater poets or our greater poet-critics. The 'poetry' of this most Celtic—even at times most 'wild and woolly Western'—of the Powys brothers is rather to be found in his *Autobiography* and in what he has himself well described as 'the sort of mystic-humorous, Pantagruelian, Shandean, Quixotic Romance' that is seen at its best in the novel whose 'heroine is the Grail'. *A Glastonbury Romance* has never been everyone's reading; it requires for its appreciation, not only sympathy with the idiom of its author, but a series of suspensions of disbelief that are by no means easy to sustain in the twentieth century. In spite of its popular and humorous aspects—John Cowper's superlative opinion of Theodore's more ironic humour is a compliment that can sometimes be repaid to his own—it is clearly a work destined to be fully enjoyed only by scholars.

Llewelyn Powys has two styles of writing, which appeal to two distinct publics—or to two generations. His more allusive and affected style is reminiscent of the Lamb-Hazlitt circle as known to us through their essays; his biographer Malcolm Elwin says truly that he 'may eventually claim his place as a prose-writer in the dynasty of Landor and Pater'. But there is another Llewelyn, of a plainer style, who appeals more to the taste of the mid-twentieth century. In some of the chapters of *Black Laughter* the very feel of Africa is given to us in a relatively unadorned prose that is the reverse of Lamb's or Pater's and whose nearest modern equivalent is George Orwell's.

The first public critic of the Powys brothers was their

friend Louis Wilkinson, and after the lapse of nearly half a century it must be admitted that Mr. Wilkinson's early judgement has been proved right. The classic of the family, one can but agree, is T. F. Powys, though not by any means in the whole of his work nor to the detriment of his brothers. Theodore's subject is often Man rather than men and women; in their treatment of individuals, John Cowper and Llewelyn are sometimes superior. Where Theodore gives the type, they give the personality: the old sexton in *Love and Death*, for instance, compared with old Sextonhood in the *Fables*.

The Powys brothers—all three 'poets' in the widest sense of the word, though their poetic, religious view of life has mostly been expressed in prose—present a somewhat isolated picture in the English literature of the twentieth century. Belonging to no current school or contemporary trend, they have never been widely popular, never been honoured with Nobel Prizes or Orders of Merit, and at different times have been rashly dismissed as old-fashioned. In the Marxist hey-day of the thirties, their concern with ultimate problems seemed bourgeois; and when ultimate problems—or ultimate answers—became the rage in the forties, the heretical Powyses were swept aside in the flood of an orthodox Christian revival. Their insistence on the brutal as well as the peaceful aspects of country life removed them from the 'culture-agriculture' equation of contemporary back-to-the-land theorists, as their Rabelaisian delight in what Shakespeare called 'country matters' from the more urban and cosmopolitan varieties of the erotic. But writers who have never been in fashion cannot logically be accused of becoming out of it.

THE POWYS FAMILY

A Select Bibliography

(Place of publication London unless stated otherwise)

JOHN COWPER POWYS

Bibliography:

A BIBLIOGRAPHY OF THE FIRST EDITIONS OF JOHN COWPER POWYS, by
L. E. Siberell. Cincinnati (1934).

Separate Works:

ODES AND OTHER POEMS (1896).

POEMS (1899).

THE WAR AND CULTURE. New York (1914). *Polemic*
—English edition, entitled *The Menace of German Culture*, 1915.

VISIONS AND REVISIONS. New York (1915). *Criticism*
—revised edition with new preface by the author, 1955.

WOOD AND STONE. New York (1915). *Novel*
—English edition, 1917.

CONFESSIONS OF TWO BROTHERS. Rochester, N.Y. (1916). *Autobiography*
—with Llewelyn Powys.

WOLF'S BANE RHYMES. New York (1916). *Verse*

ONE HUNDRED BEST BOOKS. New York (1916). *Commentary*

RODMOOR. New York (1916). *Novel*

SUSPENDED JUDGMENTS. New York (1916). *Criticism*

MANDRAGORA. New York (1917). *Verse*

THE COMPLEX VISION. New York (1920). *Philosophy*

SAMPHIRE. New York (1922). *Verse*

PSYCHOANALYSIS AND MORALITY. San Francisco (1923). *Philosophy*

THE ART OF HAPPINESS. Girard, Kansas (1925). *Philosophy*

THE RELIGION OF A SCEPTIC. New York (1925). *Philosophy*

DUCDAME (1925). *Novel*

THE SECRET OF SELF-DEVELOPMENT. Girard, Kansas (1926.) *Philosophy*

ESSAYS ON MONTAIGNE, PASCAL, VOLTAIRE. Girard, Kansas (c.1926).
Criticism

THE ART OF FORGETTING THE UNPLEASANT. Girard, Kansas (1928).
Philosophy

WOLF SOLENT (1929). *Novel*
—new edition with preface by the author, 1961.

THE MEANING OF CULTURE. New York (1929). *Philosophy*
—English edition, 1930. New edition with new introduction by the
author, 1939.

IN DEFENCE OF SENSUALITY (1930). *Philosophy*

THE OWL, THE DUCK, AND—MISS ROWE! MISS ROWE! Chicago (1930).
Short stories

DEBATE! IS MODERN MARRIAGE A FAILURE? New York (1930.) *Polemic*
—with Bertrand Russell.

DOROTHY M. RICHARDSON (1931). *Criticism*

A GLASTONBURY ROMANCE. New York (1932). *Novel*
—English edition, 1933. New edition with preface by the author,
1955.

A PHILOSOPHY OF SOLITUDE (1933). *Philosophy*
—American and English editions have different prefaces.

WEYMOUTH SANDS. New York (1934). *Novel*
—English edition (with modified text) entitled *Jobber Skald*, 1935.

AUTOBIOGRAPHY (1934).

THE ART OF HAPPINESS (1935). *Philosophy*
—not identical with American pamphlet with the same title.

MAIDEN CASTLE. New York (1936). *Novel*
—English edition, 1937.

MORWYN (1937). *Novel*

THE PLEASURES OF LITERATURE (1938). *Essays*

OWEN GLENDOWER. New York (1940). *Novel*
—English edition, 1941.

MORTAL STRIFE (1941). *Commentary*

THE ART OF GROWING OLD (1944). *Philosophy*

DOSTOIEVSKY (1946). *Criticism*

PAIR DADENI OF THE CAULDRON OF REBIRTH. Carmarthen (1946). *Pamphlet*

OBSTINATE CYMRIC: ESSAYS 1935–1947. Carmarthen (1947). *Criticism*

RABELAIS (1948). *Biography*
—with new translations and critical commentary.

PORIUS (1951). *Novel*

THE INMATES (1952). *Novel*

IN SPITE OF (1953). *Philosophy*

ATLANTIS (1954). *Novel*

THE BRAZEN HEAD (1956). *Novel*

LUCIFER (1956). *Verse*

UP AND OUT (1957). *Stories*
—contains also 'the Mountains of the Moon'.

THE LETTERS OF JOHN COWPER POWYS TO LOUIS WILKINSON: 1935–1956 (1958)
—edited by L. Wilkinson.

HOMER AND THE AETHER (1959). *Paraphrase of 'The Iliad'*.

ALL OR NOTHING (1960). *Novel*

Note: J. C. Powys's introductions to books by other writers have been omitted from this check-list.

LLEWELYN POWYS

Separate Works:

EBONY AND IVORY (1923). *Stories and Sketches*
—with a preface by E. Shanks. American edition has a preface by T. Dreiser.

THIRTEEN WORTHIES. New York (1923). *Biographical Essays*
—English edition, 1924, with preface by Van W. Brooks.

HONEY AND GALL. Girard, Kansas (1924). *Essays*

CUP-BEARERS OF WINE AND HELLEBORE. Girard, Kansas (1924). *Literary Studies*

BLACK LAUGHTER. New York (1924). *Stories and Sketches*
—English edition, 1925. New edition with foreword by N. Farson, 1953.

SKIN FOR SKIN. New York (1925). *Autobiography*
—English edition, 1926.

THE VERDICT OF BRIDLEGOOSE. New York (1926). *Autobiography*
—English edition, 1927. This was reprinted in one volume with *Skin for Skin*, 1948.

HENRY HUDSON (1927). *Biography*

OUT OF THE PAST. Pasadena, California (c.1928). *Essay*
—later included in *Earth Memories*.

THE CRADLE OF GOD (1929). *Philosophy*
—new edition with preface by E. Carr, 1949.

AN HOUR ON CHRISTIANITY. New York (1930). *Philosophy*
—English edition (entitled *The Pathetic Fallacy: A Study of Christianity*), 1930, reprinted in *The Thinker's Library*, 1931.

APPLES BE RIPE (1930). *Novel*
—reprinted in *Big Ben Books*, 1940.

A PAGAN'S PILGRIMAGE (1931). *Travel*

IMPASSIONED CLAY (1931). *Philosophy*

THE LIFE AND TIMES OF ANTHONY A'WOOD (1932)
—abridged from A. Clark's edition with introductory essay. Reprinted in *World's Classics*, 1961.

NOW THAT THE GODS ARE DEAD. New York (1932). *Philosophy*
—English edition, with *The Glory of Life*, 1949.

GLORY OF LIFE (1934). *Philosophy*
—a *Golden Cockerell Press* limited edition, with wood engravings by R. Gibbings, 1930.

EARTH MEMORIES (1934). *Essays*
—with woodcuts by G. M. Powys.

DAMNABLE OPINIONS (1935). *Philosophy*

DORSET ESSAYS (1935). *Essays*
—twelve of these were reprinted (New York, 1938), with *Earth Memories* and introduction by Van W. Brooks.

THE TWELVE MONTHS (1936). *Essays*

SOMERSET ESSAYS (1937). *Essays*
—republished with *Dorset Essays*, 1957, with introduction by J. C. Powys.

RATS IN THE SACRISTY (1937). *Biographical and Critical essays*
—with preface by J. C. Powys and wood engravings by G. M. Powys.

THE BOOK OF DAYS (1937). *Philosophy*
—thoughts selected from the philosophy of Ll. Powys by J. Wallis, with introduction by Ll. Powys.

LOVE AND DEATH: AN IMAGINARY AUTOBIOGRAPHY (1939)
—with introduction by A. Gregory.

A BAKER'S DOZEN. Herrin, Ill. (1939). *Essays*
—with introduction by L. E. Siberell and illustrations by M. Noheimer. English edition, 1941, has introduction by J. C. Powys and decorations by G. M. Powys.

THE LETTERS OF LLEWELYN POWYS (1943)
—selected and edited by L. Wilkinson, with introduction by A. Gregory.

SWISS ESSAYS (1947).

ADVICE TO A YOUNG POET (1949). *Letters*
—to Kenneth Hopkins.

LLEWELYN POWYS: A SELECTION OF HIS WRITINGS (1952)
—selected by K. Hopkins, contains 20 letters first published and 3 essays here first collected.

THEODORE FRANCIS POWYS

Collected Stories:

THE WHITE PATERNOSTER (1930).

BOTTLE'S PATH (1946).

GOD'S EYES A-TWINKLE, selected and introduced by C. Prentice (1947).

Separate Works:

AN INTERPRETATION OF GENESIS (1908). *Meditations*
—privately printed. New edition, 1929.

THE SOLILOQUY OF A HERMIT. New York (1916). *Meditations*
—English edition, 1918, entitled *Soliloquies of a Hermit*.

THE LEFT LEG: HESTER DOMINY: ABRAHAM MEN (1923). *Stories*

BLACK BRYONY (1923). *Novel*
—woodcuts by R. A. Garnett.

MARK ONLY (1924). *Novel*

MR. TASKER'S GODS. New York (1924). *Novel*
—English edition, 1925. (Written 1916-17).

MOCKERY GAP (1925). *Novel*

A STUBBORN TREE (1926). *Story*

INNOCENT BIRDS (1926). *Novel*

FEED MY SWINE (1926). *Story*
—later included in *The White Paternoster*.

A STRONG GIRL and THE BRIDE (1926). *Stories*
—the latter included in *The White Paternoster*.

MR. WESTON'S GOOD WINE (1927). *Novel*
—illustrations by G. Charlton. *Penguin* edition 1937.

THE RIVAL PASTORS (1927). *Story*
—later included in *The White Paternoster*.

WHAT LACK I YET? (1927). *Story*
—later included in *The White Paternoster*.

THE HOUSE WITH THE ECHO (1928). *Stories*
—the title story written 1917-18.

THE DEWPOND (1928).
—later included in *Bottle's Path*.

FABLES (1929)
—new edition, 1934, entitled *No Painted Plumage*.

THE KEY OF THE FIELD (1930). *Story*
—later included in *Bottle's Path*.

URIAH ON THE HILL. Cambridge (1930). *Story*

KINDNESS IN A CORNER (1930). *Novel*

CHRIST IN THE CUPBOARD (1930). *Story*
—later included in *The White Paternoster*.

UNCLE DOTTERY. Bristol (1930). *Story*

WHEN THOU WAST NAKED (1931). *Story*
—later included in *Bottle's Path*.

THE ONLY PENITENT (1931) *Story*
—later included in *Bottle's Path*.

UNCLAY (1931). *Novel*

THE TITHE BARN and THE DOVE AND THE EAGLE (1932). *Stories*
—the latter included in *Bottle's Path*.

THE TWO THIEVES: GOD: IN GOOD EARTH (1932). *Stories*

MAKE THYSELF MANY (1935). *Story*

CAPTAIN PATCH (1935). *Stories*

GOAT GREEN (1937). *Story*
—engravings by G. Morgan. Later included in *Bottle's Path* under the
title of *The Better Gift*.

LITTLETON CHARLES POWYS

THE JOY OF IT (1937). *Memoirs*

THE POWYS FAMILY. Yeovil (1952). *Pamphlet*

STILL THE JOY OF IT (1956). *Memoirs*

ALBERT REGINALD POWYS

THE ENGLISH HOUSE (1929). *Pamphlet*

REPAIR OF ANCIENT BUILDINGS (1929).

THE ENGLISH PARISH CHURCH (1930)
—with an introduction by E. Ferrers.

ORIGINS OF BAD ARCHITECTURE (1931). *Pamphlet*

FROM THE GROUND UP (1937)
—with an introduction by J. C. Powys.

PHILIPPA POWYS

DRIFTWOOD (1930). *Verse*

THE BLACKTHORN WINTER (1930). *Novel*

MARIAN POWYS

LACE AND LACE-MAKING. Boston (1953).

THE POWYS FAMILY

Some Biographical and Critical Studies:

BLASPHEMY AND RELIGION: Dialogue about WOOD AND STONE by J. C. Powys and THE SOLILOQUY OF A HERMIT by T. F. Powys, by L. U. Wilkinson. New York (1916).

THE BUFFOON, by L. U. Wilkinson. New York (1916). *Novel*
—contains fictional portrait of J. C. Powys under the name Jack Welsh.

CRITICAL WOODCUTS, by S. Sherman. New York (1926)
—on Llewelyn Powys, pp. 138-155.

THE NOVELS AND STORIES OF T. F. POWYS, by W. Hunter. Cambridge (1930).

SWAN'S MILK, by L. Marlow (1934)
—an autobiographical novel which contains many reminiscences of the Powys Brothers. Marlow is a pen name of L. Wilkinson.

CRUMBS ARE ALSO BREAD, by M. Burrell (1934)
—contains notes on Llewelyn and J. C. Powys, pp. 128-140.

THE POWYS BROTHERS, by R. H. Ward (1936).

WELSH AMBASSADORS, by L. Marlow (1936)
—contains check-list of publications.

GENIUS OF ENGLAND, by H. J. Massingham (1937)
—contains a chapter on Llewelyn Powys.

JOHN COWPER POWYS, by W. C. Derry. Boston (1938)
—an interpretation.

THE TERRIBLE CRYSTAL, by M. S. Chaning-Pearce (1940)
—contains a section on J. C. Powys, pp. 180-193.

THE LIFE OF LLEWELYN POWYS, by M. Elvin (1946)
—new edition, 1953.

THE NEW SPIRIT, ed. E. W. Martin (1946)
—contains a chapter on Llewelyn Powys, pp. 42-53.

'The Path of T. F. Powys', by R. C. Churchill in *The Critic* (Spring, 1947).

LIVING WRITERS, edited by G. H. Phelps (1947)
—a broadcast symposium which contains an essay on T. F. Powys, pp. 151-157.

THE BROTHERS POWYS, by L. Wilkinson. Cincinnati (1947)
—reprinted in *Essays by Divers Hands*, 1948.

'J. C. Powys', by K. Hopkins in *World Review* (March, 1958).

'Llewelyn Powys: A village Radical' by W. G. Allen in *The Wind and the Rain* (Winter, 1949).

SEVEN FRIENDS, by L. Marlow (1953).

CATALOGUE OF MANUSCRIPTS OF LLEWELYN POWYS, by G. F. Simms. Hurst, Berks. (1953).

'The Quiet Man of Dorset' [T. F. Powys] by F. Powys in *The Adelphi* (Fourth Quarter, 1954).

J. C. Powys Number of *Dock Leaves*, ed. by R. Garlick. (Spring, 1956).

'A Famous Family', by A. Gregory in *The London Magazine* (March 1958).

T. F. POWYS, by H. Coombes (1960).

THE MODERN AGE, edited by B. Ford (1961)
—in Pelican Books: contains a chapter on T. F. Powys and Dylan Thomas, pp. 415-428.

'Lawrence, Joyce and [J.C.] Powys,' by G. Wilson Knight, in *Essays in Criticism* (October 1961).

Shakespeare:

The Histories

by L. C. KNIGHTS

Published for The British Council
and The National Book League
by Longmans, Green & Co.

Two shillings and sixpence net

in this essay Professor Knights, Winterstoke Professor of English at Bristol University, discusses Shakespeare's *Richard III*, *King John*, *Richard II* and *Henry V*.

As is the case with certain companion essays in the Shakespeare series, the illustrations have been chosen with particular reference to the most significant productions of their time. The bibliographies follow a uniform plan. They assume that Mr. J. R. Brown's bibliography in *Writers and Their Work* No. 58 is available to the reader, and in the main they confine themselves to the plays under immediate consideration. Essays and papers are not ordinarily included in the bibliographies of the Series but, as it is not possible to keep up with Shakespeare studies unless they are added, they here duly appear.

Forthcoming:

ROMAN PLAYS: T. J. B. Spencer   FINAL PLAYS: Frank Kermode
                    THE POEMS: J. W. Lever

Already Published:

SHAKESPEARE by C. J. Sisson: bibliography by J. R. Brown: a Student's Guide to the texts and the literature.
THE EARLY COMEDIES by Derek Traversi.
THE GREAT TRAGEDIES by Kenneth Muir.
THE PROBLEM PLAYS by Peter Ure.
THE LATE COMEDIES by G. K. Hunter.
THE CHRONICLES by Clifford Leech.

Bibliographical Series
of Supplements to 'British Book News'
on Writers and their Work

★

GENERAL EDITOR
Bonamy Dobrée

WILLIAM SHAKESPEARE

The Histories

Richard III. King John. Richard II. Henry V

by

L. C. KNIGHTS

. . . the truth of what we are
shows us but this   RICHARD II

Published for the British Council and
The National Book League by
LONGMANS GREEN & CO.

LONGMANS, GREEN & CO. LTD.,
48 Grosvenor Street, London, W.1.
Railway Crescent, Croydon, Victoria, Australia
Auckland, Kingston (Jamaica), Lahore, Nairobi

LONGMANS SOUTHERN AFRICA (PTY) LTD.
Thibault House, Thibault Square, Cape Town,
Johannesburg, Salisbury

LONGMANS OF NIGERIA LTD.
W.R. Industrial Estate, Ikeja

LONGMANS OF GHANA LTD.
Industrial Estate, Ring Road South, Accra

LONGMANS GREEN (FAR EAST) LTD.
443 Lockhart Road, Hong Kong

LONGMANS OF MALAYA LTD.
44 Jalan Ampang, Kuala Lumpur

ORIENT LONGMANS LTD.
Calcutta, Bombay, Madras
Delhi, Hyderabad, Dacca

LONGMANS CANADA LTD.
137 Bond Street, Toronto 2

First published in 1962
© L. C. Knights, 1962

Printed in Great Britain by
F. Mildner & Sons, London, E.C.1

CONTENTS

I.   SHAKESPEARE'S HISTORIES: The Background   *page* 7

II.   *RICHARD III*   16

III. *KING JOHN*   26

IV.   *RICHARD II*   31

V.   *HENRY V*   39

      A Select Bibliography   49

ILLUSTRATIONS

I.   David Garrick (1717-1779) as Richard III. *Reproduced from the painting by William Hogarth at the Walker Art Gallery, Liverpool.*

II. Alec Guinness as Richard II, in the Old Vic production of 1947.

III. Robert Helpmann as the dying King John.
Stratford-on-Avon Memorial Theatre production 1948.

IV. Design for production of Henry V by Charles Keane (1811-1868) by Thomas Grieves and L. Lloyds. *Reproduced from the water-colour at the Victoria and Albert Museum.*

¶ WILLIAM SHAKESPEARE was born at Stratford-on-Avon and was christened in the Parish Church on 26 April 1564. There, too, he died, on 23 April 1616, and was buried in the chancel, where a monument was erected before 1623.

SHAKESPEARE'S HISTORIES

I

SHAKESPEARE'S HISTORIES:
THE BACKGROUND

SHAKESPEARE wrote ten plays on subjects taken from English history, and although only four of them will be dealt with in this essay some general observations on 'the Histories' may be allowed to introduce the discussion of *Richard III*, *King John*, *Richard II* and *Henry V*.

To start with, although we shall all go on using the term 'Shakespeare's Histories', it would be as well if we could free ourselves from some misleading notions that go with it. 'The Histories' are better thought of not simply as History Plays—the dramatisation of past events—but as political plays. The Histories or Political Plays, moreover, do not form an entirely distinct and homogeneous species of Shakespearean drama: as with 'Shakespearean Tragedy' the blanket-term covers very great variety, and we need to be aware of this as well as of important common elements; there is continuity, development, but there is no mere repetition, no common formula for each member of the series. Finally, even though a rough grouping of plays on 'historical' themes clearly has its uses, these plays are properly understood only when they are seen in relation to others that are not historical or, in any obvious sense, political.

The political plays have of course a more obvious reference to events and accepted ideas outside themselves than is the case, for example, with *Othello*, and this raises the question of the kind of equipment necessary for the student. Here again there are a few simple distinctions to be made. To understand, to enjoy and to profit from these plays what we most need is of course an interest in men and affairs, a lively feeling for literature, and a capacity for responding to each play as a work of art. Given that basic and indispensable equipment however (and without it book-loads of information are of little use), some kinds of knowledge extraneous to the plays can help to sharpen our vision. Shakespeare was not, as was once believed, almost entirely ignorant of formal history, keeping by him, as was suggested in the eighteenth century, a 'chuckle-pated Historian' to give him facts which he afterwards vamped up.[1] He read for himself in Hall and Holinshed, and his reading did more than give him events that could be represented on the stage; it prompted his thinking about actions and reactions in the public world. As readers of the Histories therefore we need to know something of the Tudor view of history; even more, perhaps, we need to know something of the main assumptions behind men's thinking about politics in the sixteenth century, of the clash of ideas about such subjects as law, power, government, and the relations of men in society. It remains to add that when we have equipped ourselves with some information of this kind we shall be very careful not to assume that Shakespeare, in any play, is simply reflecting 'Tudor ideas', or that he is accepting them uncritically as premise for a dramatic action—not, at all events, unless we have good warrant from the play itself. In almost all his plays Shakespeare combined in a remarkable way a sense of tradition—the ability to assimilate and learn from the past— and the freshness and independence of one who sees and thinks for himself; even when he seems to put most emphasis on traditional and received ideas he has a way of subjecting those ideas to the keenest scrutiny: which of course is how tradition is kept alive, and part of the debt we owe to genius.

The major themes and assumptions of English historical writing in the sixteenth century have been admirably described by E. M. W. Tillyard in the second chapter of his

[1] E. K. Chambers, *A Short Life of Shakespeare*, (1933) pp. 242-3.

Shakespeare's History Plays—a book indispensable to the student. In the historians' treatment of the comparatively recent past the great theme was of course the slow and painful working out of the consequences of the deposition of Richard II and the providential accession of Henry Tudor by which the civil strife of more than half a century was brought to an end: 'So that all men'—in Hall's often quoted words—'(more clearer than the sun) may apparently perceive, that as by discord great things decay and fall to ruin, so the same by concord be revived and erected.' Nowadays we may feel a little ironic about the Tudor view of history, so convenient for the Tudor monarchs, just as we find it hard to stomach the use of Homilies appointed to be read in churches for absolutist propaganda. Perhaps fully to enter into the Tudor dread of renewed internal dissention it would be necessary to have some first-hand experience of the miseries of civil war—of how 'one doth rend the other of those that one wall and one foss shuts in' (*Purgatorio*, vi, 83–84). But a very little historical imagination should be enough to check our irony. When in 1548 Hall asked, 'what noble man liveth at this day or what gentleman of any ancient stock . . . whose lineage hath not been infested and plagued with this unnatural division?' it was no mere rhetorical flourish. For sixteenth-century Englishmen it must have been virtually self-evident that 'the union of the two noble and illustre families of Lancaster and York' was an act of Providence.

But the events that loomed largest in the eyes of English historians of the sixteenth century—the miseries of the Wars of the Roses—were only the most striking examples of processes at work in all times and all places. History, for all its immediate appeal to the human interest in story, in character and action, was essentially the record of a moral process: it taught lessons that could be applied to the understanding of the present and the conduct of affairs. As Louis B. Wright says, in his great work on the reading habits of the Elizabethans: 'The faith in the didactic value of history

was not confined . . . to any social group in Tudor and
Stuart England, because the belief was almost universal that
a knowledge of the past furnished a valuable guide to the
present.'[1] And when history was transposed into semi-
fictional forms it was still the moral issue that was predominant. It was, in the words of one of the most popular
compilations of the mid-sixteenth century, 'a mirror'.
Thomas Baldwin, in his dedication of the first edition of
A Mirror for Magistrates (1559) to 'the nobility and all other
in office', declaring that God dealt sternly with corrupt
governors, wrote:

> How he hath dealt with some of our countrymen your ancestors,
> for sundry vices not yet left, this book . . . can show: which there-
> fore I humbly offer unto your honours, beseeching you to accept
> it favourably. For here as in a looking glass, you shall see (if any
> vice be in you) how the like hath been punished in other heretofore,
> whereby admonished, I trust it will be a good occasion to move
> you to the sooner amendment.[2]

We need not concern ourselves just now with the rather
sweeping assumption behind this (Baldwin himself admits
that 'some have for their virtue been envied and murdered');
the important fact is that those who bought the *Mirror* in its
successive editions—and its popularity continued until well
into the seventeenth century—expected something more
than information or entertainment; they expected moral
examples drawn from the field of public life and great
affairs.

[1] *Middle-Class Culture in Elizabethan England*, Chap. IX, 'The Utility
of History', p. 301.
[2] *A Mirror for Magistrates*, ed. Lily B. Campbell, pp. 65-66. The motto
on the title page of the early editions is, '*Felix quem faciunt aliena pericula
cautum*'. On the conception of history as a mirror see Miss Campbell's
Introduction, pp. 48-55. Compare *Gorboduc* (acted 1562), I.i. Chorus:
> And this great king, that doth divide his land,
>   And change the course of his descending crown. . . .
> A mirror shall become to princes all,
> To learn to shun the cause of such a fall.

Similar expectations and interests were also satisfied in the theatre. It is a matter of common knowledge that the last ten or fifteen years of the reign of Queen Elizabeth I saw the performance of a very large number of plays on subjects drawn from English history. Some of these can properly be covered by the familiar description of 'chronicle play'—'a history transformed into a play' (Schelling); but a considerable number, including the most distinguished, are related more closely to the old political and social moralities —like, say, Skelton's *Magnificence* (1516), Sir David Lindsay's *A Satire of the Three Estates* (1540-52), or the anonymous *Respublica* (1553)—than they are to the straight 'chronicles': to use the convenient term coined by A. P. Rossiter, they were Moral Histories—'chronicle patterned on an abstract design'. In the Preface to his edition of the anonymous *Woodstock* (c.1591-94) Mr. Rossiter wrote:

> 'Moral History' is a form to be critically recognized, not as a primitive survival, with flat Abstractions masking as characters; but as a useful name for history-plays where the shadow-show of a greater drama of state plays continually behind the human characters, sometimes (as in Shakespeare) upon something as large as the cyclorama of the stars ... However historical an Elizabethan play is, it is very little 'period': the writer's mind, like the stage itself (with its Elizabethan dresses and weapons), largely operated in a timeless sphere. Within that sphere, history was often presented as the conflict of principles.[1]

'Moral History'—in the sense in which *Woodstock* is a Moral History—is a category into which none of Shakespeare's plays fits with any ease,—at all events, after the Henry VI sequence. (Rossiter himself makes this plain in his later book, *Angel with Horns*.) All the same, to recognize the existence of this *kind* of play is to bring about an important shift of focus when we try to see Shakespeare's

[1] *Woodstock: a Moral History*, Preface, pp. 9-10 and *passim*. *Woodstock* itself 'is no "Chronicle-history-play". The chronicle materials are lifted from their time-sequence to operate in a timeless conflict of moral forces, in a strictly patterned plot' (p. 25).

Histories for what they are: for they too use historical material as a means of exploring fundamental principles of man's life in a political society.

Little can be said by one who is not a specialist in these matters about the political principles most likely to have influenced the mind of the young Shakespeare. Perhaps the best known principle of state concerned the necessity for authority, order and degree. There was as yet no fully developed theory of the divine right of kings, but it was natural that supporters of the Tudor monarchy should put a good deal of weight on the virtue of obedience in the subject. Not only was firm order in the state the only alternative to anarchy (in the later part of the century contemporary France seemed to reinforce the lesson of the Wars of the Roses), society was seen as part of the cosmic order with its parallel and corresponding 'planes of being', so that disorder at one level was echoed in the others. In the First Book of Homilies (1547), *An Exhortation Concerning Good Order and Obedience to Rulers and Magistrates* speaks of order in the heavens, on the earth, in man's body and mind, and in the state, and proceeds:

> So that in all things is to be lauded and praised the goodly order of God: without the which no house, no city, no commonwealth can continue and endure; for, where there is no right order, there reigneth all abuse, carnal liberty, enormity, sin and Babylonical confusion. Take away kings, princes, rulers, magistrates, judges, and such estates of God's order, no man shall ride or go by the highway unrobbed; no man shall sleep in his own house or bed unkilled; no man shall keep his wife, children, and possessions in quietness; all things shall be in common; and there must needs follow all mischief and utter destruction both of souls, bodies, goods and commonwealths.[1]

This is the note that, after the failure of the Rebellion of the North, is formidably developed in the *Homily against*

[1] *The Two Books of Homilies Appointed to be Read in Churches*, ed. John Griffiths (1859), pp. 104-5.

Disobedience and Wilful Rebellion (1570). Since the miseries of mankind sprang from Adam's disobedience, 'it is evident that obedience is the principal virtue of all virtues, and indeed the very root of all virtues, and the cause of all felicity'. Rebellion, on the other hand, is 'worse than the worst government of the worst prince'.

> How horrible a sin against God and man rebellion is, cannot possibly be expressed according to the greatness thereof. For he that nameth rebellion nameth not a singular or one only sin, as is theft, robbery, murder and such like; but he nameth the whole puddle and sink of all sins against God and man; against his prince, his country, his countrymen, his parents, his children, his kinsfolk, his friends, and against all men universally; all sins, I say, against God and all men heaped together nameth he that nameth rebellion.[1]

This aspect of Tudor theory has been admirably described in recent works of scholarship, and in a general way is now sufficiently well known to students of Elizabethan literature.[2] But it is also important to remember that at no time did absolutist propaganda have an entirely free field. Besides positive law, there was Natural law (so powerfully expounded by Hooker); besides the idea of royal supremacy there was the idea of the moral responsibility of the ruler —the idea, even, of the ruler as the 'representative' of the commonwealth: 'kings and princes . . . are but members . . . without a commonwealth there can be no king.' This last quotation is from John Ponet's *A Shorte Treatise of Politicke Power* (1556) which, according to Ponet's modern editor, was one of the signs, in mid-century, of a partial return to medieval conceptions of the limits of a prince's power: 'Even with the rise of strong national monarchy, the old restrictions did not entirely disappear from the English consciousness'.[3] How far these different currents of thought

---

[1] *Op. cit.*, p. 568.
[2] See the books by Tillyard, Spencer and Hart listed in the bibliography.
[3] Winthrop S. Hudson, *John Ponet* (1516?-1556), *Advocate of Limited Monarchy*. See also J. W. Allen, *A History of Political Thought in the Sixteenth Century*, Part II, Chap. III, 'The Very and True Commonweal'.

—derived from contemporary need and practice and from medieval tradition, from the Bible, Aristotle and Aquinas, and from many other sources—conflicted with and modified each other is something not easily determined. For the literary student there are perhaps two points in especial to be emphasized. The first is the simple fact that 'Tudor thought' on social and political matters was not entirely homogeneous: there was at all events sufficient diversity— indeed contradiction—to incite thoughtful men to thinking. The second is that a loyal and intelligent subject of Elizabeth I was likely to be conscious of other political matters besides what was due to the Prince. At the beginning of his masterly and lucid survey, *Political Thought in England: Tyndale to Hooker*, Mr. Christopher Morris remarks of sixteenth-century Englishmen:

> Most of all they discussed the importance to Society of obedience to authority, although they remained aware of limits which, in a healthy society, no authority would think of over-stepping. The King, moreover, was only one of the authorities. There were others—the Law, the People, the Church, God, and (according to some thinkers) Conscience. None of these authorities had as yet been conflated or confused with any other; and the problem facing social theorists was that of rendering to each authority its due.

In the early 1590's the author of *Woodstock* knew what response he would get from his audience when he made the bad Judge, Tresilian, say, 'It shall be law, what I shall say is law . . . I rule the law'.[1]

Where, then, did Shakespeare take his start? To that question only a study of the plays can provide an adequate answer. It can safely be asserted however that he was well aware of the 'educated' view of English history since the deposition of Richard II, and of the prevailing doctrine of

[1] *Cf.* Morris, *op. cit.*, p. 83: 'Without doubt there was general agreement among Elizabethans that the king was not absolute in any but a highly technical sense, that he was not above the law, that law was not what he willed, that in so far as he ever made law, he made it in and through his parliament.'

the need for strong rule, order and degree, and of the heinousness of rebellion: aware of them, but not uncritical of them; for each view, right up to a point, oversimplified. The belief in historical nemesis, with its corollary of some kind of mundane happy ending once guilt had been expiated, left no room for a fact of history as fully attested as the coming home of sins to roost.

> Just or unjust alike seem miserable,
> For oft alike both come to evil end.

For neither Shakespeare nor Milton was that a final answer: all the same it represents a different order of thinking from the easy moralizing of *A Mirror for Magistrates*, and it was a thought not unlikely to have occurred to the author of *King Lear*. As for the necessity for order, so often expounded in this period, I know it is sometimes claimed that Shakespeare was a convinced exponent of what we should nowadays call the right-wing assumptions of his time; and there are indeed passages in his work that testify to a horror of anarchy. But order—especially order dependent on absolute rule and unargued acceptance of the powers that be—was not for Shakespeare a simple and unquestioned value: essential order, simultaneously political and more-than-political, was something that needed his full mature powers to define and assert. What he gained from the historical writing and the political assumptions of his time, though not from these alone, was a conviction that politics and morals cannot be separated without falsification and disaster. That conviction lasted him a lifetime. More narrowly formulated doctrines of the kind touched on above served him in organizing historical material in his earliest work; but as his mind played on them the current simplifications were dissolved into something more subtle, more far-reaching, more firmly related to the pressures of experience. As A. P. Rossiter said: 'The Tudor myth system of Order, Degree, etc., was too rigid, too black-and-white, too doctrinaire and narrowly moral for Shakespeare's mind: it falsified his fuller experience of men.'[1] The plays now to be examined show Shakespeare developing a view of history, of politics and public life, more searching than anything to be found in his 'sources'.

II

RICHARD III

To call Shakespeare's Histories 'political' plays is simply one way of indicating that they deal with such matters as the nature of power—and the conflict of powers—within a constituted society, and with the relation of political exigencies to the personal life of those caught up in them. In other words, they belong not with the limited class of Elizabethan chronicle plays, but with that extensive range of world literature that includes *Antigone*, *Athalie*, *The Possessed* and *Under Western Eyes*. To say this is not of course to offer a definition: it merely suggests the nature of the interest that we bring to bear. What that interest finds to engage and direct it in such plays as *Richard III* and *Julius Caesar* is a matter for particular criticism: there is no formula that will help us. But there is one preliminary generalization that may be made. Shakespeare's early plays show an increasingly subtle relation between observation and what—for want of a better word—we may call inwardness. It is observation that strips off pretence, shows us how the world goes, points a useful moral. But at its furthest reach it can do no more than offer a truth that we acknowledge about other people—the Bastard's 'Commodity, the bias of the world . . .', or Dr. Stockman's summing up in *An Enemy of the People*:

[1] *Angel with Horns, and Other Shakespeare Lectures*, 3, 'Ambivalence: the Dialectic of the Histories', p. 59.

I only want to drum into the heads of these curs the fact that the liberals are the most insidious enemies of freedom—that party programmes strangle every young and vigorous truth—that considerations of expediency turn morality and justice upside down.

Inwardness on the other hand is not only the probing of character and motive, it involves the observer: some revelation of what is usually concealed prompts not only dramatic sympathy but a sense that something potential in the spectator is being touched on. It is the development of this quality that, above all, links the political plays with the great tragedies—with *Macbeth*, for example, which is simultaneously political play and universal tragedy. In the plays before us there is indeed no clear line of progression, but we shall, I think, appreciate more vividly what each play has to offer if we see it not simply as an isolated achievement but as pointing towards the masterpieces that lie outside the scope of this study.

Richard III (1592-3) is clearly linked to the three parts of *Henry VI* by what Dr. Tillyard calls 'the steady political theme: the theme of order and chaos, of proper political degree and civil war, of crime and punishment'; but, unlike its predecessors, it is very much more than a dramatic presentation of the Tudor view of history. It is not simply a play about the providential accession of the House of Tudor, it is, in the first place, an elaborately formal drama-tization of power-seeking in a corrupt world, held together by what Rossiter calls a 'basic pattern of retributive justice'.[1]

The formal pattern of the play has often been described, and certainly it is a contrivance of great ingenuity. Basically (as Dover Wilson, following Moulton, points out), it is composed of a complicated system of nemeses: crime brings punishment, for, in the words of York in *3 Henry VI*,

[1] Whether directly, or mediately through the chronicles, Shakespeare was deeply indebted to More's Life of Richard, which was 'an attack on the non-moral statecraft of the early Sixteenth Century.'—R.W. Chambers, *Thomas More*, (1935) p. 117.

'Measure for measure must be answered', or, in the words of Buckingham in this play, 'Wrong hath but wrong, and blame [sc. fault] the due of blame'. Clarence (who broke his promise to Warwick and was one of those who killed Edward, the Lancastrian Prince of Wales) goes to his death in the Tower just as Hastings is released. Hastings, hearing of the death of the Queen's kindred at Pomfret, exults in his own security:

> Think you, but that I know our state secure,
> I would be so triumphant as I am?   (III.ii.81-82)

just before he is hustled to his death by Richard and Buckingham. Buckingham, 'the deep revolving, witty Buckingham', who plays his part as Richard's 'other self' with something of his master's swagger, breaks with Richard partly because of the proposed murder of the Princes, partly because he can't get payment for his services: when he too falls and is led to execution, he recalls the false oath with which he sealed his reconciliation with the Queen's party:

> That high All-seer, which I dallied with,
> Hath turn'd my feigned prayer on my head,
> And giv'n in earnest what I begg'd in jest.   (V.i.20-22)

As for the arch-contriver, there is the succession of eleven ghosts before Bosworth to remind him—and us—what he is now paying for. This kind of repetition in the action gives an effect of irony both to the mutual pledges and to the boastful self-assertion of the characters; whilst at the same time the device of formal accusation of one character by another keeps the crimes committed constantly in view —each is, as it were, his brother's bad conscience. The effect is to present almost all these people as interlocked in a 'destiny' made of 'avoided grace' (IV.iv.219).

The formal patterning of the action is of course paralleled in the verbal structure: 'the patterned speech of the dialogue . . . is fundamentally one with the ironic patterns of the plot' (Rossiter). I do not know whether rhetorical devices are more numerous here than in any other of Shakespeare's plays; they are certainly more obtrusive. No purpose would be served by listing the various figures of speech—alliteration, repetition, antithesis, stichomythia, and more recondite Elizabethan 'figures'—it is enough if we notice the stiff formal texture of so much of the verse:

> *Anne.* Lo, in these windows that let forth thy life
>   [the wounds of the dead Henry VI]
> I pour the helpless balm of my poor eyes.
> O cursed be the hand that made these holes!
> Cursed be the heart that had the heart to do it!
> More direful hap betide that hated wretch,
> That makes us wretched by the death of thee,
> Than I can wish to adders, spiders, toads,
> Or any creeping venom'd thing that lives!   (I.ii.12-20)

> *Gloucester.* Fairer than tongue can name thee, let me have
> Some patient leisure to excuse myself.
> *Anne.* Fouler than heart can think thee, thou canst make
> No excuse current but to hang thyself.
> *Glou.* By such despair, I should accuse myself.
> *Anne.* And, by despairing, shouldst thou stand excused
> For doing worthy vengeance on thyself,
> That did unworthy slaughter upon others.   (I.ii.81-88)

> *Q. Elizabeth.* If you will live, lament: if die, be brief
>   (II.ii.43)

> *Duchess of York.* Dead life, blind sight, poor mortal living
>   ghost,
> Woe's scene, world's shame, grave's due by life usurp'd,
> Brief abstract and record of tedious days,
> Rest thy unrest on England's lawful earth,
> Unlawfully made drunk with innocent blood!   (IV.iv.26-30)

These are characteristic examples; and the internal patterning of the verse is emphasized by the formal stance of the characters, as when Richard and Anne engage in a 'keen encounter of our wits', or when Queen Margaret makes a late appearance (clean contrary to historical fact and probability—'Here in these confines slily have I lurk'd') solely that she may join with Queen Elizabeth and the Duchess of York in a prolonged antiphonal lament that serves, once more, to recall the crimes and miseries of the past that have made the wretched present. Together, the elements of rhetorical speech and carefully balanced action combine to produce a complicated echoing effect of revenge and mutual wrong.

Yet what we have to do with is not a self-enclosed world of evil. The characters, it is true, move in a dense atmosphere of hatred, suspicion, treachery and fear, but the standards against which we, the spectators, are expected to judge 'the grossness of this age',[1] are firmly presented. This is not only a matter of explicit religious reference, as when the Second Murderer of Clarence surprisingly quotes Scripture—

> How fain, like Pilate, would I wash my hands
> Of this most grievous murder—   (I.iv.272)

Shakespeare had already at command more varied means of awakening the moral imagination. When compared with the second part of Clarence's dream, which is explicitly about hell, the first part may at first seem almost extraneous to the matter in hand: in fact it is an effective symbolist transformation of the more explicit moral commentary:

> Methought I saw a thousand fearful wracks,
> A thousand men that fishes gnaw'd upon,
> Wedges of gold, great anchors, heaps of pearl,
> Inestimable stones, unvalu'd jewels,

---

[1] Buckingham, objecting to the Cardinal's reluctance to fetch the young Duke of York from sanctuary:
> You are too senseless-obstinate, my lord,
> Too ceremonious and traditional.
> Weigh it but with the grossness of this age,
> You break not sanctuary in seizing him.   (III.i.44-47)

> All scatter'd in the bottom of the sea.
> Some lay in dead men's skulls; and, in the holes
> Where eyes did once inhabit, there were crept,
> As 'twere in scorn of eyes, reflecting gems. . . .   (I.iv.24-31)

This, we may say, is a Shakespearean condensation of the contrast that runs all through Tourneur's *The Revenger's Tragedy*. At the other extreme is the dialogue on conscience between the murderers of Clarence:

> *First Murderer.* How dost thou feel thyself now?
> *Second Murderer.* Faith, some certain dregs of conscience are yet within me.
> *First Murderer.* Remember our reward, when the deed's done.
> *Second Murderer.* 'Zounds! he dies! I had forgot the reward.
> *First Murderer.* Where's thy conscience now?
> *Second Murderer.* O, in the Duke of Gloucester's purse.
> *First Murderer.* So when he opens his purse to give us our reward, thy conscience flies out.
> *Second Murderer.* 'Tis no matter, let it go: there's few or none will entertain it.
> *First Murderer.* What if it come to thee again?
> *Second Murderer.* I'll not meddle with it: it makes a man a coward: a man cannot steal, but it accuseth him; a man cannot swear, but it checks him; a man cannot lie with his neighbour's wife, but it detects him. 'Tis a blushing shamefast spirit, that mutinies in a man's bosom; it fills a man full of obstacles; it made me once restore a purse of gold that by chance I found; it beggars any man that keeps it; it is turn'd out of towns and cities for a dangerous thing; and every man that means to live well endeavours to trust to himself and live without it.   (I.iv.120ff)

Irrelevant from the point of view of 'plot', this—which has obvious parallels in the later plays—is clearly a low-life variation on the main theme. ('Conscience', says Richard, when he has just suffered his worst defeat at its hands, 'is but a word that cowards use.'). Nor, if we remember the Seven Deadly Sins in *Piers Plowman*, shall we find anything incongruous in the humour. The serious comedy of this scene is one more reminder that behind *Richard III* is the tradition of the morality play.[1]

Now all this, although necessary, has done little to bring into focus what it is that makes the play worth watching or reading, what makes it indeed characteristically Shake-spearean: that is, the felt presence of a creative energy centering in, but not confined to, the figure of Richard of Gloucester. It is something that takes possession of our imagination as soon as Richard declares himself in his opening soliloquy.

> . . . Grim-visag'd War hath smooth'd his wrinkled front;
> And now, instead of mounting barbed steeds,
> To fright the souls of fearful adversaries,
> He capers nimbly in a lady's chamber,
> To the lascivious pleasing of a lute.
> But I, that am not shap'd for sportive tricks,
> Nor made to court an amorous looking-glass;
> I, that am rudely stamp'd, and want love's majesty,
> To strut before a wanton ambling nymph;
> I, that am curtail'd of this fair proportion,
> Cheated of feature by dissembling Nature,
> Deform'd, unfinish'd, sent before my time
> Into this breathing world, scarce half made up,
> And that so lamely and unfashionable,
> That dogs bark at me as I halt by them;
> Why, I, in this weak piping time of peace,
> Have no delight to pass away the time,
> Unless to spy my shadow in the sun,
> And descant on mine own deformity.
> And therefore, since I cannot prove a lover,
> To entertain these fair well-spoken days,
> I am determined to prove a villain. . . .   (I.i.9ff)

There is a colloquial vividness here that reminds us of Mosca's self-revelation at the opening of the third act of

---

[1] *Cf.* Dover Wilson's Introduction to his edition of the play, pp. xvi-xvii. There is of course more sardonic humour in the scene (III.vii.) in which Gloucester is 'persuaded' to accept the crown.

Volpone, but the total effect is quite un-Jonsonian. The idiomatic gusto—the pleasure in speaking words that have the well-directed aim of caustic popular speech—points forward to the Bastard, and will be an element in the poetry of all the greater plays. And this blends unobtrusively with effects of rhetoric and artifice: consider, for example, how the alliteration insists on a slight meaningful pause after 'spy' and 'descant' in the lines,

> Unless to spy my shadow in the sun,
> And descant on mine own deformity.

What is not Jonsonian is the felt presence of a world behind the lines—a world of strutting gallants and affected ladies, with, by contrast, the dogs barking at the malformed Richard; and behind this, pressing on it, is the private world of the man who has always felt himself to be outside the world's game and will, in consequence, simply play his own.[1]

It is the energy with which Richard plays his part— forthright wooer, plain blunt man, reluctant king ('O! do not swear, my Lord of Buckingham'), satirical commentator on the world's affairs and machiavellian schemer—it is this that makes him into a commanding figure. But we should certainly be wrong to regard him solely as an 'engaging monster' to whose successful contrivance we give a reluctant admiration. Not only is Richard, like the other political figures, placed firmly within a framework of explicit moral reference, the energy that informs his language also manifests itself in other ways. I do not intend to take up again the question of 'character' in Shakespeare.[2] It is clear that if Shakespeare was intent on something more than—something different from—the presentation of life-like characters,

[1] There is an excellent account of this soliloquy by D. A. Traversi in his essay, 'Shakespeare: the Young Dramatist', *The Pelican Guide to English Literature*, 2, *The Age of Shakespeare*, pp. 180-2.
[2] See my essay, 'The Question of Character in Shakespeare', in *More Talking of Shakespeare* (1959), edited by John Garrett.

his figures are never merely embodied abstractions: in some sense we feel them as if they were persons, and we are made explicitly aware of those aspects of their assumed life history (Othello's generalship, Coriolanus' ties to his mother) that are relevant to the main design. In the case of Richard of Gloucester this means that Shakespeare compels us to take into account, and to give full weight to, his deformity—and his rancour at his deformity—that is insisted on in his first soliloquy. When, in Act II, scene iv, young York retails the gossip, picked up from his mother, that his uncle Gloucester was born with teeth, it seems a mere repetition of the legend to which Gloucester had himself subscribed in *3 Henry VI* (V.vii.53–54 and 70ff.). The effect, however, is very different; for whereas in the earlier play the abnormality seemed little more than part of the stock legend of the monster ('which plainly signified That I should snarl and bite and play the dog'), the present context enforces a change of tone and implication. Gloucester—his mother has just told us—'was the wretched'st thing when he was young', and this unobtrusive substitution of the real for the conventional momentarily shifts the balance of our sympathies and antipathies, just as when, later, young York gives his uncle a 'scorn' about his hunchback (III.i.128–135). There is to be sure no attempt to blur judgement with a sentimental 'understanding'. But the fact remains that in the presentation of the zestfully sardonic villain there are some disturbing reverberations.

> A grievous burthen was thy birth to me;
> Tetchy and wayward was thy infancy;
> Thy school-days frightful, desperate, wild and furious. . . .
>
> (IV.iv.168–70)

It does not seem fanciful to say that this—from a further exchange between mother and son—presents in miniature the Delinquent's Progress to a manhood that is 'proud, subtle, sly, and bloody' (IV.iv.172).[1]

[1] See Grace Stuart, *Narcissus: a Psychological Study of Self Love* (1956).

In *Richard III*, although the various conventions are not yet welded into a unity, the connexion between linguistic vitality and energy of moral insight is already apparent. It is not only that Richard's lively idiom 'cuts through the muffled hypocrisies of language'.[1] Even in the elaborately stylized scenes Shakespeare is aiming at something more subtle that a self-conscious display of rhetorical skill: these too can precipitate a moment of lucid truth about human nature; as when Anne gives a somnambulistic half-assent to Richard (' I would I knew thy heart') when he has woven round her his net of sophistries, which she knows to be such (I.ii.33–224), or when Queen Elizabeth, engaged in a formal rhetorical duel with Richard (IV.iv.376–80), shows him, step by step, that there is nothing he can swear by and be believed—neither honour, nor self, nor religion:

Q. Eliz. Swear then by something that thou hast not wrong'd.
K. Rich. Then, by myself—
Q. Eliz.   Thyself is self-misus'd.
K. Rich. Now, by the world—
Q. Eliz.   'Tis full of thy foul wrongs.
K. Rich. My father's death—
Q. Eliz.   Thy life hath it dishonour'd.
K. Rich. Why then, by God—
Q. Eliz.   God's wrong is most of all.

But perhaps the most striking example of artifice working in the service of psychological realism is the climactic scene of Richard's visitation before Bosworth by the ghosts of his victims (V.iii.119ff.). Judged by the standards of the later Shakespeare the stiffly formal projection of suppressed guilt is crudely done. But this 'morality masque', this 'homily in fancy dress', does not stand alone; it leads directly to Richard's soliloquy on awakening:

[1] 'In scorn or indignation, such writers as Dickens, Heine and Baudelaire sought to cut through the muffled hypocrisies of language'. George Steiner, *Tolstoy or Dostoevsky* (1960), p. 25.

> O coward conscience, how dost thou afflict me!
> The lights burn blue. It is now dead midnight.
> Cold fearful drops stand on my trembling flesh.
> What do I fear? myself? there's none else by:
> Richard loves Richard; that is, I am I.
> Is there a murderer here? No. Yes, I am.
> Then fly. What, from myself? Great reason: why?
> Lest I revenge. What, myself upon myself?
> Alack, I love myself. Wherefore? for any good
> That I myself have done unto myself?
> O, no! alas, I rather hate myself
> For hateful deeds committed by myself. . . .

Touches of melodrama should not prevent us from seeing that Richard's dialogue with himself is, as Palmer says, 'no empty catechism, but a dialogue pointed at the heart of the eternal problem of conscience and personality'. It not only points forward to the deeper searchings of the self-division caused by evil in *Macbeth*, it helps to explain why *Richard III* is so much more than an historical pageant, more even than a political morality play. It is one instance among others of Shakespeare's sure sense—his sane, sure probing—of what lies behind the heavy entanglements of public action.

III

KING JOHN

Shakespeare's *King John* (c.1594) has no relation to Bale's *King Johan* (c.1539; revised 1560–63), which may be mentioned here for two reasons. Bale's play is violent Protestant propaganda, his King virtually a martyr to the corrupt power of Rome:

> This noble King John, as a faithful Moses,
> Withstood proud Pharaoh, for his poor Israel,
> Minding to bring it out of the land of darkness. . . .

Some at least of Shakespeare's first audience must have been familiar with this tradition and have noticed what he did *not* say. Secondly, although John is supposed to stand for an historical person, the other characters either are allegorical ('England, a widow') or hover uneasily between allegory and history (Sedition is also Stephen Langton, and Private Wealth, Cardinal Pandulph): in other words the play takes its place in a category only recently recognized in which the old morality technique is used for contemporary religious or social purposes.

Shakespeare's direct source is the anonymous *Troublesome Reign of King John*, published in two parts in 1591, in which the action makes some claim to being historical. *The Troublesome Reign*, although not so tedious as Bale's play, and although it provides a first sketch of the Bastard, is a sprawling affair. If Shakespeare's dramatic skill is evident in the form that he imposed on mere chronicle material it is because he shaped his original, and thereby transformed it, in the light of an idea—something of which *The Troublesome Reign* is innocent. It wasn't merely a matter of toning down the anti-Roman Catholic bias, or of excising the less promising scenes and reshaping the rest, or, even, of developing the Bastard into a vigorous 'character'. What Shakespeare set himself to do was to present international power politics in the realistic spirit in which he had presented the manoeuvring for power within one country in *Richard III*.

The attempt, it must be admitted, is not entirely successful. Partly this is because the chronicle material was recalcitrant. More important, if we exclude Constance and Arthur (and the rhetoric of Constance's laments has little to do with true feeling), there is no point at which any kind of inward life is seen: the play is entirely governed by 'observation'. Within these marked limitations what we are given is of course often superb; and Faulconbridge, the main commentator on the action, represents the clear emergence in Shakespeare's work of an element that he was to transcend but never entirely to abandon. In spite of his royal blood the Bastard is, in the society in which he finds himself, an outsider—the shrewd young man up from the country; and his vigorous colloquial speech matches the keenness of his perception of all forms of humbug, whether social or diplomatic. The tone is set in the sprightly imaginary dialogue in which he sees himself engaging in the inanities of polite conversation in 'worshipful society' (I.i.189ff.). He is the solvent of all that is pretentious and unreal, whether it is the political rhetoric of the Citizen of Angiers ('He speaks plain cannon fire, and smoke and bounce'), or the love rhetoric of the Dauphin and some Elizabethan sonneteers, or diplomatic profession not matched by performance.

The world into which he is introduced is the world of 'policy', of Machiavellian statecraft. John is a usurper, whose 'strong possession' is much more than his 'right'. This however does not prevent him from publicly announcing himself as 'God's wrathful agent'. On the other side King Philip of France, joining the Duke of Austria in 'a just and charitable war', makes much of the religious sanctions of his support of Arthur, of his 'hospitable zeal' in the young Prince's cause, and so on. None of which prevents him from patching up a peace with England by means of a politic marriage between John's niece and the Dauphin, in which the bride is to bring four provinces as her dowry. That the peace is immediately broken at the instigation of the papal Legate does not affect the force of the Bastard's pivotal speech on 'commodity', or self-interest, which closes the first section of the play.

> Mad world! mad kings! mad composition!
> John, to stop Arthur's title in the whole,
> Hath willingly departed with a part:
> And France, whose armour conscience buckled on,
> Whom zeal and charity brought to the field
> As God's own soldier, rounded in the ear
> With that same purpose-changer, that sly devil,
> That broker, that still breaks the pate of faith,
> That daily break-vow, he that wins of all,

I. David Garrick (1717-1779) as Richard III

Reproduced from the painting by William Hogarth at the Walker Art Gallery, Liverpool

II. Alec Guinness as Richard II, in the Old Vic production of 1947

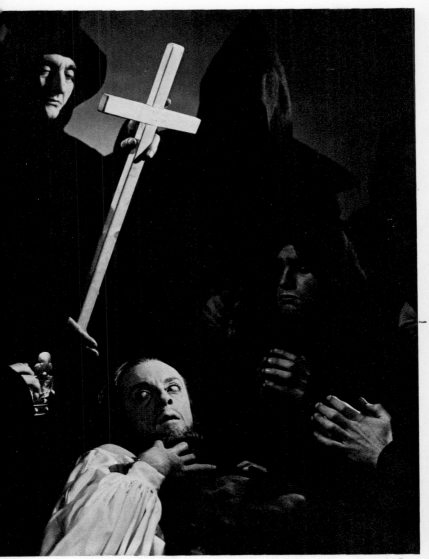

III. Robert Helpmann as the dying King John
Stratford on Avon Memorial Theatre production 1948

IV. Design for production of Henry V by Charles Kean (1811-1868)

> Of kings, of beggars, old men, young men, maids,
> Who, having no external thing to lose
> But the word 'maid', cheats the poor maid of that,
> That smooth-faced gentleman, tickling Commodity. . . .
> And this same bias, this Commodity,
> This bawd, this broker, this all-changing word,
> Clapp'd on the outward eye of fickle France,
> Hath drawn him from his own determined aid,
> From a resolved and honourable war,
> To a most base and vile-concluded peace. . . .   (II.i.561ff.)

This looks forward to the remainder of the action as well as back. There is indeed none of the anti-Catholic bias of the earlier John plays, but Pandulph is a worldly prelate, playing the world's game: having broken the league between the French and English kings he coolly expounds to the Dauphin how the news of his invasion of England is likely to cause John to put Arthur to death, thus strengthening the Dauphin's claim to the English throne. On John's politic submission he thinks to dismiss the French forces that he has used for his own purposes:

> It was my breath that blew this tempest up,
> Upon your stubborn usage of the Pope;
> But since you are a gentle convertite,
> My tongue shall hush again this storm of war. . . . (V.i.17-20)

The 'gentle convertite' meanwhile has become a murderer —in intention if not in effect—whose bad conscience is reflected in political ineptitude and an inglorious end. The Dauphin, on the other hand, has attempted to double-cross the English lords who, deserting from a bad king to a foreign invader, are caught in the contradictions of political action:

> . . . such is the infection of the time,
> That, for the health and physic of our right,
> We cannot deal but with the very hand
> Of stern injustice and confused wrong.   (V.ii.20-23)

The weakness of the play is seen in the conclusion. The revolted English lords, learning of the Dauphin's treachery, return to their allegiance. Salisbury has a lofty speech about this:

> We will untread the steps of damnéd flight,
> And like a bated and retired flood,
> Leaving our rankness and irregular course,
> Stoop low within those bounds we have o'erlooked,
> And calmly run on in obedience,
> Even to our ocean, to our great King John. . . .   (V.iv.52-57)

The last line, severely qualified though it is by the context of the play, does not seem to be intended ironically: it is simply preparing the way for the patriotic finale which can be contrived when John is dead and a new king proclaimed who does not share his guilt.

> This England never did, nor never shall
> Lie at the proud foot of a conqueror,
> But when it first did help to wound itself . . .
> . . . Naught shall make us rue,
> If England to itself do rest but true.   (V.vii.112ff)

This passage is certainly an improvement on the corresponding lines in *The Troublesome Reign*, and there is no reason to doubt Shakespeare's patriotism. But it is difficult to see here, as some have done, an explicit statement of the main theme of the play. In none of Shakespeare's plays does the ending simply cancel out—though it may modify—anything that has been strongly built into the body of the action, and on most of what has been unfolded before us our comment can only be the Bastard's 'Smacks it not something of the policy?' It is 'policy' and its entanglements that is engaging Shakespeare's interest. And although this may be seen with an almost cynical amusement, as in the Commodity speech, there are hints of a deeper awareness of what is involved in the clash of rival interests, as in the sombre poetry of the Bastard's comment as Hubert carries away the body of the dead Arthur.

> I am amazed, methinks, and lose my way
> Among the thorns and dangers of this world.
> How easy dost thou take all England up!
> From forth this morsel of dead royalty,
> The life, the right and truth of all this realm
> Is fled to heaven: and England now is left
> To tug and scamble and to part by th'teeth
> The unowed interest of proud-swelling state. . . .
> Now happy he whose cloak and cincture can
> Hold out this tempest.   (IV.iii.140ff)

Observation of the public world, when as keen-edged as the Bastard's, ends in perplexity and misgiving, and by itself can go no further. In order to explore the nature of the 'tempest' caused when right and truth are fled, leaving only appetite and interest, naked or disguised, Shakespeare needed to relate more firmly his portrayed public action to the inner lives of men.[1]

IV

RICHARD II

Richard II (1595) is a political play with a difference. Drawing on events known to everyone as leading to the English civil wars of the fifteenth century, it presents a political fable of permanent interest: for what it shows is how power—hardly conscious of its own intentions until the event fulfills them—must necessarily fill a vacuum caused by the withdrawal of power[2]. But behind the public frame-

[1] See John F. Danby, *Shakespeare's Doctrine of Nature*, pp. 68-69.

[2] See Brents Stirling, *Unity in Shakespearean Tragedy*, Chap. III. As so often with Shakespeare's Histories, Marvell's *An Horatian Ode* provides a useful gloss:
> Nature that hateth emptiness,
> Allows of penetration less. . . .

work attention is concentrated on *the kind of man* who plays
the central role. Richard is more than an unkingly king, he
is an egotist who, like egotists in humbler spheres, constructs
an unreal world that finally collapses about him. And it is
because the political interest cannot be separated from the
psychological interest—is indeed dependent on it—that
Richard II is a different kind of play from *King John:* in some
important ways it looks back to *Richard III* and forward to
Julius Caesar and *Macbeth.*

That Richard is a king, and not simply a man, and that
the play is about the deposition of a king—these are cardinal
dramatic facts; and most of Richard's actions have to do
with the exercise of kingly power, or the failure to exercise
it. What we should think of the King the play leaves in no
doubt. Of the king-becoming graces named in *Macbeth*
(IV.iii.91ff.) Justice stands first, and Richard is not just. The
matter of Gloucester's death though referred to with some
explicitness (I.ii), lies outside the action of the play, but the
whole of the first two acts portrays an arbitrariness and self-
will that respects neither persons nor established rights.
Richard is an extortionate landlord of his realm; he is
brutal and unjust towards Gaunt; and in depriving Bolingbroke of his inheritance he strikes at the foundations of his
own power.

> Take Hereford's rights away, and take from time
> His charters and his customary rights;
> Let not tomorrow then ensue to-day;
> Be not thyself; for how art thou a king
> But by fair sequence and succession?   (II.i.195-99)

Action is reinforced by explicit commentary. Richard's
behaviour is a 'rash fierce blaze of riot' (II.i.33); it is 'vanity'
(II.i.38); it is a 'surfeit' that will inevitably bring its 'sick
hour' (II.ii.84). At the turning point of the action the
gardeners are introduced for no other purpose than to
moralize the event.

First Servant. Why should we, in the compass of a pale,
Keep law and form and due proportion,
Showing, as in a model, our firm estate,
When our sea-walled garden, the whole land,
Is full of weeds? . . .
Gardener.   Hold thy peace—
He that hath suffered this disordered spring
Hath now himself met with the fall of leaf . . .
                . . . And Bolingbroke
Hath seiz'd the wasteful king. O, what pity is it
That he had not so trimm'd and dress'd his land
As we this garden! . . .
                Superfluous branches
We lop away, that bearing boughs may live;
Had he done so, himself had borne the crown,
Which waste of idle hours hath quite thrown down.[1]

(III.iv.40ff)

If however 'the political moral of *Richard II* is clear . . . it is not simple' (Brents Stirling). Richard's misdeeds do not justify his deposition—and this not because Shakespeare has passively accepted the doctrine of the sanctity of kingship and the sinfulness of rebellion. Gaunt, it is true, proclaims passive obedience before 'God's substitute, His deputy anointed in His sight', but this is balanced by the unavoidable questions prompted by Richard's own development of the theory of divine right (III.ii.36ff.). What guides us here is simply Shakespeare's appraisal of necessary consequences. It may be argued that Carlisle's impassioned prophecy before the deposition is prophecy only in appearance—Shakespeare had read Holinshed and knew what happened in the fifteenth century. But Shakespeare is not merely offering wisdom after the event; he is intent on causes and consequences, on the laws of human behaviour, as in Richard's rebuke to Northumberland after the deposition:

[1] It is a mistake to play this scene as a simple mixture of humour and pathos: the Gardener, who is not a stage rustic, has a genuine 'authority'. For the history of the comparison of the state to a garden see Peter Ure's Introduction to the New Arden edition, pp. li–lvii.

> thou shalt think,
> Though he divide the realm and give thee half,
> It is too little, helping him to all. . . .
> The love of wicked men converts to fear,
> That fear to hate. . . .   (V.i.6off.)

This is the way things happen in the game of power, and although Bolingbroke returns initially to claim what is justly his, he is no more—even if, confronting Richard's 'vanity', he is no less—than a man of power. In short, the play presupposes no possibility of a simple solution to the political situation: as Rossiter says, 'Richard is wrong, but Bolingbroke's coronation is not right; and Richard's murder converts it to the blackest wrong'. York's words apply to *both* sides—'To find out right with wrong—it may not be' (II.iii.145).

Within this clearly delineated framework of a political dilemma—this soberly realistic mapping of one of history's cunning passages—interest centres on the man who is Richard II. He is early shown as petulant and wilful; but what the play focuses with especial clarity is the fact that he is a self-deceiver, a man who imagines that a habitable world can be constructed from words alone. As with many figures in the later plays, essential attitudes are embodied in a manner of speech which simultaneously 'places' them. On Richard's return from Ireland some sixty lines are devoted to this purpose alone:

> I weep for joy
> To stand upon my kingdom once again.
> Dear earth, I do salute thee with my hand,
> Though rebels wound thee with their horses' hoofs.
> As a long-parted mother with her child
> Plays fondly with her tears and smiles in meeting,
> So weeping, smiling, greet I thee, my earth,
> And do thee favours with my royal hands;
> Feed not thy sovereign's foe, my gentle earth,
> Nor with thy sweets comfort his ravenous sense,
> But let thy spiders that suck up thy venom

And heavy-gaited toads lie in their way,
Doing annoyance to the treacherous feet,
Which with usurping steps do trample thee;
Yield stinging nettles to mine enemies. . . .   (III.ii.4ff.)

—and so on. There follows Richard's elaborate comparison of the king to the sun, leading into an assertion of divine right:

Not all the water in the rough rude sea
Can wash the balm off from an anointed king:
The breath of wordly men cannot depose
The deputy elected by the Lord;
For every man that Bolingbroke hath press'd
To lift shrewd steel against our golden crown,
God for his Richard hath in heavenly pay
A glorious angel. . . .   (III.ii.54ff.)

The sequence prompts various reflections. Most obviously Richard has not been a 'mother' to his land (we last saw him ordering the seizure of Bolingbroke's possessions, and we have been told of his other exactions): this bit of make-believe is almost as fantastic as the notion that Bolingbroke would be troubled by spiders. Richard of course does not expect to be taken seriously—'Mock not my senseless conjuration, lords', he says: the trouble is that it is impossible to draw a line between this fanciful self-dramatization and the more seriously intended assertion of royal power that follows. Not only does the repeated use of the first person singular ('my earth'!) undermine the royal 'we' when it appears (III.ii.49–50), Richard's assumption that heavenly powers will aid a king is seen, in this context, as not very different from the admittedly fanciful invocation of the English soil; indeed the religious references—as with the 'three Judases' later (III.ii.132)—only serve to underline the fearful discrepancy between Richard's self-deceiving rhetoric and reality. On a later speech in which self-dramatization is followed by foolish and irrelevant fantasy

(III.iii.143ff.) Dr. Johnson commented, 'Shakespeare is very apt to deviate from the pathetic to the ridiculous'; but it is Richard, not Shakespeare, who thus deviates.

Shakespeare however is using the figure of Richard for a more serious purpose than the exhibition of a particular kind of kingly incompetence. *Richard II* is not universal tragedy, as *Macbeth* is; nevertheless what lifts it above the previous political plays is the way in which reality breaks into the closed world of the self-deceiver. The deposition scene (IV.i.162ff.) begins equivocally: there is dignity and pathos, but there is also the familiar self-regarding dramatization and habit of word-play. It is at the end of a passage of restrained rhetoric—beginning, characteristically, 'Now, mark me how I will undo myself'—that the process of recognition begins. There is indeed no sudden illumination, and the process is difficult to define without extensive quotation, but there is something that can properly be called a break-through from the depths of the nature that Shakespeare has imagined. It can be felt in the changed tone. Whereas Richard's earlier manner had been almost feminine, it is now masculine and direct. At the end of Richard's speech of self-deposition, the question, 'What more remains?' (IV.i.222) may be read as 'exhausted' (Traversi) or as an abrupt descent from rhetoric. What can be in no doubt is that from now on Richard sees himself without disguise:

> Must I do so? and must I ravel out
> My weaved-up follies? . . .
> Nay, if I turn mine eyes upon myself,
> I find myself a traitor with the rest. . . .
>   . . . I'll read enough
> When I do see the very book indeed
> Where all my sins are writ, and that's myself.   (IV.i.228ff)

It is this new tone that underprops the pathos ('Mine eyes are full of tears, I cannot see'), and makes of the subsequent play with the mirror something different from mere self-indulgent theatricality: as Derek Traversi says, 'artificiality, conscious self-exhibition, and true self-exploration are typically blended'.

> Was this face, the face
> That every day under his household roof
> Did keep ten thousand men? Was this the face
> That like the sun did make beholders wink?
> *Is this the face that faced* [trimmed] *so many follies . . . ?*
>
> (IV.i.281ff)

In more senses than one Richard is a man at bay, for he is exposed to himself as well as to his enemies.[1] It is a bleak awakening, as he admits with a sparse directness in the moving scene of his parting from his wife (V.i):

> Learn, good soul,
> To think our former state a happy dream;
> From which awak'd, the truth of what we are
> Shows us but this.

Richard still *sees* his own story (V.i.40ff.); but he also sees his own 'profane hours', and the verse in which he fore-tells to Northumberland the consequences of usurpation (V.i.55ff.) is unusually forthright.

The scene of the murder firmly establishes this new move-ment. Richard's thought is still fanciful (something not un-likely in solitary confinement) and his expression 'conceited'; but the more fanciful passages end with a return to the idiomatic and forthright:

> While I stand fooling here, his Jack o'the clock. . . .
>
> Spurr'd, gall'd, and tir'd by jauncing Bolingbroke;

and there is no turning away from the painful reality. Richard

---

[1] It is worth noticing how Shakespeare contrives to give the *feel* of Richard's isolation, not only by what is said but by what is not said: like Richard, we are aware of Bolingbroke's meaningful taciturnity ('Mark, silent king . . .') and of the eyes fixed on the central figure. The climax ('Then give me leave to go.'—'Whither?'—'Whither you will, so I were from your sights.') is masterly.

recognizes his own sins:

> And here have I the daintiness of ear
> To check time broke in a disorder'd string;
> But for the concord of my state and time
> Had not an ear to hear my true time broke:
> I wasted time, and now doth time waste me. . . .   (V.v.45ff.)

And this in turn is accompanied by a recognition of the vanity of a life lived without some transforming principle that takes the self beyond the self:

> Nor I, nor any man that but man is,
> With nothing shall be pleas'd, till he be eas'd
> With being nothing.   (V.v.39ff)

The expected death comes abruptly—'How now! what means death in this rude assault?' Editors find this line perplexing, but the meaning is surely clear: death has not come in any of its fancifully imagined forms (III.ii.155ff.), it is simply brutal. In a sense the play ends with the heavily stressed monosyllabic line,

> thy fierce hand
> Hath with the king's blood stain'd the king's own land.
>   (V.v.109-110)

Those scenes of the last act from which Richard is absent, showing glimpses of the new world in which Bolingbroke rules, seem in some ways perfunctory and immature, and it is hard to take much interest in Aumerle's abortive conspiracy or the scene in which the Duchess of York pleads for her son's life. Sometimes the verse descends to doggerel, which may perhaps be, as Dover Wilson thinks, left over from an older play—though it is hard to see why Shakespeare should have let his attention lapse at just these points. It is indeed difficult to be sure of the reason for the unevenness of the last act, but certainly the poor verse of V.iii and V.vi makes the scene of the murder (V.v) stand out in strong contrast—and this not only in an easy theatrical effectiveness. Bolingbroke exercises kingly power with more firmness than Richard had done, and he shows clemency to Aumerle; but—and there is a parallel here with the opening scenes of the play—behind the public exercise of kingly rights lies illegality, and an act so bad that it can only be hinted at. It seems at least possible that the explanation of the silly rhymes and the almost farcical note of parts of the Aumerle scenes is that all this is intended to emphasize the superficial character of authority divorced from the moral foundations of rule. The reality is murder:

> Riddles lie here, or in a word—
> Here lies blood. . . .

As Traversi suggests, Bolingbroke's 'absorbing pursuit of power' is, in the nature of things, not likely to lay firmer foundations than Richard's abnegation of responsibility. The world of the unsuccessful egotist has collapsed; the nature of the world constructed by the realist politician, Henry IV, will be shown in the plays that bear his name.

V

HENRY V

Between *Richard II* and *Henry V* stands *Henry IV*, and neither of the two Parts of that play fits very happily into any generalizations we might be tempted to make about 'the Histories'. Indeed, as I have suggested elsewhere, the second Part is at least as closely related to the tragedies as it is to the historical sequence. All the same, *Henry IV* is in one of its aspects a political Morality of the kind that Dover Wilson describes in *The Fortunes of Falstaff*: Justice triumphs over Iniquity, and Hal, escaping from Feigning Flatterers, emerges as the type of the Prince, the Ruler. Now, in

Henry V (1599), Shakespeare—a popular playwright after all—finds himself committed to showing the Ruler in action. If the play doesn't entirely succeed it is partly because it is ostensibly devoted to a public theme in which we cannot quite believe; and the impression we get from the play is that Shakespeare didn't believe in it either.

Certainly there is much in the play that can be cited by those who believe that Shakespeare's king is simply the hero of popular legend:

> Never came reformation in a flood,
> With such a heady currance, scouring faults. . . .   (I.i.33-34)

Canterbury and Ely describe him at length as the Renaissance complete man—able to reason in divinity and state affairs, eloquent, and yet a man of action. We may not entirely trust these wordly prelates, but it is a Chorus that speaks of him as 'the mirror of all Christian kings'; Henry emphatically declares that his 'passions' are subject to his 'grace' (I.ii.242); and he wishes to wage war with equity:

> . . . we give express charge that in our marches through the country there be nothing compelled from the villages, nothing taken but paid for, none of the French upbraided or abused in disdainful language; for when lenity and cruelty play for a kingdom, the gentler gamester is the soonest winner.   (III.vi.105ff.).

He is aware of 'the fault my father made in compassing the crown', and he hopes by penitence to cleanse his rule of that stain. He is the embodiment of military heroism, the successful leader in war; he is 'free from vainness and self-glorious pride' (V. Chorus); and he shows himself capable of mixing easily with the common people. Nevertheless the play is something very different from a simple glorification of the warrior king. When we give full weight to all its parts—not simply to those in which Henry is favourably presented—we see that Shakespeare's attitude is complex and critical.

The patriotic theme is developed in the declamatory and unsubtle verse of the Choruses.[1] But what they give is only the public view of the public theme—'an abstract of average public opinion' (Goddard): there are also realistic 'close-ups' which bring in some deflationary irony. The second Chorus for example ('Now all the youth of England are on fire . . . and honour's thought Reigns solely in the breast of every man') is immediately followed by the first meeting of Bardolph, Nym and Pistol. Pistol 'shall sutler be Unto the camp, and profits will accrue'. As he says later (II.iii.52-4):

> Yoke-fellows in arms,
> Let us to France; like horse-leeches, my boys,
> To suck, to suck, the very blood to suck.

We shouldn't of course make too much of the sociological significance of Pistol & Co.: they are obviously stage-comics, and Bates and Williams are the genuinely representative figures among the common soldiers. But Shakespeare knew that they were among the 'cull'd and choice-drawn cavaliers' eulogized in the third Chorus; he knew what the war meant to them; and he knew what was likely to happen to the disbanded riff-raff when the war was over (V.i.83-5):

> Old I do wax, and from my weary limbs
> Honour is cudgelled. Well, bawd I'll turn,
> And something lean to cut-purse of quick hand. . . .

A similar qualifying irony plays round some (not all) of the more famous passages of military exhortation. In Henry's long speech calling on the citizens of Harfleur to capitulate, Shakespeare's voice speaks through—and in a sense opposed to—the voice of the King, thus firmly 'placing' the sentiments expressed:

---

[1] 'The lines given to the Chorus have many admirers; but the truth is, that in them a little may be praised, and much must be forgiven'.—Dr. Johnson.

> The gates of mercy shall be all shut up,
> And the flesh'd soldier, rough and hard of heart,
> In liberty of bloody hand shall range
> With conscience wide as hell, mowing like grass
> Your fresh-fair virgins and your flowering infants. . . .
> What rein can hold licentious wickedness
> When down the hill he holds his fierce career?
> We may as bootless spend our vain command
> Upon the enraged soldiers in their spoil
> As send precepts to the leviathan
> To come ashore. . . .   (III.iii.10ff.)

There is much more to the same effect. Now Henry is of
course painting the bloodiest possible picture in order to
win Harfleur without fighting: when the city gives in his
order is, 'Use mercy to them all'. All the same, Shakespeare
has been at pains to describe in detail some of the almost
inevitable consequences of war. And this is not the only
occasion on which he reminds the audience that there is
more than one way of responding to a successful military
campaign. We can for example put side by side the English
and the French versions of the battle of Crecy:

> *Canterbury.*   . . . Edward, the Black Prince,
> Who on the French ground play'd a tragedy,
> Making defeat of the full power of France;
> Whiles his most mighty father on a hill
> Stood smiling to behold his lion's whelp
> Forage in blood of French nobility.   (I.ii.105ff.)

> *French King.*   . . . Edward, Black Prince of Wales;
> Whiles that his mountain sire, on mountain standing,
> Up in the air, crown'd with the golden sun,
> Saw his heroical seed, and smil'd to see him,
> Mangle the work of nature, and deface
> The patterns that by God and by French fathers
> Had twenty years been made.   (II.iv.56ff.)

We have here in little—in the clash between the admiring
'Forage in blood' and the regretful 'Mangle the work of

nature . . . '—an example of something that is not made
fully explicit until the play is near its end: it is the contrast
between a limited and inadequate ideal of manliness and
one that is fully adequate and mature. Henry's first speech
before Harfleur—'Once more unto the breach, dear friends
. . .' (III.i)—does not represent the war poetry of the play at
its best. It is rhetorical in the bad sense, the imagery is forced
and unnatural, and it compares very unfavourably with the
King's address to his men before the battle of Agincourt
(IV.iii). All the same, it is not only the speech from the play
that every schoolboy knows, it represents an important part
of the attitude to life embodied in the figure of the hero-
king. How inadequate this is is fully revealed when, in the
last scene, Burgundy makes his great plea for peace
(V.ii.31ff.):

> . . . let it not disgrace me
> If I demand before this royal view,
> What rub or what impediment there is,
> Why that the naked, poor, and mangled Peace,
> Dear nurse of arts, plenties, and joyful births,
> Should not in this best garden of the world,
> Our fertile France, put up her lovely visage?
> Alas, she hath from France too long been chas'd,
> And all her husbandry doth lie on heaps,
> Corrupting in its own fertility.
> Her vine, the merry cheerer of the heart,
> Unpruned dies; her hedges even-pleach'd,
> Like prisoners wildly overgrown with hair,
> Put forth disorder'd twigs; her fallow leas
> The darnel, hemlock and rank fumitory
> Doth root upon; while that the coulter rusts
> That should deracinate such savagery;
> The even mead, that erst brought sweetly forth
> The freckled cowslip, burnet, and green clover,
> Wanting the scythe, all uncorrected, rank,
> Conceives by idleness, and nothing teems
> But hateful docks, rough thistles, kecksies, burrs,
> Losing both beauty and utility.

> And as our vineyards, fallows, meads, and hedges,
> Defective in their natures, grow to wildness,
> Even so our houses and ourselves and children
> Have lost, or do not learn for want of time,
> The sciences that should become our country;
> But grow like savages, as soldiers will,
> That nothing do but meditate on blood,
> To swearing and stern looks, defus'd attire,
> And every thing that seems unnatural. . . .

This beautiful passage—which in its ease and complexity reminds us that Shakespeare is now reaching the height of his powers—is not only free from the emotional straining that marks the Harfleur speech; it offers a positive ideal of civilization that is no mere abstraction but that brings with it the felt presence of the lived activities in which the ideal may be embodied. 'Behind the image of life and nature run wild for lack of human care is the implied ideal of natural force tended and integrated into a truly human civilization';[1] human, but still rooted in nature: in Milton's words, 'Growth, sense, reason, all summ'd up in man'.

Seen in this light it is hard to regard the play as a simple glorification of heroic leadership, even if, with Dover Wilson, we find that Henry's character is deepened and humanized after Harfleur. Rather I should agree with Mr. Traversi that the effect of the play as a whole is 'to bring out certain contradictions, human and moral, which seem to be inherent in the notion of a successful king'. Although Shakespeare presents with understanding the heightened fellowship of those sharing a common danger, and the responsiveness of the good general to the needs of the situation, there is only one scene where Henry gains a full measure of our sympathy—and that in spite of the fact, or because of the fact, that we don't entirely agree with him. I refer of course to the masterly scene near the opening of Act IV, where the King, disguised and under cover of darkness, talks with the common soldiers before the battle of

---

[1] L. C. Knights, *Some Shakespearean Themes*, p. 128.

Agincourt. There is no need to comment on the surface realism—admirably done—of the soldiers' comments.

> *Bates.* He [the King] may show what outward courage he will, but I believe, as cold a night as 'tis, he could wish himself in Thames up to the neck; and so I would he were, and I by him, at all adventures, so we were quit here. (IV.i.112ff.)

The ensuing conversation—so unforced in tone, and yet so telling in all its details—poses the dilemma of political leadership when force is accepted as a necessary instrument of policy: and it is a real dilemma, not one admitting of any simple solution. To the King's claim that his cause is just and his quarrel honourable Williams replies with a curt, 'That's more than we know'; and he goes on to insist on the grave moral responsibility of the ruler:

> But if the cause be not good, the king himself hath a heavy reckoning to make, when all those legs and arms and heads, chopped off in a battle, shall join together at the latter day, and cry all 'We died at such a place'; some swearing; some crying for a surgeon; some upon their wives left poor behind them; some upon the debts they owe; some upon their children rawly left. . . . Now, if these men do not die well, it will be a black matter for the king that led them to it; who to disobey were against all proportion of subjection.
>
> (IV.i.133ff.)

Henry replies with a variety of arguments, too long to quote here, leading to the conclusion, 'Every subject's duty is the king's; but every soldier's soul is his own': *how* each soldier dies is his own concern. It is an interesting speech, in conscious intention sincere, and each statement in it taken singly is true or, at least, more than merely plausible. But it doesn't all add up to what Henry thinks it does. The analogies on which Henry relies so heavily are not perfect analogies: the master who sends his servant on a journey, in which the servant is set upon and killed 'in many irreconciled iniquities', is not an exact equivalent for the king who leads his subjects to war. The king has brought his men to fight ('Then imitate the action of the tiger . . .'), and, says Williams, 'I am afeard there are few die well that die in battle; for how can they charitably dispose of any thing when blood is their argument?' That contention could, I think, be answered, but Henry does not answer it. He simply shifts the responsibility. And the mood of the whole tragic argument finds its natural issue in the famous soliloquy:

> Upon the king—let us our lives, our souls,
> Our debts, our careful wives,
> Our children, and our sins lay on the king.
> We must bear all. O hard condition,
> Twin born with greatness. . . .   (IV.i.126-30.)

—ending with the nostalgic vision of a life free from the weight of responsibility which is all the king gets in return for his vain 'ceremony'.

The even division of sympathy in this scene—with the cutting edge of the argument, all the same, directed against Henry—suggests something of the complexity of attitude that informs the play as a whole. It is not resolved. As M. Fluchère says, 'While making the necessary concessions to patriotic feeling . . . Shakespeare lets us see . . . that the political problem, linked with the moral problem, is far from being solved by a victorious campaign.' In short, the political problem, conceived purely in terms of politics and the political man, is insoluble.

In *Julius Ceasar*, written in the same year as *Henry V*, freed from the embarrassments of a patriotic theme, and with the problem projected into a 'Roman' setting, Shakespeare examined even more closely the contradictions and illusions involved in political action. But is *Julius Caesar* a History, a Political Play, or a Tragedy? In a sense the futility of the question provides an answer to it. When history is conceived in terms of a living present, it becomes a spur to the political intelligence; when the political intelligence is that of a Shakespeare—nourished, moreover, by a tradition in which political action is seen primarily as social, and ultimately as individual, action—then the action of that intelligence on its material will almost necessarily bring into view some of the profoundest questions of human nature. What gives Shakespeare's early political plays their distinctive quality is the fact that they are part of the same continuous, and continually deepening, exploration of the nature of man that includes the great tragedies. Why that should be so I have tried to indicate in the preceding pages, and by way of summary I should like to use the words of a critic whose understanding of Shakespeare was informed by a rare wisdom and humanity. Speaking of the material that Shakespeare made use of for the very first of his Histories, the late Professor Goddard wrote: 'Here, writ large, was the truth that chaos in the state is part and parcel of chaos in the minds and souls of individuals, that the political problem is, once and for all, a function of the psychological problem'. Later in the same study Professor Goddard says: 'Perhaps education will some day revert to a perception of what was so like an axiom to Shakespeare: that psychology goes deeper than politics and that a knowledge of man himself must precede any fruitful consideration of the institutions he has created.'[1]

---

[1] Harold C. Goddard, *The Meaning of Shakespeare*, 1951 (Phoenix Books, 1960), Vol. I, pp. 29, 147. This remarkable book came to my hands when this essay was virtually complete. I am glad to call attention to it not only for the profound understanding of Shakespeare's political plays that one finds in its pages.

THE HISTORY PLAYS
Richard III · King John · Richard II · Henry V

A SELECT BIBLIOGRAPHY

(Books published in London, unless stated otherwise)

Full bibliographical descriptions of the separate quarto editions and of the first collected edition of *Mr. William Shakespeare's Comedies, Histories & Tragedies*, 1623 (the FIRST FOLIO) are given in W. W. Greg, *A Bibliography of the English printed drama to the Restoration*, 4 vols. 1940–59.

ABBREVIATIONS

E.E.T.S.:	*Early English Text Society*
ELH:	*Journal of English Literary History*
JEGP:	*Journal of English and Germanic Philology*
MLQ:	*Modern Language Quarterly*
MLR:	*Modern Language Review*
PMLA:	*Publications of the Modern Languages Association of America*
PQ:	*Philological Quarterly*
RES:	*Review of English Studies*
SB:	*Studies in Bibliography*
ShJ:	*Shakespeare Jahrbuch*
ShQ:	*Shakespeare Quarterly*
ShS:	*Shakespeare Survey*
SP:	*Studies in Philology*

TEXTUAL STUDIES

CHAMBERS, E. K. *William Shakespeare: a study of facts and problems.* Oxford, 1930. I., pp. 294–305, 348–56, 364–7, 388–96.

WALKER, A. *Textual problems of the First Folio.* Cambridge, 1953.

GREG, W. W. *The editorial problem in Shakespeare.* 3rd ed. Oxford, 1954. pp. 68–70, 77–88, 120–1, 142–3.

——*The Shakespeare First Folio.* Oxford, 1955, pp. 190–9, 236–9, 248–55, 282–8.

SISSON, C. J. *New readings in Shakespeare*, II. 1956 (1961).

CRAIG, H. *A new look at Shakespeare's Quartos.* Stanford, 1961.

CONTEMPORARY BACKGROUND SOURCES

BROOKE, C. F. T. (ed). *The Shakespeare Apocrypha*. Oxford, 1908. (Edward III, Sir Thomas More).

BULLOUGH, G. (ed.) *Narrative and dramatic sources of Shakespeare*. III (1960), pp. 221–349, 353–491; IV (1962), pp. 1–151, 347–432.

ELYOT, Sir T. *The Boke named the Governour*, 1531. (Everyman, 1907).

HALL, E. *The Union of the two noble and illustre famelies of Lancastre and York*, 1548. (ed. Sir H. Ellis, 1809).

GRIFFITHS, J. (ed.) *The two books of Homilies appointed to be read in churches*. Oxford, 1859. ('An Exhortation concerning good order and obedience, 1547; 'An Homilie agaynst disobedience and wylful rebellion', 1570.)

HOLINSHED. *Chronicles of England, Scotland and Irelande*, 1577. (Selection, ed. by A. and J. Nicoll, Everyman, 1927.)

HOOKER, R. *Of the lawes of ecclesiasticall politie*, 1594. (Book I and Introduction, Everyman, 1954.)

LINDSAY, Sir D. *Ane Satyre of the thrie estaitis*, 1602. (ed. J. Kinsley, 1954 or in 'Works', ed. D. Hamer, Scottish Text Society, 1931–6).

A Mirror for Magistrates, 1559. (ed. L. B. Campbell. Cambridge, 1938.)

Respublica, 1553. (ed. W. W. Greg. E.E.T.S., 1952).

ROSSITER, A. P. (ed.) *Woodstock: a moral history*. 1946.

SACKVILLE, T. & NORTON, T. *Gorboduc*, 1565. (ed. A. K. McIlwraith, 'Five Elizabethan tragedies', World's Classics, 1938.)

SKELTON, J. *Magnyfycence*, 1529. (ed. R. L. Ramsey, E.E.T.S., 1908.)

BACKGROUND; SECONDARY

COLERIDGE, S. T. 'On the principles of political knowledge'. (First section of *The Friend*, 1809, reprinted 1904 etc.)

SCHELLING, F. E. *The English chronicle play*. 1902.

POLLARD, A. W. and others. *Shakespeare's hand in the play of Sir Thomas More*. Cambridge, 1923.

ALEXANDER, P. *Shakespeare's Henry VI and Richard III*. Cambridge, 1929.

HART, A. *Shakespeare and the Homilies*. Melbourne, 1934.

D'ENTREVES, A. P. *The medieval contribution to political thought*. Oxford, 1939.

ALLEN, J. W. *A history of political thought in the sixteenth century*. 2nd ed. 1941.

HUDSON, W. S. *John Ponet (1516?–1556), advocate of limited monarchy*. Chicago, 1942.

TILLYARD, E. M. W. *The Elizabethan world picture*. 1943.

CAMPBELL, L. B. *Shakespeare's history plays: mirrors of Elizabethan policy*. San Marino, 1947.

HALLIDAY, F. E. *Shakespeare companion, 1550–1950*. 1952.

MORRIS, C. *Political thought in England: Tyndale to Hooker*. 1953.

HONIGMANN, E. A. J. 'Shakespeare's lost source-plays'. *MLR*, XLIX, 1954, 293–307.

KNIGHTS, L. C. *Poetry, politics and the English tradition*. 1954.

——'Shakespeare's politics: with some reflections on the nature of tradition'. *Proceedings of the British Academy*, XLIII, 1957, 115–32.

RIBNER, I. *The English history play in the age of Shakespeare*. Princeton, 1957.

WRIGHT, L. B. *Middle-class culture in Elizabethan England*. 1959. (ch. IX 'The utility of history'.)

MUIR, K. 'Source problems in the histories' *ShJ*. XCVI, 1960, 47–63.

GENERAL CRITICISM

MOULTON, R. G. *Shakespeare as a dramatic artist*. Oxford, 1885.

MURRY, J. Middleton. *Shakespeare*. 1936.

ALEXANDER, P. *Shakespeare's life and art*. 1939.

CHAMBERS, R. W. *Man's unconquerable mind*. 1939.

TILLYARD, E. M. W. *Shakespeare's history plays*. 1944 (1962).

PALMER, J. *Political characters of Shakespeare*. 1945 (1961).

CRAIG, H. 'Shakespeare and the history play' [In *Joseph Quincy Adams Memorial Studies*. Washington, 1948. Pp. 55–64].

DANBY, J. F. *Shakespeare's doctrine of nature: a study of King Lear*. 1949.

MUIR, Edwin. 'The politics of King Lear'. [In *Essays in literature and society* .1949. Pp. 31–48.]

SPENCER, T. *Shakespeare and the nature of man*. 2nd ed. New York, 1949.

GODDARD, H. C. *The meaning of Shakespeare*. Chicago, 1951.

CLEMEN, W. H. 'Anticipation and foreboding in Shakespeare's early histories'. *ShS*., VI, 1953, 25–35.

FLUCHÈRE, H. *Shakespeare*. 1953 (1961).

JENKINS, H. 'Shakespeare's history plays: 1900–1951'. *ShS*., VI, 1953, 1–15.

TRAVERSI, D. A. 'Shakespeare, the young dramatist'. [In *The Pelican Guide to English Literature*, II, The Age of Shakespeare, ed. Boris Ford. 1955. Pp. 179–200]

STIRLING, B. *Unity in Shakespearian tragedy*. New York, 1956. (Chapter on Richard III.)

TRAVERSI, D. A. *Shakespeare from Richard II to Henry V.* 1958.
KNIGHTS, L. C. *Some Shakespearean themes.* 1959.
STRIBRNY, Z. *Shakespeare's history plays.* Prague, 1959.
REESE, M. M. *The cease of majesty: a study of Shakespeare's history plays.*
    1961.
ROSSITER, A. P. *Angel with horns.* 1961.

RICHARD III

First editions: (i) The Tragedy of King Richard the third . . . 1597.
    [first Quarto. Facsimile, ed. W. W. Greg (1959)]; (ii) five further
    Quartos, 1598–1622; (iii) in the First Folio, 1623.
Modern editions: Arden, ed. A. H. Thompson (1907); New Variorum,
    ed. H. H. Furness, jr. (Philadelphia, 1908); Yale, ed. J. R. Crawford
    (1927); New Temple, ed. M. R. Ridley (1935); Penguin, ed. G. B.
    Harrison (1953); New Cambridge, ed. J. Dover Wilson (1954);
    Pelican, ed. G. B. Evans (Baltimore, 1959).

TEXTUAL STUDIES & SOURCES

GRIFFIN, W. J. 'An omission in the Folio text of Richard III' *RES.*,
    XIII, 1937, 329–32.
WILSON, J. Dover. 'Shakespeare's Richard III and the True Tragedy of
    Richard the Third, 1594'. *ShQ.*, III, 1952, 299–306.
WALTON, J. K. *The copy for the Folio text of Richard III.* Auckland, 1955.
    (Reviewed by F. Bowers in *Sh.Q.*, X, 1959, 91–6.)
CAIRNCROSS, A. S. 'The Quartos and the Folio text of Richard III'
    RES., VIII, 1957, 225–33.
GEREVINI, F. S. *Il testo del Riccardo III.* Pavia, 1957.
WALTON, J. K. 'The Quarto copy for the Folio Richard III'. *RES.*,
    X, 1959, 127–40.
BOWERS, F. 'The copy for the Folio Richard III' *ShQ.*, X, 1959, 541–44.

CRITICAL STUDIES

ALEXANDER, P. *Shakespeare's Henry VI and Richard III.* 1929.
ROSSITER, A. P. 'The structure of Richard the Third' *Durham University
    Journal*, XXXI, 1938, 44–75.
THOMAS, S. *The antic Hamlet and Richard III.* New York, 1943.
LAW, R. A. 'Richard III: a study in Shakespeare's composition' *PMLA.*,
    LX, 1945, 689–96.

SMITH, F. M. 'The relation of Macbeth to Richard III' *PMLA.*, LX, 1945, 1003–20.

CLEMEN, W. H. 'Tradition and originality in Shakespeare's Richard III'. *ShQ.*, V, 1954, 247–57.

——*Kommentar zu Shakespeare's Richard III: Interpretation eines Dramas.* Göttingen, 1957.

KING JOHN

First edition: in the First Folio, 1623.

Modern editions: New Variorum, ed. H. H. Furness, jr. (Philadelphia, 1919); Yale, ed. S. T. Williams (1927); New Temple, ed. M. R. Ridley (1935); New Cambridge, ed. J. Dover Wilson (1936); Arden, ed. E. A. J. Honigmann (1954); Penguin, ed. G. B. Harrison (1957).

TEXTUAL STUDIES & SOURCES

ELSON, J. 'Studies in the King John plays'. [In *Joseph Quincy Adams Memorial Studies*. Washington, 1948. Pp. 183–97].

LAW, R. A. 'On the date of King John' *SP.*, LIV, 1957, 119–27.

MCDIARMID, M. P. 'Concerning the Troublesome Reign of King John'. *Notes and Queries*, CCII, 1957, 435–8.

CRITICAL STUDIES

ASH, D. F. 'Anglo-French relations in King John'. *Études anglaises*, III, 1939, 349–58.

PETIT-DUTAILLIS, C. *Le roi Jean et Shakespeare*. Paris, 1944.

SALTER, F. M. 'Problem of King John' *Royal Society of Canada Transactions*, XLIII, 1949, 115–36.

BONJOUR, A. 'The road to Swinstead Abbey: a study of the sense and structure of King John'. *ELH.*, XVIII, 1951, 253–74.

PETTET, E. C. 'Hot irons and fever: a note on some of the imagery of King John'. *Essays in Criticism*, IV, 1954, 128–44.

VAN DE WATER, J. C. 'The Bastard in King John'. *ShQ.*, XI, 1960, 137–46.

RICHARD II

First editions: (i) The Tragedie of King Richard the second . . . 1597. [first Quarto. Facsimile ed. W. A. Harrison (1888)]; (ii) four further Quartos, 1598–1615; (iii) in the First Folio, 1623.

Modern editions: New Temple, ed. M. R. Ridley (1935); Penguin, ed. G. B. Harrison (1937); New Clarendon, ed. J. M. Lothian (1938); New Cambridge, ed. J. Dover Wilson (1939); ed. G. L. Kittredge (New York, 1941); Arden, ed. P. Ure (1956); New Variorum, ed. M. W. Black (Philadelphia, 1956); Yale, ed. R. T. Petersson (1957); Pelican, ed. M. Black (Baltimore, 1957).

TEXTUAL STUDIES AND SOURCES

BLACK, M. W. 'The sources of Shakespeare's Richard II'. [In *Joseph Quincy Adams Memorial Studies*. Washington, 1948. Pp. 199–216.]
HASKER, R. E. 'The copy of the First Folio Richard II'. *SB.*, V, 1953, 53–72.

CRITICAL STUDIES

DRAPER, J. W. 'The character of Richard II'. *PQ.*, XXI, 1942, 228–36.
ALTICK, R. D. 'Symphonic imagery in Richard II'. *PMLA.*, LXII, 1947, 339–65.
RIBNER, I. 'Bolingbroke, a true Machievellian'. *MLQ.*, IX, 1948, 177–84.
BONNARD, G. A. 'The actor in Richard II'. *ShJ.*, LXXXVII–VIII, 1952, 87–101.
SUZMAN, A. 'Imagery and symbolism in Richard II'. *ShQ.*, VII, 1956, 355–70.
BRYANT, J. A. jnr. 'The linked analogies of Richard II'. *Sewanee Review*, LXV, 1957, 420–33.
THOMPSON, K. F. 'Richard II, martyr'. *ShQ.*, VIII, 1957, 159–66.
QUINN, M. 'The King is not himself: the personal tragedy of Richard II'. *SP.*, LVI, 1959, 169–86.
DORIUS, R. J. 'A little more than a little'. *ShQ.*, XI, 1960, 13–26.
PHIALAS, P. G. 'The medieval in Richard II'. *ShQ.*, XII, 1961, 305–10.

HENRY V

First editions: (i) The Cronicle History of Henry the fift . . . 1600. [a 'bad' Quarto. Facsimile ed. W. W. Greg (1957)]; (ii) in the First Folio, 1623.

Modern editions: New Temple, ed. M. R. Ridley (1935); Penguin, ed. G. B. Harrison (1937); New Clarendon, ed. R. F. W. Fletcher (1941);

ed. G. L. Kittredge (New York, 1945); New Cambridge, ed. J. Dover Wilson (1947); Arden, ed. J. H. Walter (1954); Yale, ed. R. J. Dorius (1955); Pelican, ed. L. B. Wright and V. Freund (Baltimore, 1957).

TEXTUAL STUDIES AND SOURCES

Smith, W. D. 'The Henry V choruses in the First Folio' *JEGP*, LIII, 1954, 38–57.

Cairncross, A. S. 'Quarto copy for Folio Henry V'. *SB.*, VIII, 1956, 67–93.

Walker, A. 'Some editorial principles, with special reference to Henry V'. *SB.*, VIII, 1956, 95–112.

Pitcher, S. M. *The case for Shakespeare's authorship of The Famous Victories.* New York, 1961.

CRITICAL STUDIES

Traversi, D. A. 'Henry the Fifth'. *Scrutiny*, IX, 1941, 352–74.

Wilson, J. Dover. *The fortunes of Falstaff.* Cambridge, 1943.

Jorgensen, P. A. 'Accidental judgments, casual slaughters and purposes mistook: critical reactions to Shakespere's Henry V'. *Shakespeare Association Bulletin*, XXII, 1947, 51–61.

——'The courtship scene in Henry V'. *MLQ.*, XI, 1950, 180–8.

Ribner, I. 'The political problem in Shakespeare's Lancastrian tetralogy'. *SP.*, XLIX, 1952, 171–84.

Braddy, H. 'Shakespeare's Henry V and the French nobility'. *Texas Studies in Literature and Language*, III, 1961, 189–96.

George Herbert

by

T. S. ELIOT

Published for The British Council
and The National Book League
by Longmans, Green & Co.

Two shillings and sixpence net

Every new publication by Mr. Eliot attracts world-wide attention, and in considering George Herbert (1593-1633) author of some of the loveliest and most profound religious verse in the language, he has a subject which he regards with affection, sympathy and admiration. His assessment comes with the authority which is an attribute of everything that Mr. Eliot writes. '*The Temple*', he says, 'is not to be regarded simply as a collection of poems, but . . . as a record of the spiritual struggles of a man of intellectual power and emotional intensity who gave much toil to perfecting his verses. As such, it should be a document of interest to all those who are curious to understand their fellow men; and as such, I regard it as a more important document than all of Donne's *religious* poems taken together.'

Bibliographical Series
of Supplements to 'British Book News'
on Writers and Their Work

★

GENERAL EDITOR
Bonamy Dobrée

¶ George Herbert was born at Montgomery Castle on 3 April 1593. He died on 3 March 1633 and was buried at Bemerton, Wiltshire.

GEORGE HERBERT
after an engraving by R. White which first
appeared in Izaac Walton's *Life*, 1670, and
in the 1674 edition of *The Temple*.

GEORGE HERBERT

by T. S. Eliot

PUBLISHED FOR
THE BRITISH COUNCIL
and the NATIONAL BOOK LEAGUE
by LONGMANS, GREEN & CO.

LONGMANS, GREEN & CO. LTD.,
48 Grosvenor Street, London, W.1.
Railway Crescent, Croydon, Victoria, Australia
Auckland, Kingston (Jamaica), Lahore, Nairobi

LONGMANS SOUTHERN AFRICA (PTY) LTD.
Thibault House, Thibault Square, Cape Town,
Johannesburg, Salisbury

LONGMANS OF NIGERIA LTD.
W.R. Industrial Estate, Ikeja

LONGMANS OF GHANA LTD.
Industrial Estate, Ring Road South, Accra

LONGMANS GREEN (FAR EAST) LTD.
443 Lockhart Road, Hong Kong

LONGMANS OF MALAYA LTD.
44 Jalan Ampang, Kuala Lumpur

ORIENT LONGMANS LTD.
Calcutta, Bombay, Madras
Delhi, Hyderabad, Dacca

LONGMANS CANADA LTD.
137 Bond Street, Toronto 2

First Published in 1962
© T. S. Eliot 1962

820
W939
no. 152

Printed in Great Britain by
F. Mildner & Sons, London, E.C.1

GEORGE HERBERT

I

THE family background of a man of genius is always of interest. It may show evidence of powers which blaze forth in one member, or it may show no promise of superiority of any kind. Or it may, like that of George Herbert, show distinction of a very different order. There is a further reason for knowing something of the ancestry of George Herbert: it is of interest to us because it was important to him.

The family of Herbert was, and still is, notable among the British aristocracy. I say British rather than English, because one branch of the family, that to which the poet belonged, had established itself in Wales and had intermarried with Welsh landed families. The Herberts lay claim to being of Norman-French origin, and to having been land-holders since the Norman conquest. At the time of the Wars of the Roses the Herberts of Wales had supported the Yorkist cause; but after the battle of Bosworth they transferred their allegiance to the new monarch, the Lancastrian Henry Tudor, himself a Welshman on his father's side, who ascended the throne as Henry VII. Under the new dynasty the Herberts continued to flourish. Henry VII was determined to exert in Wales the same authority that he enjoyed in England—a control to which the local chieftains of Wales were not accustomed. Among those Welshmen of position and authority who supported and advanced King Henry's law and order in Wales was Sir Richard Herbert of Montgomery Castle. Montgomery lies in North Wales; in the South another Herbert was (and is) Earl of Pembroke; and still another branch of the family is represented by the Earl of Carnarvon.

George Herbert's ancestors and kinsmen were active both in the service of the King and in local affairs. Their rank was among the highest. Several of the family were distinguished for their courage, their prowess in war and duel and their astonishing feats of arms. An exceptional race, but giving no indication of literary tastes and ability before the time of George Herbert and his brother Edward. That two poets, brothers, should appear in a family so conspicuous for warlike deeds, administrative gifts and attendance at Court, can only be accounted for by the fact that their mother, the wife of Sir Richard Herbert of Montgomery, was a woman of literary tastes and of strong character and of exceptional gifts of mind as well as beauty and charm. She was Magdalen, daughter and heiress of Sir Richard Newport, a wealthy landowner in Shropshire.

George Herbert was born in 1593. Three years later his father died, leaving the mother with ten children, seven boys and three girls. Edward was the eldest son; the younger sons would have, of course, to make their own way in life—presumably, as other Herberts had done, in the wars or in some public service—but Lady Herbert's standards were high and she was determined to give them all a good education. The eldest, Edward, the other poet of the family and the heir to the estates, was thirteen and already an undergraduate at Oxford when his father died. At fifteen Edward was married off to an heiress (a Herbert of another branch) but continued at Oxford, where his mother moved her family to be near him and to supervise his education. There she made friends, and even held a kind of salon, among the more brilliant of the learned dons.

It is worth while to say something of Edward Herbert, the eldest brother, not merely to mention his poetry but to point the striking contrast between the two gifted brothers. Edward was ambitious to live abroad, to enjoy court life in foreign capitals and to engage in rather dilletante diplomacy; and to this end he learned French, Italian and Spanish. He seems to have been a man of great physical strength, and was noted for his address at sports and success in love-making: in short, he was a man of abounding vitality. He was later raised to the peerage as Lord Herbert of Cherbury, by which name he is known as author of at least two very fine poems familiar to readers of anthologies. He was not only a poet, but something of a philosopher, and entertained distinctly heretical views in religious matters. On the other hand, John Donne spoke well of him, and Ben Jonson was a friend and correspondent. For he enjoyed the society of men of letters, among whom he moved as an equal as well as among the courtiers of Europe and among ladies and gentlemen of fashion. In Edward the characteristic traits of the Herberts and some of the particular traits of Magdalen Herbert, his mother, appear to have been combined. In George, of frailer constitution and contemplative mind, we seem to find more of Magdalen; yet he was as proudly conscious of being a Herbert as any other Herbert, and at one period had the family inclination to life in the world of public affairs.

By far the most important for our study of George Herbert, of the men of letters and the scholars who delighted in the company of Magdalen Herbert, was John Donne. He was enough older in years to have the admiration of the younger man and to influence him: he was enough beneath Lady Herbert in rank to be almost a protégé. The friendship between Donne and Lady Herbert is commemorated in one of Donne's best known and most loved poems, 'The Autumnal', in which is found the couplet which every lover of Donne's poetry knows by heart:

> No Spring, nor Summer Beauty hath such grace
> As I have seen in one Autumnal face.

To the influence of Donne's poetry upon that of Herbert we shall return presently. Meanwhile it is in place to provide a brief survey of Herbert's life and a sketch of his character.

At the age of twelve George Herbert was sent to Westminster School, where he became proficient in the usual disciplines of Latin and Greek, and gained also— what is equally important for mention here—an advanced practice in music: not only in the choral singing for which that famous school was well known because of its association with the services in Westminster Abbey, but also with a difficult instrument—the lute. If we remember Herbert's knowledge of music, and his skill at the instrument, we appreciate all the better his mastery of lyric verse. From Westminster he went on to Trinity College Cambridge, being one of three boys of Westminster School who were given scholarships to that College at that time.

At Westminster School Herbert had an exemplary record. The relation of the school to the Abbey had also familiarised him with the church offices, in which the boys took part. (Their close attention to the sermon was ensured by the requirement that they should afterwards compose a summary of it in Latin.) At the university Herbert was equally forward; sober and staid in his conduct and diligent in his studies, he was given particular attention by the Master. It was said of him, however, that he was careful to be well, even expensively dressed; and that his attitude towards his fellow undergraduates of lower social position was distant, if not supercilious. Even Isaac Walton (his most nearly contemporary biographer) who tends to emphasise Herbert's saintliness, admits that Herbert, at this stage of his life, was very much aware of the consideration which he thought due to his exalted birth.

At the age of twenty-three Herbert was made a Fellow of his own college of Trinity. He began by instructing the younger undergraduates in Greek grammar; later he taught rhetoric and the rules of oratory. His health was never good; and the climate of Cambridge was somewhat harsh for a young man of frail constitution. His income as Fellow and Tutor was eked out by a small allowance from his brother Edward (the head of the family) and occasionally by gifts from his step-father. For his mother had, in middle age, married again, and was now the wife of Sir John Danvers. But Herbert's poor health meant doctors' bills and occasional absences from Cambridge; as a learned scholar of an active and curious mind he needed constantly to purchase books, and books were expensive, especially those which had to be imported from the continent. He therefore sought to improve his finances, and at the same time attain a position of considerable dignity, by obtaining appointment as Public Orator to the University.

Herbert had not yet formed the design of passing his life as a country parson. Indeed, the post of Public Orator was one which would bring him into the great world and even into contact with the court of James I. He achieved his aim; and during his tenure of this office acquired an extensive acquaintance, which his family connections and his own wide sympathies helped to enlarge. He greatly admired Sir Francis Bacon, a man of a type of mind very different from his own; another elder friend with whom he was on affectionate terms was the saintly Bishop Lancelot Andrewes. Nor did a wide divergence of religious attitude and belief diminish the warm regard between him and his elder brother Edward.

A Fellow of a College was expected to take holy orders in the Church of England within seven years of his appointment, or resign his Fellowship. Herbert was, like his mother, a practising and devout Anglican, but at this time his ambition looked toward the world of Court and Government. His violent attack, in the form of a Latin thesis, upon the Puritan position in the person of one of its most outrageous zealots, Andrew Melville, was his only sortie into religious controversy; though undoubtedly wholly sincere, Herbert probably aimed at winning the approval of King James. He would certainly have liked public office, but had neither the wiles of ingratiation, nor the means or the wish to buy his way in. His next step was to become Member of Parliament for Montgomery—an election which came to him almost as a matter of course as a member of the Herbert family. But this period of his life was not marked by success: two great noblemen of whose patronage he felt assured died, and the death of King James himself, in the following year, seems to have left him with little hope of a Secretaryship of State.

It was necessary to review this much of Herbert's early life to make the point that Herbert, though from childhood a pious member of the Anglican Church, and a vigorous opponent of the Puritans and Calvinists, felt no strong vocation to the priesthood until his thirty-first year. There were at least four persons in his life who may, by precept or example, have influenced him to this decision. His mother, to whom he was devotedly attached, was, we know, a woman not only of strong character, but of great piety. Two friends much older than himself have already been mentioned: Dr. John Donne and Bishop Andrewes. And finally, there was his dear friend Nicholas Ferrar of Little Gidding, an exemplar of High Churchmanship, whose domestic life approached that of a religious community. To Ferrar it was that he consigned, upon his death, the manuscript collection of verse upon which his fame is founded, the collection *The Temple* which we should not know had Ferrar not chosen to publish it; this he did in the same year in which Herbert died.[1]

---

[1] Four editions of *The Temple* appeared within three years of its first publication; its popularity continued to the end of the century. In the eighteenth century Herbert's poems were generally disparaged: Cowper, for instance, though he found in them a strain of piety which he admired, regarded them as 'gothick and uncouth', and this was the universal opinion of that age. The restoration of Herbert's reputation was begun by Coleridge who, in a letter to William Collins, dated 6 December 1818, writes: '. . . I find more substantial comfort now in pious George Herbert's 'Temple' which I used to read to amuse myself with his quaintness—in short, only to laugh at—than in all the poetry since the poems of Milton. If you have not read Herbert, I can recommend the book to you confidently. The poem entitled 'The Flower' is especially affecting; and, to me, such a phrase as 'and relish versing' expresses a sincerity, a reality, which I would unwillingly exchange for the more dignified 'and once more love the Muse' &c. And so, with many other of Herbert's homely phrases.' (Letters, vol. IV, edited by Earl Leslie Griggs, 1959.)

Writing to Lady Beaumont in 1826, Coleridge says: 'My dear old friend Charles Lamb and I differ widely (and in point of taste and moral feeling this is a rare occurrence) in our estimate and liking of George Herbert's sacred poems. He greatly prefers Quarles—nay he dislikes Herbert.' (The Letters of Charles Lamb, edited by E. V. Lucas, vol. I, 1935.)

Herbert's mother died in 1626. George Herbert was for a time a guest in the house of his step-father's elder brother, Lord Danvers, and in 1629, having already taken holy orders, he married Jane Danvers, the daughter of a cousin of Lord Danvers. It was a happy marriage. Six years after Herbert's death, his widow married Sir Robert Cook. In her widowhood, Isaac Walton says:

> . . . She continued mourning, till time and conversation had so moderated her sorrows, that she became the happy wife of Sir Robert Cook of Highnam in the County of Gloucester, Knight. And though he put a high value on the excellent accomplishments of her mind and body; and was so like Mr. Herbert, as not to govern like a Master, but as an affectionate Husband; yet she would even to him take occasion to mention the name of Mr. George Herbert, and say that name must live in her memory, till she put off mortality.

George Herbert died of consumption at the age of forty. For the last years of his life he had been Rector of the parish of Bemerton in Wiltshire. That he was an exemplary parish priest, strict in his own observances and a loving and generous shepherd of his flock, there is ample testimony. And we should bear in mind, that at the time when Herbert lived, it was most unusual that a man of George Herbert's social position should take orders and be content to devote himself to the spiritual and material needs of a small parish of humble folk in a rural village. From Walton's *Life* I must quote one anecdote:

> In another walk to *Salisbury*, he saw a poor man, with a poorer horse, that was fall'n under his Load; they were both in distress, and needed present help; which Mr. *Herbert* perceiving, put off his Canonical Coat, and help'd the poor man to unload, and after, to lead his horse: The poor man blest him for it: and he blest the poor man; and was so like the *good Samaritan* that he gave him money to refresh both himself and his horse; and told him, *That if he lov'd himself, he should be merciful to his Beast.* Thus he left the poor man, and at his coming to his musical friends at *Salisbury,*

they began to wonder that Mr. *George Herbert* which us'd to be so trim and clean, came into the company so soyl'd and discompos'd; but he told them the occasion: And when one of the company told him, *He had disparag'd himself by so dirty an employment*; his answer was, *That the thought of what he had done, would prove Musick to him at Midnight; and that the omission of it would have upbraided and made discord in his Conscience, whensoever he should pass by that place; for, if I be bound to pray for all that be in distress, I am sure that I am bound so far as it is in my power to practise what I pray for. And though I do not wish for the like occasion every day, yet let me tell you, I would not willingly pass one day of my life without comforting a sad soul, or shewing mercy; and I praise God for this occasion:* And now let's tune our instruments.

In this context is worth mention a prose treatise of Herbert's entitled *A Priest to the Temple Or The Country Parson His Character etc.* In this treatise he sets forth the duties and responsibilities of the country parson to God, to his flock, and to himself; and from what we know of Herbert we can be sure that he practised, and always strove to practise, what he here prescribes to other priests. The story of the poor man and his horse is all the more touching when we read that the Parson's apparell should be

plaine, but reverend, and clean, without spots, or dust, or smell; the purity of his mind breaking out, and dilating it selfe even to his body, cloaths, and habitation.

We are told elsewhere in the same treatise that a priest who serves as domestic chaplain to some great person is not to be

over-submissive, and base, but to keep up with the Lord and Lady of the house, and to preserve a boldness with them and all, even so farre as reproofe to their very face, when occasion calls, but seasonably and discreetly.

The pride of birth natural to Herbert is transformed into

the dignity of the Servant of God. The parson, he continues, should be a man of wide reading: Herbert mentions the Church Fathers and the Scholastics, and tells us that the parson should be attentive to later writers also. The parson must give careful attention to his sermon, taking due account of the needs and capacities of his parishioners, and keeping their attention by persuading them that his sermon is addressed to this particular congregation and to one and all of them. And he should, especially when visiting the sick, or otherwise afflicted, persuade them to particular confession, 'labouring to make them understand the great good use of this antient and pious ordinance'.

We are not to presume, however, that George Herbert was naturally of a meek and mild disposition. He was, on the contrary, somewhat haughty; proud of his descent and social position; and, like others of his family, of a quick temper. In his poems we can find ample evidence of his spiritual struggles, of self-examination and self-criticism, and of the cost at which he acquired godliness.

I struck the board, and cry'd, No more.
I will abroad.
What? shall I ever sigh and pine?
My lines and life are free; free as the rode,
Loose as the winde, as large as store.
Shall I be still in suit?
Have I no harvest but a thorn
To let me bloud, and not restore
What I have lost with cordiall fruit?
Sure there was wine
Before my sighs did drie it: there was corn
Before my tears did drown it.
Is the yeare onely lost to me?
Have I no bayes to crown it?
No flowers, no garlands gay? all blasted?
All wasted?
Not so, my heart: but there is fruit
And thou hast hands.

Recover all they sigh-blown age
On double pleasures: leave thy cold dispute
Of what is fit and not. Forsake thy cage,
            Thy rope of sands,
Which pettie thoughts have made, and made to thee
    Good cable, to enforce and draw,
            And be thy law,
Whilst thou didst wink and wouldst not see.
            Away; take heed;
            I will abroad.
Call in thy deaths head there: tie up thy fears.
            He that forbears
        To suit and serve his need
            Deserves his load.
But as I rav'd and grew more fierce and wilde
            At every word,
Me thoughts I heard one calling, *Child*!
            And I reply'd, *My Lord*.

                                (*The Collar*)

To think of Herbert as the poet of a placid and comfortable
easy piety is to misunderstand utterly the man and his
poems. Yet such was the impression of Herbert and of the
Church of England given by the critic who wrote the
introduction to the World's Classics edition of Herbert's
Poems in 1907. For this writer, the Church of England, in
Herbert's day as well as in his own, is typified by a peaceful
country churchyard in the late afternoon:

> Here, as the cattle wind homeward in the evening light, the
> benign, white-haired parson stands at his gate to greet the cowherd,
> and the village chimes call the labourers to evensong. For these
> contented spirits, happily removed from the stress and din of
> contending creeds and clashing dogmas, the message of the gospel
> tells of divine approval for work well done. . . . And among these
> typical spirits, beacons of a quiet hope, no figure stands out more
> brightly or more memorably than that of George Herbert.

This rustic scene belongs to the world of Tennyson and
Dickens; but no more to the world of George Herbert than

to our world to-day. It is well that the latest World's Classics
edition (the text based on that established by F. E.
Hutchinson) has a new introduction by a learned and sensitive critic, Miss Helen Gardner. The earlier introduction
gave a false picture both of Herbert and his poetry, and of
the Church itself in an age of bitter religious conflict and
passionate theology: it is worth quoting in order to point
out how false a picture this is.

II

The poems on which George Herbert's reputation is based
are those constituting the collection called *The Temple*.
About *The Temple* there are two points to be made. The
first is that we cannot date the poems exactly. Some of
them may be the product of careful re-writing. We cannot
take them as being necessarily in chronological order: they
have another order, that in which Herbert wished them to
be read. *The Temple* is, in fact, a structure, and one which
may have been worked over and elaborated, perhaps at
intervals of time, before it reached its final form. We cannot
judge Herbert, or savour fully his genius and his art, by any
selection to be found in an anthology; we must study *The
Temple* as a whole.

To understand Shakespeare we must acquaint ourselves
with all of his plays; to understand Herbert we must
acquaint ourselves with all of *The Temple*. Herbert is, of
course, a much slighter poet than Shakespeare; nevertheless
he may justly be called a major poet. Yet even in anthologies
he has for the most part been underrated. In Sir Arthur
Quiller-Couch's *Oxford Book of English Verse*, which was
for many years unchallenged in its representative character,
George Herbert was allotted five pages—the same number
as Bishop King and much less than Robert Herrick, the
latter of whom, most critics of to-day would agree, is a poet
of very much slighter gifts. For poetic range Herbert was

commonly considered more limited than Donne; and for intensity he was compared unfavourably with Crashaw. This is the view even of Professor Grierson, to whom we are greatly indebted for his championship of Donne and those poets whose names are associated with that of Donne.

And here we must exercise caution in our interpretation of the phrase 'the school of Donne'. The present writer once contemplated writing a book under that title; and lately the title has been used by a distinguished younger critic for a study covering the same ground. The phrase is legitimate and useful to designate that generation of men younger than Donne whose work is obviously influenced by him, but we must not take it as implying that those poets who experienced his influence were for that reason lesser poets. (Professor Grierson, indeed, seems to consider Andrew Marvell the greatest, greater even than Donne.) That Herbert learned directly from Donne is self-evident. But to think of 'the school of Donne', otherwise 'the metaphysical poets', as Donne's inferiors, or to try to range them on a scale of greatness, would be to lose our way. What is important is to apprehend the particular virtue, the unique flavour of each one. Comparing them with any other group of poets at any other period, we observe the characteristics which they share: when we compare them with each other, their differences emerge clearly.

Let us compare a poem by Donne with a poem by Herbert; and as Herbert's poetry deals always with religious matter, we shall compare two religious sonnets. First, Donne:

> Batter my heart, three person'd God; for, you
> As yet but knocke, breathe, shine, and seeke to mend;
> That I may rise, and stand, o'erthrow mee', and bend
> Your force, to breake, blowe, burn and make me new.
> I, like an usurpt towne, to'another due,
> Labour to 'admit you, but Oh, to no end,
> Reason your viceroy in mee, mee should defend,
> But is captiv'd, and proves weake or untrue.

Yet dearely' I love you,' and would be loved faine,
But am betroth'd unto your enemie:
Divorce mee, 'untie, or break that knot againe;
Take mee to you, imprison mee, for I
Except you 'enthrall mee, never shall be free,
Nor ever chast, except you ravish mee.

And here is George Herbert:

Prayer (1)

Prayer the Churches banquet, Angels age,
　　Gods breath in man returning to his birth,
　　The soul in paraphrase, heart in pilgrimage,
The Christian plummet sounding heav'n and earth;
Engine against th' Almightie, sinners towre,
　　Reversed thunder, Christ-side-piercing spear,
　　The six-daies world transposing in an houre,
A kinde of tune, which all things heare and fear;
Softnesse, and peace, and joy, and love, and blisse,
　　Exalted Manna, gladnesse of the best,
　　Heaven in ordinarie, man well drest,
The milkie way, the bird of Paradise,
　　　　Church-bels beyond the starres heard, the souls bloud,
　　　　The land of spices; something understood.

The difference that I wish to emphasise is not that between
the violence of Donne and the gentle imagery of Herbert, but
rather a difference between the dominance of intellect over
sensibility and the dominance of sensibility over intellect.
Both men were highly intellectual, both men had very keen
sensibility: but in Donne thought seems in control of
feeling, and in Herbert feeling seems in control of thought.
Both men were learned, both men were accustomed to
preaching—but not to the same type of congregation. In
Donne's religious verse, as in his sermons, there is much more
of the *orator*: whereas Herbert, for all that he had been
successful as Public Orator of Cambridge University, has a
much more intimate tone of speech. We do not know what
Herbert's sermons were like; but we can conjecture that

in addressing his little congregation of rustics, all of whom he knew personally, and many of whom must have received both spiritual and material comfort from him and from his wife, he adopted a more homely style. Donne was accustomed to addressing large congregations (one is tempted to call them 'audiences') out of doors at Paul's Cross, Herbert only the local congregation of a village church.

The difference which I have in mind is indicated even by the last two lines of each sonnet. Donne's

> . . . for I
> Except you'enthrall me, never shall be free,
> Nor ever chast, unless you ravish mee

is, in the best sense, *wit.* Herbert's

> Church-bels beyond the starres heard, the souls bloud,
> The land of spices, something understood

is the kind of poetry which, like

> magic casements, opening on the foam
> Of perilous seas, in faery lands forlorn

may be called *magical.*

Of all the poets who may be said to belong to 'the school of Donne', Herbert is the only one whose whole source of inspiration was his religious faith. Most of the poetry upon which rests the reputation of Donne is love poetry, and his religious verse is of a later period in his life; his reputation, and his influence upon other poets would have been as great had he written no religious poetry at all. Richard Crashaw, who had himself frequented the community of Nicholas Ferrar at Little Gidding before his conversion to the Church of Rome, might still have been a notable poet had he written no religious verse—even though his devotional poems are his finest. Herbert, before becoming Rector of Bemerton, had never been a recluse: he had, in his short life, wide acquaintance in the great world, and he enjoyed a happy marriage. Yet it was only in the Faith, in hunger and thirst after godliness, in his self-questioning and his religious meditation, that he was inspired as a poet. If there is another example since his time of a poetic genius so dedicated to God, it is that of Gerard Hopkins. We are certainly justified in presuming that no other subject-matter than that to which he confined himself could have elicited great poetry from George Herbert. Whether we regard this as a limitation, or as the sign of solitary greatness, of a unique contribution to English poetry, will depend upon our sensibility to the themes of which he writes.

It would, however, be a gross error to assume that Herbert's poems are of value only for Christians—or, still more narrowly, only for members of his own church. For the practising Christian, it is true, they may be aids to devotion. When I claim a place for Herbert among those poets whose work every lover of English poetry should read and every student of English poetry should study, irrespective of religious belief or unbelief, I am not thinking primarily of the exquisite craftmanship, the extraordinary metrical virtuosity, or the verbal felicities, but of the *content* of the poems which make up *The Temple*. These poems form a record of spiritual struggle which should touch the feeling, and enlarge the understanding of those readers also who hold no religious belief and find themselves unmoved by religious emotion. Professor L. C. Knights, in an essay on George Herbert in his *Explorations*, both expresses this doubt on the part of the non-Christian and dispels it:

> Even Dr. Hutchinson, whose superbly edited and annotated edition of the Complete Works is not likely to be superseded . . . remarks that 'if to-day there is a less general sympathy with Herbert's religion, the beauty and sincerity of its expression are appreciated by those who do not share it'. True, but there is much more than the 'expression' that we appreciate, as I shall try to show. Herbert's poetry is an integral part of the great English tradition.

Whether the religious poems of Donne show greater pro-
fundity of thought, and greater intensity of passion, is a
question which every reader will answer according to his
own feelings. My point here is that *The Temple* is not to be
regarded simply as a collection of poems, but (as I have said,)
as a record of the spiritual struggles of a man of intellectual
power and emotional intensity who gave much toil to
perfecting his verses. As such, it should be a document of
interest to all those who are curious to understand their
fellow men; and as such, I regard it as a more important
document than all of Donne's *religious* poems taken
together.

On the other hand, I find Herbert to be closer in spirit to
Donne than is any other of 'the school of Donne'. As the
personal bond, through Lady Herbert, was much closer,
this seems only natural. Other powerful literary influences
formed the manner of Crashaw, the Roman Catholic
convert: the Italian poet Marino and the Spanish poet
Gongora, and, we are told,[1] the Jesuit poets who wrote in
Latin. Vaughan and Traherne were poets of mystical
experience: each appears to have experienced early in life
some mystical illumination which inspires his poetry. And
the other important poet of the 'metaphysical' school,
Andrew Marvell, is a master of secular and religious poetry
equally. In my attempt to indicate the affinity of Herbert to
Donne, and also the difference between them, I have spoken
earlier of a 'balance' between the intellect and the sensibility.
But equally well (for one has recourse to diverse and even
mutually contradictory metaphors and images to express
the inexpressible) we can speak of a 'fusion' of intellect and
sensibility in different proportions. In the work of a later
generation of 'metaphysicals'—notably Cleveland, Benlowes
and Cowley—we encounter a kind of emotional drought,
and a verbal ingenuity which, having no great depth of
feeling to work upon, tends towards corruption of language,

[1] By Mario Praz, whose *Seicentismo e marinismo in Inghilterra* is essential
for the study of Crashaw in particular.

and merits the censure which Samuel Johnson applies
indiscriminately to all the 'school of Donne'.

To return to the import of *The Temple* for all perceptive
readers whether they share Herbert's faith or no. Professor
Knights quotes with approval Dr. Hutchinson's description
of the poems as

> colloquies of the soul with God or self-communings which seek
> to bring order into that complex personality of his which he analyses
> so unsparingly,

but goes on to make a qualification which seems to me very
important. Dr. Hutchinson believes that Herbert's principal
temptation was *ambition*. We need not deny that Herbert
had been, like many other men, ambitious; we know that
he had a hot temper; we know that he liked fine clothes
and fine company, and would have been pleased by pre-
ferment at Court. But beside the struggle to abandon thought
of the attractions offered to worldly ambition, Professor
Knights finds 'a dejection of spirit that tended to make him
regard his own life, the life he was actually leading, as
worthless and unprofitable'. Mr. Knights attributes the cause
partly to ill-health, but still more to a *more ingrained distrust.*
It was perhaps distrust of himself, or fear of testing his powers
among more confident men, that drove him to the shelter
of an obscure parsonage. He had, Mr. Knights suggests, to
rid himself of the torturing sense of frustration and impotence
and accept the validity of his own experience. If this is so,
Herbert's weakness became the source of his greatest power,
for the result was *The Temple*.

I have called upon Mr. Knights's testimony in evidence
that Herbert is not a poet whose work is significant only
for Christian readers; that *The Temple* is not to be taken
as simply a devotional handbook of meditation for the
faithful, but as the personal record of a man very conscious
of weakness and failure, a man of intellect and sensibility
who hungered and thirsted after righteousness. And that
by its *content,* as well as because of its technical accomplish-

ment, it is a work of importance for every lover of poetry. This is not, however, to suggest that it is unprofitable for us to study the text for closer understanding, to acquaint ourselves with the liturgy of the Church, with the traditional imagery of the Church, and identify the Biblical allusions. One long poem which has been subjected to close examination is 'The Sacrifice'. There are sixty-three stanzas of three lines each, sixty-one of which have the refrain 'Was ever grief like Mine?' I mention this poem, which is a very fine one, and not so familiar as are some of the shorter and more lyrical pieces, because it has been carefully studied by Professor William Empson in his *Seven Types of Ambiguity*, and by Miss Rosamund Tuve in her *A Reading of George Herbert*. The lines are to be taken as spoken by Christ upon the Cross. We need, of course, enough acquaintance with the New Testament to recognise references to the Passion. But we are also better prepared if we recognise the Lamentations of Jeremiah, and the Reproaches in the Mass of the Presanctified which is celebrated on Good Friday.

> *Celebrant:* I led thee forth out of Egypt, drowning Pharaoh in the Red Sea: and thou hast delivered me up unto the chief priests.
> *Deacon & Subdeacon:* O my people, what have I done unto thee, or wherein have I wearied thee? Testify against me.

It is interesting to note that Mr. Empson and Miss Tuve differ in their interpretation of the following stanza:

> *O all ye who passe by, behold and see;*
> Man stole the fruit, but I must climbe the tree;
> The tree of life to all, but onely me:
>   Was ever grief like mine?

Mr. Empson comments: 'He climbs the tree to repay what was stolen, as if he were putting the apple back'; and develops this explanation at some length. Upon this interpretation Miss Tuve observes rather tartly: 'All (Mr. Empson's) rabbits roll out of one small hat—the fact that

Herbert uses the time-honoured 'climb' for the ascent of the Cross, and uses the word 'must', to indicate a far deeper necessity than that which faces a small boy under a big tree.' Certainly, the image of *replacing* the apple which has been plucked is too ludicrous to be entertained for a moment. It is obvious that Christ 'climbs' or is 'lifted' up on the Cross in atonement for the sin of Adam and Eve; the verb 'climb' being used traditionally to indicate the *voluntary* nature of the sacrifice for the sins of the world. Herbert was, assuredly, familiar with the imagery used by the pre-Reformation Church. It is likely also that Donne, learned in the works of the scholastics, and also in the writings of such Roman theologians contemporary with himself as Cardinal Bellarmine, set a standard of scholarship which Herbert followed.

To cite such an instance as this, however, is not to suggest that the lover of poetry needs to prepare himself with theological and liturgical knowledge *before* approaching Herbert's poetry. That would be to put the cart before the horse. With the appreciation of Herbert's poems, as with all poetry, enjoyment is the beginning as well as the end. We must enjoy the poetry before we attempt to penetrate the poet's mind; we must enjoy it before we understand it, if the attempt to understand it is to be worth the trouble. We begin by enjoying poems, and lines in poems, which make an immediate impression; only gradually, as we familiarise ourselves with the whole work, do we appreciate *The Temple* as a coherent sequence of poems setting down the fluctuations of emotion between despair and bliss, between agitation and serenity, and the discipline of suffering which leads to peace of spirit.

The relation of enjoyment to belief—the question whether a poem has more to give us if we share the beliefs of its author, is one which has never been answered satisfactorily: the present writer has made some attempt to contribute to the solution of the problem, and remains dissatisfied with his attempts. But one thing is certain: that even if the reader enjoys a poem more fully when he shares the beliefs of the author, he will miss a great deal of possible enjoyment and of valuable experience if he does not seek the fullest understanding possible of poetry in reading which he must 'suspend his disbelief'. (The present writer is very thankful for having had the opportunity to study the *Bhagavad Gītā* and the religious and philosophical beliefs, so different from his own, with which the *Bhagavad Gītā* is informed.)

Some of the poems in *The Temple* express moods of anguish and sense of defeat or failure:

> At first thou gav'st me milk and sweetnesses;
> > I had my wish and way:
> My dayes were straw'd with flow'rs and happinesse;
> > There was no moneth but May.
> But with my yeares sorrow did twist and grow,
> And made a partie unawares for wo. . . .
>
> Yet, though thou troublest me, I must be meek;
> > In weaknesse must be stout.
> Well, I will change the service, and go seek
> > Some other master out.
> Ah my deare God! though I am clean forgot,
> Let me not love thee, if I love thee not.

The foregoing lines are from the first of five poems all of which bear the title 'Affliction'. In the first of two poems both of which are entitled 'The Temper', he speaks of his fluctuations of faith and feeling:

> How should I praise thee, Lord! how should my rymes
> > Gladly engrave thy love in steel,
> > If what my soul doth feel sometimes,
> > > My soul might ever feel!

The great danger, for the poet who would write religious verse, is that of setting down what he would like to feel rather than be faithful to the expression of what he really feels. Of such pious insincerity Herbert is never guilty. We need not look too narrowly for a steady progress in Herbert's religious life, in an attempt to discover a chronological order. He falls, and rises again. Also, he was accustomed to working over his poems; they may have circulated in manuscript among his intimates during his lifetime. What we can confidently believe is that every poem in the book is true to the poet's experience. In some poems there is a more joyous note, as in 'Whitsunday':

> Listen sweet Dove unto my song,
> And spread thy golden wings in me;
> Hatching my tender heart so long,
> Till it get wing, and flie away with thee. . . .

> Lord, though we change, thou art the same;
> The same sweet God of love and light:
> Restore this day, for thy great name,
> Unto his ancient and miraculous right.

In 'The Flower' we hear the note of serenity, almost of beatitude, and of thankfulness for God's blessings:

> How fresh, O Lord, how sweet and clean
> Are thy returns! ev'n as the flowers in spring;
> To which, besides their own demean,
> The late-past frosts tributes of pleasure bring.
> > Grief melts away
> > Like snow in May,
> As if there were no such cold thing.
> > . . . . . .

> And now in age I bud again,
> After so many deaths I live and write;
> I once more smell the dew and rain,
> And relish versing: O my onely light,
> > It cannot be
> > That I am he
> On whom thy tempests fell all night.[1]

[1] A. Alvarez in *The School of Donne* says justly of this stanza: 'This is, I suppose, the most perfect and most vivid stanza in the whole of Herbert's work. But it is, in every sense, so natural that its originality is easily missed.' (See also Coleridge on this poem: footnote to p.10.)

I cannot resist the thought that in this last stanza—itself a miracle of phrasing—the imagery, so apposite to express the achievement of faith which it records, is taken from the experience of the man of delicate physical health who had known much illness. It is on this note of joy in convalescence of the spirit in surrender to God, that the life of discipline of this haughty and irascible Herbert finds conclusion: *In His will is our peace.*

III

Of all the 'school of Donne' Herbert is the closest to the old Master. Two other fine poets of the group might just as well be said to belong to the 'school of Herbert'. The debt of Vaughan to Herbert can be shown by quotation; Herbert's most recent and authoritative editor, Dr. F. E. Hutchinson, says: 'there is no example in English literature of one poet adopting another poet's work so extensively.' As for Crashaw, he undoubtedly admired Herbert. Nevertheless, in spite of a continuity of influence and inspiration, we must remember that these four poets, who form a constellation of religious genius unparalleled in English poetry, are all highly individual, and very different from each other.

The resemblances and differences between Donne and Herbert are peculiarly fascinating. I have suggested earlier that the difference between the poetry of Donne and Herbert shows some parallel to the difference between their careers in the Church. Donne the Dean of St. Paul's, whose sermons drew crowds in the City of London; Herbert the shepherd of a little flock of rustics, to whom he laboured to explain the meaning of the rites of the Church, the significance of Holy Days, in language that they could understand. There are, however, lines which might have come from either, where we seem to hear the same voice— Herbert echoing the idiom or reflecting the imagery of Donne. There is at least one poem of Herbert's in which he plays with extended metaphor in the manner of Donne.

It is 'Obedience' where he uses legal terms almost throughout:

> My God, if writings may
> Convey a Lordship any way
> Whither the buyer and the seller please;
> Let it not thee displease,
> If this poore paper do as much as they.

> .   .   .   .   .

> He that will passe his land,
> As I have mine, may set his hand
> And heart unto this Deed, when he hath read;
> And make the purchase spread
> To both our goods, if he to it will stand.

Such elaboration is not typical of Herbert. But there is *wit*
like that of Donne in 'The Quip'. One feels obliged to quote
the whole poem:

> The merrie world did on a day
> With his train-bands and mates agree
> To meet together, where I lay,
> And all in sport to geere at me.

> First, Beautie crept into a rose,
> Which when I pluckt not, Sir, said she,
> Tell me, I pray, Whose hands are those?
> *But thou shalt answer, Lord, for me.*

> Then Money came, and chinking still,
> What tune is this, poore man? said he:
> I heard in Musick you had skill.
> *But thou shalt answer, Lord, for me.*

> Then came brave Glorie puffing by
> In silks that whistled, who but he?
> He scarce allow'd me half an eie.
> *But thou shalt answer, Lord, for me.*

> Then came quick Wit and Conversation,
> And he would needs a comfort be,
> And, to be short, make an Oration.
> *But thou shalt answer, Lord, for me.*

> Yet when the houre of thy designe
> To answer these fine things shall come;
> Speak not at large; say, I am thine:
> And then they have their answer home.

Professor Knights observes very shrewdly: 'the personifications here have nothing in common with Spenser's
allegorical figures or with the capitalised abstractions of the
eighteenth century: "brave Glorie puffing by in silks that
whistled" might have come straight from *The Pilgrim's
Progress.*' How audible are these silks 'that whistled'!
'Puffing' is equally apt: the same participle is used, to
produce another but equally striking effect, elsewhere:

> Sometimes Death, puffing at the doore,
> Blows all the dust about the floore.
>
> (*The Church Floore*)

Herbert is a master of the simple everyday word in the
right place, and charges it with concentrated meaning, as
in 'Redemption', one of the poems known to all readers
of anthologies:

> Having been tenant long to a rich Lord,
> Not thriving, I resolved to be bold,
> And make a suit unto him, to afford
> A new small-rented lease, and cancell th'old.
> In heaven at his manour I him sought:
> They told me there, that he was lately gone
> About some land, which he had dearly bought
> Long since on earth, to take possession.
> I straight return'd, and knowing his great birth,
> Sought him accordingly in great resorts;
> In cities, theatres, gardens, parks, and courts:
> At length I heard a ragged noise and mirth
> Of theeves and murderers: there I him espied,
> Who straight, *Your suit is granted*, said, & died.

The phrase 'ragged noise and mirth' gives us, in four words,
the picture of the scene to which Herbert wishes to introduce us.

There are many lines which remind us of Donne:

> What though my bodie runne to dust?
> Faith cleaves unto it, counting evr'y grain
> With an exact and most particular trust,
>   Reserving all for flesh again.
>   (*Faith*)

> My God, what is a heart?
> Silver, or gold, or precious stone,
> Or starre, or rainbow, or a part
> Of all these things, or all of them in one?
>   (*Mattens*)

>   . . . learn here thy stemme
> And true descent; that when thou shalt grow fat,

> And wanton in thy cravings, thou mayst know,
> That flesh is but the glasse, which holds the dust
> That measures all our time; which also shall
> Be crumbled into dust. . . .
>   (*Church-monuments*)

> Lord, how can man preach thy eternall word ?
>   He is a brittle crazie glasse: . . .
>   (*The Windows*)

> My bent thoughts, like a brittle bow,
>   Did flie asunder: . . .
>   (*Deniall*)

Herbert must have learned from Donne the cunning use of both the learned and the common word, to give the sudden shock of surprise and delight.

> But man is close, reserv'd, and dark to thee:
>   When thou demandest but a heart,
>   He cavils instantly.
>   In his poore cabinet of bone
>   Sinnes have their box apart,
> Defrauding thee, who gavest two for one.
>   (*Ungratefulnesse*)

> The fleet Astronomer can bore,
> And thred the spheres with his quick-piercing minde:
> He views their stations, walks from doore to doore,
>   Surveys, as if he had design'd
> To make a purchase there: he sees their dances,
>   And knoweth long before
> Both their full-ey'd aspects, and secret glances.
>   (*Vanitie*)

> My thoughts are all a case of knives, . . .
>   (*Affliction IV.*)

The following lines are very reminiscent of Donne:

> How soon doth man decay!
> When clothes are taken from a chest of sweets
> To swaddle infants, whose young breath
>   Scarce knows the way;
> Those clouts are little winding sheets,
> Which do consigne and send them unto death.
>   (*Mortification*)

Here and there one can believe that Herbert has unconsciously used a word, or a rhythm of Donne, in a very
different context from that of the original, as perhaps in the
first line of 'The Discharge':

> Busie enquiring heart, what wouldst thou know?

Donne begins 'The Sunne Rising' with the line

> Busie old foole, unruly Sunne. . .

If Herbert's line be an echo and not a mere coincidence—
the reader must form his own opinion—it is all the more
interesting because of the difference in subject matter between
the two poems. If Herbert, in writing a poem of religious
mortification, could echo a poem of Donne which is an
aubade of the lover's complaint that day should come so

soon, it suggests that the literary influence of the elder man upon the younger was profound indeed.

Herbert's metrical forms, however, are both original and varied. To have invented and perfected so many variations in the form of lyrical verse is evidence of native genius, hard work and a passion for perfection. Two of his poems are such as would be considered, if written by a poet to-day, merely elegant trifles: 'The Altar' and 'Easter Wings'. In each, there is a disposition of longer and shorter lines so printed that the poem has the shape, the one of an altar and the other of a pair of wings. Such a diversion, if employed frequently, would be tedious, distracting and trying to the eyesight and we must be glad that Herbert did not make further use of these devices: yet it is evidence of Herbert's care for workmanship, his restless exploration of variety, and of a kind of gaiety of spirit, a joy in composition which engages our delighted sympathy. The exquisite variations of form in the other poems of *The Temple* show a resourcefulness of invention which seems inexhaustible, and for which I know no parallel in English poetry. Here, we can only quote a stanza from each of a brief selection to suggest the astonishing variety:

> O my chief good,
> How shall I measure out thy bloud?
> How shall I count what thee befell,
> And each grief tell?
>
> > (*Good Friday*)

> O blessed bodie! Whither are thou thrown?
> No lodging for thee, but a cold hard stone?
> So many hearts on earth, and yet not one
> > Receive thee?
> > (*Sepulchre*)

Poems in such measures as these, and more obviously 'The Sacrifice', which we have quoted earlier, seem to indicate an ear trained by the music of liturgy.

Rise heart; thy Lord is risen. Sing his praise
Without delayes,
Who takes thee by the hand, that thou likewise
With him mayst rise:
That, as his death calcined thee to dust,
His life may make thee gold, and much more, just.

                         (*Easter*)

The slow movement of the last line quoted above has something of the movement of the exquisite line which ends
Donne's 'Nocturnall upon S. Lucies Day':

Both the yeares, and the dayes deep midnight is.

Somewhat similar to the movement of 'Good Friday'
(quoted above) is:

Since, Lord, to thee
A narrow way and little gate
Is all the passage, on my infancie
Thou didst lay hold, and antedate
My faith in me.

                         (*Holy Baptisme I*)

Close enough to the form of 'Holy Baptisme' for its
difference to be all the more striking is:

Lord, I confesse my sinne is great;
Great is my sinne. Oh! gently treat
With thy quick flow'r, thy momentarie bloom;
Whose life still pressing
Is one undressing,
A steadie aiming at a tombe.

                         (*Repentance*)

The next quotation has a solemn liturgical movement
suited to the subject-matter and the title:

> O Do not use me
> After my sinnes! look not on my desert,
> But on thy glorie! then thou wilt reform
> And not refuse me: for thou onely art
> The mightie God, but I a sillie worm;
>   O do not bruise me!
>   (*Sighs and Grones*)

Herbert knows the effect of denying a rhyme where it is expected:

> When my devotions could not pierce
>   Thy silent eares;
> Then was my heart broken, as was my verse:
> My breast was full of fears
>   And disorder:
>   (*Deniall*)

The roughness of metre of the line

> Then was my heart broken, as was my verse

is exactly what is wanted to convey the meaning of the words. The following stanza has an apparent artlessness and conversational informality which only a great artist could achieve:

> Lord, let the Angels praise thy name.
> Man is a foolish thing, a foolish thing,
>   Folly and Sinne play all his game.
> His house still burns, and yet he still doth sing,
>   *Man is but grasse,*
>   *He knows it, fill the glasse.*
>   (*Miserie*)

The next poem to be quoted is one of several poems of Herbert which, while being, like all the rest of his work, personal, have been set to music and sung as hymns:

> King of Glorie, King of Peace,
>   I will love thee:
> And that love may never cease,
>   I will move thee.
>   (*Praise II*)

The same masterly simplicity is visible in:

> Throw away thy rod,
> Throw away thy wrath:
>> O my God,
> Take the gentle path.
>
>> *(Discipline)*

I wish to end by giving in full the poem which, significantly, I think, ends *The Temple*. It is named 'Love III', and indicates the serenity finally attained by this proud and humble man:

> Love bade me welcome: yet my soul drew back,
>> Guiltie of dust and sinne.
> But quick-ey'd Love, observing me grow slack
>> From my first entrance in,
> Drew nearer to me, sweetly questioning,
>> If I lack'd any thing.
>
> A guest, I answer'd, worthy to be here:
>> Love said, You shall be he.
> I the unkinde, ungratefull? Ah my deare,
>> I cannot look on thee.
> Love took my hand, and smiling did reply,
>> Who made the eyes but I?
>
> Truth Lord, but I have marr'd them: let my shame
>> Go where it doth deserve.
> And know you not, sayes Love, who bore the blame?
>> My deare, then I will serve.
> You must sit down, sayes Love, and taste my meat:
>> So I did sit and eat.

GEORGE HERBERT
A Select Bibliography

(Place of publication London, unless stated otherwise)

Bibliography:

A HERBERT BIBLIOGRAPHY, by G. H. Palmer. Cambridge, Mass. (1911)
—a privately printed catalogue of the compiler's collection of books by and about Herbert. Useful but incomplete.

Collected Editions:

THE WORKS, with a Preface by W. Pickering and Notes by S. T. Coleridge. 2 vols. (1835-6).

THE COMPLETE WORKS, edited by A. B. Grosart. 3 vols. (1874)
—textually most unreliable, but the first edition to make use of the Williams MS.

THE ENGLISH WORKS NEWLY ARRANGED, edited by G. H. Palmer. 3 vols. (1905-1907)
—an important edition, notwithstanding some editorial liberties and speculations.

WORKS, edited by F. E. Hutchinson. Oxford (1941)
—the definitive edition in the Oxford English Texts Series. The World's Classics reprint, 1961, has a valuable introduction by H. Gardner.

Separate Works:

THE TEMPLE, SACRED POEMS AND PRIVATE EJACULATIONS, Cambridge (1633)
—13 editions were published before 1709 but none thereafter until 1799. The Nonesuch Press edition (1927) edited by F. Meynell (with a bibliographical note by G. Keynes) is based on the Bodleian MS (Tanner 307) which was the copy licensed in 1633 for the printer by the Cambridge Vice-Chancellor and his assessors.

WITTS RECREATIONS. WITH A THOUSAND OUTLANDISH PROVERBS SELECTED BY MR. G. H. (1640)
—the proverbs attributed to Herbert were published separately in 1651 as *Jacula Prudentum*.

HERBERT'S REMAINS (1652)
—contains most of *A Priest to the Temple* and *Jacula Prudentum*.

A PRIEST TO THE TEMPLE, OR, THE COUNTREY PARSON HIS CHARACTER, AND RULE OF HOLY LIFE (1671)
—a selection, edited by G. M. Forbes, was published in 1949.

Herbert contributed Latin and Greek poems to the following memorial collections: *Epicedium Cantabrigiense, in Obitum Henrici Principis Walliae.* Cambridge, 1612 (2 Latin poems); *Lacrymae Cantabrigienses, in Obitum Reginae Annae.* Cambridge, 1619 (1 Latin poem); *True Copies of all the Latine Orations, made at Cambridge on the 25 and 27 of Februarie last past,* 1623 (1 Latin oration with English translation); *Oratio qua Principis Caroli Reditum ex Hispaniis Celebravit Georgius Herbert.* Cambridge, 1623 (1 Latin oration); *Memoriae Francisci, Baronis de Verulamio, Sacrum,* 1626 (1 Latin poem); *A Sermon of Commemoration of the Lady Danvers by John Donne. Together with other Commemorations of her, called Parentalia by her Sonne, G. Herbert,* 1627 (19 Latin and Greek poems).

Some Critical and Biographical Studies:

THE LIFE OF LORD HERBERT OF CHERBURY (1764)
—see also Lord Herbert's *Poems,* edited Moore Smith, Oxford, 1923.
THE LIFE OF MR. GEORGE HERBERT, by I. Walton (1670)
—reprinted in Walton's *Lives,* 1670 (World's Classics edition, 1923).
BIOGRAPHIA LITERARIA, by S. T. Coleridge (1817)
—chapters XIX and XX.
METAPHYSICAL POEMS AND LYRICS OF THE SEVENTEENTH CENTURY, edited with an introduction by H. Grierson. Oxford (1921).
SEICENTISMO E MARINISMO IN INGHILTERRA, di M. Praz. Florence (1925).
A CONCORDANCE TO THE ENGLISH POEMS, by C. Mann. Boston, Mass. (1927).
SEVEN TYPES OF AMBIGUITY, by W. Empson (1930).
THE DONNE TRADITION, by G. Williamson. Cambridge, Mass. (1930).
FOUR METAPHYSICAL POETS, by J. Bennett. Cambridge (1934; revised edition, 1953).
THE METAPHYSICAL POETS, by J. B. Leishman. Oxford (1934).
EXPLORATION: ESSAYS IN LITERARY CRITICISM, by L. C. Knights (1946)
—contains his essay on Herbert first printed in *Scrutiny,* 1933.
A READING OF GEORGE HERBERT, by R. Tuve. Chicago (1952).
GEORGE HERBERT, by M. Bottrall (1954).
GEORGE HERBERT, by J. H. Summers. Cambridge, Mass. (1954).
TWO GENTLE MEN, by M. Chute. New York (1959)
—biographies of Herbert and Herrick. English edition, 1960.
THE SCHOOL OF DONNE, by A. Alvarez (1961).

Ronald Firbank

and

John Betjeman

by JOCELYN BROOKE

Published for The British Council
and The National Book League
by Longmans, Green & Co.

Two shillings and sixpence net

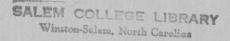

These two writers of comedy are presented together for contrast rather than for comparison.

Ronald Firbank (1886-1926) is a writer who is being 'discovered' by a new generation. He was a master of felicitous dialogue, and his novels, among them *Valmouth*, *Vainglory*, *The Flower Beneath the Foot* and the *Artificial Princess*, have never lacked admirers. As Mr. Jocelyn Brooke says, 'though not a great artist,' Firbank is 'that rare phenomenon in English literature, a *pure* artist, and as such he deserves our respect'.

John Betjeman, long known for his highly individual verse, and for his essays on architectural taste, has had this said of him by Sir Kenneth Clark: 'his influence', he wrote in a Prefatory Letter to a recent edition of *The Gothic Revival*, 'has not been exerted through learned articles, but through poetry and conversation . . . One of the few original minds of our generation.' Sir Kenneth also wrote of Mr. Betjeman's 'sensitive response to everything which expresses human needs and affections', and the tribute is apt. Mr. Betjeman has now added the distinction of having made his poetry popular to an extent to which there has not been a parallel in our own time.

Mr. Jocelyn Brooke, who has already contributed studies of *Elizabeth Bowen* (No. 28) and *Aldous Huxley* (No. 55) to this Series, is the author of distinguished novels. His fuller consideration of Firbank, which was published in 1951, is among the best studies of that writer.

Bibliographical Series
of Supplements to 'British Book News'
on Writers and their Work

GENERAL EDITOR
Bonamy Dobrée

RONALD FIRBANK
*from a photograph by
Bertram Park*

JOHN BETJEMAN
*from a photograph by
Mark Gerson*

RONALD FIRBANK

and

JOHN BETJEMAN

by

JOCELYN BROOKE

PUBLISHED FOR

THE BRITISH COUNCIL

and the NATIONAL BOOK LEAGUE

by LONGMANS, GREEN & CO.

LONGMANS, GREEN & CO. LTD.
48 Grosvenor Street, London, W.1
Railway Crescent, Croydon, Victoria, Australia
Auckland, Kingston (Jamaica), Lahore, Nairobi

LONGMANS SOUTHERN AFRICA (PTY) LTD.
Thibault House, Thibault Square, Cape Town
Johannesburg, Salisbury

LONGMANS OF NIGERIA LTD.
W.R. Industrial Estate, Ikeja

LONGMANS OF GHANA LTD.
Industrial Estate, Ring Road South, Accra

LONGMANS, GREEN (FAR EAST) LTD.
443 Lockhart Road, Hong Kong

LONGMANS OF MALAYA LTD.
44 Jalan Ampang, Kuala Lumpur

ORIENT LONGMANS LTD.
Calcutta, Bombay, Madras
Delhi, Hyberabad, Dacca

LONGMANS CANADA LTD.
137 Bond Street, Toronto 2

First Published in 1962
© Jocelyn Brooke 1962

Printed in Great Britain by
F. Mildner & Sons, London, E.C.1

RONALD FIRBANK

I

RONALD FIRBANK, though he seems to us so very much a child of his own period, might also, paradoxically, be described as a man born out of his time. Apart from a fragment of juvenilia, all his books appeared between the years 1915 and 1926,[1] and one tends to think of them—along with Eliot's *Prufrock* and Huxley's *Antic Hay*—as typical products of the nineteen-twenties; yet Firbank's true affinities were with the *fin de siècle*, the epoch of Wilde, Beardsley and *The Yellow Book*. Had he, in fact, been born a decade or so earlier, he would almost certainly not have written the kind of novels he did, and quite possibly would have produced nothing memorable at all, for his work owes its unique quality to a kind of literary cross-breeding: his innate ninetyishness is, as it were, hybridised with the more cynical and disillusioned spirit of a later age. He himself remained a good old-fashioned aesthete, his approach to life and literature was deliberately precious and artificial; but the chronological gap which separated him from the nineties enabled him to view the 'Mauve Decade' with a certain detachment, and to appreciate its more comical aspects; he possessed, moreover, a pronounced faculty for self-mockery, and was quite capable of laughing at his own preciosity.

In his lifetime and for some years after his death Firbank's work appealed only to a select few; solemn critics were apt to dismiss him as an intellectual playboy, a purveyor of frivolous trifles, though even as early as 1929 such eminent fellow-writers as E. M. Forster, Osbert Sitwell and Arthur Waley had recognized his claim to be judged—despite his apparent triviality—as a serious literary artist.[2] During the

---

[1] *The Artificial Princess* was published posthumously in 1934, but was probably written in about 1914.

[2] The first collected edition, published in 1929, contained introductory essays by Osbert Sitwell and Arthur Waley; E. M. Forster's essay on Firbank, dated the same year, appears in *Abinger Harvest*.

second world war, and for some years after it, his books
were all but unobtainable; in 1949, however, Messrs. Duckworth issued five of the novels in one volume, following it
up with further reprints, and Firbank began to be rediscovered by a younger generation. His only published
play, *The Princess Zoubaroff*, received its first performance,
and one of his best novels, *Valmouth*, was dramatized, in a
musical version, by Sandy Wilson. Firbank, in fact, more
than thirty years after his death, had achieved a celebrity
which, denied him in his lifetime, could hardly have been
foreseen even by his warmest admirers, and must have
greatly surprised those of his surviving contemporaries who
had failed to recognize, behind the frivolous façade, a
writer of enduring merit.

Arthur Annesley Ronald Firbank was born in London
in 1886, of rich upper-middle-class parents; his grandfather,
Joseph Firbank, had started life as a Durham miner, but
later amassed a large fortune as a railway contractor.
Ronald was a delicate child, and was educated, for the
most part, by private tutors. With some idea of studying
for the diplomatic service, he spent some time at Tours and
Madrid, and in 1906 went up to Trinity Hall, Cambridge.
He sat for no examinations, and left the University after
two and a half years, without a degree. Perhaps the most
noteworthy event of his time at Cambridge was his recep-
tion into the Roman Catholic church, though his catholicism
might be described, perhaps, as *pratiquant* rather than
croyant: the appeal of the Church, in fact, was for Firbank
more aesthetic than theological, and in his later novels he
adopts an attitude of affectionate mockery towards the
hierarchy.

The project of a diplomatic career was soon abandoned,
probably owing to Firbank's delicate health; for the same
reason, much of his life was spent abroad, in Italy, France,
North Africa and the West Indies. He was an enthusiastic
traveller, and his taste for exotic scenes is reflected in his
books; he was also fond of smart society, though his social

activities were apt to be inhibited by an extreme and paralysing shyness. His first book had been published in 1905, before he went up to Cambridge; thereafter he was to produce nothing more for ten years, but from 1915 onwards his novels appeared at approximately the rate of one a year. With the approach of middle-age, his health gradually declined, the process being hastened, no doubt, by heavy drinking and a highly irregular mode of life; he died at Rome in 1926, four months before his fortieth birthday.

II

How is one to define the peculiar, the essential quality of Firbank's novels? He has been described as a fantasist and as an exponent of artificial comedy, but such labels are not much to the point; for Firbank is a writer whom it is nearly impossible to fit into any of the accepted literary categories. He is a comic writer, certainly, but his comedy has always an undertone of poetry: it is nearer, one might say, to *A Midsummer Night's Dream* than to *The Importance of being Earnest*. The Firbankian world is a fantastic one, yet the fantasy is restricted, for the most part, to what is just humanly credible: the characters who people this world—priests, society ladies, nuns, negresses and so forth—are convincing within the context in which they occur, however eccentric and improbable their behaviour. Firbank, in fact, created a world in which, for all its remoteness from reality, one finds oneself able to believe, rather as one 'believes' in the world of *Alice in Wonderland* (which, like that of Firbank, has an interior logic of its own).

Firbank's style, though it cannot usefully be compared with that of any other writer, is full of echoes. His debt to the nineties is of course predominant, not so much to the epigrammatic or humorous writers of that period as to the more precious of the 'decadent' poets, as well as to

Maeterlinck and to Beardsley's *Under the Hill*. There are echoes too, perhaps, of the Restoration dramatists, and in many passages Firbank adopts—in inverted commas, as it were—the tone and mannerisms of such popular women novelists as Ouida or Marie Corelli. He is also fond of parodying the writers of gossip columns, and one novel, *Valmouth*, is in part a skit on those 'rural' novelists later to be satirized more directly by Stella Gibbons in *Cold Comfort Farm*.

Firbank, in fact, might be described as a *pasticheur*, yet from the strange stylistic amalgam produced by his many borrowings emerges something uniquely his own: one cannot read a page or even a paragraph of his mature work without at once recognizing its author. This technique of multiple pastiche might be compared with those surrealist collages of Max Ernst which, fabricated from the illustrations to Victorian magazines, mysteriously transcend their humdrum sources, and become something wholly personal to their creator.

Firbank's novels, though they seem so casually put to-gether, are in fact written with immense care; every word tells, each sentence is cunningly designed to produce exactly the effect required. Firbank can be perverse and even silly at times, but his writing is never slipshod, and in his close attention to verbal and syntactical values he may be said to bear some relation (though admittedly a distant one) to James Joyce. There is, moreover, a 'syncopated' quality about his prose which faintly suggests the influence of jazz music, whose beginnings were more or less con-temporaneous with Firbank's début as a novelist. This effect is produced mainly by the eccentric placing of words, particularly adverbs: thus, he will write of a young man 'grooming fitfully his hair' (*Vainglory*). He is an adept, too, at the comic juxtaposition of pompous diction and col-loquialisms, and like Joyce again, he enjoys *playing* with words, inventing new verbal combinations, and twisting his sentences into curious and unprecedented patterns. He

is fond of alliteration, and sometimes uses it with an almost
onomatopoeic effect, as when he writes 'The plaintive
pizzicato of Madame Mimosa's Pom pup, "Plum Bun",'
etc. (*Valmouth*). And here is another passage from *Valmouth*
in which the syntax is strained almost to bursting point:

> 'Lift the lid of the long casket—and pick me a relic', Mrs.
> Hurstpierpoint enjoined. . . .
> 'You used to say the toe, 'm, of the married sister of the Madonna,
> the one that was a restaurant proprietress (Look alive there with
> those devilled kidneys, and what is keeping Fritz with that sweet
> omelette?) in any fracas was particularly potent.'

Firbank's humour might be said to be a by-product of
his style: the fun lies not so much in the jokes themselves
(they are often rather feeble) as in the form and cadence of
a sentence, or in the choice of some surprising or incongruous epithet. He is at his best in his dialogue which,
though as stylized as that of I. Compton Burnett, contrives
also to catch the exact tones and modulations of real speech.
The talk in a Firbank novel, perhaps one should add,
performs no such pedestrian function as furthering the plot,
or even (in most cases) of characterizing the respective
speakers, who as often as not have a way of speaking wildly
out of character. Their conversation tends to be the merest
gossip, yet full of strange overtones, half-hints and sly
implications. Here (in *Vainglory*) two women are discussing
a new curate:

> 'Probably a creature with a whole gruesome family?' she in-
> directly enquired.
> 'Unhappily he's only just left Oxford.'
> 'Ah, handsome, then, I hope.'
> 'On the contrary, he's like one of those cherubs one sees on
> eighteenth-century fonts with their mouths stuffed with cake.'
> 'Not really?'
> '*And he wears glasses.*'
> 'But he takes them off sometimes—?'
> 'That's just what I don't know.'

This passage, even though read in isolation, might serve as a test of Firbank's capacity to make one laugh: if one doesn't find it funny (and many people do not), one is not likely to enjoy Firbank's work as a whole. Note, incidentally, the characteristic use of italics to give an equivocal emphasis to a perfectly ordinary remark: a device which has been borrowed by Evelyn Waugh, who in his earlier novels was much influenced by Firbank. Also, though seldom overtly indecent, Firbank is a master of bawdy innuendo, and can suggest, by a mere verbal echo or by a row of dots, the most outrageous obscenities, while ostensibly expressing himself with perfect propriety.

Though hardly a literary innovator on the scale of Joyce, Firbank did nonetheless break new ground as a novelist: quite apart from idiosyncrasies of style, the construction of his books is also strikingly original. Abandoning the traditional mode of direct narrative, he employed a method akin to cinematic montage, switching abruptly from scene to scene, and ruthlessly omitting all those introductory or explanatory passages which earlier novelists had thought necessary for the convenience of the reader. This technique of 'cutting', though today (owing partly, perhaps, to Firbank) it has become almost a commonplace in the writing of fiction, was decidedly a novelty forty-five years ago, and the opening sentences of *Vainglory* may well have seemed bewildering to the average reader who picked it up in 1915:

'And, then, oh yes! Atalanta is getting too pronounced.' She spoke lightly, leaning back a little in her deep armchair. It was the end of a somewhat lively review.

On such a languid afternoon how hard it seemed to bear a cross! Pleasant to tilt it a little—lean it for an instant against somebody else. . . . Her listener waved her handkerchief expressively. She felt, just then, it was safer not to speak. . . .

On a dark canvas screen were grouped some inconceivably delicate Persian miniatures.

She bent towards them. 'Oh, what gems!'

And so on, and so forth: only gradually and by a series of inferences does one learn, during that first chapter, who is speaking to whom, what they are all talking about, where they live, etc. The reader, in fact, is in the position of one who finds himself at some party at which the guests, all unknown to him, are gossiping about private topics to whose nature he has no clue; nor does the host (in the person of the narrator) make any but the most perfunctory efforts to enlighten him. In time, however, one becomes accustomed to Firbank's oblique method of presentation; one's fellow-guests no longer seem strangers, one learns their names and their habits, and the flood of gossip becomes suddenly intelligible.

III

Firbank's first book, *Odette d'Antrevernes*, was published in 1905. The title-story is a feeble pastiche of Maeterlinck at his most cloying; it gives no hint of the way in which its author was to develop, and is interesting only as exhibiting, in its pure form, that sickly *fin de siècle* romanticism which Firbank was never quite to discard, and of which traces can still be detected even in his latest and most mature work. Bound up with the original *Odette*, but not reprinted in later editions, was a short sketch, *A Study in Temperament*, which though of little intrinsic worth does foreshadow, if only dimly, Firbank's characteristic style, and in which, significantly, he is already poking fun at Maeterlinck ('It is so delightful to be seen reading Maeterlinck! So decadent!' remarks one of the characters).

Next in order of writing comes *The Artificial Princess*, though in fact this was not published until after Firbank's death; it can be assumed that he was dissatisfied with it, for a number of sentences and several whole paragraphs recur almost unchanged in *Vainglory*. The narrative style is still, relatively speaking, traditional, and Firbank's innovations in this respect are scarcely apparent. Compared with the

later books it strikes one as loosely and even carelessly
written; yet it is recognizably a Firbank novel, and marks
a complete break with the style of *Odette*. The fantastic
characters, the perverse humour, the sly allusions and
innuendoes are all there; and the setting—an imaginary
'Ruritania'—will be reproduced in *The Flower beneath the
Foot*.

Vainglory (1915) is Firbank's longest novel, and many of
his admirers, including the present writer, find it almost his
funniest, though not his best or most characteristic. It is
diffuse and overcrowded, there is even less plot than usual,
and the book is really a series of set-pieces so tenuously
connected that a new reader may easily become confused.
In his later work Firbank was to practise a greater concision
and economy, but if the writing is over-lush and the
structure somewhat top-heavy, *Vainglory* has a youthful
charm and spontaneity which make it one of his most
endearing novels.

Such plot as there is centres round the ambition of a Mrs.
Shamefoot to commemorate herself (while still alive and,
indeed, fairly young) by a stained glass window in a
cathedral. This, however, is a mere peg—and not, perhaps,
a very adequate one—to support a rich and complex verbal
tapestry, in which innumerable characters endlessly converse
against a background which is sometimes London but more
often the cathedral town of Ashringford. There are count-
less parties, not the least memorable of which is, perhaps,
that given by Mrs. Henedge (in Chapter II) to make known
a newly discovered fragment of Sappho, and at which, too,
many of the leading characters make their first appearance:
Miss Compostella ('Nobody would have guessed her to be
an actress, she was so private looking'); Mrs. Steeple who,
'one burning afternoon in July, with the thermometer at
90 . . ., had played *Rosmersholm* in Camberwell'; Monsignor
Parr, described as 'temperamental, when not otherwise . . .
employed'; Winsome Brooks, Mrs. Asp, Miss Thumbler
and many more.

The scene shifts to Ashringford, a city which, though bearing some faint generic resemblance to Winchester or Canterbury, can boast a Satanic colony and a bishop who is said to resemble 'a faun crowned with roses'. Here we are introduced to a host of new characters: Lady Anne Pantry, the Bishop's wife, who 'in the evening . . . sometimes suggested Phèdre', and her secretary Miss Hospice, whose personality Firbank evokes in a kind of poetic shorthand: 'With a rather cruel yellow at her neck, waist and feet, and a poem of fifty sheets, on *Verlaine at Bournemouth*, at her back. What is there left to say—'; Miss Wookie, Mrs. Pontypool, Lord Blueharnis, Mrs. Barrow of Dawn, and so on.

A word should perhaps be said about Firbank's use of comic names for his characters. In the hands of a less tactful writer this habit can become highly irritating, but Firbank's names, though one would find few of them in the telephone book, for the most part have just the right touch of fantasy: though intrinsically funny, they strike one as being just—though only just—credible. Another aspect of Firbank which, to the more literal-minded reader, may seem merely tiresome, is his occasional indulgence in sheer nonsense. In *Vainglory*, perhaps more than elsewhere, this nonsensical vein is much in evidence: thus, Miss Missingham, the imaginary author of a work called *Sacerdotalism and Satanism*, is made to remark that the towers of the cathedral at twilight resemble 'the helmets of eunuchs at carnival time', a comparison which, one feels, could have occurred to nobody but Firbank, and which only his confirmed addicts will value at its true worth.

The next novel, *Inclinations* (1916), is in striking contrast with its predecessor. The dense, luxuriant texture of *Vainglory* has given place to a simpler, less involuted style; it is as though an overgrown hedge of rambler roses had been ruthlessly pruned by the gardener. *Inclinations* is a 'slim' book in every sense: very short, and as light as a soufflé. The scene is laid mainly in Greece, where a fifteen

year old girl, Mabel Collins, is touring with her female
protectress, Miss O'Brookomore; Mabel elopes with an
Italian count, but the plot is vestigial, and Firbank, one feels,
became rather bored with it. The elopement is described in
what is possibly the shortest chapter ever written:

'Mabel! Mabel! Mabel! Mabel!
Mabel! Mabel! Mabel! Mabel!'

The book is written almost entirely in dialogue; some of
it displays Firbank at his best and funniest, but too often it
lapses into a rather feebly exclamatory tone, and there are
far too many dashes and exclamation marks. On the whole
it is Firbank's weakest novel, though it contains some passages of great humour, and some typically Firbankian
flights of fancy. One remembers, for instance, Miss
O'Brookomore's comment upon a hotel orchestra in
Athens: 'It sounds like the Incest-music to some new opera.'
Or Mabel's lament after leaving Paris, on the journey out:
'Tomorrow . . . six Cornish girls are to dance at the Lune
Grise. What a pity to have missed them.' One shares
Mabel's disappointment, for those Cornish girls must surely
have provided an unusual and stimulating attraction for a
Parisian cabaret.

With *Caprice* (1917) Firbank's art may be said to have
achieved maturity. Like *Inclinations*, it is a lightweight affair,
with none of the baroque elaboration of *Vainglory*; but here
Firbank has his material more fully under control, the
dialogue is more pointed, and the characters more sharply
focused. Structurally it is one of his best books, and the
narration, though typically oblique, is perfectly lucid. Its
theme is that of the 'innocent abroad', which will recur in
several of the later books: the stage-struck daughter of a
clergyman, having purloined the family jewels, escapes to
London determined to try her luck upon the boards; she
rents a theatre and appears as Juliet, but on the morning
after the first performance (having slept in the greenroom),
she falls into a well beneath the stage. It is the first (but not

the last) of Firbank's novels to have a 'tragic' ending.

There are many memorable passages: Sarah Sinquier's first visit to the Café Royal, for example, where she meets the sinister Mrs. Sixsmith (a name, incidentally, which does actually exist in real life); or her alarming interview with Mrs. Mary, the famous actress-manageress:

> 'The Boards, I believe, are new to you?'
> 'Absolutely.'
> 'Kindly stand.'
> 'I'm five full feet.'
> 'Say "Abyssinia".'
> 'Abyssinia!'
> 'As I guessed . . .'
> 'I was never there.'
> 'Now say "Joan".'
> 'Joan!'
> 'You're Comedy, my dear. Distinctly! And now sit down.'

Caprice reflects Firbank's passion for the theatre, and it seems probable that he would have preferred to write plays rather than novels. His attempts to do so, however, appear to have been unsuccessful, and his only published play, *The Princess Zoubaroff* (1920), though containing much amusing dialogue, shows little talent for dramatic construction.

The next novel, *Valmouth* (1919), is possibly Firbank's best. It has a solidity and richness of texture which recall *Vainglory*, though by now Firbank's prose has become tauter and more concise. In *Valmouth* his preoccupation with Catholicism, noticeable in *Vainglory*, is greatly intensified: the atmosphere of the book is heavy with incense, and the characters include a number of priests, nuns and choir-boys, all of them eccentric and most of them (one is allowed to infer) morally unorthodox. The scene is an imaginary corner of England where the climate is so salubrious that most of the inhabitants live to be centenarians, among them Mrs. Hurstpierpoint and Mrs. Thoroughfare, who inhabit the local manor house. These two ladies, together with Mrs. Yajñavalkya, the negress masseuse, are among Firbank's

most solidly drawn and unforgettable characters, and they
dominate the book, though they are in fact only incidental
to the plot, which is chiefly concerned with the courtship
and marriage of Mrs. Thoroughfare's son to a bewitching
young negress.

In *Valmouth* Firbank's descriptive powers are deployed
more effectively than in any of the novels since *Vainglory*,
more especially in the rustic episodes already mentioned;
these, though partly parodic in intention, show that Firbank,
when it suited him, could write a sustained and melodious
prose which compares favourably with that of many writers
far more highly esteemed as stylists. There is, as usual, a
great deal of dialogue, but it is more concentrated and more
carefully wrought than heretofore. Firbank's faculty for
catching the precise tone and rhythm of the human voice
has been referred to before, and nowhere is this employed
more happily than in the diffuse, gushing monologues of
Lady Parvula de Panzoust, a visiting *grande dame* who,
though one of Firbank's most fantastic creations, is also one
of his most plausible:

'One could count more alluring faces out with the Valmouth,
my husband used to say, than with any other pack. The Baroness
Elsassar—I can see her now on her great mauve mount with her
profile of royalty in misfortune—never missed. Neither, bustless,
hipless, chinless, did "Miss Bligh"! It was she who so sweetly
hoisted me to my saddle when I'd slid a-heap after the run of a
"fairy" fox. We'd whiffed it—the baying of the dogs is something
I shall never forget; dogs always know!—in a swede-field below
your house, from where it took us by breakneck, rapid stages—
(oh! oh!)—to the sands. There, it hurried off along the sea's edge
with the harriers in full cry; all at once, near Pizon Point, it vanished.
Mr. Rogers, who was a little ahead, drew his horse in with the
queerest gape—like a lost huntsman (precisely) in the *Bibliothèque
bleue*.'

In *Valmouth*, too, Firbank employs a device which he has
already used in *Vainglory*: the recording, as it might be by a

tape-machine, of the confused and disconnected chatter of a crowd. In the following passage, the identities of the speakers are not specified, we are eavesdropping, as it were, upon a dozen or so different conversations proceeding simultaneously (the occasion is a garden *fête*), catching a word here and a word there:

'Heroin.'

'Adorable simplicity.'

'What could anyone find to admire in such a shelving profile?'

'We reckon a duck here of two or three and twenty not so old. And a spring chicken *anything to fourteen.*'

'My husband had no amorous energy whatsoever; which just suited me, of course.'

'I suppose when there's no room for another crow's-foot, one attains a sort of peace?'

'I once said to Doctor Fothergill, a clergyman of Oxford and a great friend of mine, "Doctor", I said, "oh, if only you could see my—"'

'*Elle était jolie! Mais jolie!* . . . *C'était une si belle brune.* . . . !'

'Cruelly lonely.'

'Leery . . .'

'Vulpine.'

'Calumny.'

'People look like pearls, dear, beneath your wonderful trees.'

'. . . Milka, to-night—she is like a beautiful Cosway.'

'Above social littleness. . . .'

'Woman as I am!'

'Philanthropy.'

'. . . A Jewess in Lewisham who buys old clothes, old teeth, old plate, old lace. And gives very good prices indeed.'

' 'Er 'ealth I'm pleased to say is totally established.'

'If she pays her creditors *sixpence* in the *pound* it's the utmost they can expect.'

'Wonderful the Duchess of Valmouth's golden red hair, is it not?'

' "You lie to me", he said. "I'm not lying, and I *never* lie", I said. "It's *you* who tell the lies." Oh! I reproached him.'

'I'm tired, dear, but I'm *not* bored! . . .'

'What is a boy of twenty to me?'

'It's a little pain-racked face—not that she really suffers.'

Santal (1921) is an anomaly in the Firbankian canon: a short story which seems a throwback to the mood of *Odette*. This wistfully sentimental tale of an Arab boy in search of God must have come as a disappointment, at the time, to admirers of *Valmouth* and *Caprice*; only in a few scraps of dialogue is Firbank's characteristic humour in evidence, and though agreeable enough in its way, the story exemplifies (like *The Princess Zoubaroff*) the limitations of its author.

The Flower Beneath the Foot (1923) might be described as Firbank's most 'typical' novel, combining as it does, in about equal proportions, his habitual preoccupations with sex, religion and social grandeur. The setting, moreover— an imaginary country which may be assumed to be some- where in the Balkans—is suitably exotic, and later writers who have come under Firbank's influence seem to have had this novel, more than the rest, in mind (a good example is Evelyn Waugh's *Black Mischief*). The characters include the King and Queen, various high-born ladies about the Court, and (as usual) an attendant chorus of priests and nuns. Nor is the English colony neglected: Mrs. Montgomery, the royal governess, Mrs. Barleymoon and, best of all, Mrs. Bedley, who runs a Circulating Library:

'By the way, Miss Hopkins . . . I've to fine you for pouring tea over *My Stormy Past*.'

'It was coffee, Mrs. Bedley—not tea.'

'Never mind, dear, what it was, the charge for a stain is the same, as you know.'

This passage, incidentally, displays Firbank's skill in suggesting, without resort to phonetic spelling, the typical accent of a particular social class: Mrs. Bedley, one feels, was just a little too conscious of being a 'lady', and rather apt to overstress her own gentility.

In the same chapter Firbank himself makes an appearance, though only, as it were, off-stage:

'*The Passing of Rose* I read the other day,' Mrs. Montgomery said, 'and *so* enjoyed it.'

'Isn't that one of Ronald Firbank's books?'

'No, dear, I don't think it is. . . .'

'I suppose I'm getting squeamish! But this Ronald Firbank I can't take to at all. *Valmouth*! Was there ever a novel more coarse? I assure you I hadn't gone very far when I had to put it down.'

'It's *out*', Mrs. Bedley suavely said, 'as well', she added, 'as the rest of them.'

'I once met him', Miss Hopkins said, dilating slightly the *retinae* of her eyes. 'He told me writing books was by no means easy!'

A moment later a nun enters the shop:

'Have you *Valmouth* by Ronald Firbank, or *Inclinations* by the same author?' she asked.

'Neither: I'm sorry—both are out!'

A maid-in-waiting, Laura de Nazianzi, loves and is loved by the Crown Prince who, however, throws her over for Princess Elsie of England, with whom a match has been arranged by the two royal families. Mlle de Nazianzi, in despair, enters the Order of the Flaming Hood (like most religious orders in Firbank it appears to be remarkably lax in the matter of discipline), and ultimately, as a footnote informs us, becomes a saint. Once again the story has a quasi-tragic ending, but here, more than in *Caprice*, there are signs of an emotion genuinely felt; the theme of sexual frustration is a recurrent one in Firbank's work, and in the later novels it is given an increasing prominence.

Prancing Nigger (1925)[1] is probably Firbank's most widely known book, and was particularly successful in America. Many people consider it the best of the novels, and even if one prefers *Valmouth* or *Vainglory*, one is bound to admit

[1] The original English title was *Sorrow in Sunlight*; the book appeared in the United States, however, as *Prancing Nigger*, and the American title has been used for all subsequent reprints in this country.

that *Prancing Nigger* is, technically, one of his finest achievements. One reason for its popularity, perhaps, is that it has (though Firbank would have winced at such a humourless suggestion) what might be interpreted as a 'serious' sociological theme: racial discrimination. The scene is a West Indian republic (compounded of Cuba and Haiti); a family of negroes, socially ambitious, move from their country home to the capital, and the story is concerned with their attempts—which prove mainly abortive—to 'get into society'. Once again, as in *Caprice*, Firbank is dealing with the social embarrassments and misadventures of the Innocent Abroad, though here the theme is treated, if not exactly seriously, at least with something approaching genuine sympathy. Young Edna Mouth becomes a white man's mistress, her brother frequents the society of 'youths of a certain life, known as bwam-wam bwam-wams'; as for their elder sister, Miss Miami Mouth, her lover is killed by a shark, and she, like Mlle de Nazianzi before her, seeks consolation in religion and pious works.

Firbank was strongly attracted towards the coloured races, and if his picture of the West Indian negro is hardly an accurate one, it is drawn with real (if amused) affection; the book is admirably constructed, and the ironic tragicomedy of the final chapters, though exceedingly funny, comes nearer to being moving than anything else in Firbank's work.

Concerning the Eccentricities of Cardinal Pirelli (1926) has something of the solidity of texture which characterized *Valmouth*, and the novel contains some of Firbank's best writing. It is set in Spain, and the Cardinal's 'eccentricities' include the baptism of pet dogs in his cathedral and an unsuitable passion for choir-boys. Plot is reduced to a minimum, once again the book consists of a series of conversation-pieces; there is a brief interlude at the Vatican, where Pope Tertius II is much troubled by 'these schisms in Spain', though the passage is perhaps chiefly notable for a hitherto unrecorded sidelight on the late Queen Victoria:

'The dear *santissima* woman', the Pontiff sighed, for he entertained a sincere, if brackish, enthusiasm for the lady who for so many years had corresponded with the Holy See under the signature of *The Countess of Lostwaters*.

'Anglicans . . .? Heliolaters and sun-worshippers', she had written in her most masterful hand, 'and your Holiness may believe us', she had added, 'when we say especially our beloved Scotch.'

Cardinal Pirelli is, incidentally, the bawdiest of Firbank's novels: what elsewhere has been suggested by a mere lift of the eyebrow is here presented without the least equivocation. On the whole, the change is not for the better; Firbank's mingling of sanctity and smut is not the most attractive aspect of his work, and to a modern reader seems curiously dated. The Cardinal's pursuit of the choir-boy, in the last chapter, is plainly intended to produce the half-funny, half-moving effect of the final passages in *Prancing Nigger*; the intention fails, however, for in these concluding pages of his last book[1], Firbank relapses once again into the sentimental and too consciously 'literary' style of *Odette* and *Santal*. It is as though the two contrasted elements in his personality, so happily blended in his best work, had here refused to mingle, and the effect is of an uneasy collaboration between two quite disparate writers.

Firbank is not an author who lends himself to facile literary judgments: he cannot be fitted into any of the normal categories, and to dissect his novels as one might, say, those of George Eliot, is, as E. M. Forster has wisely said, equivalent to breaking a butterfly upon a wheel.[2] In any case, one must first catch one's butterfly, and Firbank, more than most writers, eludes pursuit, and refuses to be

---

[1] Since this was written, a fragment of *The New Rhythum*, a novel about New York which Firbank was at work on when he died, has been published, together with several pieces of juvenilia. The latter are of some interest, written as they were in the transitional phase between *Odette* and *The Artificial Princess;* the novel-fragment, though amusing enough, seems hardly up to the standard of its predecessors.

[2] Essay on Firbank in *Abinger Harvest*.

pinned down. Any judgement upon him is bound to be highly personal: either one enjoys his work or one does not, and it is all but impossible to explain its merits to those who dislike it.

Firbank has been compared, in an earlier passage of this essay, with James Joyce, and though no two writers seem, on the face of it, more dissimilar, the comparison could be extended. Neither Joyce nor Firbank, in their earliest work, appeared to possess more than the slenderest of talents: *Odette* can be paralleled by the vapid and derivative poems in *Chamber Music*. Both, however, were gifted with great literary virtuosity and a talent for pastiche, and were thus enabled to produce works totally different in quality and scope from anything which could have been predicted from their juvenilia. But whereas Joyce was tempted to work on a vast scale (and thereby, as some may think, to dissipate much of his natural talent), Firbank was content to recognise his own limitations, and to write in the manner which he found easiest and most pleasing to himself.

Firbank is without doubt a minor writer (whether Joyce, for all his present *réclame*, is a major one, is a question which can only be settled by posterity), but one who, for the most part, achieved precisely what he set out to do. Sometimes his inspiration flags, he can be irritating and downright silly; yet he is one of those artists who, as Cyril Connolly has said, 'attempt, with a purity and a kind of dewy elegance, to portray the beauty of the moment, the gaiety and sadness, the fugitive distress of hedonism'.[1] Such artists are not, perhaps, very fashionable today; yet among them can be numbered (as Mr. Connolly goes on to say) such names as Horace, Watteau and Mozart. Firbank, of course, is not their peer, but he is a citizen, so to speak, of the same country; though not a great artist, he is that rare phenomenon in English literature, a *pure* artist, and as such he deserves our respect.

[1] *The Condemned Playground.*

RONALD FIRBANK

A Select Bibliography

(Place of publication, London unless stated otherwise)

Bibliography:

RONALD FIRBANK: A BIBLIOGRAPHY, by M. Benkovitz (to be published 1963)
—in the Soho Bibliographies.

Collections and Selections:

WORKS, 5 vols. (1929)
—limited edition, with an Introduction by A. Waley and a Memoir by O. Sitwell.

FIVE NOVELS (1949)
—contains *Valmouth, The Flower Beneath the Foot, Prancing Nigger, Concerning the Eccentricities of Cardinal Pirelli,* and *The Artificial Princess,* with an Introduction by O. Sitwell.

THREE NOVELS (1950)
—contains *Vainglory, Inclinations,* and *Caprice,* with an introduction by Ernest Jones.

THE COMPLETE RONALD FIRBANK (1961), with a preface by Anthony Powell.

THE NEW RYTHUM AND OTHER PIECES (1962)
—a posthumous collection, including a fragment (40 pp.) of an unfinished novel and miscellaneous writings and photographs from his unpublished papers, sold in London in 1962, with a preface by Alan Harris.

Separate Works:

ODETTE D'ANTREVERNES and A STUDY IN TEMPERAMENT (1905) *Story and Sketch*

VAINGLORY (1915) *Novel*

INCLINATIONS (1916) *Novel*

CAPRICE (1917) *Novel*

VALMOUTH (1919) *Novel*

THE PRINCESS ZOUBAROFF (1920) *A Comedy*

SANTAL (1921) *Story*

THE FLOWER BENEATH THE FOOT (1923) *Novel*

SORROW IN SUNLIGHT (1925) *Novel*
—reprinted in 1929 with the title *Prancing Nigger*.

CONCERNING THE ECCENTRICITIES OF CARDINAL PIRELLI (1926) *Novel*

THE ARTIFICIAL PRINCESS (1934) *Novel*
—with an Introduction by C. Kennard.

Some Critical and Biographical Studies:

RONALD FIRBANK, A MEMOIR, by I. K. Fletcher (1930)
—with reminiscenses by Lord Berners, A. John, V. B. Holland, and
O. Sitwell.

ABINGER HARVEST—A MISCELLANY, by E. M. Forster (1936)
—contains an essay on Firbank.

RONALD FIRBANK, by J. Brooke (1951).

Gerald Duckworth & Co. Ltd. publish Ronald Firbank's works,
and quotations are made by their kind permission.

JOHN BETJEMAN

I

ONE is tempted to say of John Betjeman that he is an architect *manqué* and a poet only by accident, for architecture has always been his chief preoccupation, both as a man and as a writer, and his various books and articles on the subject far exceed, in mere bulk, his output as a poet. Since, however, he describes himself in *Who's Who* as 'poet and hack', we must assume that he regards architecture as a mere side-line, subsidiary to his poetry (upon which, nonetheless, it has exercized a fertilizing influence). To be a poet, moreover—as he tells us in *Summoned by Bells*—was his earliest ambition:

> I knew as soon as I could read and write
> That I must be a poet,

and farther on, describing his early attempts at verse, he writes:

> The muse inspired my pen:
> The sunset tipped with gold St. Michael's Church,
> Shouts of boys bathing came from Highgate Ponds,
> The elms that hid the houses of the great
> Rustled with mystery, and dirt-grey sheep
> Grazed in the foreground; but the lines of verse
> Came out like parodies of *A and M*.

The confession is significant, for the influence of *Hymns Ancient and Modern* survives in much of Betjeman's mature work, and at least one of his poems is a direct parody of a popular hymn in that famous collection. If his childhood ambition has been fulfilled, his present celebrity as a poet is hardly, perhaps, of the kind which he envisaged in those summer evenings on Hampstead Heath fifty-odd years ago. Lord Birkenhead, in his introduction to the *Collected Poems* (1958), asserts that 'John Betjeman is not a "funny" poet, and resents being regarded as one', though it is conceded

25

that 'he frequently writes supremely funny poems because solemnity is not in his nature'. But this is surely to beg the question, for nearly all Betjeman's poems are funny, though the nature and quality of the fun vary enormously. If a writer of verse makes one laugh almost continuously, how is he to avoid being regarded—resent it though he may—as a 'funny poet'?

The trouble is that, since the Romantic Revival, we have tended to draw an arbitrary and largely artificial distinction between 'serious' and 'light' verse. It is arguable, indeed, that this dichotomy had its origins at an even earlier date, and Aldous Huxley considers that 'the secret of being lyrically funny, of writing comic verses that are also beautiful' died with the Elizabethans.[1] He quotes the following lines, by an anonymous Tudor poet, as an example:

> He tickles this age that can
> Call Tullia's ape a marmosite
> And Leda's goose a swan.

It might perhaps be said of John Betjeman that he has rediscovered this long-lost faculty for being 'lyrically funny', though with him the blend of fun and lyricism has little in common with its Elizabethan counterpart. His affinities are rather, one would say, with Edward Lear, who for that matter has a better claim to have revived this particular genre. Lear's Nonsense Songs are funny, but are also (as in the 'Yonghy-Bonghy Bo' or 'My Aged Uncle Arly') hauntingly beautiful. The Elizabethan poem quoted above depends for its effect largely upon its sheer verbal felicity; with Betjeman the combination of beauty and humour is effected less by purely verbal means than by the juxtaposition of grandiose and humdrum images, by the romantic or mock-heroic treatment of themes commonly regarded as banal or trivial, by pastiche (like Lear, again, he is fond of imitating Tennyson), and above all by his strangely

---

[1] *Texts and Pretexts.*

ambivalent attitude towards the subject-matter of his poems. With many if not most of the persons, places, buildings and so forth which his poetry celebrates, he seems involved in what can only be termed a love-hate relationship, and it is this habitual (and sometimes puzzling) ambiguity which, more than anything else, makes him so original and so fascinating a writer.

Reading his earlier poems, in the nineteen-thirties, the average reader was apt to conclude, when Mr. Betjeman waxed enthusiastic over some Victorian-Gothic church of more than ordinary ugliness, that he had his tongue in his cheek; later poems, however—quite apart from his prose-writings—seemed to suggest that so simple an explanation was less than adequate. Could it be that Mr. Betjeman's tongue had become so firmly implanted in his cheek that he was unable to get it out again? Or had he, perhaps—as one was tempted to infer from his growing interest in the Anglican liturgy—'gone to mock and stayed to pray'?

Here perhaps we are nearer the heart of the matter, though Mr. Betjeman seems always to have possessed a strain of natural piety, and it might be truer to say that he went to pray and stayed to mock. This is to cast no reflection upon the genuineness of his religious beliefs, for where church matters are concerned his mockery has seldom been anything but affectionate: he never mocks at Christianity itself, only at its outward forms, as expressed in church furnishings and the nice distinctions, within the Anglican Communion, between 'High', 'Low' and 'Broad'.

This note of affection is notably lacking, however, in certain poems dealing with other subjects, for example the one which begins 'Come, friendly bombs, and fall on Slough'. Here it is plain that he genuinely and unequivocally loathes this squalid riverside town on the fringes of London, with its:

> air-conditioned, bright canteens,
> Tinned fruit, tinned meat, tinned milk, tinned beans,
> Tinned minds, tinned breath.

Such 'hate' poems, though, are exceptional, and his more characteristic pieces are marked by that emotional ambivalence which has already been noted. Thus, though he hates Slough, he will write lovingly (if ironically) of such towns as Swindon, Camberley or Westgate-on-Sea, which to many people would seem hardly more attractive or enlivening than Slough itself.

But if his dislikes often strike us as inconsistent or merely incomprehensible, it will be seen, on examining his work as a whole, that his prejudices have after all a certain logic and consistency of their own, though of a nature wholly personal and often, as many readers must think, perverse if not positively anti-social.

The truth of the matter is that Betjeman is, above all, the poet of nostalgia: any landscape, building or social custom which has survived from his childhood or young manhood evokes in him an emotion comparable with that evoked for Proust by the madeleine dipped in tea. The past, that is to say, acquires a value for him by the mere fact of *being* the past; Betjeman, one feels, would not really have much enjoyed subalterns' dances and tennis-parties at Aldershot or Camberley in the nineteen-twenties, but distance lends enchantment to his view of them. One might even hazard a guess that his admiration for Victorian church architecture has its roots—despite his learned disquisitions in defence of such architects as Gilbert Scott, J. L. Pearson, Butterfield, etc.—in his memories of those smoke-grimed Ruskinian turrets and pinnacles which loomed through the misty Highgate evenings of his childhood. Perhaps, for that matter, taste in the visual arts is never really 'pure', and is always traceable, to a greater or lesser degree, to personal sentiment. However that may be, it is the Past—the Lost Paradise of childhood and adolescence—which is the primal inspiration of Betjeman's poetry; modern 'progress' is anathema to him, he loathes 'processed' food, plastics, vita-glass, the Welfare State and (one may infer) democracy, though fortunately for us he is still able to laugh at them.

II

John Betjeman was born in 1906, the son of a well-off London merchant and manufacturer of Dutch origin whose firm had been established in 1820. Betjeman's childhood was mainly spent in London; he was educated at Marlborough and Oxford, but left the University without a degree. He worked for a time as a schoolmaster, and during part of the second world war was United Kingdom Press Attaché in Dublin. He had early begun to make a name for himself as a writer on architecture, and up till the late nineteen-thirties was probably better known as an expert upon (and champion of) the nineteenth-century Gothic revival than as a poet. His earliest book of verse, *Mount Zion*, appeared in 1933, but attracted little attention; his second, *Continual Dew* (1937), incorporated many of the poems in the previous volume, together with a number of new ones. With this book Betjeman became known, as a writer of verse, to a somewhat wider circle, though his public remained a small one. The book was bound in a quasi-'devotional' style, like an old-fashioned prayer-book, with imitation gilt clasps; in startling contrast was the surrealist dust-cover (by McKnight Kauffer) depicting a severed human hand protruding from what appeared to be a cabbage. The pages were lavishly decorated with pastiches of Victorian designs, steel engravings, *art nouveau*, etc. Such details are worth mentioning only to suggest that *Continual Dew* was presented to the public as a *humorous* book: a fact which should perhaps be emphasized, in the light of Lord Birkenhead's later disclaimer, especially as the volume, in its original form, has long been out of print, though most of the verses have reappeared in the *Collected Poems*.

Further volumes appeared at intervals during the next fifteen years: *Old Lights for New Chancels* (1940); *New Bats in Old Belfries* (1945); *Selected Poems* (1948), containing several new pieces, and with an appreciative introduction by

John Sparrow, Warden of All Souls' College, Oxford;
A Few Late Chrysanthemums (1954). Betjeman's reputation
as a poet, during this period, was still restricted to a fairly
small band of admirers, and it was not till the appearance
of Lord Birkenhead's collection, in 1958, that he achieved
a sudden and, in the circumstances, astonishing celebrity.
This may have been partly due to a growing sophistication
on the part of the reading public, but one cannot help
suspecting that Mr. Betjeman's popularity as a television
personality also played its part; so too perhaps did the poem
'How to get on in Society', a catalogue of social solecisms
which, reprinted in a Sunday newspaper some years
previously, had established him, along with Miss Nancy
Mitford, as a kind of unofficial arbiter of elegance.

Before examining Betjeman's verse, a word must be said
about his prose works. These include, apart from various
articles and reviews in magazines, *Ghastly Good Taste* (1934);
An Oxford University Chest (1938); the 'Shell Guides' to
Cornwall (1935) and Devon (1936); and *First and Last Loves*
(1952), a collection of previously published essays. This
latter volume should be read as a kind of concordance to or
commentary upon the poems, on which it casts a revealing
light. As a prose-writer Mr. Betjeman has an off-hand,
conversational style, wholly unpretentious and excessively
readable; he writes, indeed, almost exactly as he talks, and
anyone who has heard him broadcast will know that, as
a speaker, he has the virtue of being at once entirely self-
possessed and absolutely natural.

III

John Betjeman's development as a poet has been slow
and—since he writes in a number of contrasted styles, and
is liable to revert, in his later work, to earlier techniques
and mannerisms—not very easy to summarize. During a
period of thirty years or so the quality of his sensibility has

changed very little, though his verse as a whole shows a steady improvement in prosodic technique.

The first poem in the *Collected Poems*, 'Death in Leamington', is presumably one of his earliest, and may be assigned to the late twenties or very early thirties. This description of an old lady's death in a decrepit Victorian villa already foreshadows most of his later preoccupations: nineteenth-century architecture, the niceties of social usage and vocabulary and the details of English upper-middle-class domesticity; significantly, too, the poem has that element of the macabre which will recur frequently throughout his work, for Betjeman is—as T. S. Eliot has said of Webster—'much possessed by death'.

> She died in the upstairs bedroom
>> By the light of the ev'ning star
> That shone through the plate glass windows
>> From over Leamington Spa.
>
> Beside her the lonely crochet
>> Lay patiently and unstirred,
> But the fingers that would have work'd it
>> Were dead as the spoken word.
>
> And Nurse came in with the tea-things
>> Breast high 'mid the stands and chairs—
> But Nurse was alone with her own little soul,
>> And the things were alone with theirs. . . .
>
> And 'Tea!' she said in a tiny voice
>> 'Wake up! It's nearly *five*.'
> Oh! Chintzy, chintzy cheeriness,
>> Half dead and half alive! . . .

The contractions—'ev'ning', 'work'd'—are habitual with Betjeman, and like many of his other mannerisms carry an echo of minor Victorian verse. Later poems on similar themes tend to be less mannered, and it is interesting to compare 'Death in Leamington' with 'Remorse' (1954), of which I quote the first two stanzas:

> The lungs draw in the air and rattle it out again;
>> The eyes revolve in their sockets and upwards stare;
> No more worry and waiting and troublesome doubt again—
>> She whom I loved and left is no longer there.
>
> The nurse puts down her knitting and walks across to her
>> ·With quick professional eye she surveys the dead.
> Just one patient the less and little the loss to her,
>> Distantly tender she settles the shrunken head. . . .

Here the slightly mocking tone of 'Leamington' has given place to a genuine compassion; the verse, moreover, is tauter and more firmly controlled, and the whole poem is a far more proficient piece of work, though some of Betjeman's admirers may regret the casual, rather amateurish quality which gave the earlier poems a charm of their own.

In complete contrast with 'Death in Leamington' is another very early poem, 'The Varsity Students' Rag', of which I quote the first verse and chorus:

> I'm afraid the fellows in Putney rather wish they had
> The social ease and manners of a 'varsity undergrad,
> For tho' they're awf'lly decent and up to a lark as a rule
> You want to have the 'varsity touch after a public school.
>
> CHORUS:
>> *We* had a rag at Monico's. *We* had a rag at the Troc.,
>> And the one we had at the Berkeley gave the customers
>>>> quite a shock.
>> *Then* we went to the Popular, and after that—oh my!
>> I *wish* you'd seen the rag we had in the Grill Room at
>>>> the Cri.

This poem is, of course, in itself something of a 'rag', but it is a good satire upon the loutish behaviour of a certain type of undergraduate at that time. The slang and many of the incidental allusions have dated, and future students of

Mr. Betjeman's poetry may well be puzzled by such abbreviations as 'Troc.' and 'Cri.', for Trocadero and Criterion—restaurants in or near Piccadilly Circus, much frequented in those days by the rowdier element. The poem exemplifies, in fact, Betjeman's habit of addressing himself to a private—or at any rate an extremely restricted—audience, and it is fairly safe to say that only a person of approximately the poet's own age and educational background would be able to comprehend it in detail. Such locutions, for example, as 'varsity' and 'undergrad' were at that period frowned upon by the smarter kind of undergraduate; but if Mr. Betjeman's attitude seems here a trifle snobbish, it is only fair to point out that it is precisely the snobbery of the 'varsity' man—his ill-bred jeering at 'the fellows in Putney'—which is the main target of the satire.

Another early poem, 'The Garden City', is perhaps worth quoting in part (it was omitted by Lord Birkenhead from his collection); this too is broadly satirical, though here the mockery is less unkind:

> O wot ye why in Orchard Way
>   The roofs be steep and shelving?
> Or wot ye what the dwellers say
>   In close and garden delving?
>
> 'Belike unlike my hearths to yours,
>   Yet seemly if unlike them.
> Deep green and stalwart be my doors
>   With bottle glass to fryke them.
>
> 'Hand-woven be my wefts, hand-made
>   My pottery for pottage,
> And hoe and mattock, aye, and spade
>   Hang up about my cottage'. . . .

A solemn footnote informs us that 'fryke' is a mediaeval word for deck, and the whole poem hits off splendidly that spurious and suburbanized 'arty-craftiness' which was one of the less fortunate by-products of the doctrines of William Morris.

Most poets write love-poems, and John Betjeman is no exception, though as a lover he appears to have somewhat recondite tastes:

> The sort of girl I like to see
> Smiles down from her great height at me.
> She stands in strong athletic pose
> And wrinkles her *retroussé* nose. . . .
> Oh! would I were her racket press'd
> With hard excitement to her breast
> And swished into the sunlit air
> Arm-high above her tousled hair. . . .
> ('The Olympic Girl')

Elsewhere he writes appreciatively of a 'great big mountainous sports girl', with arms 'as firm and hairy as Hendren's', and the same slightly masochistic element is present in one of his most celebrated poems, 'A Subaltern's Love-song':

> Miss J. Hunter Dunn, Miss J. Hunter Dunn,
> Furnish'd and burnish'd by Aldershot sun,
> What strenuous singles we played after tea,
> We in the tournament—you against me!

The poem goes on to describe a drive:

> Into nine-o'clock Camberley, heavy with bells
> And mushroomy, pine-woody, evergreen smells,

and a dance in the town:

> Oh! full Surrey twilight! importunate band!
> Oh! strongly adorable tennis-girl's hand!

And finally:

> the scent of her wrap, and the words never said,
> And the ominous, ominous dancing ahead.
> We sat in the car park till twenty to one
> And now I'm engaged to Miss Joan Hunter Dunn.

Such poems have their closest literary parallel, perhaps, in Swinburne who, if he were alive today, might well find the charms of Miss J. Hunter Dunn no less stimulating than those of the famous *équestrienne*, Adah Menken.

For the most part these love-poems are linked with the poet's nostalgia for his childhood and adolescence; he seldom concerns himself with physical sexuality, and when he does tends to relate it to that macabre obsession with old-age and death which has already been noted:

> . . . I run my fingers down your dress
> With brandy-certain aim
> And you respond to my caress
> And maybe feel the same.
>
> But I've a picture of my own
> Of this reunion night,
> Wherein two skeletons are shewn
> To hold each other tight;
>
> Dark sockets look on emptiness
> Which once was loving-eyed,
> The mouth that opens for a kiss
> Has got no tongue inside. . . .
> ('Late-Flowering Lust')

IV

John Betjeman, one imagines, is bored by politics and by public affairs in general, except insofar as they help or hinder those causes which are nearest his heart (and for which he has done much useful work), such as the preservation of ancient—or not so ancient—buildings, and of the English countryside. By temperament he is a last-ditch Tory, far more deeply conservative than even the most right-wing member of the Party which bears that name today; yet this conservatism is almost purely aesthetic, and his hatred of 'progress' implies no inhumanity or class-prejudice on his part. What it does imply, one may suppose, is a profound pessimism, a deep-rooted distrust of the intellectual assumptions which govern our present way of life. Mr. Betjeman, one feels, wants people to be happy rather than not; but how (he would argue) can true happiness be achieved in a world growing daily uglier, a world of processed food and processed thinking, in which our natural responses become more and more inhibited, our capacity for enjoyment less keen? Mr. Betjeman would say that our sole hope of regeneration lies in the Christian religion (he is himself a staunch Anglican), but it is fairly clear from his writings that he considers the hope a forlorn one, and that our increasingly materialistic society is unlikely to undergo any such change of heart. Certainly he is no earnest salvationist, and in his poetry his personal convictions are implied unobtrusively, often by means of ironic understatement:

> Not the folk-museum's charting of man's Progress out of slime
> Can release me from the painful seeming accident of Time. . . .
>
> Not my vegetarian dinner, not my lime-juice minus gin,
> Quite can drown a faint conviction that we may be born in Sin.
> ('Huxley Hall')

This poem is of course a skit on Tennyson's 'Locksley Hall', and something should here be said about Betjeman's use of parody and his habitual borrowings from other poets. Not even his warmest admirers could claim that in his choice of metre and stanza-form he is anything but traditional, derivative and reactionary. The modern movement initiated by Pound and Eliot has passed him by, and it would be almost true to say that, formally speaking, he has never written a wholly original poem. His originality, in fact, is a matter not of technique but of thought and sensibility: thus, in his parodies of Victorian poets, his purpose is not so much to poke fun at his models as to point the contrast between their world and ours; just so did James Joyce, more pretentiously, attempt to portray modern Dublin in terms of Homer's Odyssey. Tennyson is a favourite, so is Longfellow, there are echoes of Kipling and Newbolt, and often, too, of minor nineteenth-century poets who have been all but forgotten. In 'Love in a Valley' he adopts the metre of Meredith's poem of the same title, though the Surrey he describes is hardly that of Meredith:

> Take me, Lieutenant, to that Surrey homestead!
>> Red comes the winter and your rakish car,
> Red among the hawthorns, redder than the hawberries
>> And trails of old man's nuisance, and noisier far.
> Far, far below me roll the Coulsdon woodlands,
>> White down the valley curves the living rail,
> Tall, tall, above me, olive spike the pinewoods,
>> Olive against blue-black, moving in the gale. . . .

Characteristically, a footnote informs us that Coulsdon is reached by 'Southern Electric 25 mins.', and this brings us to an important—perhaps the most important—aspect of Betjeman's work: his intense preoccupation with topographical detail. Turning the pages of his *Collected Poems*, one is struck by the fact that almost every other poem has a place-name for title, or if it has not, contains some specific reference to particular towns, villages or suburbs. Camberley, Croydon, Westgate-on-Sea, Slough, Bristol, Upper Lambourne, Harrow-on-the-Hill—the list, if completed, would probably account for at least half of Betjeman's poetic output. One almost feels that, like primitive people and children, he finds it difficult if not impossible to think of any material entity in the abstract: such concepts as 'The English Village' or 'The Suburbs' would be meaningless to him, he can only grasp them in terms of some particular village or suburb, with its own special atmosphere, its sights, smells, peculiarities of architecture and so on; and how precisely he catches those mysterious emanations of the *genius loci* which make a particular locality just a little different from other and outwardly similar ones:

> Belbroughton Road is bonny, and pinkly bursts the spray
> Of prunus and forsythia across the public way,
> For a full spring-tide of blossom seethed and departed hence,
> Leaving land-locked pools of jonquils by sunny garden fence.

> And a constant sound of flushing runneth from windows where
> The toothbrush too is airing in this new North Oxford air
> From Summerfields to Lynam's, the thirsty tarmac dries,
> And a Cherwell mist dissolveth on elm-discovering skies.
> ('May-day Song for North Oxford')

North Oxford, it may be said, is not a neighbourhood which has inspired many poets, but for anyone who has read this poem, Belbroughton Road will never be quite the dull respectable thoroughfare that it seemed before. Note, incidentally, the personal and semi-private references: 'Lynam's', for example, a boys' preparatory school called thus by its ex-*alumni* after the first headmaster, but officially known as The Dragon School.

This habit of particularization is not confined to topography. It might be said of Betjeman that he never, if he can help it, calls a spade a spade: if he happened to be writing about spades, as likely as not he would refer to them by the name of their manufacturer. For example, he seldom speaks of a motor-car *tout court*: it is nearly always an Arrol-Johnston, a Hupmobile, a Hillman Minx and so forth. Similarly with clothes, shampoos, lemonade, marmalade etc., etc.: nearly all are given their brand-names or those of their makers—e.g., Windsmoor, Drene, Kia-Ora, Cooper's Oxford. This, of course, helps to date the poems, and is doubtless meant to: for instance, in *Summoned by Bells* Betjeman mentions Cook's Farm Eggs, a form of egg-substitute in use during the First World War and (so far as the present writer is aware) not obtainable since. Such names—especially those of cars—are often deftly employed, too, to indicate the social status of those who own or use the product referred to. Whether this device is justifiable is perhaps a doubtful point; but Betjeman might well argue that previous writers—including Shakespeare—have been free with their local and topical references. In certain poems the method seems wholly successful, as for example in 'Variations on a Theme by T. W. Rolleston', in which the names of chain-stores in the London Suburbs and the Home Counties resound like the muffled tolling of a passing-bell. The poem is perhaps worth quoting in full, if only because it is unaccountably missing from the *Collected Poems* (although it reappears in the recent paperback edition):

Under the ground, on a Saturday afternoon in winter
    Lies a mother of five,
And frost has bitten the purple November rose flowers
    Which budded when *she* was alive.

They have switched on the street lamps here by the cemet'ry
                railing;
    In the dying afternoon
Men from football, and women from Timothy White's and
                McIlroy's
    Will be coming teawards soon.

But her place is empty in the queue at the International,
    The greengrocer's queue lacks one,
So does the crowd at Mac Fisheries. There's no one to go
             to Freeman's
    To ask if the shoes are done.

Will she, who was so particular, be glad to know that after
    The tears, the prayers and the priest,
Her clothing coupons and ration book were handed in at the
            Food Office
    For the files marked 'deceased'?

V

It has been suggested in an earlier section of this essay that the hard and fast distinction between 'light' and 'serious'

verse is a comparatively modern phenomenon, scarcely to
be encountered, in the sense in which we understand it,
before the beginning of the nineteenth century. When we
speak of light verse nowadays we are likely to have in mind
such popular rhymesters as A. P. Herbert and the late
A. A. Milne: inheritors of a tradition which goes back
through W. S. Gilbert to R. H. Barham and Thomas Hood.
John Betjeman, however, can hardly be fitted into this
category; on the other hand, he is quite obviously not a
'serious' poet in the sense that we regard Yeats, Eliot or
Auden as such, and the recent tendency (exemplified by
Lord Birkenhead's preface) to treat him as though he were
can only lead to confusion.

In this connection, the 'Variations on a Theme' quoted
above is perhaps worth a second glance. If not one of
Betjeman's best poems, it is a fairly typical one: characteristically, it is concerned with death; it is also a quiet but devastating satire upon the bleak impersonality of bureaucratic
methods; it is, moreover, very much a poem of its time—
the post-war period of rationing, coupons, Food Offices
and so forth, and its effect depends largely upon these
topical references, as well as upon the shop names, Timothy
White's, McIlroy's etc. The theme is serious, the tone
compassionate, yet it cannot be described as anything but
light verse. How, then, is Betjeman to be classified? Is he a
mere entertainer, a writer of parodies and *pièces d'occasion*,
or is he to be regarded as a serious literary artist?

One is tempted to answer 'yes' to both questions, for at
his best Betjeman is a poet of true originality who has
extended the range of our perceptions and sensibilities; on
the other hand, his verse is 'light' in the sense that it is
unfailingly readable and entertaining. Perhaps he can best
be described as a writer who uses the medium of light verse
for a serious purpose: not merely as a vehicle for satire or
social commentary, but as a means of expressing a peculiar
and specialized form of aesthetic emotion, in which nostalgia and humour are about equally blended. In this respect,

he may be compared with Firbank, whose nostalgic passion for the *fin de siècle* was balanced by his capacity for poking fun at it. Betjeman, it should be emphasized, is, like Firbank, a pure aesthete, and some of his more eccentric enthusiasms recall the perverse and often quasi-masochistic tastes of Huysmans's des Esseintes: the *frisson* which, for example, he obtains from the station buffet at Baker Street is comparable with that experienced by Huysmans's hero at the English 'Bodega' in the Rue d'Amsterdam.

Betjeman's particular blend of fun and nostalgia, of irony and romantic feeling, is not wholly a novelty: it is already implicit in other, earlier writers of this century, in Firbank, for example, or the early T. S. Eliot, and is perhaps peculiar to—and symptomatic of—our age. What is really remarkable about John Betjeman is his capacity to pin down, to codify as it were, this ambivalent state of mind, and to give expression to it in terms which are not only subtle and precise, but easily intelligible to a wide public.

Betjeman is an unequal poet, not only in his prosodic technique, but in the quality of his imagination. On the whole he is least good when he is trying to be most serious; some of the 'funny' poems, on the other hand ('Sun and Fun', 'How to get on in Society'), hardly rise above the level of the more sophisticated kind of revue lyric. A poem such as 'Seaside Golf' might well have been the work of some anonymous *Punch* contributor in the twenties or thirties: it is good light verse, and that is all one can say for it—or almost all, for the joke of the poem (which is not in itself particularly funny) lies, for the addict, in the mere fact that John Betjeman, that arch-aesthete, should play golf at all, much less write poems in praise of it. Esotericism in literature could hardly, one feels, be carried further.

In the early poems the occasional awkwardness of scansion can be rather endearing; in the later pieces such lapses, when they occur, are inclined to jar, because we have learned to expect a greater technical proficiency:

I pulled aside the thick magenta curtains
  —So Regency, so Regency, my dear—
And a host of little spiders
Ran a race across the ciders
    To a box of baby 'pollies by the beer. . . .
        ('Sun and Fun: The Song of a Nightclub Proprietress')

Here the final line spoils the effect of the stanza, for 'beer' is
plainly put in for the sake of the rhyme, and blurs the visual
image evoked in the previous couplet; since we do not
know where the beer was standing, we are no wiser as to
the exact position of the 'baby' pollies' in relation to it.
Such criticism may seem pedantic, but such verses as these,
if they are to be fully effective, demand the impeccable
neatness of execution which one finds in a good limerick.

Betjeman's latest work is a long autobiographical poem
covering his childhood, his schooldays and his career at
Oxford. *Summoned by Bells* is in blank verse, and on the
whole he manages this difficult form with great success:
the scansion is above reproach, and the diction adequate if
a little flat. As always, the poem is continuously entertaining,
but one cannot help feeling that Betjeman works best on a
smaller scale, and one misses (apart from a few interpolated
poems) the complex stanza-forms and rhyme-patterns of
the shorter pieces. Since, moreover, most of his earlier work
is autobiographical, the book strikes one, here and there,
as being a trifle repetitive.

John Betjeman, as we have seen, cannot conveniently be
fitted into any literary category, yet if one were compelled
to name some other poet with whom he might be compared,
one's choice might well fall—improbable though it seems—
on Rudyard Kipling. Poles apart though they are in the
quality and range of their sensibility and in their attitudes
to life and literature, both are poets who have written light
verse in a manner which transcends the limitations of their
medium. Both, moreover, are conservative by temperament
and, in their very different ways, extremely patriotic; both,
too, are totally independent of—and largely indifferent to—

the *avant garde* writing of their respective periods. Both, finally, have achieved an enormous popularity among the sort of people who would never, in the ordinary way, think of opening a book of verse.

John Betjeman has been compared, in the course of this essay, with Firbank and Huysmans on the one hand, with Kipling on the other; the very fact that he should suggest comparisons so disparate and apparently so incongruous, is perhaps the measure of his originality, both as a social phenomenon and as a writer.

JOHN BETJEMAN

A Select Bibliography

(Place of publication London, unless stated otherwise)

Collections and Selections:

SELECTED POEMS (1948)
—with a Preface by J. Sparrow.

SELECTED POEMS (1958)
—in the Pocket Poets Series (48 pp.).

COLLECTED POEMS (1958)
—with an Introduction by the Earl of Birkenhead. New paper-back edition, 1962, with additions.

Separate Works:

MOUNT ZION (1931) *Verse*

GHASTLY GOOD TASTE (1933) *Essay*

CORNWALL ILLUSTRATED (1934) *Topography*
—a 'Series of Views', re-issued as a Shell Guide, 1939.

DEVON (1936) *Topography*
—a Shell Guide.

CONTINUAL DEW (1937) *Verse*

AN OXFORD UNIVERSITY CHEST (1938) *History*

SIR JOHN PIERS, by 'Epsilon'. Mullingar [1938] *Verse Pamphlet*
—privately printed.

ANTIQUARIAN PREJUDICE (1939) *Pamphlet Essay*

OLD LIGHTS IN NEW CHANCELS (1940) *Verse*

VINTAGE LONDON (1942) *Topography*

ENGLISH CITIES AND SMALL TOWNS (1943) *Architecture*
—in Collins's Britain in Pictures Series.

NEW BATS IN OLD BELFRIES (1945) *Verse*

JOHN PIPER (1948) *Art Criticism*
—an illustrated monograph in the series of Penguin Modern Painters.

MURRAY'S BUCKINGHAMSHIRE ARCHITECTURAL GUIDE (1948) *Architecture*
—in collaboration with John Piper.

MURRAY'S BERKSHIRE ARCHITECTURAL GUIDE (1949) *Architecture*
—in collaboration with John Piper.

SHROPSHIRE (1951) *Topography*
—a Shell Guide, in collaboration with John Piper.

FIRST AND LAST LOVES (1952) *Architecture*

POEMS IN THE PORCH (1954) *Verse Pamphlet*
—'these verses [originally broadcast in the B.B.C.'s Western Regional Service] do not pretend to be poetry'. Decorations by John Piper.

A FEW LATE CHRYSANTHEMUMS (1954) *Verse*

THE ENGLISH TOWN IN THE LAST HUNDRED YEARS (1956) *Architecture*
—the Rede Lecture at Cambridge University.

ENGLISH LOVE POEMS (1957) *Anthology*
—an anthology in collaboration with G. Taylor.

COLLINS'S GUIDE TO ENGLISH PARISH CHURCHES (1958) *Architecture*

ALTAR AND PEW (1959) *Anthology*
—a small collection (48 pp.) of English devotional verse; in the Pocket Poets Series.

SUMMONED BY BELLS (1960) *Autobiography in Verse*

Messrs John Murray Ltd. publish John Betjeman's verse and much of his prose. The quotations are made by their kind leave.

E